# 25

## SEASONS AT ANFIELD

## THE COMPLETE RECORD

## 1977-78 TO 2001-02

David Powter

# CONTENTS

British Library Cataloguing in Publication Data
A catalogue record for this book is available from the British Library

ISBN 1-86223-068-4

Copyright © 2002, SOCCER BOOKS LIMITED (01472 696226)
72 St. Peter's Avenue, Cleethorpes, N.E. Lincolnshire, DN35 8HU, England
Web site    http://www.soccer-books.co.uk
e-mail    info@soccer-books.co.uk

**Printed by Bookcraft**

# LIVERPOOL FC CLUB RECORD

**Year Formed:** 1892

**Turned Professional:** 1892

**Ground:** Anfield, Anfield Road, Liverpool, L4 0TH

**Telephone:** 0151 263-2361

**Capacity:** 45,362

**Record Attendance:** 61,905 vs Wolverhampton Wanderers (1951-52)

**Pitch Measurements:** 111 x 74 yards

**Colours:** All red

**Nickname:** The Reds

**League History:** 1893 – Division 2 • 1894-95 – Division 1 • 1895-96 – Division 2 • 1896-1904 – Division 1 • 1904-05 – Division 2 • 1905-54 – Division 1 • 1954-62 – Division 2 • 1962-92 – Division 1 • 1992– F.A. Premier League (Founder Members)

**Record League Victory:** 10-1 v Rotherham Town (1895-96)

**Record League Defeat:** 1-9 v Birmingham City (1954-55)

**Most League Points (2 for a win):** 68 in the First Division (1978-79)

**Most League Points (3 for a win):** 90 in the First Division (1987-88)

**Most League Goals:** 106 in the Second Division (1895-96)

**Highest League Scorer (in aggregate):** 245 goals – Roger Hunt (1959-69)

**Highest League Scorer (in a season):** 41 goals – Roger Hunt (1961-62)

**Most Goals in a game:** 5 goals – Andy McGuigan vs Stoke City (1901-02), John Evans vs Bristol Rovers (1954-55) & Ian Rush vs Luton Town (1983-84)

**Most League appearances:** 640 – Ian Callaghan (1960-78)

**Longest Sequence of League Wins:** 12 (from 21/4/1990 to 6/10/1990)

**Longest Sequence of League Defeats:** 9 (from 29/4/1899 to 14/10/1899)

**Longest Sequence of Unbeaten League Games:** 31 (from 4/5/1987 to 16/3/1988)

**Longest Sequence of League Games without a Win:** 14 (12/12/1953 to 20/3/1954)

**Most Capped Player:** 67 – Ian Rush (for Wales)

**Record Transfer Fee Received:** £12.5million for Robbie Fowler (to Leeds United, November 2001)

**Record Transfer Fee Paid:** £11 million for Emile Heskey (from Leicester City, March 2000)

## MAJOR HONOURS (37 TROPHIES)

**Football League Champions on 18 occasions:** 1900-01, 1905-06, 1921-22, 1922-23, 1946-47, 1963-64, 1965-66, 1972-73, 1975-76, 1976-77, 1978-79, 1979-80, 1981-82,

1982-83, 1983-84, 1985-86, 1987-88, 1989-90

**F.A. Cup Winners on 6 occasions:** 1964-65, 1973-74, 1985-86, 1988-89, 1991-92, 2000-01

**Football League Cup Winners on 6 occasions:** 1980-81, 1981-82, 1982-83, 1983-84, 1994-95, 2000-01

**European Cup Winners on 4 occasions:** 1976-77, 1977-78, 1980-81, 1983-84

**UEFA Cup on 3 occasions:** 1972-73, 1975-75, 2000-01

## OTHER HONOURS

**Football League Second Division Champions on 4 occasions:** 1893-94, 1895-96, 1904-05, 1961-62

# LIVERPOOL FC CLUB RECORD 1977-78 TO 2001-02

**Highest League Victory:** 9-0 vs Crystal Palace (1989-90)

**Highest League Defeat:** 1-5 vs Coventry City (1992-93)

**Most League Points (2 for a win):** 68 in the First Division (1978-79)

**Most League Points (3 for a win):** 90 in the First Division (1987-88)

**Most League Goals Scored:** 89 (1985-86)

**Most League Goals Conceded:** 55 (1992-93) & (1993-94)

**Highest League Scorer (in aggregate):** 229 goals – Ian Rush

**Highest League Scorer (in a season):** 32 goals – Ian Rush (1983-84)

**Most Goals in a game:** 5 goals – Ian Rush vs Luton Town (1983-84)

**Number of League Hat-tricks:** 39 (includes 5 goals in a game once and 4 goals in a game five times)

**Leading Scorer over most Seasons:** Ian Rush – 8 occasions, including once jointly

**Most League appearances:** 469 – Ian Rush

**Number of Ever-Present Players throughout a Season:** 43

**Most Seasons Ever-Present:** 7 – Phil Neal

**Highest Average Home League Attendance:** 46,406 (1977-78)

**Highest Home League Crowd:** 52,211 vs Everton (1978-79)

**Lowest Home League Crowd:** 20,746 vs Watford (1983-84)

**Longest Sequence of League Wins:** 12 (from 21/4/1990 to 6/10/1990)

**Longest Sequence of League Defeats:** 4 (from 16/4/1983 to 2/5/1983 and also from 1/9/1993 to 2/10/1993)

**Longest Sequence of Unbeaten League Games:** 31 (from 4/5/1987 to 16/3/1988)

**Longest Sequence of League Games without a Win:** 8 (12/4/1983 to 27/8/1983)

**Most Capped Player:** 67 caps – Ian Rush (Wales)

**Record Transfer Fee Received:** £12.5 million for Robbie Fowler (to Leeds United, November 2001)

**Record Transfer Fee Paid:** £11 million for Emile Heskey (from Leicester City, March 2000)

## MAJOR HONOURS (22 TROPHIES)

**Football League Champions on 8 occasions:** 1978-79, 1979-80, 1981-82, 1982-83, 1983-84, 1985-86, 1987-88, 1989-90

**F.A. Cup Winners on 4 occasions:** 1985-86, 1988-89, 1991-92, 2000-01

**League Cup Winners on 6 occasions:** 1980-81, 1981-82, 1982-83, 1983-84, 1994-95, 2000-01

**European Cup Winners on 3 occasions:** 1977-78, 1980-81, 1983-84

**UEFA Cup Winners once:** 2000-01

# LIVERPOOL 25 SEASONS 1977-78 TO 2001-02

## INTRODUCTION

Having won two major trophies in each of the previous two campaigns, Liverpool fans were on a high during the summer of 1977. They were eager for the 1977-78 campaign to commence. Their side was not only League Champions, but the holders of the European Cup. The only cloud hanging over Anfield at that time was the departure of their star man Kevin Keegan (who had joined Hamburg). There was a question-mark about his replacement Kenny Dalglish. He was obviously a fine player, but would he fit into the Liverpool side? The answer was not long in coming and by the time Dalglish hung up his boots, in 1990, most Liverpool fans considered him to be the finest player that ever pulled on a red shirt.

Dalglish's new team-mates in 1977 included many of the country's best footballers. These included: Ray Clemence, Phil Neal, Phil Thompson, Emlyn Hughes, Tommy Smith, Ray Kennedy, Jimmy Case, Steve Heighway, John Toshack, Ian Callaghan and Terry McDermott.

Keegan's last game for the Reds was the dramatic European Cup Final against Borussia Moenchengladbach, in Rome, on 25th May 1977. Liverpool won 3-1 to lift the trophy for the first time. Twelve months previously Liverpool had been successful in the UEFA Cup final. Bob Paisley was doing a wonderful job with four trophies to his name during the three seasons he had been at the helm since Bill Shankly's surprise retirement. The next quarter of century was to bring much more joy to Liverpool supporters. Their side would go on to capture 22 more trophies and ensure that Liverpool FC was one of the most respected football clubs in Europe.

Paisley was to bring another nine trophies to the club. His successor Joe Fagan brought another three (all in his debut campaign) and the sides of player-manger Dalglish won five trophies. Graeme Souness and Roy Evans won one cup each during their reigns as the Anfield, while, more recently, Gerard Houllier's 2000-01 squad added a glorious treble of cups. So, it was not quite an average of one a season – but 22 pieces of silverware in 25 seasons is quite some haul!

The quarter of a century up to the summer of 2002 brought some very sad days too. In particular 29th May 1985 – when the Heysel tragedy occurred. And 15th April 1989 – the day of the Hillsborough Disaster.

Two dreadful events which gave everybody connected with Liverpool FC a different perspective on life.

# LIVERPOOL 25 SEASONS 1977-78 TO 2001-02

## 1977-78 SEASON

The 1977-78 campaign ended on a glorious note with the retention of the European Cup, but in the League, two separate but disastrous five game spells handed the initiative to Nottingham Forest. The Reds eventually finished second, seven points adrift. Bob Paisley's side also came second to Forest in the League Cup Final, a single goal turning an Old Trafford replay the Midlanders' way.

The first game against Forest had ended scoreless; but Liverpool did score once at Wembley in 1977-78, when Kenny Dalglish netted the only goal in the European Cup Final against FC Brugge. The Reds were not at their best, but even so were easily the masters on the night and only some good goalkeeping kept the score down.

Dalglish had a wonderful first season at Anfield. He was the club's leading goalscorer with 20 League goals, twice as many as the second top scorer David Fairclough. Dalglish's sublime performances during 1977-78 more than compensated for the departure of Kevin Keegan. The King had gone, but the cry was still "Long live the King!"

The 1977-78 campaign proved to be the last at Anfield for four internationals. They were former skipper Tommy Smith, left-back Joey Jones, striker John Toshack and Ian Callaghan. Cally was the last of Bill Shankly's promotion squad to leave the club. The winger played for England in the 1966 World Cup tournament and made a club record 640 League appearances (scoring 49 times) for Liverpool before joining Swansea City.

**FACTFILE 1977-78**

**Manager:** Bob Paisley

**LEAGUE STATISTICS**

**Final Position:** 2nd place in Division One
**Games played:** 42  **Points:** 57
**Biggest Victory:** 4-0 vs Leicester City (H) and also vs Manchester City (H)
**Biggest Defeat:** 2-4 vs Derby County (A)
**Leading Goalscorer:** Kenny Dalglish (20 goals)
**Ever-Presents:** Kenny Dalglish and Phil Neal
**Hat-Trick Heroes:** None
**Average Home Attendance:** 45,546
**Highest Home Crowd:** 51,668 vs Everton
**Lowest Home Crowd:** 38,249 vs QPR

**CUPS**

**F.A. Cup:** Round 3
**League Cup:** Finalists
**European Cup:** Winners

# 1978-79 SEASON

Liverpool's grip on the European Cup was relinquished early in the 1978-79 campaign when they were paired with Nottingham Forest. Brian Clough's side won the first leg 2-0 and then held Bob Paisley's side to a goalless draw at Anfield. The Reds also experienced considerable cup disappointment later in the season, when they lost an F.A. Cup semi-final replay 1-0 to Manchester United at Goodison Park.

However, it was far from all doom and gloom as Liverpool romped to their eleventh League title, eight points clear of Forest. They lost only three games and claimed the crown with an unbeaten run of 21 games.

Stalwarts Ray Clemence, Phil Neal, Phil Thompson, Emlyn Hughes, Jimmy Case, Steve Heighway and Terry McDermott all played their part in bringing the Championship back to Anfield. As did Kenny Dalglish, Alan Hansen, Alan Kennedy and Graeme Souness, who all celebrated their first Championship medals. Dalglish was named the Footballer Writers' Association 'Footballer of the Year'.

**FACTFILE 1978-79**

**Manager:** Bob Paisley

**LEAGUE STATISTICS**

**Final position:** Champions of Division One
**Games played:** 42    **Points:** 68
**Biggest Victory:** 6-0 vs Norwich City (H)
**Biggest Defeat:** 1-3 vs Aston Villa (A)
**Leading Goalscorer:** Kenny Dalglish (21 goals)
**Ever-Presents:** Ray Clemence, Kenny Dalglish, Ray Kennedy and Phil Neal
**Hat-Trick Hero:** Jimmy Case
**Average Home Attendance:** 46,406
**Highest Home Crowd:** 52,211 vs Everton
**Lowest Home Crowd:** 35,207 vs Birmingham City

**CUPS**

**F.A. Cup:** Semi-final
**League Cup:** Round 2
**European Cup:** Round 1

# 1979-80 SEASON

1979-80 proved to be an extremely busy campaign, and it would have been longer, but for another first round European Cup exit, this time at the hands of Dynamo Tbilisi. However, the Reds did have long runs in the domestic cups, exiting them both at the semi-final stage. Nottingham Forest knocked them out of the League Cup and then Arsenal eventually managed to squeeze them out of the F.A. Cup, at Highfield Road, in a third replay.

Although Manchester United pushed them all the way, Liverpool retained their League title by two points. The Reds signalled their intentions by only dropping one point in the first eleven games. Their best win of the season came during this rip-roaring spell when they spanked Spurs (fielding their two Argentinian imports) 7-0 on 2nd September. The final goal was headed home by Terry McDermott (who had run the length of the pitch) and is often quoted as one of the best scored at Anfield.

Bob Paisley's men finished the season nearly as efficiently as they began it with a 12 match unbeaten run which included nine victories.

David Johnson finished the season as top-scorer (with 21 goals), while the tireless McDermott was voted the 'Footballer of the Year'.

**FACTFILE 1979-80**

**Manager:** Bob Paisley

## LEAGUE STATISTICS

**Final position:** Champions of Division One

**Games played:** 42    **Points:** 60

**Biggest Victory:** 4-0 vs Coventry City (H), Bristol City (H), Manchester City (A) & Middlesbrough (H)

**Biggest Defeat:** 0-2 vs Tottenham Hotspur (A)

**Leading Goalscorer:** David Johnson (21 goals)

**Ever-Presents:** Kenny Dalglish, Phil Neal and Phil Thompson

**Hat-Trick Hero:** David Fairclough

**Average Home Attendance:** 44,586

**Highest Home Crowd:** 52,201 vs Everton

**Lowest Home Crowd:** 36,415 vs Stoke City

## CUPS

**F.A. Cup:** Semi-final

**League Cup:** Semi-final

**European Cup:** Round 1

# 1980-81 SEASON

Liverpool won the League Cup for the first time in 1980-81 when they beat West Ham United in a replay at Villa Park. The first game at Wembley finished 1-1, after extra-time. Alan Kennedy netted the Reds goal towards the end of extra-time, but there was still time for the Hammers to level from the spot. Kenny Dalglish and Alan Hansen were on the score-sheet, at Villa Park, in the replay. Liverpool came from behind to win 2-1.

After a good start, Bob Paisley's side lost their way in the League. Their title hopes finally disappeared during a 17 game run which yielded only 13 goals and four victories. Liverpool's finishing position of fifth was their worst performance for ten seasons.

The 1980-81 campaign was to end on a celebratory note as the Reds went to Paris and lifted the European Cup for a third time. Full-back Kennedy found the net in a Cup Final for the second time of the season and Real Madrid were powerless to respond.

## FACTFILE 1980-81

**Manager:** Bob Paisley

## LEAGUE STATISTICS

**Final position**: 5th place in Division One

**Games played**: 42    **Points**: 51

**Biggest Victory**: 4-0 vs WBA (H)

**Biggest Defeat**: 1-4 vs Wolverhampton Wanderers (A)

**Leading Goalscorer**: Terry McDermott (13 goals)

**Ever-Present**: Phil Neal

**Hat-Trick Heroes**: None

**Average Home Attendance**: 37,547

**Highest Home Crowd**: 49,743 vs Everton

**Lowest Home Crowd**: 26,744 vs Coventry City

## CUPS

**F.A. Cup**: Round 4

**League Cup**: Winners

**European Cup**: Winners

# 1981-82 SEASON

Liverpool enjoyed more success in 1981-82, collecting another pair of trophies. However, there was disappointment in the European Cup, with CSKA Sofia getting the better of them at the quarter-final stage. However, the Reds were successful again in the League Cup. Extra-time was required, with Ronnie Whelan (twice) and Ian Rush netting in a 3-1 victory over Spurs in the Final.

Meanwhile Liverpool climbed to the top of the table after Ipswich Town, Manchester United and Southampton had done much of the pace-setting. The Anfield men finished with an unbeaten 16 game run, which included 11 straight wins, to take the title by four points from Ipswich.

Graeme Souness was proving to be an inspirational captain, while Rush was very impressive in his first full season in the the first-team. The big striker was the leading goalscorer with 17 League goals. Rush, Whelan, Bruce Grobbelaar, Mark Lawrenson, Craig Johnston and Sammy Lee had all become important members of Bob Paisley's squad.

## FACTFILE 1981-82

**Manager**: Bob Paisley

## LEAGUE STATISTICS

**Final position**: Champions of Division One

**Games played**: 42   **Points**: 87

**Biggest Victory**: 5-0 vs Manchester City (A)

**Biggest Defeat**: 1-3 vs Manchester City (H)

**Leading Goalscorer**: Ian Rush (17 goals)

**Ever-Presents**: Kenny Dalglish, Bruce Grobbelaar and Phil Neal

**Hat-Trick Hero**: Ian Rush

**Average Home Attendance**: 35,060

**Highest Home Crowd**: 48,861 vs Everton

**Lowest Home Crowd**: 24,224 vs Birmingham City

## CUPS

**F.A. Cup**: Round 5

**League Cup**: Winners

**European Cup**: Quarter-final

# 1982-83 SEASON

The 1982-83 season was to be Bob Paisley's last before he stepped up to the boardroom. His managerial career ended in style with the capture of two more trophies. He was voted 'Manager of the Year' for a record sixth time.

The League Cup (now the Milk Cup) was retained with a 2-1 victory over Manchester United. Extra-time was again required, with Ronnie Whelan and Alan Kennedy getting the goals. Liverpool again reached the quarter-final stage of the European Cup, but this time found Widzew Lodz too good for them.

In the League, the Reds picked up just one point from their last six games, but romped to another title, 11 points clear of second placed Watford. Liverpool refused to relinquish the top spot after climbing there on 30th October. David Hodgson (signed from Middlesbrough) won his only League Championship medal during the 1982-83 season.

### FACTFILE 1982-83

**Manager**: Bob Paisley

### LEAGUE STATISTICS

**Final position**: Champions of Division One

**Games played**: 42   **Points**: 82

**Biggest Victory**: 5-0 vs Southampton (H) and also vs Everton (A)

**Biggest Defeat**: 1-3 vs West Ham United (A)

**Leading Goalscorer:** Ian Rush (24 goals)

**Ever-Presents:** Kenny Dalglish, Bruce Grobbelaar, Alan Kennedy & Phil Neal

**Four-Goal Hero:** Ian Rush

**Other Hat-Trick Heroes:** Kenny Dalglish and Ian Rush

**Average Home Attendance:** 34,758

**Highest Home Crowd:** 44,737 vs Everton

**Lowest Home Crowd:** 27,145 vs Nottingham Forest

## CUPS

**F.A. Cup:** Round 5

**League Cup:** Winners

**European Cup:** Quarter-final

# 1983-84 SEASON

Bob Paisley's assistant Joe Fagan took over at the start of the 1983-84. There was to be no loss of momentum and in fact, remarkably, Liverpool's fortunes took a turn for the better. Everton held them in a goalless League Cup Final, but a goal by Graeme Souness was enough to ensure the trophy was retained in a Maine Road replay.

Meanwhile, after a mixed start, the Reds went to the top of the League in early November and, apart from a short spell in March, stayed there to the end of the season. Liverpool became only the third club (after Huddersfield Town and Arsenal) to win three titles on the trot. The gap over the strong finishing Southampton was three points. Steve Nicol and Michael Robinson had become key members of the squad, while John Wark joined late in the season from Ipswich Town. Rush netted 32 times to finish as the First Division's top-scorer and earn him the 'Footballer of the Year' award.

Liverpool won their fourth European Cup in 1983-84, defeating AS Roma in the Italian capital. Phil Neal got his name on the scoresheet, but the two teams were still locked together after extra-time. So, for the first time ever, this competition was settled by penalties. It was Fagan's side who kept their nerve, with Alan Kennedy netting the decisive penalty. Not surprisingly, Joe Fagan was named 'Manager of the Year'. He had become the first man to lead a side to the League Championship in his first season at the helm.

**Manager:** Joe Fagan

## LEAGUE STATISTICS

**Final position:** Champions of Division One

**Games played:** 42　　**Points:** 80

**Biggest Victory:** 6-0 vs Luton Town (H) and also vs West Ham United (H)

**Biggest Defeat:** 0-4 vs Coventry City (A)

**Leading Goalscorer:** Ian Rush (32 goals)

**Ever-Presents:** Bruce Grobbelaar, Alan Hansen, Alan Kennedy, Mark Lawrenson and Sammy Lee

**Five-Goal Hero:** Ian Rush

**Four-Goal Hero:** Ian Rush

**Other Hat-Trick Heroes:** Michael Robinson and Ian Rush

**Average Home Attendance:** 31,974

**Highest Home Crowd:** 45,122 vs Manchester United

**Lowest Home Crowd:** 20,746 vs Watford

## CUPS

**F.A. Cup:** Round 4

**League Cup:** Winners

**European Cup:** Winners

# 1984-85 SEASON

After the massive high of the previous campaign, 1984-85 was always likely to be an anti-climax. Nobody, though, could have expected it to be so tragic.

Everton took the 1984-85 title with the Reds trailing home 13 points behind as runners-up. In fact things looked a lot bleaker for much of the season. Missing Graeme Souness (who had transferred to Sampdoria), they were as low as 18th towards the end of October and still only in tenth spot on Boxing Day. A fine late burst sent them through the pack, but Everton were out of sight and the Anfield men had to be content with runners-up medals. There was not even the compensation of a fifth successive League Cup triumph. Liverpool's love-affair with this competition was halted at White Hart Lane (in the third round).

Meanwhile Liverpool reached their fifth European Cup Final; but the night of 29th May 1985 will forever be remembered as one of great tragedy. Sadly, 39 spectators died (and several hundred more were injured) in a stampede before the kick-off inside Brussels' Heysel Stadium. A Michel Platini penalty gave Juventus the trophy and, for the very first time, Liverpool had lost in the Final of this competition. After the game Joe Fagan confirmed he was retiring.

**Manager:** Joe Fagan

## LEAGUE STATISTICS

**Final position:** 2nd place in Division One

**Games played:** 42   **Points:** 77

**Biggest Victory:** 5-0 vs WBA (A)

**Biggest Defeat:** 1-3 vs Arsenal (A) and also vs Chelsea (A)

**Leading Goalscorer:** John Wark (18 goals)

**Ever-Presents:** Bruce Grobbelaar and Phil Neal

**Hat-Trick Hero:** John Wark

**Average Home Attendance:** 35,854

**Highest Home Crowd:** 45,545 vs Everton

**Lowest Home Crowd:** 27,145 vs Coventry City

## CUPS

**F.A. Cup:** Semi-final

**League Cup:** Round 3

**European Cup:** Finalists

# 1985-86 SEASON

Kenny Dalglish took over as player-manager for 1985-86 and helped steer Liverpool back on track. The Scot captured the much prized League and F.A. Cup 'Double' in his first term. It might have been a clean sweep, but QPR got the better of them in the semi-final of the League Cup. The League race was a three horse affair between Liverpool, Everton and West Ham United. The Reds were only confirmed champions on the final Saturday of the season, with Dalglish himself scoring the only goal in a win at Chelsea. It was a vital win as second placed Everton finished only two points adrift.

The Toffees were also the bridesmaids in the F.A. Cup final. Liverpool came from behind to win 3-1 with two goals by Rush and one from Craig Johnston.

Jan Molby, Jim Beglin, Paul Walsh, Steve McMahon, Gary Gillespie and Kevin MacDonald had all become integral members of the squad in 1985-86. Ian Rush was the top-scorer (with 22 goals) and Dalglish became the first player-manager to receive the 'Manager of the Year' award.

### FACTFILE 1985-86

**Manager:** Kenny Dalglish

### LEAGUE STATISTICS

**Final position:** Champions of Division One

**Games played:** 42    **Points:** 88

**Biggest Victory:** 6-0 vs Oxford United (H)

**Biggest Defeat:** 0-2 vs Arsenal (A) and also vs Everton (H)

**Leading Goalscorer:** Ian Rush (22 goals)

**Ever-Present:** Bruce Grobbelaar

**Hat-Trick Heroes:** Gary Gillespie and Ronnie Whelan

**Average Home Attendance:** 35,854

**Highest Home Crowd:** 45,545 vs Everton

**Lowest Home Crowd:** 26,219 vs QPR

## CUPS

**F.A. Cup:** Winners

**League Cup:** Semi-final

# 1986-87 SEASON

Liverpool had to be satisfied with second place in 1986-87 as Everton took the League title by nine points. The Anfield men dropped silly points at regular intervals. They lost four of their opening 12 games and a run of five defeats inside seven springtime fixtures sealed their fate. The ever-present Ian Rush was the club's leading scorer (with 30 League goals).

Kenny Dalglish's side also came second at Wembley Stadium in the League Cup final. Arsenal defeated them 2-1 after Ian Rush had opened the scoring. Incredibly, Liverpool had never lost a match in which the Welshman had scored prior to this Final.

Any hopes Liverpool had of retaining the F.A. Cup disappeared in the third round. Luton Town got the better of them in a second replay.

## FACTFILE 1986-87

**Manager:** Kenny Dalglish

## LEAGUE STATISTICS

**Final position:** 2nd place in Division One

**Games played:** 42    **Points:** 77

**Biggest Victory:** 6-2 vs Norwich City (H)

**Biggest Defeat:** 1-4 vs Luton Town (A)

**Leading Goalscorer:** Ian Rush (30 goals)

**Ever-Present:** Ian Rush

**Hat-Trick Heroes:** Ian Rush and Paul Walsh
**Average Home Attendance:** 36,285
**Highest Home Crowd:** 44,827 vs Everton
**Lowest Home Crowd:** 25,856 vs Chelsea

## CUPS

**F.A. Cup:** Round 3
**League Cup:** Finalists

# 1987-88 SEASON

With Peter Beardsley, John Aldridge, John Barnes, Ray Houghton, Barry Venison and Gary Ablett added to the squad, Liverpool bounced back to take the League Championship again in 1987-88. They led the League for most of the season and finished nine points clear with a club record 90 points. Rush had departed to Juventus for £2.75 million, but Aldridge proved to be more than an adequate deputy and was the First Division's top-scorer with 26 goals.

However, one goal Aldridge missed was a penalty, at Wembley, in the F.A. Cup Final against Wimbledon. It was the first spot-kick to be missed in a Wembley F.A. Cup Final. That Dave Beasant save and a first-half header by Lawrie Sanchez prevented the Reds from clinching another 'Double'.

Kenny Dalglish collected another 'Manager of the Year' award in 1987-88, while Barnes was the 'Footballer of the Year' in his first campaign at Anfield after his £900,000 move from Watford.

## FACTFILE 1987-88

**Manager:** Kenny Dalglish

## LEAGUE STATISTICS

**Final position:** Champions of Division One
**Games played:** 40    **Points:** 90
**Biggest Victory:** 5-0 vs Nottingham Forest (H)
**Biggest Defeat:** 1-2 vs Nottingham Forest (A)
**Leading Goalscorer:** John Aldridge (26 goals)
**Ever-Presents:** Steve Nicol and Steve McMahon
**Hat-Trick Heroes:** John Aldridge and Steve Nicol
**Average Home Attendance:** 39,582
**Highest Home Crowd:** 44,798 vs Tottenham Hotspur

**CUPS**

**F.A. Cup:** Finalists
**League Cup:** Round 3

# 1988-89 SEASON

Liverpool returned to Wembley for their ninth F.A. Cup Final in 1988-89. They deservedly defeated their great rivals from across Stanley Park 3-2 after extra-time. John Aldridge netted early on, but the Reds failed to cash in on a boat load of chances and Everton scored late on to force extra-time. Ian Rush (back at Anfield after just one term in Italy) came off the bench to put Liverpool in front and, after the Toffees equalised again, it was also the Welshman who netted the decisive fifth goal of the game. The Reds' road to the Final was paved with great tragedy as their Hillsborough semi-final with Nottingham Forest was abandoned following the worst disaster in British sporting history (with 96 spectators killed and over two hundred injured). Liverpool won the hollow 'replay' 3-1 at Old Trafford.

Having won the F.A. Cup, Liverpool still had the League to concentrate on. The title was to be decided in the final game at Anfield on Friday 26th May – for the first time in history – live on TV. It was the ultimate clash of the top two, with Arsenal (three points behind) needing to secure a two goal win to leap-frog the Reds (on the number of goals scored). Liverpool looked safe as they had not lost in 24 League games, while the Gunners (who had led the League for most of the term) had lost their previous seven visits to Anfield.

A 53rd minute Alan Smith goal set up a memorable finish and, deep in injury-time, Michael Thomas shocked the Kop to pull off a remarkable 2-0 victory. The 1988-89 title had been ripped from Liverpool's grasp with virtually the last kick of the season. On a happier note, the Football Writers' Association voted Steve Nicol as the 'Footballer of the Year'.

**FACTFILE 1988-89**

**Manager:** Kenny Dalglish

**LEAGUE STATISTICS**

**Final position:** 2nd place in Division One
**Games played:** 38   **Points:** 76
**Biggest Victory:** 5-0 vs Luton Town (H)
**Biggest Defeat:** 1-3 vs Manchester United (A)

**Leading Goalscorer**: John Aldridge (21 goals)

**Ever-Presents**: Ray Houghton and Steve Nicol

**Hat-Trick Hero**: John Aldridge (on two occasions)

**Average Home Attendance**: 38,574

**Highest Home Crowd**: 42,518 vs Derby County

**Lowest Home Crowd**: 30,283 vs Charlton Athletic

## CUPS

**F.A. Cup**: Winners

**League Cup**: Round 4

# 1989-90 SEASON

After the great disappointment of losing the title in the last game of 1988-89, the Reds responded in style. They won the League Championship for a record 18th time. A 9-0 thrashing of Crystal Palace announced their intentions, and a run of 23 games in which they lost just once secured them the crown by a margin of nine points. John Barnes was top scorer with 22 goals; while David Burrows, Glenn Hysen and Steve Staunton picked up their first Championship medals.

Kenny Dalglish brought himself on for one end-of-season substitute appearance to close his Liverpool playing career after 355 League games (in which he scored 118 goals). Aged 39 years and 58 days on that emotional night, Kenny remains the oldest man to play for Liverpool.

Another fine F.A. Cup run ended only at the semi-final stage. Palace inflicted revenge for their early season mauling, by winning an amazing tie 4-3, after extra-time, at Villa Park.

## FACTFILE 1989-90

**Manager**: Kenny Dalglish

## LEAGUE STATISTICS

**Final position**: Champions of Division One

**Games played**: 38   **Points**: 79

**Biggest Victory**: 9-0 vs Crystal Palace (H)

**Biggest Defeat**: 1-4 vs Southampton (A)

**Leading Goalscorer**: John Barnes (22 goals)

**Ever-Presents**: Bruce Grobbelaar & Steve McMahon (includes one sub. appearance)

**Hat-Trick Heroes**: John Barnes and Ronny Rosenthal

**Average Home Attendance:** 36,589
**Highest Home Crowd:** 38,730 vs Everton
**Lowest Home Crowd:** 33,319 vs Wimbledon

## CUPS

**F.A. Cup:** Semi-final
**League Cup:** Round 3

# 1990-91 SEASON

The 1990-91 season started very brightly with all but one of the first 13 League games ending in victory. The Reds stayed unbeaten until December, but that first defeat at Highbury proved to be very significant. It gave the Gunners a psychological edge in what turned out to be a two-horse race.

Certainly Kenny Dalglish was feeling the strain. The Scot astonished the football world by resigning the day after his side had been involved in a pulsating 4-4 draw with Everton, in an F.A. Cup fifth round replay at Goodison Park.

Ronnie Moran stepped up from the coaching staff to lead the side on a caretaker basis. The Reds immediately lost at Luton and then, more significantly, to Arsenal in front of the Kop. Liverpool's chance of winning the title had all but disappeared by the time (in April) that Graeme Souness moved from Ibrox to take the reins. Liverpool still finished as runners-up (seven points behind the Gunners), in spite of losing five of their last nine games.

## FACTFILE 1990-91

**Managers:** Kenny Dalglish & Graeme Souness

## LEAGUE STATISTICS

**Final position:** 2nd place in Division One
**Games played:** 38 **Points:** 76
**Biggest Victory:** 7-1 vs Derby County (A)
**Biggest Defeat:** 0-3 vs Arsenal (A)
**Leading Goalscorers:** John Barnes and Ian Rush (16 goals each)
**Ever-Presents:** None
**Hat-Trick Hero:** Peter Beardsley
**Average Home Attendance:** 36,589
**Highest Home Crowd:** 38,463 vs Everton
**Lowest Home Crowd:** 31,063 vs Coventry City

**CUPS**

**F.A. Cup:** Round 5
**League Cup:** Round 3

# 1991-92 SEASON

A lack of goalscoring power severely handicapped Graeme Souness's side during 1991-92. Only 12 goals were netted in the final 15 games and Dean Saunders finished top scorer with ten out of the inadequate total of 47. Liverpool had to be content with a finishing position of sixth – the club's lowest in 27 years.

However, there was the considerable consolation of a fifth F.A. Cup triumph in 1991-92. Mark Wright lifted the trophy aloft after goals by Michael Thomas (who had signed from Arsenal) and Ian Rush proved enough to defeat Second Division Sunderland 2-0. Coach Ronnie Moran led the the team out at Wembley as Graeme Souness was still convalescing after his triple heart by-pass operation. The Scot, looking rather gaunt, was just well enough to watch the victory from the bench.

Liverpool defeated just one top-flight side (Aston Villa) in the 1991-92 F.A. Cup. They earned a place in the Final by defeating second-flight Portsmouth in a Semi-final replay at Villa Park. The tie was decided on penalties, with the Reds triumphing 3-1. Liverpool thus became the first club to reach an F.A. Cup Final via a penalty shoot-out.

## FACTFILE 1991-92

**Manager:** Graeme Souness

## LEAGUE STATISTICS

**Final position:** 6th place in Division One
**Games played:** 42    **Points:** 64
**Biggest Victory:** 4-0 vs Notts County (H)
**Biggest Defeat:** 0-4 vs Arsenal (A)
**Leading Goalscorer:** Dean Saunders (10 goals)
**Ever-Presents:** None
**Hat-Trick Heroes:** None
**Average Home Attendance:** 34,799
**Highest Home Crowd:** 39,072 vs Everton
**Lowest Home Crowd:** 25,457 vs Notts County

## CUPS

**F.A. Cup:** Winners

League Cup: Round 4
UEFA Cup: Quarter-final

# 1992-93 SEASON

Success in the F.A. Cup Final gave the Reds a chance of another tilt at the European Cup Winners' Cup in 1992-93. However, they crashed out in the second round to Spartak Moscow, 6-2 on aggregate. Liverpool fared no better in the F.A. Cup, exiting to third-flight Bolton Wanderers in a fourth round replay at Anfield.

Success was also thin on the ground in the inaugural Premier League. In fact Graeme Souness's side were struggling in 15th place with just 12 games remaining. However, a late spurt of good form – in which seven matches were won – allowed them to finish in sixth spot again.

That rather flattering final position did not reflect what a poor season it had been for Liverpool. Their worst run embraced an 11 match spell during the winter, in which only one victory (at Highbury) was secured.

## FACTFILE 1992-93

**Manager:** Graeme Souness

## LEAGUE STATISTICS

**Final position:** 6th place in the F.A. Premier League
**Games played:** 42   **Points:** 59
**Biggest Victory:** 5-0 vs Crystal Palace (H)
**Biggest Defeat:** 1-5 vs Coventry City (A)
**Leading Goalscorer:** Ian Rush (14 goals)
**Ever-Presents:** None
**Hat-Trick Hero:** Mark Walters
**Average Home Attendance:** 37,004
**Highest Home Crowd:** 44,619 vs Everton
**Lowest Home Crowd:** 29,574 vs Wimbledon

## CUPS

**F.A. Cup:** Round 3
**League Cup:** Round 4
**European Cup Winners' Cup:** Round 2

# 1993-94 SEASON

The Reds were rather unconvincing during the early stages of 1993-94. A nine game unbeaten run pulled them up to fifth place towards the end of January. However, yet another another embarrassing F.A. Cup defeat, at home to third-flight Bristol City (in a third round replay), hastened Graeme Souness's resignation.

The club reverted to the policy of promoting from the boot-room and appointed assistant-manager Roy Evans as their manager. Six of the last nine games ended in defeat, condemning Liverpool to eighth place. It was the club's worst finishing position since 1962-63 (their first campaign back in the top-flight).

1993-94 was the campaign in which Robbie Fowler made his initial first-team appearance. He rattled in 12 League goals in his debut campaign, only two fewer than Ian Rush, who was the club's top scorer.

This was also the last season of the famous Kop. The last League game played in front of standing supporters on the Kop was, on 30th April 1994, against Norwich City. The party-pooping Canaries won 1-0.

## FACTFILE 1993-94

**Managers**: Graeme Souness and Roy Evans

### LEAGUE STATISTICS

**Final position**: 8th place in the F.A. Premiership
**Games played**: 42    **Points**: 60
**Biggest Victory**: 5-0 vs Swindon Town (A)
**Biggest Defeat**: 0-3 vs Newcastle United (A)
**Leading Goalscorer**: Ian Rush (14 goals)
**Ever-Present**: Rush (includes one substitute appearance)
**Hat-Trick Hero**: Robbie Fowler
**Average Home Attendance**: 38,493
**Highest Home Crowd**: 44,339 vs Norwich City
**Lowest Home Crowd**: 24,561 vs QPR

### CUPS

**F.A.Cup**: Round 3
**League Cup**: Round 4

# 1994-95 SEASON

After the many problems of 1993-94, Roy Evans' first full season at the helm was a much more successful one. His side finished a creditable fourth, reached the quarter-final stage of the F.A. Cup (where they lost to Spurs) and won the League Cup (now called the Coca-Cola Cup).

The League campaign started on a high, with a 6-1 hammering of Crystal Palace at Selhurst Park. Only four of the first 23 fixtures ended in defeat, but Liverpool could not quite stay in contention for the title and finished 15 points behind the champions Blackburn Rovers. The ever-present Robbie Fowler had a golden season and finished as the leading scorer (with 25 League goals). However, it was Steve McManaman who netted the two goals which secured Liverpool their fifth League Cup – beating second-flight Bolton Wanderers 2-1 in the Final.

Evans broke the club transfer record during the summer of 1995 when he paid Nottingham Forest £8.5 million for striker Stan Collymore.

## FACTFILE 1994-95

**Manager:** Roy Evans

### LEAGUE STATISTICS

**Final position:** 4th place in the F.A. Premiership
**Games played:** 42 **Points:** 74
**Biggest Victory:** 6-1 vs Crystal Palace (A)
**Biggest Defeat:** 0-3 vs West Ham United (A)
**Leading Goalscorer:** Robbie Fowler (25 goals)
**Ever-Presents:** Robbie Fowler and David James
**Hat-Trick Hero:** Robbie Fowler
**Average Home Attendance:** 34,176
**Highest Home Crowd:** 40,014 vs Blackburn Rovers
**Lowest Home Crowd:** 27,183 vs Coventry City

### CUPS

**F.A. Cup:** Quarter-final
**League Cup:** Winners

# 1995-96 SEASON

Roy Evans' side made a bright start to 1995-96, winning seven of their first 11 League fixtures. The Reds stuttered in November, picking up only one point and losing three times (including at home to Everton). However, they remained unbeaten in all but two of their remaining 23 fixtures and finished in third place, 11 points behind the champions Manchester United.

It was the side from Old Trafford who proved too good for Liverpool at Wembley in the F.A. Cup Final. Robbie Fowler (who netted 36 times in all competitions) had scored in every round en route to the Final, but failed to get on the scoresheet at Wembley. The only goal there coming from the boot of Eric Cantona.

Liverpool stumbled out of the UEFA Cup at the second round stage to Brondby on after a very disappointing night at Anfield. The Danes won 1-0, after the first match ended goalless. One man who played his last match for Liverpool in 1995-96 was Ian Rush. He moved to Leeds United, after scoring 229 goals in 469 League games (during his two spells) for the Reds.

### FACTFILE 1995-96
**Manager:** Roy Evans

### LEAGUE STATISTICS
**Final position:** 3rd place in the F.A. Premiership
**Games played:** 38   **Points:** 71
**Biggest Victory:** 6-0 vs Manchester City (H)
**Biggest Defeat:** 1-2 vs Newcastle United (A), vs Everton (H) and vs Middlesbrough (A)
**Leading Goalscorer:** Robbie Fowler (28 goals)
**Ever-Presents:** Robbie Fowler (includes two substitute appearances), David James and Steve McManaman
**Four-Goal Hero:** Robbie Fowler
**Hat-Trick Hero:** Robbie Fowler
**Average Home Attendance:** 39,533
**Highest Home Crowd:** 40,820 vs Chelsea
**Lowest Home Crowd:** 34,063 vs Wimbledon

### CUPS
**F.A. Cup:** Finalists
**League Cup:** Round 4
**UEFA Cup:** Round 2

## 1996-97 SEASON

There were stages of the 1996-97 campaign when Liverpool looked capable of collecting their first Premiership title. They remained unbeaten during the first eight fixtures to head the field and got their heads back in front again during the festive season. However, they lost four of their final 11 fixtures and finished fourth (with the same number of points as the second and third clubs), nine points behind the champions Manchester United.

Robbie Fowler netted 18 times and Stan Collymore scored 12 goals (to add to his first season tally of 14), but not enough goals came from midfield during 1996-97. There was little joy in the domestic cups with Middlesbrough and Chelsea proving too strong for them in the League Cup and F.A. Cup, respectively.

However, Liverpool did enjoy a good run in the European Cup Winners' Cup in 1996-97. They defeated MyPa, Sion and Brann; but found Paris St Germain too good for them at the semi-final stage. The French side won the first leg 3-0 and, despite goals from Robbie Fowler and Mark Wright, Liverpool could not quite pull level at Anfield.

## FACTFILE 1996-97

**Manager:** Roy Evans

### LEAGUE STATISTICS

**Final position:** 4th place in the F.A. Premiership
**Games played:** 38  **Points:** 68
**Biggest Victory:** 5-1 vs Chelsea (H) and also vs Middlesbrough (A)
**Biggest Defeat:** 0-3 vs Blackburn Rovers (A)
**Leading Goalscorer:** Robbie Fowler (18 goals)
**Ever-Presents:** Stig Inge Bjornebye and David James
**Four-Goal Hero:** Robbie Fowler
**Other Hat-Trick Heroes:** None
**Average Home Attendance:** 39,777
**Highest Home Crowd:** 40,892 vs Manchester United
**Lowest Home Crowd:** 36,126 vs Nottingham Forest

### CUPS

**F.A. Cup:** Round 4
**League Cup:** Quarter-final
**European Cup-Winners' Cup:** Semi-final

# 1997-98 SEASON

After scoring on his debut at the end of the previous campaign, teenage sensation Michael Owen was a regular member of the first team in 1997-98. Owen underlined his potential, and booked a World Cup place, with 22 goals (18 in the League) to become the club's leading goalscorer. When he made his England debut (against Chile) he became the youngest player (at 18 years and 59 days) to represent England in the 20th Century.

The Reds overcame a sluggish start to move into the top four over the Christmas period. A winless five match run torpedoed their title chance; but they were still good enough to cement third place (behind Arsenal and Manchester United).

Liverpool looked on course to reach Wembley and another League Cup Final after defeating West Bromwich Albion, Grimsby Town and Newcastle United. However, they were edged out 3-2, on aggregate, by Middlesbrough in the two-legged semi-final. The Anfield men also tumbled out of the UEFA Cup in the second round at the hands of Strasbourg. The French side won 3-0 on their own soil and, despite goals from Robbie Fowler and Karlheinz Riedle, there was no way back for Evans' side on Merseyside. However, that 2-0 success was Liverpool's 100th victory in major European competitions.

## FACTFILE 1997-98

**Manager:** Roy Evans

## LEAGUE STATISTICS

**Final position:** 3rd place in the F.A. Premiership
**Games played:** 38   **Points:** 65
**Biggest Victory:** 5-0 vs West Ham United (H)
**Biggest Defeat:** 1-4 vs Chelsea (A)
**Leading Goalscorer:** Michael Owen (18 goals)
**Ever-Presents:** None
**Hat-Trick Heroes:** Patrik Berger and Michael Owen
**Average Home Attendance:** 40,628
**Highest Home Crowd:** 44,532 vs Bolton Wanderers
**Lowest Home Crowd:** 34,705 vs Sheffield Wednesday

## CUPS

**F.A. Cup:** Round 3
**League Cup:** Semi-final
**UEFA Cup:** Semi-final

# 1998-99 SEASON

During the summer of 1988 it was announced that former French national team coach Gerard Houllier would manage Liverpool on a joint basis with Roy Evans. The Reds made a bright start to the campaign but then started to stutter. In November Evans resigned, with Liverpool lying in 11th place, leaving Houllier alone at the helm. Former skipper Phil Thompson was appointed assistant-manager. Houllier's side exited the UEFA Cup in early December, after losing (home and away) to Celta Vigo in the third round.

Four wins (including the 7-1 thumping of Southampton) from five fixtures around the turn of the year propelled Liverpool into the top six. However, two sloppy home defeats (to Leicester City and Aston Villa) meant the Reds eventually had to be content with seventh place. Michael Owen was the leading scoring in 1998-99 with 18 goals, four more than the haul of his co-striker Robbie Fowler. Both men missed the final clutch of matches. Owen through injury and Fowler because of a four match F.A. suspension for mimicking cocaine-snorting after scoring a penalty in the 3-2 local derby win at Anfield.

There was a very moving tribute to the 96 fans who lost their lives the Hillsborough Disaster during 1998-99. There was a minute's silence at 15:06 on 15th April, the tenth anniversary of the Disaster, with 14,000 standing silent for a minute on the 'Kop'.

## FACTFILE 1998-99

**Managers:** Roy Evans & Gerard Houllier

## LEAGUE STATISTICS

**Final position:** 7th place in the F.A. Premiership
**Games played:** 38  **Points:** 54
**Biggest Victory:** 7-1 vs Southampton (H)
**Biggest Defeat:** 1-3 vs Leeds United (H)
**Leading Goalscorer:** Michael Owen (18 goals)
**Ever-Presents:** None
**Four-Goal Hero:** Michael Owen
**Hat-Trick Heroes:** Robbie Fowler (on two occasions) and Michael Owen
**Average Home Attendance:** 43,231
**Highest Home Crowd:** 44,852 vs Everton
**Lowest Home Crowd:** 36,019 vs Leicester City

## CUPS

**F.A. Cup:** Round 4
**League Cup:** Round 4
**UEFA Cup:** Round 3

# 1999-2000 SEASON

With a new goalkeeper in Sander Westerveld (who replaced Aston Villa bound David James) and a new centre-half in Sami Hyypia, Liverpool took time to find their feet in 1999-2000. They won only three of their first eight fixtures, but then lost only two of their next 26 League fixtures to glide through the pack.

Buoyed by the arrival of defender Stephane Henchoz (from Blackburn Rovers) and the magnificent form of the ever-present Hyypia, Liverpool only conceded as many as three goals on one occasion (at home to Manchester United). In fact they conceded only 30 goals in total (their best defensive record since 1988-89). Unfortunately the Reds also found goals to come by, netting just 51 in total. In a bid to shake up the team, Gerard Houllier paid Leicester City a club record £11 million for Emile Heskey.

Liverpool looked on course for second place (behind champions-elect Manchester United) after a brace by Heskey clinched a 2-1 win at Wimbledon in April. It was their fifth successive victory. However, they stumbled during the run-in, collecting just two points from five fixtures. They had to be content with fourth place, two points behind third placed Leeds United and seven points behind the runners-up Arsenal. A Champions League place had slipped from their grasp, but at least there was the opportunity of another tilt at the UEFA Cup!

## FACTFILE 1999-2000

**Manager:** Gerard Houllier

## LEAGUE STATISTICS

**Final position:** 4th place in the F.A. Premiership
**Games played:** 38   **Points:** 67
**Biggest Victory:** 4-1 vs Sheffield Wednesday (H)
**Biggest Defeat:** 0-2 vs Chelsea (A) and also vs Leicester City (H)
**Leading Goalscorer:** Michael Owen (11 goals)
**Ever-Present:** Sami Hyypia
**Hat-Trick Heroes:** None
**Average Home Attendance:** 44,074

**Highest Home Crowd**: 44,929 vs Manchester United
**Lowest Home Crowd**: 40,483 vs Bradford City

## CUPS

**F.A. Cup**: Round 4
**League Cup**: Round 3

# 2000-01 SEASON

2000-01 was a glorious campaign for Liverpool. Gerard Houllier's side lifted both major domestic cups and followed up by winning the UEFA Cup with a golden goal. It was a tremendous team effort with 18 different men making appearances in at least one of the three Finals. Sadly, one man who played no part was club captain Jamie Redknapp, who was side-lined by injury. The arrival of Markus Babbel further strengthened the defence and, from mid-October onwards, Liverpool never slipped lower than sixth place. They won six of their final seven games to grab third place and an opportunity to play in the premier European Champions competition.

Two of the Reds' cup successes were at Cardiff's Millennium Stadium. Skipper Robbie Fowler netted a super goal in the Worthington Cup Final, but second-flight Birmingham City took the Reds to extra-time. In the end it was the Merseysiders' cooler nerves from the spot that won the day. Arsenal held the edge in the F.A. Cup Final and went ahead in the second half. However, Liverpool responded superbly and an excellent brace by Michael Owen broke the Londoners' hearts.

The UEFA Cup Final against CD Alaves was staged in Dortmund. It turned out to be a nine goal thriller. The Reds went 2-0 ahead and later 3-1 in front before being pegged back by the Spaniards. Substitute Fowler appeared to won the game with a 73rd minute goal, but Alaves scored near the end to force extra-time. The unlikely Liverpool hero turned out to be Delfin Geli, whose 117th minute own-goal brought the thriller to a halt as the golden goal law applied.

## FACTFILE 2000-01

**Manager**: Gerard Houllier

## LEAGUE STATISTICS

**Final position**: 3rd place in the F.A. Premiership
**Games played**: 38  **Points**: 69
**Biggest Victory**: 4-0 vs Derby County (A), vs Arsenal (H) and vs Charlton Athletic (A)
**Biggest Defeat**: 0-3 vs Chelsea (A)

**Leading Goalscorer:** Michael Owen (16 goals)

**Ever-Presents:** Markus Babbel and Sander Westerveld

**Hat-Trick Heroes:** Michael Owen (on two occasions) and Emile Heskey

**Average Home Attendance:** 43,699

**Highest Home Crowd:** 44,806 vs Manchester United

**Lowest Home Crowd:** 38,474 vs Southampton

## CUPS

**F.A. Cup:** Winners

**League Cup:** Winners

**UEFA Cup:** Winners

# 2001-02 SEASON

Despite the early exits from both domestic cups, 2001-02 was another extremely busy campaign which included 16 nights of European football. The Reds easily side-stepped Haka to reach the first stage of the Champions League. They finished top of their group (which contained Boavista, Borussia Dortmund and Dynamo Kiev) to reach the last 16 and the second group stage. Liverpool again qualified, this time in second place (behind Barcelona), at the expense of Roma and Galatasaray. They eventually exited the competition after a thrilling quarter-final second leg in Leverkusen. The German side trailed 1-0 from the first leg but looked favourites to progress when they led 3-1 on the night, with only a quarter of the home leg remaining. However, Jari Litmanen popped up in the 79th minute to level the aggregate scores and give the Anfield men an advantage in terms of away goals. Sadly, however, the Germans responded with their fourth goal of the evening to end Liverpool's adventure.

Arsenal got revenge for the previous season's defeat in the F.A. Cup Final by edging Liverpool out of the same competition at a turbulent Highbury. The Gunners finished with nine men, while the Reds had Jamie Carragher dismissed for 'returning' a coin to the crowd.

Health matters had dominated Liverpool's thoughts during the early months of 2001-02. Markus Babbel contracted a mystery virus, which weakened his immune system and truncated his season to just the first two League games. Then, on 13th October during the home match with Leeds United, Gerard Houllier was rushed to hospital for major heart surgery after experiencing chest pains during his half-time talk. Phil Thompson took the reins while the Frenchman recuperated and it was five months later before Houllier made an emotional return to Anfield. Meanwhile the

Reds had been involved in the tightest fight for the Premiership for years. They led the table for a month just before to Christmas and won eleven out of 12 matches from the back-end of January to lay down a serious challenge to Manchester United, Arsenal and Newcastle United.

Liverpool headed the table at the end of March (having played more games), but defeat at Tottenham, at the end of April, finally ended any hopes of a 19th title. They won their last two matches, though, to secure second spot (seven points behind champions Arsenal) and finish above Manchester United (for the first time since 1990-91). Polish keeper Jersey Dudek had an excellent debut campaign, as did John Arne Riise. Playing either on the left of the defence or midfield, the Norwegian was superb (and contributed seven useful League goals). In addition, Portuguese defender Abel Xavier provided an extra option at the back after his move across Stanley Park. Among the departures from Anfield in 2001-02 were Sander Westerveld and Robbie Fowler. After much soul-searching, Fowler departed to Leeds for a club record £12.5 million fee. Then, towards the end of the campaign, the injury-jinxed Jamie Redknapp left Anfield for Spurs as Houllier made room in the dressing-room for another set of arrivals.

## FACTFILE 2001-02

**Manager:** Gerard Houllier

### LEAGUE STATISTICS

**Final position:** 2nd place in the F.A. Premiership
**Games played:** 38   **Points:** 80
**Biggest Victory:** 6-0 vs Ipswich Town (A)
**Biggest Defeat:** 0-4 vs Chelsea (A)
**Leading Goalscorer:** Michael Owen (19 goals)
**Ever-Presents:** None
**Hat-Trick Hero:** Robbie Fowler
**Average Home Attendance:** 43,389
**Highest Home Crowd:** 44,371 vs Everton
**Lowest Home Crowd:** 37,163 vs Fulham

### CUPS

**F.A. Cup:** Round 4
**League Cup:** Round 3
**European Champions Cup:** Quarter-final

# THE FUTURE

Although the Reds did not win a major trophy in 2001-02 there were a lot of positives to take from the campaign. Not least the fact that the Reds had finished in their highest position since 1990-91. Liverpool fans eagerly awaited the coming season with a strong notion that their side had their best chance to date of claiming that elusive first Premiership crown.

Gerard Houllier sensibly declined the opportunity to travel to Japan and Korea for the World Cup. Quite rightly he put his health first and by the end of the summer of 2002 he was almost his old self. He was not dormant on the transfer front, though, with four new faces joining the squad in return for an outlay of £19 million. Patrice Luzi arrived on a free transfer from Monaco, while midfielder Bruno Cheyrou joined from Lille for £4 million. Two members of Senegal's exciting World Cup squad were also brought to Anfield. Midfielder Saif Diao cost £5 million (from Sedan), while the most expensive purchase was striker El Hadji Diouf (from Lens). The 'African Footballer of the Year' cost £10 million.

Houllier also nearly signed Lee Bowyer from Leeds United. However, the Liverpool manager changed his mind about him when it was clear that the midfielder's attitude was not quite right. Houllier was quoted as saying "he did not have the 100% desire to play for Liverpool".

In addition former Arsenal striker Nicolas Anelka, who made 20 League appearances on loan (from Paris St Germain) during 2001-02, was not offered a permanent contract. Meanwhile Nicky Barmby moved on to Leeds United just two seasons after making the move from Everton. Another to leave Liverpool, also after two terms, was Gary McAllister, who returned to Coventry City to become the club's player-manager.

With a brand new 55,000 seater stadium in Stanley Park planned to open in 2005-06, Liverpool fans had a lot to look forward to in the medium term. More immediately, though in the summer of 2002, high on their wish list was surely that there be another long run in the Champions League (and perhaps even success this time). But Liverpool's number one priority was clearly the Premiership title. Houllier's squad was undoubtedly hungry enough, but would they prove good enough?

# LIVERPOOL 25 SEASONS 1977-78 TO 2001-02

## A-Z OF THE 25 MOST INFLUENTIAL PLAYERS

## JOHN ALDRIDGE

During his early days at Anfield, John Aldridge was written off by one newspaper as a "£750,000 misfit". However, Aldo responded by proving that he not only looked a little like Ian Rush but could score goals like him, too. He only started 66 League games for the Reds but rattled in a round half century of goals. He proved to be the perfect replacement for Rush, in 1987-88, and his form remained of a sufficient high quality to help restrict the Welshman's starting appearances on his return to the club in 1988-89.

Aldridge was the leading scorer in each of his two full seasons at Anfield. He collected a League Championship medal in 1987-88 and scored the opener in the F.A. Cup Final triumph of 1989. It helped a little to erase the painful memory of 12 months earlier, when he became the first man to miss a penalty in a Wembley F.A. Cup Final. He won 67 caps for the Republic of Ireland, 19 of these being awarded while he was on Liverpool's books.

A true Liverpudlian, who supported the Reds from the Kop as a boy, John's last important act at Anfield was to slot home a penalty after coming on as a substitute in the 9-0 hammering of Crystal Palace. He was sold to Real Sociedad for £1 million and later became player-manager of Tranmere Rovers (where he gave a League debut to his son Paul). Rovers reached the League Cup Final under Aldridge. However, he left Prenton Park in 2001, with his side heading towards the Second Division.

John Aldridge made his Football League debut for Newport County (after signing from South Liverpool) and later scored a bucket full of goals for Oxford United (helping them win the League Cup and the Second Division title). He was an unlikely hero, but a real hero of the Kop. And Aldo was definitely no misfit.

### FACTFILE

**Born**: Liverpool, 18th August 1958
**Position**: Striker
**Liverpool 25 Seasons League Record**: 83 appearances – 50 goals
**Liverpool Career League Record**: As above
**Other League apps (Pre-Liverpool)**: Newport County (170 apps. – 69 goals),
Oxford United (114 apps. – 72 goals)

**Other League apps (Post-Liverpool):** Tranmere Rovers (242 apps. – 138 goals)

## 25 SEASONS LIVERPOOL LEAGUE RECORD

| Season | Apps | Goals |
|---|---|---|
| 1986-1987 | 10 | 2 |
| 1987-1988 | 36 | 26 |
| 1988-1989 | 35 | 21 |
| 1989-1990 | 2 | 1 |
| 25 Seasons Total | 83 | 50 |

# JOHN BARNES

Only seven men played more League games for Liverpool than John Barnes in the quarter of a century up to the summer of 2002, a period when the Jamaican-born England international netted the fourth highest tally of goals for the club. He made his name with Watford before Kenny Dalglish secured his signature in the summer of 1987 for £900,000.

He was a naturally skilful performer who could play on either wing, or up front. His close control was top-class and he was a fine crosser of the ball. He bagged 84 League goals for Liverpool, 22 of which came in 1988-89 when he was the club's top scorer. He was also the leading scorer (jointly with Ian Rush) the following campaign. John won two League Championship medals and was a member of the sides which won the League Cup in 1995 and the F.A. Cup in 1992. He missed the 1992 F.A. Cup because of a thigh injury. He played in the 1988 Final, though, and also experienced the emotion of defeat in an F.A. Cup Final with Watford and Newcastle United.

John skippered Liverpool towards the end of his Anfield career. He joined Newcastle on a free in the summer of 1997 and finished his playing career with Charlton Athletic. He later managed Celtic (under Dalglish), but not with any great success. John Barnes was capped by England on 73 occasions (48 while with Liverpool), the most memorable occasion being in Rio de Janeiro (in 1984) when he scored a wonderful solo goal. He was awarded an MBE for his services to football and was voted 'Footballer of the Year' in 1988 and 1990. He was also the PFA 'Player of the Year' in 1988.

## FACTFILE

**Born:** Jamaica, 7th November 1963
**Position:** Midfield/Forward

**Liverpool 25 Seasons League Record**: 314 appearances – 84 goals
**Liverpool Career League Record**: As above
**Other League apps (Pre-Liverpool)**: Watford (233 apps. – 65 goals)
**Other League apps (Post-Liverpool)**: Newcastle United (27 apps – 6 goals),
Charlton Athletic (12 apps. – 0 goals)

## 25 SEASONS LIVERPOOL LEAGUE RECORD

| Season | Apps | Goals |
| --- | --- | --- |
| 1987-1988 | 38 | 15 |
| 1988-1989 | 33 | 8 |
| 1989-1990 | 34 | 22 |
| 1990-1991 | 35 | 16 |
| 1991-1992 | 12 | 1 |
| 1992-1993 | 27 | 5 |
| 1993-1994 | 26 | 3 |
| 1994-1995 | 38 | 7 |
| 1995-1996 | 36 | 3 |
| 1996-1997 | 35 | 4 |
| 25 Seasons Total | 314 | 84 |

# PETER BEARDSLEY

Peter Beardsley was a key component of the Kenny Dalglish's sides of the late 1980's. He won two League Championship medals and was part of the team that defeated Everton in the 1989 F.A. Cup Final. He spent just four seasons at Anfield before making the short trek across Stanley Park to Everton (for £1 million) in the summer of 1991.

He was an intelligent player who could play up front, behind the front two or in midfield. He bagged 46 League goals for the Reds and set up countless chances for his team-mates. He cost £1.9 million when he signed from Newcastle United in 1987.

Peter won 34 of his 59 England caps during his spell at Anfield. He began his career with Carlisle United and had spells with Vancouver Whitecaps and Manchester United (making just one League Cup appearance), before making his name with the Magpies. Five other League clubs (including Newcastle again) utilised his enthusiasm and experience after he left Goodison Park. He also had a spell in Australia with Melbourne Knights.

## FACTFILE

**Born:** Newcastle-Upon-Tyne, 18th January 1961

**Position:** Forward/Midfield

**Liverpool 25 Seasons League Record:** 131 appearances – 46 goals

**Liverpool Career League Record:** As above

**Other League apps (Pre-Liverpool):** Carlisle United (104 apps. – 22), Newcastle United (147 apps. – 61 goals)

**Other League apps (Post-Liverpool):** Everton (81 apps. – 25 goals), Newcastle United (129 apps. – 46 goals), Bolton Wanderers (17 apps. – 2 goals), Manchester City (on loan 6 apps. – 0 goals), Fulham (on loan 21 apps. – 4 goals), Hartlepool United (22 apps. – 2 goals)

## 25 SEASONS LIVERPOOL LEAGUE RECORD

| Season | Apps | Goals |
|---|---|---|
| 1987-1988 | 38 | 15 |
| 1988-1989 | 37 | 10 |
| 1989-1990 | 29 | 10 |
| 1990-1991 | 27 | 11 |
| 25 Seasons Total | 131 | 46 |

# RAY CLEMENCE

Ray Clemence was Liverpool's number one for virtually the whole of the 1970's, missing only six League games in 11 seasons. He was as competent as he was consistent. He controlled his area superbly and marshalled his defence expertly. Bill Shankly signed Ray from Scunthorpe United in 1968-69 and, after a spell in the Central League team, he took over the gloves from Tommy Lawrence.

All-told Clemence was an ever-present during six seasons, the last being in 1978-79 when he kept 28 clean sheets and only conceded 16 goals as the Reds raced to the title. He keep a mammoth 227 clean sheets all-told in 470 League games for Liverpool. He was an key member of five League Championship winning sides, won an F.A. Cup winners' medal (in 1974) and a League Cup winners' medal (in 1981).

Ray moved to Spurs in the summer of 1981 and played against his old mates in the 1981-82 League Cup Final. He won the F.A. Cup with the London side later that season. He later coached Spurs and managed Barnet. Ray Clemence would have won over one hundred England caps – if he was not a contemporary of Peter Shilton.

He actually won 61 (56 while at Anfield). He is the father of Tottenham midfielder Stephen Clemence.

## FACTFILE

**Born:** Skegness, 5th August 1948

**Position:** Goalkeeper

**Liverpool 25 Seasons League Record:** 164 appearances – 0 goals

**Liverpool Career League Record:** 470 appearances – 0 goals

**Other League apps (Pre-Liverpool):** Scunthorpe United (48 apps. – 0 goals)

**Other League apps (Post-Liverpool):** Tottenham Hotspur (240 apps. – 0 goals)

## 25 SEASONS LIVERPOOL LEAGUE RECORD

| Season | Apps | Goals |
| --- | --- | --- |
| 1977-1978 | 40 | 0 |
| 1978-1979 | 42 | 0 |
| 1979-1980 | 41 | 0 |
| 1980-1981 | 41 | 0 |
| 25 Seasons Total | 164 | 0 |

# KENNY DALGLISH

Kenny Dalglish MBE was arguably the finest footballer to play for Liverpool. There was a cloud hanging over Anfield when Kevin Keegan moved to Hamburg during the summer of 1977. However, Bob Paisley certainly knew what he was doing when he signed Dalglish (for £440,000) from Celtic (where he won nine trophies). The Scot scored on his League debut at Middlesbrough and in fact only failed to score in one of his first six League outings. He was the club's top scorer (with 20 League goals) at the end of that 1977-78 campaign. A season that he crowned by scoring the only goal against FC Brugge in the European Cup Final at Wembley.

Kenny was ever-present in five out of his first six campaigns at the club. He was leading scorer again in 1977-78. All-told he won 17 winners' medals while he was at Anfield. He won the League title eight times, won two F.A. Cups (one as a player and one as a manager), collected four League Cup winners' medals (scoring in the 1981 Final replay) and was a member of three sides which won the European Cup. He was both the 'Footballer of the Year' in 1979 and 1983. He was also voted the PFA 'Player of the Year' in 1983. Kenny won 102 Scottish caps, the last 55 of them while he was a Liverpool player.

Dalglish had an excellent eye for goal and had superb technical ability. He was most effective up front, or in the hole, but in his later days proved he could be a very creative midfielder. Kenny became player-manager of Liverpool when Joe Fagan retired in the summer of 1985. He hit the ground running by becoming the first player-manager to steer a side to the First Division title. His side also won the F.A. Cup in that 'Double' winning campaign of 1985-86. Liverpool won two more titles and another F.A. Cup before the pressure told and Dalglish resigned from his managerial post. However, he bounced back to steer Blackburn Rovers to the Premiership title and later took Newcastle United to an F.A. Cup Final. A spell in Celtic's boardroom proved less satisfactory.

The great Bob Paisley is the only manager to have steered the Reds to more trophies than Kenny Dalglish (who was 'Manager of the Year' on three occasions). Kenny had few equals on the pitch and none of them pulled on a Liverpool shirt during the quarter of a century up to the summer of 2002.

## FACTFILE

**Born**: Dalmarnock, 4th March 1951
**Position**: Striker/Midfield
**Liverpool 25 Seasons League Record**: 355 appearances – 118 goals
**Liverpool Career League Record**: As above

## 25 SEASONS LIVERPOOL LEAGUE RECORD

| Season | Apps | Goals |
| --- | --- | --- |
| 1977-1978 | 42 | 20 |
| 1978-1979 | 42 | 21 |
| 1979-1980 | 42 | 16 |
| 1980-1981 | 34 | 8 |
| 1981-1982 | 42 | 13 |
| 1982-1983 | 42 | 18 |
| 1983-1984 | 33 | 7 |
| 1984-1985 | 36 | 6 |
| 1985-1986 | 21 | 3 |
| 1986-1987 | 18 | 6 |
| 1987-1988 | 2 | 0 |
| 1988-1989 | 0 | 0 |
| 1989-1990 | 1 | 0 |
| 25 Seasons Total | 335 | 118 |

# ROBBIE FOWLER

Only Ian Rush, his mentor, scored more League goals for Liverpool in the quarter of a century up to the summer of 2002 than the 120 netted by Robbie Fowler. So, it was hardly surprising that so many at Anfield had heavy hearts when the talented striker joined Leeds United in November 2001, when aged 26.

An 18 year-old Robbie made an immediate impact during his debut campaign for the Reds, netting a dozen League goals at a rate of nearly one every other game. He was an ever-present member of the side in 1994-95 (when he won a League Cup winners' medal) and 1995-96. He was the club's top scorer in each of those two campaigns, and emulated the feat again in 1996-97.

Plagued by injuries, Fowler dropped down Gerard Houllier's pecking order behind his England colleagues Michael Owen and Emile Heskey. Even so he made some important contributions during the glorious 'three cups' campaign of 2001-02. With a wonderful 30 yard dipping volley, he was Liverpool's goalscorer in the Worthington Cup success. He also made appearances from the bench in the F.A. Cup and UEFA Cup Finals, scoring a crucial goal in the latter. Robbie Fowler netted 12 times to be top scorer for Leeds, in 2001-02, after his £12.5 million move (a Liverpool club record). Up to the summer of 2002 he had won 26 England caps, the first 22 were awarded while he was a Liverpool player.

## FACTFILE

**Born**: Liverpool, 9th April 1975
**Position**: Striker
**Liverpool 25 Seasons League Record**: 236 appearances – 120 goals
**Liverpool Career League Record**: As above
**Other League appearances (Post-Liverpool)**: Leeds United (22 apps. – 12 goals)

## 25 SEASONS LIVERPOOL LEAGUE RECORD

| Season | Apps | Goals |
|---|---|---|
| 1993-1994 | 28 | 12 |
| 1994-1995 | 42 | 25 |
| 1995-1996 | 38 | 28 |
| 1996-1997 | 32 | 18 |
| 1997-1998 | 20 | 9 |
| 1998-1999 | 25 | 14 |
| 1999-2000 | 14 | 3 |

| | | |
|---|---|---|
| 2000-2001 | 27 | 8 |
| 2001-2002 | 10 | 3 |
| 25 Seasons Total | 236 | 120 |

# BRUCE GROBBELAAR

Bruce Grobbelaar was one of the most colourful players to represent Liverpool. Only Ian Rush made more appearances for Liverpool in the quarter of a century up to the summer of 2002. Bruce was born in South Africa, but made 20 international appearances between the sticks for Zimbabwe.

Grobbelaar made his Football League debut for Crewe Alexandra, after joining on trial from Vancouver Whitecaps. It was the Canadian club who collected the £250,000 fee after the keeper joined Liverpool in March 1981. Ray Clemence's departure to Spurs gave Bruce the opportunity to play in the first-team at the start of 1981-82 campaign. He grasped his big chance with both hands and was ever-present for five consecutive seasons (and six times altogether).

In addition to being an excellent shot-stopper, Bruce dominated his area more than any of his predecessors. Like all good goalkeepers, Bruce was certainly crazy. In fact he was crazier than most, but also better at his art than all but a few. He was full of idiosyncrasies and often clown-like, but was much-loved on the terraces.

Bruce won five League titles, kept goal in three victorious F.A. Cup Finals and helped the Reds win four League Cups. His 'wobble' in the 1984 European Cup Final shoot-out will never be forgotten. He was loaned out to Stoke City during 1992-93, but returned to Anfield to make another 29 League appearances in 1993-94. He joined Southampton, on a free transfer, in the summer of 1994.

After two years at the Dell, Bruce moved to Plymouth Argyle. He was later on the books of Oxford United and Sheffield Wednesday, before making four appearances for Oldham Athletic. He was playing for Non-League Chesham United in September 1998, when he was invited to fill in in an emergency for Bury. At the age of 40 years and 337 days he became the oldest player ever in the Shakers' history. He made his final League appearances for Lincoln City in December 1998. He later coached in Zimbabwe and South Africa. Bruce Grobbelaar certainly had his critics, but he was a fine goalie.

## FACTFILE

**Born**: Durban (South Africa), 6th October 1957
**Position**: Goalkeeper

**Liverpool 25 Seasons League Record**: 440 appearances – 0 goals

**Liverpool Career League Record**: As above

**Other League apps (Pre-Liverpool)**: Crewe Alexandra (24 apps. – 1 goal)

**Other League apps (on loan from Liverpool)**: Stoke City (4 apps. – 0 goals)

**Other League apps (Post-Liverpool)**: Southampton (32 apps. – 0 goals), Plymouth Argyle (36 apps. – 0 goals), Oldham Athletic (4 apps. – 0 goals), Bury (1 app. – 0 goals), Lincoln City (2 apps. – 0 goals)

## 25 SEASONS LIVERPOOL LEAGUE RECORD

| Season | Apps | Goals |
| --- | --- | --- |
| 1981-1982 | 42 | 0 |
| 1982-1983 | 42 | 0 |
| 1983-1984 | 42 | 0 |
| 1984-1985 | 42 | 0 |
| 1985-1986 | 42 | 0 |
| 1986-1987 | 31 | 0 |
| 1987-1988 | 38 | 0 |
| 1988-1989 | 21 | 0 |
| 1989-1990 | 38 | 0 |
| 1990-1991 | 31 | 0 |
| 1991-1992 | 37 | 0 |
| 1992-1993 | 5 | 0 |
| 1993-1994 | 29 | 0 |
| 25 Seasons Total | 440 | 0 |

# ALAN HANSEN

Alan Hansen was one of the most intelligent and effective defenders that has ever worn a red shirt. In a Liverpool career clocking 13 seasons, the Scot won 16 winners' medals. He won eight League Championship medals, two F.A. Cup winners' medals, three League Cup winners' medals and three European Cup winners' medals. He became a first-team regular in 1978-79, nudging out Emlyn Hughes, and was an important member of the side (apart from 1988-89, most of which he missed through injury) until he hung up his boots in 1990.

Bob Paisley bought Alan from Partick Thistle for a bargain £100,000 fee in April 1977. He made his Football League debut the following September in a victory over

Derby County. Hansen was a forceful tackler whose powers of anticipation added an extra yard to his game. He was ever-present in the League in 1983-84 and missed only one League game in each of the subsequent two campaigns. He became a fine skipper of some of Liverpool's best teams.

Alan Hansen won all of his 26 Scottish caps while on Liverpool's books. He was 34 years-old when he retired from playing, after helping the Reds clinch the 1989-90 title. He is now an eloquent member of the BBC TV 'Match of the Day' team of pundits.

## FACTFILE

**Born**: Alloa, 13th June 1955
**Position**: Defender
**Liverpool 25 Seasons League Record**: 438 appearances – 8 goals
**Liverpool Career League Record**: As above

## 25 SEASONS LIVERPOOL LEAGUE RECORD

| Season | Apps | Goals |
|---|---|---|
| 1977-1978 | 18 | 0 |
| 1978-1979 | 34 | 1 |
| 1979-1980 | 38 | 4 |
| 1980-1981 | 36 | 1 |
| 1981-1982 | 35 | 0 |
| 1982-1983 | 34 | 0 |
| 1983-1984 | 42 | 1 |
| 1984-1985 | 41 | 0 |
| 1985-1986 | 41 | 0 |
| 1986-1987 | 39 | 0 |
| 1987-1988 | 39 | 1 |
| 1988-1989 | 6 | 0 |
| 1989-1990 | 31 | 0 |
| 25 Seasons Total | 434 | 8 |

# DAVID JAMES

Only Bruce Grobbelaar, the man he ultimately replaced, stood between the sticks more times for Liverpool in the quarter of a century up to the summer of 2002 than

David James. Signed from Watford (for a £1 million fee) in July 1992, the 6 foot 5 inch James was a very competent performer for the Reds during the best part of seven seasons of the 1990's.

James commands his area with great presence and there a few better shot-stoppers in the country. His distribution of the ball is generally excellent; but occasionally he is found wanting with high crosses. Graeme Souness signed him to replace Grobbelaar, but it was not until 1994-95 that the Anfield goalkeeper jersey fully belonged to him. He helped Liverpool win the League Cup during 1994-95, the first of three successive campaigns in which he was ever present in the League.

After making 214 League appearances for Liverpool, David transferred to Aston Villa for £1.8 million. Two summers later he was on the move again, this time to West Ham United. He had an excellent first season in East London and secured a place in England's World Cup squad. David James won nine England caps up to the summer of 2002, the first being while he was with Liverpool.

## FACTFILE

**Born**: Welwyn Garden City, 1st August 1970
**Position**: Goalkeeper
**Liverpool 25 Seasons League Record**: 214 appearances – 0 goals
**Liverpool Career League Record**: As above
**Other League appearances (Pre-Liverpool)**: Watford (89 apps. – 0 goals)
**Other League appearances (Post-Liverpool)**: Aston Villa (67 apps. – 0 goals), West Ham United (26 apps – 0 goals)

## 25 SEASONS LIVERPOOL LEAGUE RECORD

| Season | Apps | Goals |
|---|---|---|
| 1992-1993 | 29 | 0 |
| 1993-1994 | 14 | 0 |
| 1994-1995 | 42 | 0 |
| 1995-1996 | 38 | 0 |
| 1996-1997 | 38 | 0 |
| 1997-1998 | 27 | 0 |
| 1998-1999 | 26 | 0 |
| 25 Seasons Total | 214 | 0 |

# DAVID JOHNSON

Only five men scored more goals for Liverpool in the quarter of a century up to the summer of 2002 than David Johnson – even though he held a regular first-team place for just three seasons. He netted 55 League goals for Liverpool, 21 coming in 1979-80 – when he was the club's leading scorer. He dove-tailed well with Kenny Dalglish, but lost his place after the emergence of Ian Rush.

Johnson won four League Championship medals and played in the 1981 European Cup Final. He also played in the 1977 F.A. Cup Final and came off the bench in the League Cup Final five years later. David re-joined Everton, his first club, after he left Anfield in 1982. He also played for Ipswich Town and Manchester City before dropping down the divisions. David Johnson won eight England caps, five of them being awarded while he was with Liverpool.

## FACTFILE

**Born**: Liverpool, 23rd October 1951
**Position**: Striker
**Liverpool 25 Seasons League Record**:  123 appearances – 50 goals
**Liverpool Career League Record**:  149 appearances – 55 goals
**Other League apps (Pre-Liverpool)**:  Everton (50 apps. – 11 goals),
Ipswich Town (137 apps. – 45 goals)
**Other League apps (Post-Liverpool)**:  Everton (40 apps. – 4 goals),
Barnsley (on loan 4 apps. – 1 goal),  Manchester City (24 apps. – 3 goals)

## 25 SEASONS LIVERPOOL RECORD

| Season | Apps | Goals |
|---|---|---|
| 1977-1978 | 12 | 3 |
| 1978-1979 | 30 | 16 |
| 1979-1980 | 37 | 21 |
| 1980-1981 | 29 | 8 |
| 1981-1982 | 15 | 2 |
| 25 Seasons Total | 123 | 50 |

# ALAN KENNEDY

Alan Kennedy was Liverpool's regular left-back during the late 1970s and early 1980s. He was a solid defender who had the happy knack of scoring in big matches.

He was signed from Newcastle United (for whom he played against Liverpool in 1974 F.A. Cup Final) in the summer of 1978. Alan made an immediate impact and became Phil Neal's usual full-back partner.

Kennedy won five League Championships, four League Cup winners' medals and played in Liverpool's last three European Cup Finals. Alan scored the only goal against Real Madrid on that unforgettable night in Paris and converted the decisive penalty in the shoot-out three years later (against AS Roma). He also scored in the League Cup Finals of 1981 and 1983. Alan was ever-present in the League in 1983-84 and 1984-85.

Kennedy signed for his native Sunderland after leaving Anfield (a comical own-goal at Oxford hastened his departure) in 1985. He dropped down the divisions afterwards and also had spells with Belgian side Beerschot and Non-League Colne Dynamoes. Alan Kennedy won both of his England caps while he was with Liverpool.

## FACTFILE

**Born:** Sunderland, 31st August 1954
**Position:** Defender
**Liverpool 25 Seasons League Record:** 251 appearances – 15 goals
**Liverpool Career League Record:** As above
**Other League apps (Pre-Liverpool):** Newcastle United (158 apps. – 9 goals)
**Other League apps (Post-Liverpool):** Sunderland (54 apps. – 2 goals),
Hartlepool United (5 apps. – 0 goals), Wigan Athletic (22 apps. – 0 goals),
Wrexham (16 apps. – 0 goals)

## 25 SEASONS LIVERPOOL LEAGUE RECORD

| Season | Apps | Goals |
|---|---|---|
| 1978-1979 | 37 | 3 |
| 1979-1980 | 37 | 1 |
| 1980-1981 | 19 | 2 |
| 1981-1982 | 34 | 3 |
| 1982-1983 | 42 | 3 |
| 1983-1984 | 42 | 2 |
| 1984-1985 | 32 | 1 |
| 1985-1986 | 8 | 0 |
| 25 Seasons Total | 251 | 15 |

# RAY KENNEDY

Signed by Bill Shankly, Ray Kennedy never had the chance to play under the great Scot. Ray was part of the strike-force that helped Arsenal win the 'Double' in 1970-71. Yet, at Anfield, he was turned into an international midfielder. Although he did not know it at the time, even while he was the peak of his career, he was suffering from Parkinson's Disease (which is the curse of his life).

Kennedy struggled up front for Liverpool, but Bob Paisley had a brain-wave and moved him back into midfield. Excellent at shielding the ball and an accurate passer, he soon made the number 5 shirt his own. He won five League Championship medals, a League Cup winners' medal and appeared in three European Cup Finals while with Liverpool. In addition to winning the 'Double' at Highbury, Ray also was part of the Arsenal side that won the European Fairs Cup.

Ray's biggest seasonal tally of League goals for Liverpool was ten, in 1978-79, when he was ever-present. Probably his most important goal came in 1981 when he scored the valuable away goal seven minutes from time which allowed the Reds to side-step Bayern Munich. He played for Swansea City and Hartlepool United after leaving Anfield. But for being a contemporary of Trevor Brooking, Ray Kennedy would have won far more than 17 England caps (all awarded while he was with Liverpool).

## FACTFILE

**Born:** Seaton Delaval, 28th July 1951
**Position:** Midfield/Striker
**Liverpool 25 Seasons League Record:** 182 appearances – 33 goals
**Liverpool Career League Record:** 275 appearances – 51 goals
**Other League apps (Pre-Liverpool):** Arsenal (158 apps. – 53 goals)
**Other League apps (Post-Liverpool):** Swansea City (42 apps. – 2 goals), Hartlepool United (23 apps. – 3 goals)

## 25 SEASONS LIVERPOOL LEAGUE RECORD

| Season | Apps | Goals |
|---|---|---|
| 1977-1978 | 41 | 4 |
| 1978-1979 | 42 | 10 |
| 1979-1980 | 40 | 9 |
| 1980-1981 | 41 | 8 |
| 1981-1982 | 15 | 2 |
| 25 Seasons Total | 179 | 33 |

# MARK LAWRENSON

Mark Lawrenson was a classy defender and a key component of the very best Liverpool sides of the 1980s. He won five League Championships, one F.A. Cup winners' medal and three League Cup winners' medals. He also played in the 1984 and 1985 European Cup Finals. He won 38 caps for the Republic of Ireland, 24 of them while he was a Liverpool player.

Mark began his Football League career with his home-town club Preston North End (for whom his father Tommy had played). He joined Liverpool from Brighton & Hove Albion for £900,000 (then a record fee for both clubs) in the summer of 1981. He was ever-present in 1983-84 and missed very few games in his first six campaigns at the club. However, a nasty achilles injury forced him to retire in 1987-88. He later had two short spells in management, with Oxford United and Peterborough United. In between he played in the USA for Tampa Bay Rowdies. Mark Lawrenson is now a football journalist and a pundit on BBC TV's 'Match of the Day' programme.

## FACTFILE

**Born**: Preston, 2nd June 1957
**Position**: Defender
**Liverpool 25 Seasons League Record**: 241 appearances – 11 goals
**Liverpool Career League Record**: As above
**Other League apps (Post-Liverpool)**: Preston North End (73 apps. – 2 goals),
Brighton & Hove Albion (152 apps. – 5 goals)

## 25 SEASONS LIVERPOOL LEAGUE RECORD

| Season | Apps | Goals |
|---|---|---|
| 1981-1982 | 39 | 2 |
| 1982-1983 | 40 | 5 |
| 1983-1984 | 42 | 0 |
| 1984-1985 | 33 | 1 |
| 1985-1986 | 38 | 3 |
| 1986-1987 | 35 | 0 |
| 1987-1988 | 14 | 0 |
| 25 Seasons Total | 241 | 11 |

# SAMMY LEE

Sammy Lee was an industrious member of Liverpool's midfield during the first half of the 1980s. He capped his League debut with a flukey goal against Leicester City, in 1977-78. It was somewhat ironic that he made a scoring start as the little man was never to become renowned for his goalscoring (only netting another 12 goals in nearly 200 League appearances). Sammy eventually became a first-team regular in 1980-81. All-told he collected four League Championship medals, four League Cup winners' medals and appeared in two European Cup winning sides.

Despite his lack of height (5 foot 7 inches in his socks), he was a good ball-winner and a neat passer. He was particularly outstanding in 1983-84, but lost form soon afterwards and moved on to QPR in 1986. He later played for Spanish outfit Osasuna before making a few appearances for Southampton and Bolton Wanderers. All 14 of Sammy Lee's England caps were won while he was with Liverpool. He has since represented his country again in a coaching capacity. Sammy Lee is now an important member of the Anfield backroom staff.

## FACTFILE

**Born**: Liverpool, 7th February 1959
**Position**: Midfield
**Liverpool 25 Seasons League Record**: 197 appearances – 13 goals
**Liverpool Career League Record**: As above
**Other League apps (Post-Liverpool)**: QPR (30 apps. – 0 goals),
Southampton (2 apps. – 0 goals), Bolton Wanderers (4 apps. – 0 goals)

## 25 SEASONS LIVERPOOL LEAGUE RECORD

| Season | Apps | Goals |
|--------|------|-------|
| 1977-1978 | 2 | 1 |
| 1978-1979 | 2 | 0 |
| 1979-1980 | 7 | 0 |
| 1980-1981 | 37 | 4 |
| 1981-1982 | 35 | 3 |
| 1982-1983 | 40 | 3 |
| 1983-1984 | 42 | 2 |
| 1984-1985 | 17 | 0 |
| 1985-1986 | 15 | 0 |
| 25 Seasons Total | 197 | 13 |

# TERRY McDERMOTT

Terry McDermott was one of the first names Bob Paisley wrote on his team-sheet during the second half of the 1970s and early 1980s. He was a tireless midfielder, whose unselfish play helped create boat loads of chances for his colleagues. He had an eye for goal with his long-range shooting, netting 54 times for the club in the League. He reached double figures in three successive campaigns in the 1980s, but one of his most important goals came in 1976-77, when he scored Liverpool's opener in the European Cup Final.

McDermott won three League Championship medals, was a member of three victorious European Cup Final sides and collected two League Cup winners' medals. He was voted the 'Footballer of the Year' and the PFA 'Player of the Year' in 1980. He won 25 England caps, all of which were awarded while he was at Anfield.

Terry was a Liverpool fan as a boy, but made his League debut for Bury. He joined the Reds from Newcastle United and returned there in 1983 when he was surplus to requirements at Anfield. After spells in Ireland and Cyprus, he later returned to St James' Park to become assistant-manager to Kevin Keegan. Terry McDermott was one of most tactically astute midfielders to play for Liverpool.

## FACTFILE

**Born**: Liverpool, 8th February 1951
**Position**: Midfield
**Liverpool 25 Seasons League Record**: 182 appearances – 50 goals
**Liverpool Career League Record**: 232 appearances – 54 goals
**Other League apps (Pre-Liverpool)**: Bury (90 apps. – 8 goals),
Newcastle United (56 apps. – 6 goals)
**Other League apps (Post-Liverpool)**: Newcastle United (74 apps. – 12 goals)

## 25 SEASONS LIVERPOOL LEAGUE RECORD

| Season | Apps | Goals |
|---|---|---|
| 1977-1978 | 37 | 4 |
| 1978-1979 | 37 | 8 |
| 1979-1980 | 37 | 11 |
| 1980-1981 | 40 | 13 |
| 1981-1982 | 29 | 14 |
| 1982-1983 | 2 | 0 |
| 25 Seasons Total | 182 | 50 |

# STEVE McMAHON

Steve McMahon was a key member of Liverpool's squad during the second half of the 1990s. Kenny Dalglish recruited the former Evertonian, from Aston Villa (for £375,000), in 1985-86, to add bite to his midfield. In addition to being a great tackler, Steve proved during his spell at Anfield that he also had great vision. He hit a stream of telling passes, and could score valuable goals, too.

Liverpool did the 'Double' in Steve's first season although he did not play in the F.A. Cup Final. However, he was a member of the F.A. Cup Final teams of 1988 and 1989. He was ever-present in 1987-88 and 1989-90, helping the Reds claim two more League titles. He won all 17 of his England caps while with Liverpool. His days at Anfield were numbered when Graeme Souness took over and he was sold to Manchester City for £900,000 in December 1991. Steve McMahon later became player-manager of Swindon Town. He left the County Ground in 1999. He became Blackpool's manager in January 2000 and steered them out of the Third Division in his first full campaign at the Bloomfield Road helm.

## FACTFILE

**Born**: Liverpool, 20th August 1961
**Position**: Midfield
**Liverpool 25 Seasons League Record**: 204 appearances – 29 goals
**Liverpool Career League Record**: As above
**Other League apps (Pre-Liverpool)**: Everton (100 apps. – 11 goals),
Aston Villa (75 apps. – 7 goals)
**Other League apps (Post-Liverpool)**: Manchester City (87 apps. – 1 goal),
Swindon Town (41 apps. – 0 goals)

## 25 SEASONS LIVERPOOL LEAGUE RECORD

| Season | Apps | Goals |
|---|---|---|
| 1985-1986 | 23 | 6 |
| 1986-1987 | 37 | 5 |
| 1987-1988 | 40 | 9 |
| 1988-1989 | 29 | 3 |
| 1989-1990 | 38 | 5 |
| 1990-1991 | 22 | 0 |
| 1991-1992 | 15 | 1 |
| 25 Seasons Total | 204 | 29 |

# STEVE McMANAMAN

Steve McManaman was an important member of most of the Liverpool sides of the 1990's. A fine dribbler, with close control and good balance, he brought a degree of intelligence to the Reds' attack. He made his debut in 1990-91 and, just over 12 months later, collected an F.A. Cup winners' medal when he played against Sunderland. He was the creator of Liverpool's first goal in that game (scored by Mickey Thomas), but got on the score-sheet himself in Liverpool's next Cup Final, three years later. Steve netted both goals that day, in the League Cup Final, in the 2-1 defeat of Bolton Wanderers.

McManaman's most fruitful season in a red shirt was in 1997-98, when he found the net 11 times in League games. He decided to try his luck abroad and joined Real Madrid after his Liverpool contract expired, on a free transfer, in the summer of 1999. He appeared for Real Madrid in the European Cup Finals of 1999-2000 (scoring the second goal) and 2001-02 (coming on as a substitute), collecting a winners' medal on each occasion. Steve McManaman had won 37 England caps up to the summer of 2002, the first 24 were awarded while he was a Liverpool player.

## FACTFILE

**Born**: Liverpool, 11th February 1972
**Position**: Midfield/Forward
**Liverpool 25 Seasons League Record**: 272 appearances – 46 goals
**Liverpool Career League Record**: As above

## 25 SEASONS LIVERPOOL LEAGUE RECORD

| Season | Apps | Goals |
|--------|------|-------|
| 1990-1991 | 2 | 0 |
| 1991-1992 | 30 | 5 |
| 1992-1993 | 31 | 4 |
| 1993-1994 | 30 | 2 |
| 1994-1995 | 40 | 7 |
| 1995-1996 | 38 | 6 |
| 1996-1997 | 37 | 7 |
| 1997-1998 | 36 | 11 |
| 1998-1999 | 28 | 4 |
| 25 Seasons Total | 272 | 46 |

# JAN MOLBY

Jan Molby was a key performer during a career at Anfield that spanned 11 and a half years. He missed chunks of several campaigns but still managed to collect two League Championship medals, two F.A. Cup winners' medals and was a member of the side which won the League Cup in 1995. The Dane moved to Merseyside from Ajax for £575,000 in August 1984. He was a powerful midfielder who could pass the ball with great accuracy. He scored valuable goals from midfield. His most fruitful campaign was in 1985-86, when he found the net 14 times in the League.

Molby was impressive in the F.A. Cup Finals of 1986 and 1992. He helped make two goals in the 1986 Final and orchestrated most of the Reds' attacks in the latter Final. A series of injuries, a stretch in prison for 'drink-driving' and weight problems caused him to be in and out of the side. However, on his best form, he was a very fine player. He was versatile as well, performing competently whenever used as a sweeper. Jan was loaned out to Barnsley and Norwich City before leaving Anfield for Swansea City, where he became player-manager. He was sacked in 1987-88 but bounced back with great success as the manager of Kidderminster, where he took the Harriers into the Football League, in 1999-2000. He left Kidderminster for a similar role at Hull City in 2002. Jan Molby played for Denmark on 67 occasions.

## FACTFILE

**Born**: Kolding (Denmark), 4th July 1963
**Position**: Midfield/Defender
**Liverpool 25 Seasons League Record**: 218 appearances – 44 goals
**Liverpool Career League Record**: As above
**Other League appearances (On Loan from Liverpool)**: Barnsley (5 apps. – 0 goals), Norwich City (3 apps. – 0 goals)
**Other League apps (Post-Liverpool)**: Swansea City (41 apps. – 8 goals)

## 25 SEASONS LIVERPOOL LEAGUE RECORD

| Season | Apps | Goals |
|--------|------|-------|
| 1984-1985 | 22 | 1 |
| 1985-1986 | 39 | 14 |
| 1986-1987 | 34 | 7 |
| 1987-1988 | 7 | 0 |
| 1988-1989 | 13 | 2 |
| 1989-1990 | 17 | 1 |

| | | |
|---|---|---|
| 1990-1991 | 25 | 9 |
| 1991-1992 | 26 | 3 |
| 1992-1993 | 10 | 3 |
| 1993-1994 | 11 | 2 |
| 1994-1995 | 14 | 2 |
| 25 Seasons Total | 218 | 44 |

## PHIL NEAL

Phil Neal was one of the finest right-backs to pull on a Liverpool shirt. He was 'Mr Dependable', missing only one League fixture in ten seasons, and a super cool penalty-taker. He joined Liverpool in October 1974 from his local side Northampton Town for £60,000 and made his first-team debut against Everton at Goodison Park the following month.

The super-fit Neal was ever-present on nine occasions. All-told he made 455 League appearances for the Reds, 348 of them in the quarter of a century up to the summer of 2002. Only five men pulled on a Liverpool jersey more times during that period. His overall tally of League goals for the Reds was swollen by many from the spot. Phil scored in two of the five European Cup Finals in which he played. He netted from the spot in Rome in 1977 and struck the opening goal on the same ground seven years later (when he was also on target in the shoot-out). He also won eight League Championship medals and four League Cup winners' medals while at Anfield.

Phil holds the Liverpool record for making the most consecutive first-team appearances in all competitions. He played in 417 consecutive games between 23rd October 1976 and 24th September 1983. He was a skilful attacking full-back with good positional sense and a crisp tackle. He won 50 England caps and later assisted Graham Taylor when he was in charge of the national team. Phil Neal left Anfield to become Bolton Wanderers' player-manager in December 1985. He later managed Coventry City and Cardiff City.

### FACTFILE

**Born:** Irchester, 20th February 1951
**Position:** Defender
**Liverpool 25 Seasons League Record:** 348 appearances – 28 appearances
**Liverpool Career League Record:** 455 appearances – 41 appearances
**Other League apps (Pre-Liverpool):** Northampton Town (186 apps. – 29 goals)

**Other League apps (Post-Liverpool):** Bolton Wanderers (64 apps. – 3 goals)

## 25 SEASONS LIVERPOOL LEAGUE RECORD

| Season | Apps | Goals |
|--------|------|-------|
| 1977-1978 | 42 | 4 |
| 1978-1979 | 42 | 5 |
| 1979-1980 | 42 | 1 |
| 1980-1981 | 42 | 2 |
| 1981-1982 | 42 | 2 |
| 1982-1983 | 42 | 8 |
| 1983-1984 | 41 | 1 |
| 1984-1985 | 42 | 4 |
| 1985-1986 | 13 | 1 |
| 25 Seasons Total | 348 | 28 |

# STEVE NICOL

Steve Nicol was a popular and versatile member of the Liverpool squad for eleven full seasons during the 1980s and early 1990s. His best position was right-back, but he was also a fine central defender and, whenever asked, did an admirable job in midfield.

Nicol joined the Reds from his local side, Ayr United, in October 1981 for £300,000. He gradually broke into the Liverpool side and eventually replaced Phil Neal at right-back. He won four League Championship medals and was a member of three triumphant F.A. Cup Final sides. He came on as a substitute in the 1983-84 European Cup Final and had the 'bottle' to take his side's first penalty in the shoot-out. He missed, but deservedly collected a winners' medal in Rome on that glorious night.

Steve was ever-present in the League, in 1988-89, the campaign in which he was voted 'Footballer of the Year'. He netted one hat-trick for Liverpool, at Newcastle, in 1987-88. He left Anfield in January 1995, on a free transfer, and later that year joined Sheffield Wednesday. He also played for WBA on loan and for Doncaster Rovers in the Conference. He later moved across the Atlantic to coach New England Revolution. Steve Nicol won 27 caps for Scotland, all of them while he was on Liverpool's books.

## FACTFILE

**Born:** Irvine, 11th December 1961
**Position:** Defender

**Liverpool 25 Seasons League Record**: 343 appearances – 36 goals

**Liverpool Career League Record**: As above

**Other League apps (Post-Liverpool)**: Notts County (32 apps. – 2 goals), Sheffield Wednesday (49 apps. – 0 goals), WBA (on loan 9 apps. – 0 goals)

## 25 SEASONS LIVERPOOL LEAGUE RECORD

| Season | Apps | Goals |
| --- | --- | --- |
| 1982-1983 | 4 | 0 |
| 1983-1984 | 23 | 5 |
| 1984-1985 | 31 | 5 |
| 1985-1986 | 34 | 4 |
| 1986-1987 | 14 | 3 |
| 1987-1988 | 40 | 6 |
| 1988-1989 | 38 | 2 |
| 1989-1990 | 23 | 6 |
| 1990-1991 | 35 | 3 |
| 1991-1992 | 34 | 1 |
| 1992-1993 | 32 | 0 |
| 1993-1994 | 31 | 1 |
| 1994-1995 | 4 | 0 |
| 25 Seasons Total | 343 | 36 |

# MICHAEL OWEN

Most of Merseyside was aware of Michael Owen's talent before he was given his League baptism at the end of 1996-97. So, it came as no surprise that he scored on his debut. He has maintained that high standard ever since and has been Liverpool's leading scorer in each of his five full campaigns in the first team. Michael has been equally impressive for England, winning 41 caps (and scoring 18 goals) up to the summer of 2002. He was the youngest man to play for England in the 20th Century when he made his international debut, in 1997-98, aged 18 years and 59 days.

With his electric pace, close control and a poacher's instinct, Owen is one of the most valuable players in the Premiership. A series of injuries have dogged him in recent seasons and these have marginally dampened his effectiveness. He was an unused substitute when the Worthington Cup was won, in Cardiff, in 2000-01.

However, later in that campaign he was the 'Man of the Match' at the Millennium Stadium, netting the brace which torpedoed Arsenal. He also created two of Liverpool's goals in the UEFA Cup Final victory over CD Alaves four days later. Michael is the son of former professional footballer Terry Owen.

## FACTFILE

**Born**: Chester, 14th December 1979

**Position**: Striker

**Liverpool 25 Seasons League Record**: 152 appearances – 83 goals

**Liverpool Career League Record**: As above

## 25 SEASONS LIVERPOOL LEAGUE RECORD

| Season | Apps | Goals |
|--------|------|-------|
| 1996-1997 | 2 | 1 |
| 1997-1998 | 36 | 18 |
| 1998-1999 | 30 | 18 |
| 1999-2000 | 27 | 11 |
| 2000-2001 | 28 | 16 |
| 2001-2002 | 29 | 19 |
| 25 Seasons Total | 152 | 83 |

# JAMIE REDKNAPP

Jamie Redknapp was one of Liverpool's most influential midfielders of the 1990s. Yet, he might have achieved so much more with the club if it was not for a series of injuries. He became club captain but missed a significant number of games. He was absent for the whole of 2000-01 when his side won three major trophies. He was again absent for much of 2001-02 and left Merseyside for Tottenham Hotspur towards the end of that campaign.

Redknapp made his Football League debut for Bournemouth in 1989-90 and transferred to Liverpool for £350,000 in January 1991. His main strength is his ability to stroke the ball accurately around the pitch. He never flinches from the tackle and contributes his share of goals from midfield. He had been awarded 17 England caps up to the summer of 2002, all of them while he with Liverpool. He shone brightly for England during the Euro '96 tournament (before getting injured), but missed out on selection for the 1998 and 2002 World Cups.

Jamie is the son of Portsmouth boss Harry Redknapp (who sold him to Liverpool when manager of Bournemouth) and is a cousin of Chelsea midfielder Frank Lampard Junior. Jamie Redknapp was a part of the side which won the 1994-95 League Cup and was one of the most popular men to pull on a red shirt in the quarter of a century up to the summer of 2002.

**FACTFILE**

**Born:** Barton-on-Sea, 25th June 1973
**Position:** Midfield
**Liverpool 25 Seasons League Record:** 243 appearances – 30 goals
**Liverpool Career League Record:** As above
**Other League appearances (Pre-Liverpool):** Bournemouth (13 apps. – 0 goals)

**25 SEASONS LIVERPOOL LEAGUE RECORD**

| Season | Apps | Goals |
|---|---|---|
| 1991-1992 | 6 | 1 |
| 1992-1993 | 29 | 2 |
| 1993-1994 | 35 | 4 |
| 1994-1995 | 41 | 3 |
| 1995-1996 | 23 | 3 |
| 1996-1997 | 23 | 2 |
| 1997-1998 | 20 | 3 |
| 1998-1999 | 34 | 8 |
| 1999-2000 | 22 | 3 |
| 2000-2001 | 0 | 0 |
| 2001-2002 | 10 | 1 |
| 25 Seasons Total | 243 | 30 |

# IAN RUSH

Nobody made more appearances, or scored more goals, for Liverpool than Ian Rush in the quarter of a century up to the summer of 2002. The Welsh striker bagged 229 goals in 469 League appearances. A legend on Anfield, he holds the record (jointly with two others) for the number (5) of goals scored in a League game, is the club's most capped player, and has netted more times than any other man in Merseyside derbies.

Ian joined Liverpool for £30,000 from Chester City in 1980. He served his apprenticeship in the Central League side before making his League debut in 1980-81. His second first-team appearance was in the League Cup Final replay. He made a huge impact in 1981-82, netting 30 times in all competitions to help Liverpool lift the title and retain the League Cup. His tally of 17 League goals made him the club's leading scorer. All-told he was the club's top scorer in the League on eight occasions (once jointly). He was ever-present in both 1986-87 and 1993-94 (when he made appearance from the bench).

After netting 109 times in 182 League games, Rush left Anfield for the challenge of Serie A football in the summer of 1986. Juventus paid £3.2 million for his services. He failed to settle in Italy and returned to Anfield the following summer. Initially he was on loan, but eventually he was bought back for a £2.8 million fee. He scored only seven League goals during his first term back in a red shirt, but did score two important goals when he came off the bench in the 3-2 F.A. Cup victory over Everton. All-told Ian collected three F.A. Cup winners' medals (scoring a record five goals in finals), won five League Cup winners' medals and was a key member of the side which won the European Cup in 1983-84. He won 73 caps for Wales, all but six were won while he was a Liverpool player. He was voted as both the 'Footballer of the Year' and the PFA 'Player of the Year' in 1984.

Ian Rush left Anfield again at the end of the 1995-96 campaign and joined Leeds United on a free transfer. His one term at Elland Road yielded only three goals and, in some matches, was deployed in midfield. He looked a pale shadow of his former self when he was on Newcastle United's books. He also played for Sheffield United (on loan) and finished his career at Wrexham (where he helped coach the reserves). His final playing days may have been very undistinguished, but Ian Rush will forever be an 'Anfield Great'.

## FACTFILE

**Born:** St Asaph, 20th October 1961
**Position:** Striker
**Liverpool 25 Seasons League Record:** 469 appearances – 229 goals
**Liverpool Career League Record:** As above
**Other League apps (Pre-Liverpool):** Chester City (34 apps. – 14 goals)
**Other League apps (Post-Liverpool):** Leeds United (36 apps. – 3 goals), Newcastle United (10 apps. – 0 goals), Sheffield United (on loan 4 apps. – 0 goals), Wrexham (17 apps. – 0 goals)

## 25 SEASONS LIVERPOOL LEAGUE RECORD

| Season | Apps | Goals |
| --- | --- | --- |
| 1980-1981 | 7 | 0 |
| 1981-1982 | 32 | 17 |
| 1982-1983 | 34 | 24 |
| 1983-1984 | 41 | 32 |
| 1984-1985 | 28 | 14 |
| 1985-1986 | 40 | 22 |
| 1986-1987 | 42 | 30 |
| 1988-1989 | 24 | 7 |
| 1989-1990 | 36 | 18 |
| 1990-1991 | 37 | 16 |
| 1991-1992 | 18 | 4 |
| 1992-1993 | 32 | 14 |
| 1993-1994 | 42 | 14 |
| 1994-1995 | 36 | 12 |
| 1995-1996 | 20 | 5 |
| 25 Seasons Total | 469 | 229 |

# GRAEME SOUNESS

Graeme Souness was an inspirational captain and a key cog in the successful Liverpool teams of the late 1970s and early 1980s. His rather turbulent spell as manager in the early 1990s can not be forgotten, but it should not be allowed to diminish his great achievements in a red shirt. Only nine men made more appearances for Liverpool in the quarter of a century up to the summer of 2002. He won five League Championships, four League Cup winners' medals (he scored the winner in the 1983-84 replay) and was a member of three European Cup winning sides. He won 54 Scottish caps, 37 of them while he was with Liverpool.

The tough tackler's first League club was Spurs (with whom he won an F.A. Youth Cup winners' medal); but it was with Middlesbrough that he made his Football League debut. He made his name with Jack Charlton's battling side and helped them seal the Second Division Championship in 1973-74. He transferred to Liverpool (for £352,000) in January 1978. He was an excellent tackler, fine passer and possessed a fierce shot. Liverpool sorely missed him after he moved to Sampdoria (for £650,000) in the summer of 1984.

Graeme took over as player-manager at Ibrox in May 1986 and in his five years there led Rangers to the Scottish title on three occasions and to success in four Scottish League Cup Finals. He returned to Anfield in April 1991 after Kenny Dalglish's resignation. His spell at Liverpool's helm was disappointing, but his side did win the F.A. Cup in 1992. He attended the Final even though it came only 32 days after he had a triple heart by-pass. Graeme Souness left Anfield in 1994 after his side were bundled out of the F.A. Cup by Bristol City. He later managed Galatasaray, Southampton, Torino, Benfica and Blackburn Rovers.

## FACTFILE

**Born:** Edinburgh, 6th May 1953
**Position:** Midfield
**Liverpool 25 Seasons League Record:** 247 appearances – 38 goals
**Liverpool Career League Record:** As above
**Other League apps (Pre-Liverpool):** Middlesbrough (176 apps. – 22 goals)

## 25 SEASONS LIVERPOOL LEAGUE RECORD

| Season | Apps | Goals |
|---|---|---|
| 1977-1978 | 15 | 2 |
| 1978-1979 | 41 | 8 |
| 1979-1980 | 41 | 1 |
| 1980-1981 | 37 | 6 |
| 1981-1982 | 35 | 5 |
| 1982-1983 | 41 | 9 |
| 1983-1984 | 37 | 7 |
| 25 Seasons Total | 247 | 38 |

# RONNIE WHELAN

Ronnie Whelan was an important member of Liverpool's midfield throughout most of the 1980s. He made an immediate impact, scoring on his League debut as a 19 year-old, stayed loyal to the Reds and was given the responsibility of captaincy towards the end of his career. He was awarded 53 caps by the Republic of Ireland, all of which were won while he was on Liverpool's books.

The son of a useful footballer (also called Ronnie), Whelan joined Liverpool from Irish side Home Farm. He made his Football League debut in 1980-81. He was a battling midfielder with an abundance of skill. He contributed many useful goals and twice netted as many as ten League goals in a season. He scored twice to help his side defeat Spurs in the 1981-82 League Cup Final. He also netted at Wembley 12 months later when his side retained the trophy.

Ronnie was a member of the F.A. Cup winning sides of 1986 and 1989 (when he was captain). He won the League Championship on six occasions and was a member of the side which won the European Cup in 1983-84. He moved to Southend United in 1994 and later became the Shrimpers' player-manager. Ronnie Whelan left Roots Hall in 1997 and has subsequently coached in Greece and Cyprus.

## FACTFILE

**Born**: Dublin, 25th September 1961
**Position**: Midfield
**Liverpool 25 Seasons League Record**: 362 appearances – 46 goals
**Liverpool Career League Record**: As above
**Other League apps (Post-Liverpool)**: Southend United (34 apps. – 1 goals)

## 25 SEASONS LIVERPOOL LEAGUE RECORD

| Season | Apps | Goals |
|---|---|---|
| 1979-1980 | 1 | 1 |
| 1980-1981 | 32 | 10 |
| 1981-1982 | 28 | 2 |
| 1982-1983 | 23 | 4 |
| 1983-1984 | 37 | 7 |
| 1984-1985 | 39 | 10 |
| 1985-1986 | 39 | 3 |
| 1986-1987 | 28 | 1 |
| 1987-1988 | 37 | 4 |
| 1988-1989 | 34 | 1 |
| 1989-1990 | 14 | 1 |
| 1990-1991 | 10 | 0 |
| 1991-1992 | 17 | 1 |
| 1992-1993 | 23 | 1 |
| 25 Seasons Total | 362 | 46 |

# LIVERPOOL 25 SEASONS 1977-78 TO 2001-02

## JUST ABOUT MANAGING!

Six men managed Liverpool during the quarter of a century up to the summer of 2002. For a short period (in 1998), two men – Roy Evans and Gerard Houllier – shared the job. The reigns of the Liverpool managers embraced the following periods.

| | |
|---|---|
| JULY 1974 TO JUNE 1983 | BOB PAISLEY |
| JUNE 1983 TO MAY 1985 | JOE FAGAN |
| JUNE 1985 TO FEBRUARY 1991 | KENNY DALGLISH |
| APRIL 1991 TO JANUARY 1994 | GRAEME SOUNESS |
| FEBRUARY 1994 TO JULY 1998 | ROY EVANS |
| JULY 1998 TO NOVEMBER 1998 | ROY EVANS & GERARD HOULLIER |
| FROM NOVEMBER 1998 | GERARD HOULLIER |

## BOB PAISLEY – JULY 1974 TO JUNE 1983

Bob Paisley was the very nice man who worked his way up through the ranks to become the most successful club manager in British football. He continued the excellent work of his predecessor Bill Shankly, led Liverpool to 13 major trophies and was voted 'Manager of the Year' on six occasions.

Never one to seek publicity, Paisley relied on his team to do the talking for him. He had a deep understanding of every part of the football spectrum whether it be injuries, pitches, tactics or knowing how to get the best out of his players. He brought some great players to Anfield, including Kenny Dalglish, Graeme Souness, Alan Hansen, Ian Rush, Mark Lawrenson, Phil Neal, Alan Kennedy, Steve Nicol and Terry McDermott. He also had the brain-wave to convert struggling striker Ray Kennedy, Shankly's last buy, into a midfielder. The former Arsenal man became so good in his new role that he won 17 caps for England.

Paisley became an apprentice bricklayer after leaving school. He joined Northern League Bishop Auckland in 1938 and collected an F.A. Amateur Cup winners' medal the following year. His performances at wing-half were spotted by Liverpool and he joined the Reds in May 1939.

His early years as a professional were wiped away by the war. He served with the Royal Artillery although was able to make the odd guest appearance for Bristol City. He made his Football League debut in 1946-47 and helped Liverpool to the title in his first season. He went on to appear in 252 League games (scoring ten times). A crisp tackle and a useful long throw were his trademarks. He retired from playing in the summer of 1954. His biggest disappointment was being left out of the 1950 F.A. Cup final side despite playing in all but one of the earlier rounds (scoring in the semi-final). Liverpool asked the F.A. to strike a special medal for Paisley, but it was a losers' medal as Arsenal won the final 2-0. Ironically Paisley was not able to lead Liverpool to F.A. Cup glory during his nine years at the helm.

Having been dissuaded from returning to bricklaying, Bob remained at Anfield as the assistant-trainer. He later became trainer, physiotherapist and then Shankly's assistant-manager. He was the obvious successor when Shanks surprisingly retired in the summer of 1974. His side took a season to gel, but in 1975-76 they won the UEFA Cup and the first of six League titles in eight years. A year later they won the first of three European Cups under his stewardship. In addition, Liverpool captured the League Cup three seasons running at the end of his reign.

Bob was awarded the OBE in 1977 and was voted 'Manager of the Year' in 1976, 1977, 1979, 1980, 1982 and 1983. He stepped up to become a Director after handing over the reins to Joe Fagan in May 1983. After nearly 53 years at Anfield, ill-health forced him to retire from the board in February 1992. He died, after a long illness, on St Valentine's Day 1996.

Bob Paisley may have had less charisma than many other managers, but very few were more liked and only Sir Alex Ferguson has been as successful.

## FACTFILE

**Born:** Hetton-le-Hole, 23rd January 1919

## LIVERPOOL MANAGERIAL RECORD

|            | Played | Won | Drew | Lost |
|------------|--------|-----|------|------|
| League     | 378    | 212 | 99   | 67   |
| F.A. Cup   | 36     | 20  | 7    | 9    |
| League Cup | 53     | 32  | 14   | 7    |

| Europe | 57 | 37 | 10 | 10 |
|--------|-----|-----|-----|-----|
| Total | 524 | 301 | 130 | 93 |

**Honours:** Three European Cups, Six League Championships & three League Cups
**Highest League finish:** Champions in 1975-76, 1976-77, 1978-79, 1979-80, 1981-82 and 1982-83
**Lowest League finish:** 5th in 1980-81
**Best F.A. Cup Run:** Final in 1976-77
**Best League Cup Run:** Winners in 1980-81, 1981-82 and 1982-83
**Best European Run (European Cup):** Winners in 1976-77, 1977-78 and 1980-81
**(UEFA Cup):** Winners in 1975-76
**First Match in charge:** 17th August 1974 vs Luton Town First Division (won 2-1)
**Last Match in charge:** 14th May 1983 vs Watford First Division (lost 2-1)

# JOE FAGAN JUNE – 1983 TO MAY 1985

Joe Fagan managed Liverpool for two eventful years following Bob Paisley's resignation. He carried on the true Liverpool spirit and, in his first season at the helm, became the first manager in England to steer a side to a 'Treble'. The Reds captured the League Cup, the European Cup and the League title in 1983-84.

As a player, Joe was a solid reliable centre-half who joined Manchester City, in 1938, from Earlestown Bohemians. However, it was not until after the war, in 1946-47 that he made his League debut. He made 148 appearances for the Citizens before joining Altrincham in 1950. He later played for Bradford Park Avenue and then joined Nelson as their player-manager.

Fagan was Rochdale's trainer when Bill Shankly recruited him to do a similar job for the Reds. He became Paisley's assistant after Shanks' retirement in 1974. Joe took the ultimate step up the ladder when Paisley retired in 1983. He inherited an excellent young side who collected those three trophies in 1983-84. Fagan's achievement was recognised when he was voted 'Manager of the Year'.

The next season was nowhere nearly as satisfactory. Liverpool came from a long way back, through the pack, to take second place (to Everton) in the League and the only extended cup joy came in the European Cup. Fagan had already made up his mind before the Final with Juventus. The hollow 1-0 defeat and Fagan's announcement of his departure were both naturally overshadowed by

*Bruce Grobbelaar was born in South Africa but made 20 international appearances for Zimbabwe. Well-known as an eccentric character, Bruce was a talented keeper who played 440 games for the Reds and won many trophies while at the club.*

*Kenny Dalglish joined Liverpool from Celtic in 1977 and, at only £440,000, must be counted as one of the club's best buys! In addition to winning numerous trophies as a player, Kenny managed the Reds to three League Championships and two F.A. Cups.*

*John Aldridge pictured in Oxford United's colours shortly before his transfer to Liverpool in 1986. John was bought in to replace the outgoing Ian Rush but actually managed a strike rate better than a goal every two games during his time at the club!*

*Super-fit Phil Neal was one of Liverpool's finest-ever full-backs. Phil made 455
League appearances for the club (scoring 41 goals) and missed just one game
between 1975-76 and 1984-85.*

*Mark Lawrenson – pictured before he achieved fame as a TV pundit!*
*Mark was a classy defender who made 241 League appearances for the Reds*
*during the 1980's.*

*Sammy Lee pictured in Liverpool colours towards the end of his playing career. After retiring from playing, Sammy took on a coaching role at Anfield in the famous 'Boot Room'.*

*Bob Paisley is rightly described as a Liverpool Legend and is the one of the most successful managers of all time. Bob led Liverpool to 13 major trophies and was voted 'Manager of the Year' on six occasions.*

*The Hillsborough Memorial Service –*
*The manager, players and supporters united to remember those lost on that terrible day in Sheffield.*

the news of so many dead and injured in the 'Heysel Disaster'.

Joe was 62 years of age when he accepted the manager's role, so it was not really a surprise that his reign was to be so brief. It was a pity it ended so tearfully, but it should never be forgotten that Joe Fagan was the first man in English football to pull off a 'Treble' as a manager. He died, after a long illness, aged 80 in July 2001.

### FACTFILE

**Born**: Liverpool, 12th March 1921

### LIVERPOOL MANAGERIAL RECORD

|            | Played | Won | Drew | Lost |
|------------|--------|-----|------|------|
| League     | 84     | 44  | 25   | 15   |
| F.A. Cup   | 9      | 5   | 2    | 2    |
| League Cup | 16     | 8   | 7    | 1    |
| Europe     | 16     | 11  | 3    | 2    |
| Total      | 125    | 68  | 37   | 20   |

**Honours**: European Cup, League Championship and League Cup
**Highest League finish**: Champions in 1983-84
**Lowest League finish**: Runners-up in 1984-85
**Best F.A. Cup Run**: Semi-final in 1984-85
**Best League Cup Run**: Winners in 1983-84
**Best European Run (European Cup)**: Winners in 1983-84
**First Match**: 27th August 1983 vs Wolverhampton Wanderers First Division (drew 1-1)
**Last Match in charge**: 29th May 1985 vs Juventus European Cup (lost 0-1)

# KENNY DALGLISH – JUNE 1985 TO FEBRUARY 1991

Just as Kenny Dalglish the player was undaunted by the prospect of replacing Kevin Keegan at Anfield, Dalglish the manager quickly proved that he was the right man to follow in the footsteps of Joe Fagan and Bob Paisley. Kenny was invited to become manager in the summer of 1985, after Fagan retired. He was an instant success. In his first campaign in charge he became the first player-manager to lead a side to the League Championship, only the second man (after Fagan) to take title in his initial term and became only the fifth man to lead a side to the 'Double'.

Liverpool went on to collect the title again in 1987-88 and 1989-90 under Dalglish's stewardship. They also lifted the F.A. Cup again in 1988-89 (for the second time in three seasons beating Everton at Wembley). Dalglish's side nearly repeated the 'Double' in 1987-88, when Wimbledon beat them in the F.A. Cup Final, and in the last seconds of the 1988-89 campaign (when Arsenal ripped the League title out of their hands at Anfield). Dalglish won the League Cup four times as a player, but only once led his side to the Final of this competition as a manager, in 1986-87, when they lost to Arsenal.

Although often described as "dour", Kenny managed to get the best out of his playing force. He brought some fine players to Anfield, including John Barnes, Peter Beardsley, Steve MacMahon and Ray Houghton. And, to the chagrin of several thousand doubters, his faith in John Aldridge was rewarded with a stack of goals. Kenny was voted 'Manager of the Year on three occasions (in 1986, 1988 and 1990).

It is almost certain that Dalglish's side would have tasted European glory; but his reign coincided with the ban on English clubs from entering European competitions. Even so, his side never finished lower than second in the table and a haul of five major trophies in as many full seasons at the helm was a very healthy return. If Kenny had remained at Anfield longer it is inconceivable that the club would not have lifted an extra clutch of trophies. However, his shock resignation, on 21st February 1991, left a huge hole that took a long time to fill.

Kenny's resignation, the day after his side had drawn 4-4 with Everton in the F.A. Cup, was an even bigger bombshell than the one that hit Merseyside when Bill Shankly announced his retirement in 1974. He cited "pressure and stress" as the reasons and, with the great reluctance of the board, was allowed to leave immediately. His side were three points clear at the top of the table and another 'Double' was still a distinct possibility.

While Liverpool's fortunes were dipping under new manager Graeme Souness, Dalglish recuperated with his family and enjoyed extra time on the golf course. Then in October 1991, just eight months after leaving Anfield, Kenny Dalglish found the lure of the challenge of managing Second Division Blackburn Rovers too tempting an offer to refuse.

Kenny Dalglish MBE underlined what a great manager he was by steering unfashionable Rovers to the Premiership title in 1994-95. That was a phenomenal achievement even allowing for the deepness of Jack Walker's pockets. His later slightly less distinguished spells with Newcastle United (as manager) and Celtic (in the boardroom) in no way dilutes his achievement of winning four titles and two F.A. Cups as a manager. This coming on top of the 21 major trophies (and 102 caps) he won purely as a player. Kenny is the father of Blackpool player Paul Dalglish.

## FACTFILE

**Born:** Dalmarnock, 4th March 1951

### LIVERPOOL MANAGERIAL RECORD

|  | Played | Won | Drew | Lost |
|---|---|---|---|---|
| League | 224 | 136 | 56 | 32 |
| F.A. Cup | 37 | 23 | 11 | 3 |
| League Cup | 31 | 19 | 6 | 6 |
| Europe | 0 | 0 | 0 | 0 |
| Total | 292 | 178 | 73 | 41 |

**Honours:** Three League Championships, two F.A. Cups
**Highest League finish:** Champions in 1985-86, 1987-88 and 1989-90
**Lowest League finish:** Runners-up in 1986-87 and 1988-89
**Best F.A. Cup Run:** Winners in 1985-86 and 1988-89
**Best League Cup Run:** Final in 1986-87
**First Match in charge:** 17th August 1985 vs Arsenal First Division (won 2-0)
**Last Match in charge:** 20th February 1991 vs Everton F.A. Cup (drew 4-4)

# GRAEME SOUNESS APRIL 1991 TO JANUARY 1994

Graeme Souness's excellent record in his five year spell at Ibrox made him the obvious choice to take over as Liverpool manager from his fellow team-mate Kenny Dalglish in April 1991. Unfortunately Souness never properly got to grips with the task in hand and left less than three years later. His side won one cup, an acceptable prize at most other grounds, but a less than satisfactory haul for a club so used to being embraced by glory.

To be fair to Souness, he did not inherit as nearly as good a squad as either Kenny Dalglish or Joe Fagan. It is also not true that all his buys were bad. Mark

Wright, Stig Inge Bjornebye, Rob Jones and Don Hutchison were all of sufficient quality. Admittedly his list of 'failures' is a longer one. Souness's biggest mistakes were to turn a deaf-ear to the boot-room and to shift out some of his more experienced heads (particularly Peter Beardsley and Steve McMahon) too quickly.

Liverpool finished sixth in each of Graeme's two full seasons at the helm. The first occasion was Liverpool's worst finishing position for 27 years. The second time was very flattering as only a late rush of Ian Rush goals propelled the Reds into a moderately decent position. Liverpool clearly went backwards under Souness and his spell at helm brought some loss of respect for him on Merseyside.

Many Liverpool supporters felt let down by Souness when he sold his story about his heart condition. Otherwise the speed in which he rushed back to work (and his appearance at Wembley) after his triple heart by-pass would have been seen as heroic. By the time of his departure (after the F.A. Cup defeat to Bristol City), in 1994, many were very glad that ship was in the hands of the far less turbulent Roy Evans.

After leaving Anfield Graeme Souness had spells as manager of Galatasaray, Southampton, Torino, Benfica and Blackburn Rovers. Graeme led Blackburn to promotion in his full campaign at Ewood Park and Rovers lifted the League Cup during his second season at the helm.

## FACTFILE

**Born**: Edinburgh, 6th May 1953

### LIVERPOOL MANAGERIAL RECORD

|  | Played | Won | Drew | Lost |
|---|---|---|---|---|
| League | 115 | 47 | 34 | 34 |
| F.A. Cup | 13 | 5 | 6 | 2 |
| League Cup | 16 | 7 | 7 | 2 |
| Europe | 12 | 6 | 0 | 6 |
| Total | 156 | 65 | 47 | 44 |

**Honours**: F.A. Cup
**Highest League finish**: Runners-up in 1990-91
**Lowest League finish**: 6th in 1991-92 and 1992-93
**Best F.A. Cup Run**: Winners in 1991-92
**Best League Cup Run**: Fourth Round in 1991-92, 1992-93 and 1993-94

**Best European Run (UEFA Cup):** Quarter-final in 1991-92

**First Match in charge:** 20th April 1991 vs Norwich City First Division (won 3-0)

**Last Match in charge:** 25th January 1994 vs Bristol City F.A. Cup (lost 1-0)

# ROY EVANS – FEBRUARY 1994 TO JULY 1998

The appointment of Roy Evans as Liverpool manager in February 1994 was generally heralded as a welcome return to the philosophy of the boot-room following the turbulent reign of Graeme Souness. Liverpool only won one trophy (the 1994-95 League Cup) under Evans, however he did a lot of good work in steadying the ship. Evans' spadework made it easier for Gerard Houllier to take the Reds to glory.

Evans joined Liverpool during Bill Shankly's reign as a 15 year-old, but faced stiff competition for a first-team place. The full-back made only nine League appearances, one League Cup appearance and played one match in Europe. His last two matches were in 1973-74 when he deputised for Alec Lindsay. The pragmatic Evans realised he was not going to make it as a player and, aged only 25, retired to become the reserve-team coach. He responded well to what was required of him behind the scenes and Liverpool won the Central League nine times in 11 years under his stewardship. He worked his way through the ranks to become Souness's assistant-manager.

Roy stepped up to become manager in early February 1994. His first signing was keeper Michael Stensgaard. However, his most costly purchases were Stan Collymore (£8.5 million), Jason McAteer (£4.5 million), Paul Ince (£4.2 million), Oyvind Leonhardsen (£4 million), Phil Babb (£3.6 million), Patrik Berger (£3.25 million) and John Scales (£3 million). Berger is still an important member of Liverpool's squad; however all those other 'big money' signings left Anfield for reduced fees.

Liverpool finished eighth in 1993-94, after losing six of their last nine matches. It was their lowest finishing position since 1962-63, the first campaign back in the top-flight. Liverpool finished fourth in Roy's first full season at the helm, when they also defeated Bolton Wanderers to lift the Coca-Cola Cup. The Reds subsequently finished third, fourth and third again under Evans. It was almost as if they were hitting a glass ceiling, just failing to climb above Manchester United and Arsenal. Liverpool managed to reach the F.A. Cup Final, in 1995-96, but lost 1-0 to Manchester United. They also reached the semi-final of the European Cup Winners' Cup, in 1996-97, during Evans' reign.

For some time the board wanted to inject some continental thinking into club and, in July 1998, former French national coach Gerard Houllier was appointed co-manager with Roy Evans.

## FACTFILE

**Born**: Bootle, 4th October 1948

### LIVERPOOL MANAGERIAL RECORD

|  | Played | Won | Drew | Lost |
|---|---|---|---|---|
| League | 172 | 83 | 46 | 43 |
| F.A. Cup | 17 | 8 | 5 | 4 |
| League Cup | 21 | 17 | 1 | 3 |
| Europe | 16 | 8 | 5 | 3 |
| Total | 226 | 116 | 57 | 53 |

**Honours**: League Cup
**Highest League finish**: 3rd in 1995-96 and 1997-98
**Lowest League finish**: 8th in 1993-94
**Best F.A. Cup Run**: Final in 1995-96
**Best League Cup Run**: Winners in 1994-95
**Best European Run (European Cup Winners' Cup)**: Semi-final in 1996-97
**First Match in charge**: 5th February 1994 vs Norwich City Premiership (drew 2-2)
**Last Match in charge**: 10th May 1998 vs Derby County Premiership (lost 0-1)

# ROY EVANS AND GERARD HOULLIER
# JULY 1998 TO NOVEMBER 1998

The general consensus was that it "would all end in tears" and it did. The co-managership lasted just 18 games before Roy Evans resigned. Their last match together at the helm was a League Cup tie against Tottenham Hotspur, in November 1998, which ended in a 3-1 defeat.

The only man signed during the Evans/Houllier reign was Norwegian defender Vegard Heggem. Roy Evans was manager of cash-strapped Swindon Town in 2001-02, but left the County Ground mid-season.

## LIVERPOOL MANAGERIAL RECORD

|  | Played | Won | Drew | Lost |
|---|---|---|---|---|
| League | 12 | 4 | 4 | 4 |
| F.A. Cup | 0 | 0 | 0 | 0 |
| League Cup | 2 | 1 | 0 | 1 |
| Europe | 4 | 2 | 2 | 0 |
| Total | 18 | 7 | 6 | 5 |

**Honours**: None

**Best League Cup Run**: Fourth Round in 1998-99

**First Match**: 16th August 1998 vs Southampton Premiership (won 2-1)

**Last Match**: 10th November 1998 vs Tottenham Hotspur League Cup (lost 1-3)

# GERARD HOULLIER FROM NOVEMBER 1998

Gerard Houllier fell in love with the city of Liverpool and the Kop in the late 1960's when he visited as a student. The first match he watched was the 10-0 hammering of Dundalk City (in the European Cup) in 1969. He trained to be a teacher, but was player-manager of French side Le Tourquet between 1973 and 1976. He then became head coach at Noeux Les Mines. He later managed Lens and then moved on to Paris St Germain (who he led to the championship). Gerard became coach of the French national side in the early 1990s. He also managed the French Under-21 squad.

Houllier took sole control of the Liverpool side after Roy Evans departed in November 1998. Phil Thompson was appointed as his assistant.

The most productive season during Houllier's reign was in 2000-2001, when his side lifted three cups. The League Cup was won towards the end of February, while the F.A. Cup and UEFA Cup were added during a five-day spell in May. Gerard became only the second man (after Joe Fagan, in 1983-84) to lead the Reds to three major trophies in a season.

Unfortunately, Gerard Houllier had a major health scare during 2001-02. On 13th October 2001, during the home match with Leeds United, he was rushed to hospital for major heart surgery after experiencing chest pains during his half-time talk. Thompson took the reins while Houllier recuperated and it was five months before the Frenchman was fit enough to make an emotional return to Anfield. His side reached the quarter-final of the European Cup (getting through both group stages in the process) and finished as the runners-up to Arsenal in the Premiership.

It was the Reds' highest finish since 1990-91 and was the fourth successive campaign that they had improved under Houllier. Liverpool finished seventh in 1998-99, but gradually progressed each term afterwards, with fourth, third and, then in 2001-02, second place finishes.

## FACTFILE

**Born**: Therouanne, 3rd September 1947

### LIVERPOOL MANAGERIAL RECORD (UP TO JULY 2002)

|  | Played | Won | Drew | Lost |
|---|---|---|---|---|
| League | 140 | 74 | 32 | 34 |
| F.A. Cup | 12 | 9 | 0 | 3 |
| League Cup | 10 | 6 | 1 | 3 |
| Europe | 15 | 8 | 4 | 3 |
| Total | 177 | 97 | 37 | 43 |

**Honours**: UEFA Cup, F.A. Cup, League Cup
**Highest League finish**: Runners-up in 2001-02
**Lowest League finish**: 7th in 1998-99
**Best F.A. Cup Run**: Winners in 2000-01
**Best League Cup Run**: Winners in 2000-01
**Best European Run (UEFA Cup)**: Winners in 2000-01
**First Match in charge**: 14th November 1998 vs Leeds United Premiership (lost 1-3)

# LIVERPOOL 25 SEASONS 1977-78 TO 2001-02

## THE CUP FINALS

Liverpool reached 19 major Cup Finals during the quarter of a century up to the summer of 2002. The Reds appeared in six F.A. Cup Finals (winning four), four European Cup Finals (winning three) and were triumphant in the 2000-01 UEFA Cup Final. They also won six of the eight League Cup Finals that they contested, three of which went to a replay.

The Cup Finals which featured Liverpool were:

| | | | |
|---|---|---|---|
| 1977-78 | LEAGUE CUP | vs NOTTINGHAM FOREST | DREW |
| 1977-78 | LEAGUE CUP REPLAY | vs NOTTINGHAM FOREST | LOST |
| 1977-78 | EUROPEAN CUP | vs FC BRUGGE | WON |
| 1980-81 | LEAGUE CUP | vs WEST HAM UNITED | DREW |
| 1980-81 | LEAGUE CUP REPLAY | vs WEST HAM UNITED | WON |
| 1980-81 | EUROPEAN CUP | vs REAL MADRID | WON |
| 1981-82 | LEAGUE CUP | vs TOTTENHAM HOTSPUR | WON |
| 1982-83 | LEAGUE CUP | vs MANCHESTER UNITED | WON |
| 1983-84 | LEAGUE CUP | vs EVERTON | DREW |
| 1983-84 | LEAGUE CUP | vs EVERTON | WON |
| 1983-84 | EUROPEAN CUP | vs AS ROMA | WON |
| 1984-85 | EUROPEAN CUP | vs JUVENTUS | LOST |
| 1985-86 | F.A. CUP | vs EVERTON | WON |
| 1986-87 | LEAGUE CUP | vs ARSENAL | LOST |
| 1987-88 | F.A. CUP | vs WIMBLEDON | LOST |
| 1988-89 | F.A. CUP | vs EVERTON | WON |
| 1991-92 | F.A. CUP | vs SUNDERLAND | WON |
| 1994-95 | LEAGUE CUP | vs BOLTON WANDERERS | WON |
| 1995-96 | F.A. CUP | vs MANCHESTER UNITED | LOST |
| 2000-01 | LEAGUE CUP | vs BIRMINGHAM CITY | WON |
| 2000-01 | F.A. CUP | vs ARSENAL | WON |
| 2000-01 | UEFA CUP | vs CD ALAVES | WON |

## LEAGUE CUP FINAL 1977-78
## LIVERPOOL vs NOTTINGHAM FOREST

Liverpool reached the League Cup Final for the very first time in 1979. Facing them were Brian Clough's Nottingham Forest, who were destined to pip Bob Paisley's men to the Championship that season.

The Reds were the dominant side for most of the game, but they could not find a way past Forest's 18 year-old goalkeeper Chris Woods. With Peter Shilton cup-tied, Clough showed faith in the rookie goalie during his side's League Cup run. Woods, without a Football League appearance to his name, made some good saves to frustrate Liverpool and earn his side a replay after the extra half-hour proved fruitless.

### LIVERPOOL 0-0 NOTTINGHAM FOREST (AET)

**Date**: 18th March 1978

**Manager**: Bob Paisley

**Team**: Ray Clemence, Phil Neal, Tommy Smith, Phil Thompson, Ray Kennedy (sub. David Fairclough), Emlyn Hughes, Kenny Dalglish, Jimmy Case, Steve Heighway, Terry McDermott, Ian Callaghan

**Attendance**: 100,000 (Wembley Stadium)

**Clubs defeated en route to the Final**: Chelsea, Derby County, Coventry City, Wrexham and Arsenal

## LEAGUE CUP FINAL REPLAY 1977-78
## LIVERPOOL vs NOTTINGHAM FOREST

The replay of the 1977-78 League Cup Final, took place at Old Trafford on the Wednesday evening after the goalless first encounter. It was to be a night of further frustration and considerable fury for Liverpool.

The first half yielded no goals, but soon after the break Forest were awarded a penalty for Phil Thompson's foul on John O'Hare. Ray Clemence was unable to prevent John Robertson slotting home what proved to be the only goal. Liverpool were furious with referee Pat Partridge, who disallowed a perfectly good goal by Terry McDermott for 'hand-ball'. The man in black also booked Ian Callaghan for a trivial offence. Cally had never been cautioned previously in over 800 senior games.

**LIVERPOOL 0-1 NOTTINGHAM FOREST**

Date: 22nd March 1978

Manager: Bob Paisley

Team: Ray Clemence, Phil Neal, Tommy Smith, Phil Thompson, Ray Kennedy, Emlyn Hughes, Kenny Dalglish, Jimmy Case (sub. David Fairclough), Steve Heighway, Terry McDermott, Ian Callaghan

Attendance: 54,375 (Wembley Stadium)

# EUROPEAN CUP FINAL 1977-78
# LIVERPOOL vs FC BRUGGE

On 10th May 1978 Liverpool became the first British club to win the European Cup for a second time. Six of the men who collected winners' medals in Rome, 12 months previously, lined up at Wembley to face Belgian side FC Brugge. Alongside them were Kenny Dalglish, Graeme Souness, David Fairclough, Phil Thompson and Alan Hansen (who got his opportunity because of Tommy Smith's leg injury). Steve Heighway (who started in Rome) also collected a second winners' medal after coming off the bench.

The Reds dominated the whole game without being at their best. Only a string of saves by keeper Birger Jansen kept the margin of victory to the minimum. That goal was chipped in midway through the second half by Dalglish, who then hurdled the advertising boards and sprinted towards the fence to celebrate with the fans. The unambitious Belgians nearly forced extra-time with virtually their only shot, but the alert Phil Thompson cleared the ball off the goal-line. The celebrations went on deep into the night, with the bulk of the 92,000 crowd wearing red and happy faces.

**LIVERPOOL 1-0 FC BRUGGE**

Date: 10th May 1978

Manager: Bob Paisley

Team: Ray Clemence, Phil Neal, Phil Thompson, Alan Hansen, Emlyn Hughes, Terry McDermott, Ray Kennedy, Graeme Souness, Jimmy Case (sub. Steve Heighway), David Fairclough, Kenny Dalglish

Scorer: Dalglish

Attendance: 92,000 (Wembley Stadium)

**Clubs defeated en route to the final:** Dynamo Dresden, Benfica and Borussia Moenchengladbach.

## LEAGUE CUP FINAL 1980-81
## LIVERPOOL vs WEST HAM UNITED

Liverpool reached the Final of the League Cup for the second time in the 1980-81 season. Just like the first occasion, three years earlier, a replay was required to determine the victors – but in April 1981 there was a happier outcome for the Reds.

With second-flight West Ham United as the opposition, Paisley's side started as favourites to take the trophy. The East London side, the reigning F.A. Cup holders and Second Division Champions elect, proved to be no mugs though. A battling, tense, 90 minutes brought no goals and all the major incidents took place during the butt-end of extra-time.

Alan Kennedy thought he had won Liverpool the cup when he fired home with only three minutes remaining. Referee Clive Thomas (who had earlier disallowed a Liverpool 'goal' for offside) allowed the goal to stand despite the fact that Sammy Lee was lying yards offside when he ducked his head to allow his left-back's shot rocket over him into the net. The unhappy Hammers threw extra men forward and, in injury-time, forced a free-kick from which Terry McDermott was forced to handle a goalbound header from Alvin Martin. For the second time in his career, Ray Clemence was unable to stop a League Cup Final penalty (this time taken by Ray Stewart) and a replay was required.

**LIVERPOOL 1-1 WEST HAM UNITED (AET: SCORE AFTER 90 MINS 0-0)**

**Date:** 14th March 1981

**Manager:** Bob Paisley

**Team:** Ray Clemence, Phil Neal, Alan Kennedy, Colin Irwin, Ray Kennedy, Alan Hansen, Kenny Dalglish, Sammy Lee, Steve Heighway (sub. Jimmy Case), Terry McDermott, Graeme Souness

**Scorer:** Alan Kennedy

**Attendance:** 100,000 (Wembley Stadium)

**Clubs defeated en route to the Final:** Bradford City, Swindon Town, Portsmouth, Birmingham City and Manchester City

# LEAGUE CUP FINAL REPLAY 1980-81
# LIVERPOOL vs WEST HAM UNITED

The replay of the 1980-81 League Cup Final, took place nearly three weeks later, on a Wednesday night, at Villa Park. The Hammers took the lead early on through the diving-head of Paul Goddard. Sparked into action, Liverpool stepped up a gear and scored twice before half-time through Kenny Dalglish (to maintain his record of scoring in every round) and Alan Hansen (with a header that deflected in off Billy Bonds). The Second Division side never gave up, but equally the Reds spurned good chances to completely kill the game.

Liverpool held on to collect the trophy for the very first time. It would be the best part of another four years before they relinquished it! One man who enjoyed every moment of that night at Villa Park was 19 year-old Ian Rush, who was making only his second first-team appearance for Liverpool.

### LIVERPOOL 2-1 WEST HAM UNITED

**Date:** 1st April 1981
**Manager:** Bob Paisley
**Team:** Ray Clemence, Phil Neal, Alan Kennedy, Phil Thompson, Ray Kennedy, Alan Hansen, Kenny Dalglish, Sammy Lee, Ian Rush, Terry McDermott, Jimmy Case
**Scorers:** Dalglish, Hansen
**Attendance:** 36,693 (Villa Park)

# EUROPEAN CUP FINAL
# LIVERPOOL vs REAL MADRID

Liverpool lifted the European Cup for the third time when they defeated Real Madrid by a single Alan Kennedy goal in Paris.

Liverpool started brightly with Kenny Dalglish (in spite of not being 100% fit) testing the Spanish defence. The Scot almost gave the Reds the lead in the first-half. The cautious Spanish did not force a corner until the 73rd minute, but did waste a good chance to go ahead before Liverpool netted. The winner came in the 82nd minute when Alan Kennedy chested down a throw-in, raced down the wing and fired home an unstoppable shot from a very acute angle.

Neutrals labelled the Final dull, but Bob Paisley was not complaining as he became the first man to manage a side to three European Cup triumphs. Earlier in this competition, in 1980-81, Graeme Souness secured two hat-tricks to help his side progress all the way.

### LIVERPOOL 1-0 REAL MADRID

**Date:** 27th May 1981

**Manager:** Bob Paisley

**Team:** Ray Clemence, Phil Neal, Alan Kennedy, Phil Thompson, Ray Kennedy, Alan Hansen, Kenny Dalglish (sub. Jimmy Case), Sammy Lee, David Johnson, Terry McDermott, Graeme Souness

**Clubs defeated en route to the final:** OPS Oulu, Aberdeen, CKSA Sofia, Bayern Munich

**Scorer:** Alan Kennedy

**Attendance:** 48,360 (Paris)

# LEAGUE CUP FINAL 1981-82
# LIVERPOOL vs TOTTENHAM HOTSPUR

Liverpool retained the League Cup in 1981-82 and this occasion collected the trophy at Wembley. However, Spurs pushed Bob Paisley's side all the way and yet again extra-time was required. Three men – Mark Lawrenson, Ronnie Whelan and Bruce Grobbelaar – collected their first medals with Liverpool on 13th March 1982. Standing opposite Grobbelaar in the Spurs goal was his predecessor Ray Clemence (who had made the switch to White Hart Lane the previous summer).

It was Clemence who was the happier keeper at half-time after Steve Archibald had given his side the lead. The Milk Cup did not slip from Liverpool's grasp, though, with Whelan popping up to equalise. The Reds cemented victory in the extra period through Ian Rush's first Cup Final goal and another effort by Whelan.

### LIVERPOOL 3-1 TOTTENHAM HOTSPUR
### (AET: SCORE AFTER 90 MINUTES 1-1)

**Date:** 13th March 1982

**Manager:** Bob Paisley

**Team:** Bruce Grobbelaar, Phil Neal, Alan Kennedy, Mark Lawrenson, Ronnie Whelan, Phil Thompson, Kenny Dalglish, Sammy Lee, Ian Rush, Terry McDermott (sub. David Johnson), Graeme Souness

**Scorers:** Whelan 2, Rush

**Attendance**: 100,000 (Wembley Stadium)
**Clubs defeated en route to the Final**: Exeter City, Middlesbrough, Arsenal, Barnsley and Ipswich Town

# LEAGUE CUP FINAL 1982-83
# LIVERPOOL vs MANCHESTER UNITED

Liverpool became the first club to collect the League Cup for a third successive season when they overcame Manchester United in a thrilling Wembley Final. Naturally it involved a period of extra-time.

United took the lead in the first half through Norman Whiteside but the Reds replied in the second period through Alan Kennedy. It was Ronnie Whelan, the two-goal hero from the Final of this competition 12 months before, who netted the winner. Bob Paisley collected the cup, in what was his last game at Wembley before taking retirement.

### LIVERPOOL 2-1 MANCHESTER UNITED
### (AET: SCORE AFTER 90 MINUTES 1-1)

**Date**: 26th March 1983
**Manager**: Bob Paisley
**Team**: Bruce Grobbelaar, Phil Neal, Alan Kennedy, Mark Lawrenson, Ronnie Whelan, Alan Hansen, Kenny Dalglish, Sammy Lee, Ian Rush, Craig Johnston (sub. David Fairclough), Graeme Souness
**Scorers**: Kennedy, Whelan
**Attendance**: 100,000 (Wembley Stadium)
**Clubs defeated en route to the Final**: Ipswich Town, Rotherham United, Norwich City, West Ham United and Burnley

# LEAGUE CUP FINAL 1983-84
# LIVERPOOL vs EVERTON

Liverpool battled through to their fourth successive League Cup Final during the 1983-84 season. Facing them were their great rivals from across Stanley Park. The first ever all-Merseyside Wembley Cup Final was a very tight affair. It was a game that both sides were determined not to lose and a stalemate resulted. Nevertheless it was a great occasion enjoyed by a capacity crowd.

Joe Fagan's side started the game as the favourites, with Ian Rush hungry to complete the job of scoring in every round. However, it was Everton who almost drew first blood when a shot by Adrian Heath appeared to be handled by Alan Hansen. The penalty appeal was rejected by referee Alan Robinson – to the chagrin of the blue half of the stadium.

Everton had three other good opportunities to add to their score in the first half. While, at the other end, Ian Rush forced a good save from Neville Southall. It was a match which the defences held sway and, on this occasion, Liverpool could not force a winner during extra-time.

### EVERTON 0-0 LIVERPOOL

**Date:** 25th March 1984
**Manager:** Joe Fagan
**Team:** Bruce Grobbelaar, Phil Neal, Alan Kennedy, Mark Lawrenson, Ronnie Whelan, Alan Hansen, Kenny Dalglish, Sammy Lee, Ian Rush, Craig Johnston (sub. Michael Robinson), Graeme Souness
**Attendance:** 100,000 (Wembley Stadium)
**Clubs defeated en route to the Final:** Brentford, Fulham, Birmingham City, Sheffield Wednesday and Walsall

## LEAGUE CUP FINAL REPLAY 1983-84
## EVERTON vs LIVERPOOL

The Milk Cup Final replay took place at Maine Road on the Wednesday evening following the initial goalless encounter at Wembley. Joe Fagan sent out the same side and this time they did just enough to take the trophy and break Evertonian hearts.

Graeme Souness's powerful first-half strike proved to be the only goal of the game. Everton wasted a good chance to force extra-time near the end, but two of their men – Peter Reid and Adrian Heath – got in each other's way. Ian Rush was unable to get his name on the scoresheet and maintain his record of scoring in every round.

### LIVERPOOL 1-0 EVERTON

**Date:** 28th March 1984
**Manager:** Joe Fagan

**Team:** Bruce Grobbelaar, Phil Neal, Alan Kennedy, Mark Lawrenson, Ronnie Whelan, Alan Hansen, Kenny Dalglish, Sammy Lee, Ian Rush, Craig Johnston, Graeme Souness

**Scorer:** Souness

**Attendance:** 52,089 (Maine Road)

# EUROPEAN CUP 1983-84
# LIVERPOOL vs AS ROMA

Liverpool won the European Cup for a record fourth time when they held their nerve in a penalty shoot-out again Roma, on their opposition's own territory in the Italian capital's Olympic Stadium.

Joe Fagan's side edged into a 15th minute lead through the boot of Phil Neal. The match might have been immediately killed soon afterwards, but an effort by Graeme Souness was ruled out for offside. Instead Roma pulled level just before the break when their centre-forward Pruzzo headed over a helpless Bruce Grobbelaar. The Liverpool keeper did, however, make a fine save to keep his level in the second-half. Liverpool's best chance of winning the game outright fell to Kenny Dalglish but the Italian goalkeeper made a good save.

The match went to a shoot-out and it began badly for Liverpool. Substitute Steve Nicol volunteered to take the first penalty but shot over the bar. With Grobbelaar doing his best to distract them, the Italian penalty takers were not faultless either. Roma missed their second and fourth kicks and (with Phil Neal, Graeme Souness and Ian Rush all finding the target) Alan Kennedy was given the opportunity to find the net in yet another Final. He had missed every penalty he had taken in the practice session, but showed admirable coolness under immense pressure to ignite Liverpool's celebrations.

**LIVERPOOL 1-1 AS ROMA**
**(AET: 1-1 AFTER 90 MINUTES)**
**LIVERPOOL WON 4-2 ON PENALTIES**

**Date:** 30th May 1984

**Manager:** Joe Fagan

**Team:** Bruce Grobbelaar, Phil Neal, Alan Kennedy, Mark Lawrenson, Ronnie Whelan, Alan Hansen, Kenny Dalglish (sub. Michael Robinson), Sammy Lee, Ian Rush, Craig Johnston (sub. Steve Nicol), Graeme Souness

**Scorer:** Neal

**Shoot-out Scorers**: Neal, Souness, Rush, Kennedy
**Shoot-out Misser**: Nicol
**Attendance**: 69,693 (Rome)
**Clubs defeated en route to the Final**: BK Odense, Athletic Bilbao, Benfica, Dinamo Bucharest

# EUROPEAN CUP 1984-85
# LIVERPOOL vs JUVENTUS

This match was totally overshadowed by the tragic scenes from before the game when 39 Juventus fans were crushed to death and another 400 were injured. Neither team wanted to play, but the police insisted that the Final went ahead.

Mark Lawrenson's shoulder injury forced Joe Fagan to make a change after little more than two minutes. Nevertheless the Reds made the early pace with John Wark, Paul Walsh and Ronnie Whelan all testing the keeper. However, Juventus responded well and forced Bruce Grobbelaar to make two fine saves before the break.

The Italians netted the game's only goal in the 56th minute when Michel Platini slotted home a penalty (awarded for a foul on the edge of the box). Liverpool were convinced that they should have been awarded a penalty themselves, with 15 minutes remaining, when Ronnie Whelan appeared to have been fouled in the area. A succession of late corners failed to generate an equaliser and Juventus claimed a hollow first European Cup triumph.

### LIVERPOOL 0-1 JUVENTUS

**Date**: 29th May 1985
**Manager**: Joe Fagan
**Team**: Bruce Grobbelaar, Phil Neal, Jim Beglin, Mark Lawrenson (sub. Gary Gillespie), Alan Hansen, Steve Nicol, Kenny Dalglish, Ronnie Whelan, John Wark, Ian Rush, Paul Walsh (sub. Craig Johnston)
**Attendance**: 50,000 (Brussels)

# F.A. CUP FINAL 1985-86
# LIVERPOOL vs EVERTON

Despite trailing at half-time, Liverpool beat Everton to win the F.A. Cup and become only the fifth club to clinch the League and F.A. Cup 'Double' in the same season. The Toffees were also the bridesmaids to the Reds in the 1985-86 League campaign.

Everton dominated the early play and might have had a penalty when Graeme Sharp appeared to be impeded by Steve Nicol. Referee Alan Robinson waved play on – just as he did when Everton had claimed a penalty in the 1984 Milk Cup Final. However, the Toffeemen did make the breakthrough just before the half-hour mark when Gary Lineker forced the ball home.

Kenny Dalglish's side were a little fortunate not to go further behind before the course of the Final changed in the 57th minute. Gary Stevens gave the ball away and in a flash Ronnie Whelan and Jan Molby had set up Ian Rush. The Welsh striker side-stepped keeper Bobby Mimms and the scores were level. Liverpool edged ahead six minutes later when Craig Johnston converted a Rush cross. 'Man of the Match' Rush sealed the victory with the game's fourth goal in the 84th minute.

### LIVERPOOL 3-1 EVERTON

**Date:** 10th May 1986
**Manager:** Kenny Dalglish
**Team:** Bruce Grobbelaar, Mark Lawrenson, Jim Beglin, Steve Nicol, Ronnie Whelan, Alan Hansen, Kenny Dalglish, Craig Johnston, Ian Rush, Jan Molby, Kevin MacDonald
**Scorers:** Rush 2, Johnston
**Attendance:** 98,000 (Wembley Stadium)
**Clubs defeated en route to the Final:** Norwich City, Chelsea, York City, Watford and Southampton

## LEAGUE CUP FINAL 1986-87
## LIVERPOOL vs ARSENAL

The omens looked good for Liverpool in the 1986-87 Littlewoods Cup Final when Ian Rush opened the scoring in the 20th minute. However, the Gunners were soon level through Charlie Nicholas.

Both sides had opportunities to take a grip of what was a very even game between two well balanced sides. Sadly, for the Reds, it was Arsenal who took their chance, near the end, when Nicholas converted a cross by substitute Perry Groves. The result meant that for the first time in 145 games Liverpool had been defeated in a game that Rush had scored in! This Wembley occasion, on 5th

April 1987, was the last Final in which Kenny Dalglish wore a Liverpool shirt. He had brought himself late in the game for John Wark, but was unable to make any real impact.

## LIVERPOOL 1-2 ARSENAL

**Date**: 5th April 1987

**Manager**: Kenny Dalglish

**Team**: Bruce Grobbelaar, Gary Gillespie, Barry Venison, Nigel Spackman, Ronnie Whelan, Alan Hansen, John Wark (sub. Kenny Dalglish), Craig Johnston, Ian Rush, Jan Molby, Steve McMahon (sub. John Wark)

**Scorer**: Rush

**Attendance**: 96,000 (Wembley Stadium)

**Clubs defeated en route to the Final**: Fulham, Leicester City, Coventry City, Everton and Southampton

# F.A. CUP FINAL 1987-88
# LIVERPOOL vs WIMBLEDON

Liverpool stepped on to the hallowed turf, on 14th May 1988, as the hottest favourites to lift the F.A. Cup for many a year. Facing them were Wimbledon, First Division in status but not in pedigree (having battled their way up from the Fourth Division in double-quick time). It was inconceivable that the Reds would return to Merseyside without the cup. Sadly, though, that was the outcome as the determined Dons collected their first major trophy.

Lawrie Sanchez headed the only goal in the 37th minute. But there were equally as important incidents before and afterwards. Peter Beardsley put the ball in the net on for Liverpool on for it to be unluckily ruled out three minutes before Sanchez struck! Referee Brian Hill blew his whistle for a foul on Beardsley. The ref later acknowledged that he made a mistake in not "playing on".

Wimbledon grew in confidence and took the lead, against a complacent Liverpool outfit who were certainly not at their best on a very hot afternoon. Even so, the Reds looked set to equalise on the hour-mark, when Clive Goodyear fouled John Aldridge in the box. However, Wimbledon skipper Dave Beasant made a fine save to condemn Aldo (who soon afterwards left the pitch in tears) to being the first man to miss a penalty in an F.A. Cup Final at Wembley.

**LIVERPOOL 0-1 WIMBLEDON**

Date: 14th May 1988

Manager: Kenny Dalglish

Team: Bruce Grobbelaar, Gary Gillespie, Gary Ablett, Steve Nicol, Nigel Spackman (sub. Jan Molby), Alan Hansen, Peter Beardsley, John Aldridge (sub. Craig Johnston), Ray Houghton, John Barnes, Steve McMahon

Attendance: 98,203 (Wembley Stadium)

Clubs defeated en route to the Final: Stoke City, Aston Villa, Everton, Manchester City and Nottingham Forest

# F.A. CUP FINAL 1988-89
# LIVERPOOL vs EVERTON

Twelve months after being defeated by Wimbledon, Liverpool returned to Wembley for the most poignant of F.A. Cup Finals. The match against Everton came just eight weeks after the Hillsborough Disaster, which had claimed the lives of 96 Liverpool supporters. Prior to the kick-off the crowd joined Gerry Marsden in an emotional rendition of 'You'll Never Walk Alone.'

On a baking afternoon it was Liverpool who made the early pace and they took the lead in the fourth minute through John Aldridge's first-time shot. The Reds had a clear edge in midfield and only some fine goalkeeping by Neville Southall stopped them from running away with the game. However, with the clock ticking down, substitute Stuart McCall forced extra-time when he pounced on the rebound after Bruce Grobbelaar had parried a shot from Dave Watson.

Liverpool regained the lead six minutes into the extra period through a shot by substitute Ian Rush. However, Everton showed their battling qualities and equalised again through a dipping McCall shot. McCall had become the first sub to score twice in an F.A. Cup Final. Happily, for the red half of Merseyside, another substitute emulated this feat three minutes later. A header by Rush ended the game's scoring and soon afterwards skipper Ronnie Whelan held the cup aloft.

**LIVERPOOL 3-2 EVERTON (AET: 1-1 AFTER 90 MINUTES)**

Date: 20th May 1989

Manager: Kenny Dalglish

Team: Bruce Grobbelaar, Gary Ablett, Steve Staunton (sub. Barry Venison), Steve Nicol, Ronnie Whelan, Alan Hansen, Peter Beardsley, John Aldridge (sub. Ian Rush), Ray Houghton,

John Barnes, Steve McMahon
**Scorers:** Aldridge, Rush 2
**Attendance:** 82,800 (Wembley Stadium)
**Clubs defeated en route to the Final:** Carlisle United, Millwall, Hull City, Brentford and Nottingham Forest

## F.A. CUP FINAL 1991-92
## LIVERPOOL vs SUNDERLAND

Liverpool reached the F.A. Cup Final for the third time in five seasons, in 1991-92, when they met Second Division Sunderland. The Final came just 32 days after manager Graeme Souness underwent a triple heart bypass. Nevertheless he was on the bench to witness Liverpool collect the only major trophy they were to lift during the course of his reign.

The Wearsiders had the best of the early play, but Liverpool looked the better side the longer the match progressed. They were rarely troubled after breaking the deadlock two minutes into the second half. The creator was 20 year-old Steve McManaman (deputising for the injured John Barnes), who set up Michael Thomas to volley home. Jan Molby (the midfield orchestrator) and Dean Saunders (who headed against the bar) both came close to doubling the lead. However, that honour fell to Ian Rush. The Welshman notched a record fifth F.A. Cup Final goal when he side-footed home a pass by Thomas midway through the half. Sunderland had nothing left in the tank and Mark Wright joyfully held the F.A. Cup aloft.

### LIVERPOOL 2-0 SUNDERLAND

**Date:** 9th May 1992
**Manager:** Graeme Souness
**Team:** Bruce Grobbelaar, Rob Jones, David Burrows, Steve Nicol, Jan Molby, Mark Wright, Dean Saunders, Ray Houghton, Ian Rush, Steve McManaman, Michael Thomas
**Scorers:** Thomas, Rush
**Attendance:** 79,544 (Wembley Stadium)

## LEAGUE CUP FINAL 1994-95
## LIVERPOOL vs BOLTON WANDERERS

With 'Guest of Honour' Sir Stanley Matthews showing his appreciation, Steve

McManaman was in dazzling form to help the Reds defeat second-flight Bolton Wanderers 2-1. Liverpool were victorious for a record fifth time with skipper Ian Rush involved on all five occasions.

The Trotters contributed much to the game and would have taken the lead in the first half, but for a splendid diving save from David James which kept out a 30 yard drive by Alan Thompson. Liverpool responded immediately with McManaman firing into the net at the end of a fine run.

Victory seemed secure midway through the second half when 'Man of the Match' McManaman collected a ball from Jamie Redknapp, beat two men, and placed the ball in the net. However, within 60 seconds, Bolton halved the deficit through a spectacular volley from Thompson. Liverpool held on, though, to defeat a Bolton side containing a Liverpool 'old boy' in Mark Seagreaves and a 'future Red' in Jason McAteer.

## LIVERPOOL 2-1 BOLTON WANDERERS

**Date:** 2nd April 1995
**Manager:** Roy Evans
**Team:** David James, Rob Jones, Stig Inge Bjornebye, John Scales, Phil Babb, Neil Ruddock, Steve McManaman, Jamie Redknapp, Ian Rush, John Barnes, Robbie Fowler
**Scorer:** McManaman 2
**Attendance:** 75,595 (Wembley Stadium)
**Clubs defeated en route to the Final:** Burnley, Stoke City, Blackburn Rovers, Arsenal and Crystal Palace

# F.A. CUP FINAL 1995-96
# LIVERPOOL vs MANCHESTER UNITED

This was a disappointing Final in every sense. The entertainment value was low and, sadly for the Red half of Merseyside, Manchester United won by a single goal five minutes from time.

Eric Cantona's fine strike, after David James cleared a corner to the edge of the area, was incongruous with most of the rest of the play. The Reds, or more precisely the Greens (as Liverpool wore their change kit), were unable to respond and it was not long before Cantona was lifting the F.A. Cup aloft. United had claimed their second 'Double' in three campaigns.

This was the one and only Final in which Jason McAteer and Stan Collymore featured for Liverpool. Collymore bagged a hat-trick in the Reds' 7-0 third round drubbing of Rochdale. Liverpool's performance in this Final was definitely "below par". In fact it was a display to forget, very much like the squad's cream designer suits!

## LIVERPOOL 0-1 MANCHESTER UNITED

**Date:** 11th May 1996

**Manager:** Roy Evans

**Team:** David James, Jason McAteer, Rob Jones (sub. Michael Thomas), John Scales, Mark Wright, Phil Babb, Steve McManaman, Jamie Redknapp, Stan Collymore (sub. Ian Rush), John Barnes, Robbie Fowler

**Attendance:** 79,007 (Wembley Stadium)

**Clubs defeated en route to the Final:** Rochdale, Shrewsbury Town, Charlton Athletic, Leeds United and Aston Villa

# LEAGUE CUP FINAL 2000-01
# LIVERPOOL vs BIRMINGHAM CITY

Liverpool captured their first trophy of the 21st century when they defeated First Division Birmingham City in a shoot-out to lift a record sixth League Cup. In reaching the Final Liverpool only faced Premiership opposition once, in the third round, when they side-stepped Chelsea. In the fourth round the Reds recorded their record away win when they hammered Stoke City 8-0.

Birmingham gave an excellent account of themselves in the Final, the very first English domestic Final to be played at the Millennium Stadium. After a difficult schedule of matches, Liverpool looked a little fatigued, but went ahead in the first half through a magnificent shot by skipper Robbie Fowler. City's menace grew throughout the second half and they equalised with a Darren Purse penalty in injury time. The Blues' ascendancy carried over into extra-time and it was a relief for the Reds when the final whistle signalled a penalty shoot-out.

Each side missed one of their first five penalties, Dietmar Hamann was Liverpool's culprit. Jamie Carragher netted to make his side 5-4 ahead and then Sander Westerveld saved from Andrew Johnson to ensure Gerard Houllier had captured his first trophy as Liverpool's manager.

## LIVERPOOL 1-1 BIRMINGHAM CITY

**(AET: 1-1 AFTER 90 MINUTES)    LIVERPOOL WON 5-4 ON PENALTIES**

**Date:** 25th February 2001

**Manager:** Gerard Houllier

**Team:** Sander Westerveld, Steven Gerrard (sub. Gary McAllister), Jamie Carragher, Igor Biscan (sub. Christian Ziege), Stephane Henchoz, Sami Hyypia, Danny Murphy, Vladimir Smicer (sub. Nicky Barmby), Robbie Fowler, Jari Litmanen, Dietmar Hamann

**Scorer:** Fowler

**Shoot-out Scorers:** McAllister, Barmby, Ziege, Fowler, Carragher

**Shoot-out Misser:** Hamann

**Attendance:** 73,500 (Millennium Stadium)

**Clubs defeated en route to the Final:** Chelsea, Stoke City, Fulham and Crystal Palace

# F.A. CUP FINAL 2000-01 – LIVERPOOL vs ARSENAL

Liverpool's second visit to the Millennium Stadium in 2000-01 proved as successful as the first. And, for the first time (at the fourth attempt) the Reds had defeated Arsenal in a Cup Final. The 'Man of the Match' was Michael Owen, who took his goals superbly to spike the Gunners.

Arsenal enjoyed a slight edge in the first half, but it was not until the 72nd minute that they took the lead through Freddie Ljungberg. Liverpool showed their renowned fighting spirit and equalised in the 83rd minute when Owen galloped clear and finished clinically. And, within five minutes, Owen had fired in another to kill off the Londoners and clinch Liverpool's sixth F.A. Cup success.

Sami Hyypia started the game as captain, but it was substitute Robbie Fowler (together with the non-playing injured club captain Jamie Redknapp) who collected the F.A. Cup from the Duke of York. Liverpool had become the first club to win the F.A. Cup outside England.

## LIVERPOOL 2-1 ARSENAL    (AET: 1-1 AFTER 90 MINUTES)

**Date:** 12th May 2001

**Manager:** Gerard Houllier

**Team:** Sander Westerveld, Markus Babbel, Jamie Carragher, Dietmar Hamann (sub. Gary McAllister), Stephane Henchoz, Sami Hyypia, Danny Murphy (sub. Patrik Berger), Steven Gerrard, Emile Heskey, Michael Owen, Vladimir Scimer (sub. Robbie Fowler)

**Scorer:** Owen 2

**Attendance:** 74,200 (Millennium Stadium)

**Clubs defeated en route to the Final:** Rotherham United, Leeds United, Manchester City, Tranmere Rovers and Wycombe Wanderers

## UEFA CUP 2000-01 – LIVERPOOL vs CD ALAVES

It was a little like waiting for a bus. After a long wait three come at once! After six barren years, Liverpool's third trophy success of 2001 came just four days after the F.A. Cup Final. The venue was Dortmund's Westfalenstadion and the opposition in the UEFA Cup Final were Spanish outfit CD Alaves. Having defeated Roma, AC Porto and Barcelona en route, Liverpool were favourites before the kick-off; but this Final proved to be anything but predictable!

The early action proved very satisfying as Markus Babbel and Steven Gerrard put Liverpool two in front, with little more than a quarter of an hour played. Ivan Alonso pulled a goal back for Alaves, but the Reds still turned around two goals to the good courtesy of a Gary McAllister penalty. However, the Spanish side shocked Gerard Houllier's men by squaring matters quickly after the interval through a brace from Javi Moreno. Liverpool's lead was restored in the 73rd minute when substitute Robbie Fowler hit the target. Alaves kept plugging away, though, and gained parity through Jordi Cruyff. With just a minute remaining!

A lack of discipline let the Spaniards down during the 'golden goal' period and both Magno Mocelin and Antonio Karmona were dismissed. With the prospect of a shoot-out little more than three minutes away the game was brought to a joyous halt when a McAllister free-kick was deflected into his own net by Delfin Geli. After a wait of 17 years – Liverpool had captured a European trophy.

### LIVERPOOL 5-4 CD ALAVES
### (GOLDEN GOAL SCORED DURING EXTRA TIME)

**Date:** 16th May 2001

**Manager:** Gerard Houllier

**Team:** Sander Westerveld, Markus Babbel, Jamie Carragher, Dietmar Hamann, Stephane Henchoz (sub. Vladimir Smicer), Sami Hyypia, Danny Murphy, Steven Gerrard, Gary McAliister, Emile Heskey (sub. Robbie Fowler), Michael Owen (sub. Patrik Berger)

**Scorers:** Babbel, Henchoz, McAllister (pen), Fowler, Delfin Geli (og)

**Attendance:** 65,000 (Dortmund)

**Clubs defeated en route to the Final:** Rapid Bucharest, Slovan Liberec, Olympiakos, AS Roma, FC Porto and Barcelona

# LIVERPOOL 25 SEASONS 1977-78 TO 2001-02

## THE 25 MEN WHO HAVE APPEARED MOST FREQUENTLY

## LEAGUE APPEARANCES 1977-1978 TO 2001-2002

### 25 SEASONS TOTAL

| | | |
|---|---|---|
| 1 | Ian Rush | 469 |
| 2 | Bruce Grobbelaar | 440 |
| 3 | Alan Hansen | 434 |
| 4 | Ronnie Whelan | 362 |
| 5 | Kenny Dalglish | 355 |
| 6 | Phil Neal | 348 |
| 7 | Steve Nicol | 343 |
| 8 | John Barnes | 314 |
| 9 | Steve McManaman | 272 |
| 10 | Alan Kennedy | 251 |
| 11 | Graeme Souness | 247 |
| 12 | Jamie Redknapp | 243 |
| 13 | Mark Lawrenson | 241 |
| 14 | Robbie Fowler | 236 |
| 15 | Jan Molby | 218 |
| 16 | David James | 214 |
| 17 | Steve McMahon | 204 |
| 18 | Sammy Lee | 197 |
| 19 | Phil Thompson | 194 |
| 20 | Rob Jones | 183 |
| 21 | Terry McDermott | 182 |
| 22 | Ray Kennedy | 179 |
| 23 | Craig Johnston | 178 |
| 24 | Ray Clemence | 164 |
| 25 | Jamie Carragher | 159 |

## EVER-PRESENTS (43)

**7 campaigns**: Phil Neal  (1977-78, 1978-79, 1979-80, 1980-81, 1981-82, 1982-83 and 1984-85)

**6 campaigns**: Bruce Grobbelaar  (1981-82, 1982-83, 1983-84, 1985-86 and 1989-90)

**5 campaigns**: Kenny Dalglish  (1977-1978, 1978-79, 1979-80, 1981-82 and 1982-83)

**3 campaigns**: David James  (1994-95, 1995-96 and 1996-97)

**2 campaigns**: Robbie Fowler (1994-95 and 1995-96**), Alan Kennedy  (1982-83 and 1983-84),  Steve McMahon  (1987-88 and 1989-90*),  Steve Nicol  (1987-88 & 1988-89), Ian Rush  (1986-87 and 1993-94*)

**1 campaign**: Markus Babbel (2000-01), Stig Inge Bjornebye (1996-97), Ray Clemence (1978-79),  Alan Hansen  (1983-84),  Ray Houghton  (1988-89),  Sami Hyypia  (1999-2000),  Ray Kennedy  (1978-79),  Mark Lawrenson  (1983-84),  Sammy Lee  (1983-84),  Steve McManaman  (1995-96),  Phil Thompson  (1979-80) and  Sander Westerveld (2000-01)

* includes one game as substitute        ** includes two games as substitute

# THE 25 LEADING GOALSCORERS

## LEAGUE GOALS  1977-1978 TO 2001-2002

### 25 SEASONS TOTAL

| | | |
|---|---|---|
| 1 | Ian Rush | 229 |
| 2 | Robbie Fowler | 120 |
| 3 | Kenny Dalglish | 118 |
| 4 | John Barnes | 84 |
| 5 | Michael Owen | 83 |
| 6= | John Aldridge | 50 |
| 6= | David Johnson | 50 |
| 6= | Terry McDermott | 50 |
| 9= | Peter Beardsley | 46 |
| 9= | Steve McManaman | 46 |
| 9= | Ronnie Whelan | 46 |
| 13= | Jan Molby | 44 |
| 13= | Graeme Souness | 38 |
| 14 | Steve Nicol | 36 |

| 15 | Ray Kennedy | 33 |
| 16= | Craig Johnston | 30 |
| 16= | Jamie Redknapp | 30 |
| 18= | Patrik Berger | 29 |
| 18= | Steve McMahon | 29 |
| 20= | Ray Houghton | 28 |
| 20= | Phil Neal | 28 |
| 20= | John Wark | 28 |
| 23= | Stan Collymore | 26 |
| 23= | Emile Heskey | 26 |
| 25 | Paul Walsh | 25 |

## SEASON-BY-SEASON: LEADING GOALSCORERS

| 1977-1978 | 20 – Kenny Dalglish |
| 1978-1979 | 21 – Kenny Dalglish |
| 1979-1980 | 21 – David Johnson |
| 1980-1981 | 13 – Terry McDermott |
| 1981-1982 | 17 – Ian Rush |
| 1982-1983 | 24 – Ian Rush |
| 1983-1984 | 32 – Ian Rush |
| 1984-1985 | 18 – John Wark |
| 1985-1986 | 22 – Ian Rush |
| 1986-1987 | 30 – Ian Rush |
| 1987-1988 | 26 – John Aldridge |
| 1988-1989 | 21 – John Aldridge |
| 1989-1990 | 22 – John Barnes |
| 1990-1991 | 16 – John Barnes and Ian Rush |
| 1991-1992 | 10 – Dean Saunders |
| 1992-1993 | 14 – Ian Rush |
| 1993-1994 | 14 – Ian Rush |
| 1994-1995 | 25 – Robbie Fowler |
| 1995-1996 | 28 – Robbie Fowler |
| 1996-1997 | 18 – Robbie Fowler |
| 1997-1998 | 18 – Michael Owen |
| 1998-1999 | 18 – Michael Owen |

1999-2000    11 – Michael Owen
2000-2001    16 – Michael Owen
2001-2002    19 – Michael Owen

## LEADING SCORERS (10 DIFFERENT MEN)

**8 campaigns:** Ian Rush (joint top scorer in 1990-91)
**5 campaigns:** Michael Owen
**3 campaigns:** Robbie Fowler
**2 campaigns:** John Aldridge, John Barnes (joint top scorer in 1990-91), Kenny Dalglish
**1 campaign:** Peter Beardsley, David Johnson, Terry McDermott, John Wark

# INDIVIDUAL MATCH SCORING FEATS

### FIVE GOALS IN A MATCH (ONE IN TOTAL)

No Liverpool player has scored more than five goals in a League game. However, Ian Rush came close on 29th October 1983 when he netted five times against Luton Town at Anfield. Andy McGuigan (in 1901-02) and John Evans (in 1954-55) are the only other Liverpool players to have netted 5 goals in a League game.

**Ian Rush**   vs Luton Town (H) 29th October 1983

### FOUR GOALS IN A MATCH (FIVE IN TOTAL)

Three Liverpool strikers netted as many as four goals in a League game during the 25 seasons since the summer of 1977. Two did it twice – they were Ian Rush and Robbie Fowler. Michael Owen was the other man to hit four goals in a match.

**Ian Rush (on two occasions)**
vs Everton (A) 6th November 1982
vs Coventry City (H) 7th May 1984

**Robbie Fowler (on two occasions)**
vs Bolton Wanderers (H) 23rd September 1996
vs Middlesbrough (H) 14th December 1996

**Michael Owen (once)**
vs Nottingham Forest (H) 24th October 1998

### OTHER HAT-TRICKS (33 IN TOTAL)

Thirty-four other hat-tricks were bagged by players wearing Liverpool colours in League football during the quarter of a century up to the summer of 2002. Six were registered by

Fowler, while Rush and Owen both hit four. In addition John Aldridge hit three hat-tricks and Kenny Dalglish achieved the feat twice. Fourteen other men were hat-trick heroes on one occasion.

### Robbie Fowler  (6 hat-tricks)
vs Southampton (H) 30th October 1993
vs Arsenal (H) 28th August 1994
vs Arsenal (H) 23th December 1995
vs Aston Villa (A) 21th November 1998
vs Southampton (H) 16th January 1999
vs Leicester City (A) 20th October 2001

### Ian Rush  (4 hat-tricks)
vs Notts County (H) 26th January 1982
vs Coventry City (H) 13th November 1982
vs Aston Villa (A) 20th January 1984
vs Leicester City (A) 14th February 1987

### Michael Owen (4 hat-tricks)
vs Sheffield Wednesday (A) 14th February 1998
vs Newcastle United (A) 30th August 1998
vs Aston Villa (H) 6th September 2000
vs Newcastle United (H) 5th May 2001

### John Aldridge  (3 hat-tricks)
vs Derby County (H) 29th September 1987
vs Charlton Athletic (A) 27th August 1988
vs Luton Town (H) 14th March 1989

### Kenny Dalglish  (2 hat-tricks)
vs Manchester City 1st May 1978
vs Manchester City 27th December 1982

**Jimmy Case  (1 hat-trick)**   vs Bolton Wanderers (H) 30th September 1978
**David Fairclough (1 hat-trick)**   vs Norwich City (A) 9th February 1980
**Michael Robinson (1 hat-trick)**   vs West Ham United (A) 15th October 1983
**John Wark (1 hat-trick)**   vs West Bromwich Albion (A) 23rd March 1985
**Ronnie Whelan (1 hat-trick)**   vs Coventry City 12th April 1986
**Gary Gillespie (1 hat-trick)**   vs Birmingham City 26th April 1986
**Paul Walsh (1 hat-trick)**   vs Norwich City 1st November 1986

**Steve Nicol (1 hat-trick)** vs Newcastle United (A) 20th September 1987
**Ronny Rosenthal (1 hat-trick)** vs Charlton Athletic (A) 11th April 1990
**John Barnes (1 hat-trick)** vs Coventry City (A) 5th May 1990
**Peter Beardsley (1 hat-trick)** vs Manchester United (H) 16th September 1990
**Mark Walters (1 hat-trick)** vs Coventry City (H) 17th April 1993
**Patrik Berger (1 hat-trick)** vs Chelsea (H) 5th October 1997
**Emile Heskey (1 hat-trick)** vs Derby County (A) 15th October 2000

## SEASON-BY-SEASON GOALS AND AVERAGE SCORING RATES

| | | Scored | | Conceded | |
| --- | --- | --- | --- | --- | --- |
| | Games | Goals | Average | Goals | Average |
| 1977-1978 | 42 | 65 | 1.55 | 34 | 0.81 |
| 1978-1979 | 42 | 85 | 2.02 | 16 | 0.38 |
| 1979-1980 | 42 | 81 | 1.93 | 30 | 0.71 |
| 1980-1981 | 42 | 62 | 1.48 | 46 | 1.10 |
| 1981-1982 | 42 | 80 | 1.90 | 32 | 0.76 |
| 1982-1983 | 42 | 87 | 2.07 | 37 | 0.88 |
| 1983-1984 | 42 | 73 | 1.73 | 32 | 0.76 |
| 1984-1985 | 42 | 78 | 1.86 | 35 | 0.83 |
| 1985-1986 | 42 | 89 | 2.12 | 37 | 0.88 |
| 1986-1987 | 42 | 72 | 1.71 | 42 | 1.00 |
| 1987-1988 | 40 | 87 | 2.18 | 24 | 0.60 |
| 1988-1989 | 38 | 65 | 1.71 | 28 | 0.74 |
| 1989-1990 | 38 | 78 | 2.05 | 37 | 0.97 |
| 1990-1991 | 38 | 77 | 2.03 | 40 | 1.05 |
| 1991-1992 | 42 | 47 | 1.12 | 40 | 0.95 |
| 1992-1993 | 42 | 62 | 1.48 | 55 | 1.31 |
| 1993-1994 | 42 | 59 | 1.40 | 55 | 1.31 |
| 1994-1995 | 42 | 65 | 1.55 | 37 | 0.88 |
| 1995-1996 | 42 | 70 | 1.67 | 34 | 0.81 |
| 1996-1997 | 38 | 62 | 1.63 | 37 | 0.97 |
| 1997-1998 | 38 | 68 | 1.79 | 42 | 1.11 |
| 1998-1999 | 38 | 68 | 1.79 | 49 | 1.29 |
| 1999-2000 | 38 | 51 | 1.34 | 30 | 0.79 |
| 2000-2001 | 38 | 71 | 1.87 | 39 | 1.03 |
| 2001-2002 | 38 | 67 | 1.76 | 30 | 0.79 |

# LEAGUE ATTENDANCES AT ANFIELD

The largest crowd for a League game at Anfield during the quarter of a century up to the summer of 2002 was the 52,211 who watched the 1978-79 local derby. Everton attracted the largest crowds in 14 of the 25 seasons. The lowest gate was registered in 1983-84, when only 20,746 witnessed Watford's visit.

The highest average Anfield gate over a season, during the 25 seasons up until the summer of 2002, was the 46,406 recorded in 1978-79. The lowest average was recorded as 31,974, in 1983-84.

| Season | Average | Highest | Lowest |
|--------|---------|---------|--------|
| 1977-1978 | 45,546 | 51,668 vs Everton | 38,249 vs QPR |
| 1978-1979 | 46,406 | 52,211 vs Everton | 35,207 vs Birmingham City |
| 1979-1980 | 44,586 | 52,201 vs Everton | 36,415 vs Stoke City |
| 1980-1981 | 37,547 | 49,743 vs Everton | 26,744 vs Coventry City |
| 1981-1982 | 35,060 | 48,861 vs Everton | 24,224 vs Birmingham City |
| 1982-1983 | 34,758 | 44,737 vs Everton | 27,145 vs Nottingham Forest |
| 1983-1984 | 31,974 | 45,122 vs Manchester U | 20,746 vs Watford |
| 1984-1985 | 35,854 | 45,545 vs Everton | 27,237 vs Coventry City |
| 1985-1986 | 35,271 | 45,445 vs Everton | 26,219 vs QPR |
| 1986-1987 | 36,285 | 44,827 vs Everton | 25,856 vs Chelsea |
| 1987-1988 | 39,582 | 44,798 vs Tottenham H | 30,374 vs Luton Town |
| 1988-1989 | 38,574 | 42,518 vs Derby C | 30,283 vs Charlton Athletic |
| 1989-1990 | 36,589 | 38,730 vs Everton | 33,319 vs Wimbledon |
| 1990-1991 | 36,038 | 38,463 vs Chelsea | 31,063 vs Coventry City |
| 1991-1992 | 34,799 | 39,072 vs Everton | 25,457 vs Notts County |
| 1992-1993 | 37,004 | 44,619 vs Everton | 29,574 vs Wimbledon |
| 1993-1994 | 38,493 | 44,339 vs Norwich C | 24,561 vs QPR |
| 1994-1995 | 34,176 | 40,014 vs Blackburn R | 27,183 vs Coventry City |
| 1995-1996 | 39,533 | 40,820 vs Chelsea | 34,063 vs Wimbledon |
| 1996-1997 | 39,777 | 40,892 vs Manchester U | 36,126 vs Nottingham F |
| 1997-1998 | 40,628 | 44,532 vs Bolton W | 34,705 vs Sheffield W |
| 1998-1999 | 43,231 | 44,852 vs Everton | 36,019 vs Leicester City |
| 1999-2000 | 44,074 | 44,929 vs Manchester U | 40,483 vs Bradford City |
| 2000-2001 | 43,699 | 44,806 vs Manchester U | 38,474 vs Southampton |
| 2001-2002 | 43,389 | 44,371 vs Everton | 37,163 vs Fulham |

# 1977-78

| | | | | | | | | |
|---|---|---|---|---|---|---|---|---|
| 1 | Aug | 20 | (a) | Middlesbrough | D | 1-1 | Dalglish | 31,000 |
| 2 | | 23 | (h) | Newcastle U | W | 2-0 | Dalglish, McDermott | 48,267 |
| 3 | | 27 | (h) | West Brom A | W | 3-0 | Dalglish, Heighway, Case | 48,525 |
| 4 | Sep | 3 | (a) | Birmingham C | W | 1-0 | Kennedy | 28,239 |
| 5 | | 10 | (h) | Coventry C | W | 2-0 | Fairclough, Dalglish | 45,574 |
| 6 | | 17 | (a) | Ipswich T | D | 1-1 | Dalglish | 29,658 |
| 7 | | 24 | (h) | Derby Co | W | 1-0 | McDermott | 48,359 |
| 8 | Oct | 1 | (a) | Manchester U | L | 0-2 | | 55,109 |
| 9 | | 4 | (a) | Arsenal | D | 0-0 | | 47,110 |
| 10 | | 8 | (h) | Chelsea | W | 2-0 | Dalglish, Fairclough | 40,499 |
| 11 | | 15 | (a) | Leeds U | W | 2-1 | Case 2 | 45,500 |
| 12 | | 22 | (h) | Everton | D | 0-0 | | 51,668 |
| 13 | | 29 | (a) | Manchester C | L | 1-3 | Fairclough | 49,207 |
| 14 | Nov | 5 | (h) | Aston Villa | L | 1-2 | Carrodus (og) | 50,436 |
| 15 | | 12 | (a) | QPR | L | 0-2 | | 25,625 |
| 16 | | 19 | (h) | Bristol C | D | 1-1 | Dalglish | 41,053 |
| 17 | | 26 | (a) | Leicester C | W | 4-0 | Fairclough, Heighway, Dalglish, McDermott | 26,051 |
| 18 | Dec | 3 | (h) | West Ham U | W | 2-0 | Dalglish, Fairclough | 39,659 |
| 19 | | 10 | (a) | Norwich C | L | 1-2 | Thompson | 24,983 |
| 20 | | 17 | (h) | QPR | W | 1-0 | Neal (pen) | 38,249 |
| 21 | | 26 | (a) | Nottingham F | D | 1-1 | Heighway | 47,218 |
| 22 | | 27 | (h) | Wolverhampton W | W | 1-0 | Neal (pen) | 50,294 |
| 23 | | 31 | (a) | Newcastle U | W | 2-0 | Thompson, Dalglish | 36,456 |
| 24 | Jan | 2 | (h) | Middlesbrough | W | 2-0 | Johnson, Heighway | 49,305 |
| 25 | | 14 | (a) | West Brom A | W | 1-0 | Johnson | 35,809 |
| 26 | | 21 | (h) | Birmingham C | L | 2-3 | Thompson, Kennedy | 48,401 |
| 27 | Feb | 4 | (a) | Coventry C | L | 0-1 | | 28,965 |
| 28 | | 25 | (h) | Manchester U | W | 3-1 | Souness, Kennedy, Case | 49,590 |
| 29 | Mar | 4 | (a) | Chelsea | L | 1-3 | Neal (pen) | 35,550 |
| 30 | | 8 | (a) | Derby Co | L | 2-4 | Fairclough, Dalglish | 23,413 |
| 31 | | 11 | (h) | Leeds U | W | 1-0 | Dalglish | 48,233 |
| 32 | | 25 | (a) | Wolverhampton W | W | 3-1 | Case, Dalglish 2 | 27,531 |
| 33 | Apr | 1 | (a) | Aston Villa | W | 3-0 | Dalglish 2, Kennedy | 40,190 |
| 34 | | 5 | (a) | Everton | W | 1-0 | Johnson | 52,759 |
| 35 | | 8 | (h) | Leicester C | W | 3-2 | Smith 2, Lee | 42,979 |
| 36 | | 15 | (a) | Bristol C | D | 1-1 | Heighway | 31,471 |
| 37 | | 18 | (h) | Ipswich T | D | 2-2 | Dalglish, Souness | 40,044 |
| 38 | | 22 | (h) | Norwich C | W | 3-0 | Ryan (og), Fairclough 2 | 44,857 |
| 39 | | 25 | (h) | Arsenal | W | 1-0 | Fairclough | 38,318 |
| 40 | | 29 | (a) | West Ham U | W | 2-0 | McDermott, Fairclough | 37,448 |
| 41 | May | 1 | (h) | Manchester C | W | 4-0 | Dalglish 3, Neal (pen) | 44,528 |
| 42 | | 4 | (h) | Nottingham F | D | 0-0 | | 50,021 |

FINAL LEAGUE POSITION : 2nd in Division One

Appearances

Sub. Appearances

Goals

| Clemence | Neal | Jones | Thompson | Kennedy | Hughes | Dalglish | Case | Heighway | McDermott | Callaghan | Smith | Fairclough | Johnson | Hansen | Toshack | Kewley | Souness | Ogrizovic | Lee | |
|---|---|---|---|---|---|---|---|---|---|---|---|---|---|---|---|---|---|---|---|---|
| 1 | 2 | 3 | 4 | 5 | 6 | 7 | 8 | 9 | 10 | 11 | | | | | | | | | | 1 |
| 1 | 2 | 3 | | 5 | 6 | 7 | 8 | 9 | 10 | 11 | 4 | | | | | | | | | 2 |
| 1 | 2 | 3 | | 5 | 6 | 7 | 8 | 9 | 10 | 11 | 4 | | | | | | | | | 3 |
| 1 | 2 | 3 | | 5 | 6 | 7 | | 9* | 10 | 11 | 4 | 8 | 12 | | | | | | | 4 |
| 1 | 2 | 3 | | 5 | 6 | 7 | 8 | | 10 | 11 | 4 | 9 | | | | | | | | 5 |
| 1 | 2 | 3 | | 5 | 6 | 7 | 8 | 9* | 10 | 11 | 4 | 12 | | | | | | | | 6 |
| 1 | 2 | 3 | | 5 | | 7 | 8* | 9 | 10 | 11 | 4 | 12 | | 6 | | | | | | 7 |
| 1 | 2 | 3 | | 5 | | 7 | 8 | | 10 | 11 | 4 | 9 | | 6 | | | | | | 8 |
| 1 | 2 | 3 | 4 | 5 | | 7 | 8 | | 10 | 11 | | 9 | | 6 | | | | | | 9 |
| 1 | 2 | 3 | | 5 | 6 | 7 | 8 | | 10 | 11 | | 9 | 4 | | | | | | | 10 |
| 1 | 2 | 3 | | 5 | 6 | 7 | 8 | 9 | 10* | 11 | | | 4 | 12 | | | | | | 11 |
| 1 | 2 | 3 | | 5 | 6 | 7 | 8 | 9 | | 11 | | | 4 | 10 | | | | | | 12 |
| 1 | 2 | 3 | | 5 | 6 | 7 | 8 | 9 | | 11 | | 10 | 4 | | | | | | | 13 |
| 1 | 2 | 3 | | 5 | 6 | 7 | 8* | 9 | 12 | 11 | | 10 | 4 | | | | | | | 14 |
| 1 | 2 | 3 | | 5 | 6 | 7 | | 9 | 8 | 11 | | 10 | 4 | | | | | | | 15 |
| 1 | 2 | 3 | 4 | 5 | 6 | 7 | | 9 | | 11 | | 8 | | 10 | | | | | | 16 |
| 1 | 2 | | 4 | 5 | 6 | 7 | | 9 | 8 | 11 | 3 | 10 | | | | | | | | 17 |
| 1 | 2 | | 4 | 5 | 6 | 7 | | 9 | 8 | 11 | 3 | 10 | | | | | | | | 18 |
| 1 | 2 | | 4 | 5 | 6 | 7 | 11 | 9 | 10 | | 3* | 8 | 12 | | | | | | | 19 |
| 1 | 2 | | 4 | 5 | 6 | 7 | 9 | | 8* | 11 | | 10 | 12 | 3 | | | | | | 20 |
| 1 | 2 | 3 | 4 | 5 | 6 | 7 | 11* | 9 | 8 | 12 | | 10 | | | | | | | | 21 |
| 1 | 2 | 3 | 4 | 5 | 6 | 7 | | 9* | 8 | 11 | | 10 | 12 | | | | | | | 22 |
| 1 | 2 | 3 | 4 | 5 | 6 | 7 | | 9 | 8 | 11 | | 10 | | | | | | | | 23 |
| 1 | 2 | 3 | 4 | 5 | 6 | 7 | | 9 | 8* | 11 | | 10 | | | 12 | | | | | 24 |
| 1 | 2 | | 4 | 5 | 6 | 7 | | | 8 | 11 | | 9 | 3 | | | | 10 | | | 25 |
| 1 | 2 | | 4 | 5 | 6 | 7 | 12 | | 8 | 11* | | 9 | 3 | | | | 10 | | | 26 |
| 1 | 2 | | 4 | 5 | 6 | 7 | 8 | | | 11 | | 9 | 3 | | | | 10 | | | 27 |
| 1 | 2 | | 4 | 5 | 6 | 7 | 12 | 9 | 11 | | 3 | 10* | | | | | 8 | | | 28 |
| 1 | 2 | | | 5 | 6 | 7 | 12 | 9 | 8 | | 3 | 11* | 4 | | | | 10 | | | 29 |
| | 2 | | | 5 | 6 | 7 | 11 | 9 | 8* | | 3 | 12 | 4 | | | | 10 | 1 | | 30 |
| | 2 | | 4 | 5 | 6 | 7 | 8 | 9 | | | 3 | 11 | | | | | 10 | 1 | | 31 |
| 1 | 2 | | 4 | 5 | 6 | 7 | 8 | 9 | 10 | | 3 | 11 | | | | | | | | 32 |
| 1 | 2 | | 4 | 5 | 6 | 7 | 8 | 9 | 10 | | 3 | 11 | | | | | | | | 33 |
| 1 | 2 | | 4 | 5 | 6 | 7 | 8 | 9 | 10 | | 3 | 11 | | | | | | | | 34 |
| 1 | 2 | | 4 | 5 | 6 | 7 | 8 | | 10 | | 3 | 9* | | | | | 11 | 12 | | 35 |
| 1 | 2 | | 4 | 5 | 6 | 7 | 8 | 9 | 10 | | 3 | | | | | | 11 | | | 36 |
| 1 | 2 | | 4 | | 6 | 7 | 8 | 9 | 11* | | 3 | 5 | | | | | 10 | 12 | | 37 |
| 1 | 2 | | 4 | 5 | 6 | 7 | 8 | | 10 | | 3 | 9 | | | | | 11 | | | 38 |
| 1 | 2 | | 4 | 5 | 6 | 7 | 8 | | 10 | | 3 | 9 | | | | | 11 | | | 39 |
| 1 | 2 | | 4 | 5 | 6 | 7 | 8 | | 10 | | | 9 | 3 | | | | 11 | | | 40 |
| 1 | 2 | | 4 | 5 | 6 | 7 | 8 | | 10 | | | 9 | 3 | | | | 11 | | | 41 |
| 1 | 2 | | 4 | 5 | 6 | 7 | 8 | | 10 | | | 9 | 3 | | | | 11 | | | 42 |
| 40 | 42 | 20 | 27 | 41 | 39 | 42 | 30 | 28 | 36 | 25 | 22 | 26 | 7 | 18 | 2 | | 15 | 2 | | |
| | | | | | | | 3 | | 1 | 1 | | 3 | 4 | | 1 | 1 | | 2 | | |
| | 4 | | 3 | 4 | | 20 | 5 | 5 | 4 | | 2 | 10 | 3 | | | | 2 | 1 | | |

99

# 1978-79

| 1 | Aug | 19 | (h) | QPR | W | 2-1 | Dalglish, Heighway | 50,793 |
|---|---|---|---|---|---|---|---|---|
| 2 | | 22 | (a) | Ipswich T | W | 3-0 | Souness, Dalglish 2 | 28,114 |
| 3 | | 26 | (a) | Manchester C | W | 4-1 | Souness 2, Kennedy R, Dalglish | 46,710 |
| 4 | Sep | 2 | (h) | Tottenham H | W | 7-0 | Dalglish 2, Kennedy R, Johnson 2, Neal (pen), McDermott | 50,705 |
| 5 | | 9 | (a) | Birmingham C | W | 3-0 | Souness 2, Kennedy A | 31,740 |
| 6 | | 16 | (h) | Coventry C | W | 1-0 | Souness | 51,130 |
| 7 | | 23 | (a) | West Brom A | D | 1-1 | Dalglish | 33,834 |
| 8 | | 30 | (h) | Bolton W | W | 3-0 | Case 3 | 47,099 |
| 9 | Oct | 7 | (a) | Norwich C | W | 4-1 | Heighway 2, Johnson, Case | 25,632 |
| 10 | | 14 | (h) | Derby Co | W | 5-0 | Johnson, Kennedy R. 2, Dalglish 2 | 47,475 |
| 11 | | 21 | (h) | Chelsea | W | 2-0 | Johnson, Dalglish | 45,775 |
| 12 | | 28 | (a) | Everton | L | 0-1 | | 53,131 |
| 13 | Nov | 4 | (h) | Leeds U | D | 1-1 | McDermott (pen) | 51,657 |
| 14 | | 11 | (a) | QPR | W | 3-1 | Heighway, Kennedy R, Johnson | 26,626 |
| 15 | | 18 | (h) | Manchester C | W | 1-0 | Neal (pen) | 27,765 |
| 16 | | 22 | (a) | Tottenham H | D | 0-0 | | 50,393 |
| 17 | | 25 | (h) | Middlesbrough | W | 2-0 | McDermott, Souness | 39,812 |
| 18 | Dec | 2 | (a) | Arsenal | L | 0-1 | | 51,902 |
| 19 | | 9 | (h) | Nottingham F | W | 2-0 | McDermott 2 (1 pen) | 51,469 |
| 20 | | 16 | (a) | Bristol C | L | 0-1 | | 28,722 |
| 21 | | 26 | (a) | Manchester U | W | 3-0 | Kennedy R, Case, Fairclough | 54,940 |
| 22 | Feb | 3 | (h) | West Brom A | W | 2-1 | Dalglish, Fairclough | 52,211 |
| 23 | | 13 | (h) | Birmingham C | W | 1-0 | Souness | 35,207 |
| 24 | | 21 | (h) | Norwich C | W | 6-0 | Dalglish 2, Johnson 2, Kennedy A, Kennedy R | 35,754 |
| 25 | | 24 | (a) | Derby Co | W | 2-0 | Dalglish, Kennedy R | 27,859 |
| 26 | Mar | 3 | (a) | Chelsea | D | 0-0 | | 40,594 |
| 27 | | 6 | (a) | Coventry C | D | 0-0 | | 26,629 |
| 28 | | 13 | (h) | Everton | D | 1-1 | Dalglish | 52,352 |
| 29 | | 20 | (h) | Wolverhampton W | W | 2-0 | McDermott, Johnson | 39,695 |
| 30 | | 24 | (h) | Ipswich T | W | 2-0 | Dalglish, Johnson | 43,243 |
| 31 | Apr | 7 | (h) | Arsenal | W | 3-0 | Case, Dalglish, McDermott | 47,297 |
| 32 | | 10 | (a) | Wolverhampton W | W | 1-0 | Hansen | 30,857 |
| 33 | | 14 | (h) | Manchester U | W | 2-0 | Dalglish, Neal | 46,608 |
| 34 | | 16 | (a) | Aston Villa | L | 1-3 | Johnson | 44,029 |
| 35 | | 21 | (h) | Bristol C | W | 1-0 | Dalglish | 43,191 |
| 36 | | 24 | (a) | Southampton | D | 1-1 | Johnson | 23,181 |
| 37 | | 28 | (a) | Nottingham F | D | 0-0 | | 41,898 |
| 38 | May | 1 | (a) | Bolton W | W | 4-1 | Johnson, Kennedy R. 2, Dalglish | 35,200 |
| 39 | | 5 | (h) | Southampton | W | 2-0 | Neal 2 | 46,687 |
| 40 | | 8 | (h) | Aston Villa | W | 3-0 | Kennedy A, Dalglish, McDermott | 50,576 |
| 41 | | 11 | (a) | Middlesbrough | W | 1-0 | Johnson | 32,244 |
| 42 | | 17 | (a) | Leeds U | W | 3-0 | Johnson 2, Case | 41,324 |

FINAL LEAGUE POSITION : 1st in Division One

Appearances

Sub. Appearances

Goals

| Clemence | Neal | Kennedy A | Thompson | Kennedy R | Hughes | Dalglish | Case | Heighway | McDermott | Souness | Johnson | Hansen | Fairclough | Lee | |
|---|---|---|---|---|---|---|---|---|---|---|---|---|---|---|---|
| 1 | 2 | 3 | 4 | 5 | 6 | 7 | 8 | 9 | 10 | 11 | | | | | 1 |
| 1 | 2 | 3 | 4 | 5 | 6 | 7 | 8 | 9 | 10 | 11 | | | | | 2 |
| 1 | 2 | 3 | 4 | 5 | 6 | 7 | 8 | 9 | 10 | 11 | | | | | 3 |
| 1 | 2 | 3 | 4 | 5 | 6* | 7 | 8 | 9 | 10 | 11 | 12 | | | | 4 |
| 1 | 2 | 3 | 4 | 5 | | 7 | 8 | 9 | 10 | 11 | | 6 | | | 5 |
| 1 | 2 | 3 | 4 | 5 | 6 | 7 | 8 | 9 | 10 | 11 | | | | | 6 |
| 1 | 2 | 3 | 4 | 5 | 6 | 7 | 8 | 9* | 10 | 11 | 12 | | | | 7 |
| 1 | 2 | 3 | 4 | 5 | | 7 | 8 | 9 | 10 | 11 | | 6 | | | 8 |
| 1 | 2 | 3 | 4 | 5 | | 7 | 8 | 9 | | 11 | 10 | 6 | | | 9 |
| 1 | 2 | 3 | 4 | 5 | | 7 | 8 | 9 | | 11 | 10 | 6 | | | 10 |
| 1 | 2 | 3 | 4 | 5 | | 7 | 8 | 9 | | 11 | 10 | 6 | | | 11 |
| 1 | 2 | 3 | 4 | 5 | | 7 | 8* | 9 | 12 | 11 | 10 | 6 | | | 12 |
| 1 | 2 | 3 | 4 | 5 | | 7 | 8 | 9 | 12 | 11* | 10 | 6 | | | 13 |
| 1 | 2 | 3 | 4 | 5 | | 7 | 8 | 9 | | 11 | 10 | 6 | | | 14 |
| 1 | 2 | 3 | 4 | 5 | | 7 | 8 | 9 | | 11 | 10 | 6 | | | 15 |
| 1 | 2 | 3 | 4 | 5 | | 7 | 8 | 9 | 12 | 11 | 10* | 6 | | | 16 |
| 1 | 2 | 3 | 4 | 5 | | 7 | 8 | 9 | 10 | 11 | | 6 | | | 17 |
| 1 | 2 | 3 | 4* | 5 | | 7 | 8 | 9 | 10 | 11 | 12 | 6 | | | 18 |
| 1 | 2 | 3 | 4 | 5 | | 7 | 8 | 9 | 10 | 11 | | 6 | | | 19 |
| 1 | 2 | 3 | 4 | 5 | | 7 | 8 | 9* | 10 | 11 | 12 | 6 | | | 20 |
| 1 | 2 | | 4 | 5 | 3 | 7 | 8 | | 10 | 11 | | 6 | 9 | | 21 |
| 1 | 2 | 3 | | 5 | 6 | 7 | 8* | 12 | 10 | 11 | | 4 | 9 | | 22 |
| 1 | 2 | 4 | | 5 | 3 | 7 | | 8 | 10 | 11 | | 6 | 9 | | 23 |
| 1 | 2 | 4 | | 5 | 3 | 7 | | 9 | 10 | 11 | 8 | 6 | | | 24 |
| 1 | 2 | 4 | 6 | 5 | 3 | 7 | | 9 | 10 | 11 | 8 | | | | 25 |
| 1 | 2 | 4 | 6 | 5 | 3 | 7 | | 9 | 10 | 11 | 8 | | | | 26 |
| 1 | 2 | | 4 | 5 | 3 | 7 | 9 | | 10 | 11 | 8 | 6 | | | 27 |
| 1 | 2 | | 4 | 5 | 3 | 7 | 9 | | 10 | 11 | 8* | 6 | 12 | | 28 |
| 1 | 2 | | 4 | 5 | 3 | 7 | 9 | | 10 | 11 | 8 | 6 | | | 29 |
| 1 | 2 | | 4 | 5 | 3 | 7 | 9 | | 10 | 11 | 8 | 6 | | | 30 |
| 1 | 2 | 3 | 4 | 5 | | 7 | 8 | | 10 | 11 | 9 | 6 | | | 31 |
| 1 | 2 | 3 | 4 | 5 | | 7 | 9 | | 10 | 11 | 8 | 6 | | | 32 |
| 1 | 2 | 3 | 4 | 5 | | 7 | 8 | | 10 | 11 | 9 | 6 | | | 33 |
| 1 | 2 | 3 | 4 | 5 | | 7 | | 8 | 10 | 11 | 9 | 6 | | | 34 |
| 1 | 2 | 3 | 4 | 5 | | 7 | 8 | 12 | 10 | 11 | 9* | 6 | | | 35 |
| 1 | 2 | 3 | 4 | 5 | | 7 | 8 | | 10 | | 9 | 6 | | 11 | 36 |
| 1 | 2 | 3 | 4 | 5 | | 7 | 8 | 9* | 10 | 11 | | 6 | | 12 | 37 |
| 1 | 2 | 3 | 4 | 5 | | 7 | 8 | | 10 | 11 | 9 | 6 | | | 38 |
| 1 | 2 | 3 | 4 | 5 | | 7 | 8 | | 10 | 11 | 9 | 6 | | | 39 |
| 1 | 2 | 3 | 4 | 5 | | 7 | 8 | | 10 | 11 | 9 | 6 | | | 40 |
| 1 | 2 | 3 | 4 | 5 | | 7 | 8 | | 10 | 11 | 9 | 6 | | | 41 |
| 1 | 2 | 3 | 4 | 5 | | 7 | 8 | | 10 | 11 | 9 | 6 | | | 42 |
| 42 | 42 | 37 | 39 | 42 | 16 | 42 | 37 | 26 | 34 | 41 | 26 | 34 | 3 | 1 | |
| | | | | | | | | 2 | 3 | | 4 | | 1 | 1 | |
| | 5 | 3 | | 10 | | 21 | 7 | 4 | 8 | 8 | 16 | 1 | 2 | | |

101

# 1979-80

| 1 | Aug | 21 | (h) | Bolton W | D | 0-0 | | 45,900 |
|---|---|---|---|---|---|---|---|---|
| 2 | | 25 | (h) | West Brom A | W | 3-1 | Johnson 2, McDermott | 48,021 |
| 3 | Sep | 1 | (a) | Southampton | L | 2-3 | Johnson, Irwin | 21,402 |
| 4 | | 8 | (h) | Coventry C | W | 4-0 | Johnson 2, Case, Dalglish | 39,926 |
| 5 | | 15 | (a) | Leeds U | D | 1-1 | McDermott | 39,779 |
| 6 | | 22 | (h) | Norwich C | D | 0-0 | | 44,120 |
| 7 | | 29 | (a) | Nottingham F | L | 0-1 | | 28,262 |
| 8 | Oct | 6 | (h) | Bristol C | W | 4-0 | Johnson, Dalglish, Kennedy R, McDermott | 38,213 |
| 9 | | 9 | (a) | Bolton W | D | 1-1 | Dalglish | 25,571 |
| 10 | | 13 | (a) | Ipswich T | W | 2-1 | Hunter (og), Johnson | 25,310 |
| 11 | | 20 | (h) | Everton | D | 2-2 | Lyons (og), Kennedy R | 52,201 |
| 12 | | 27 | (a) | Manchester C | W | 4-0 | Johnson, Dalglish 2, Kennedy R | 48,128 |
| 13 | Nov | 3 | (h) | Wolverhampton W | W | 3-0 | Dalglish 2, Kennedy R | 49,541 |
| 14 | | 10 | (a) | Brighton & HA | W | 4-1 | Kennedy R, Dalglish 2, Johnson | 29,682 |
| 15 | | 17 | (h) | Tottenham H | W | 2-1 | McDermott 2 | 51,092 |
| 16 | | 24 | (a) | Arsenal | D | 0-0 | | 55,561 |
| 17 | Dec | 1 | (h) | Middlesbrough | W | 4-0 | McDermott, Hansen, Johnson, Kennedy R | 39,885 |
| 18 | | 8 | (a) | Aston Villa | W | 3-1 | Kennedy R, Hansen, McDermott | 41,160 |
| 19 | | 15 | (h) | Crystal Palace | W | 3-0 | Case, Dalglish, McDermott | 42,898 |
| 20 | | 22 | (a) | Derby Co | W | 3-1 | Davies (og), McDermott (pen), Johnson | 24,945 |
| 21 | | 26 | (h) | Manchester U | W | 2-0 | Hansen, Johnson | 51,073 |
| 22 | | 29 | (a) | West Brom A | W | 2-0 | Johnson 2 | 34,915 |
| 23 | Jan | 12 | (h) | Southampton | D | 1-1 | McDermott (pen) | 44,655 |
| 24 | | 19 | (a) | Coventry C | L | 0-1 | | 31,578 |
| 25 | Feb | 9 | (a) | Norwich C | W | 5-3 | Fairclough 3, Dalglish, Case | 25,624 |
| 26 | | 19 | (h) | Nottingham F | W | 2-0 | McDermott, Kennedy R | 45,093 |
| 27 | | 23 | (h) | Ipswich T | D | 1-1 | Fairclough | 47,566 |
| 28 | | 26 | (a) | Woverhampton W | L | 0-1 | | 36,693 |
| 29 | Mar | 3 | (a) | Everton | W | 2-1 | Johnson, Neal (pen) | 53,013 |
| 30 | | 11 | (h) | Manchester C | W | 2-0 | Caton (og), Souness | 40,443 |
| 31 | | 15 | (a) | Bristol C | W | 3-1 | Kennedy R, Dalglish 2 | 27,187 |
| 32 | | 19 | (h) | Leeds U | W | 3-0 | Johnson 2, Kennedy A | 37,008 |
| 33 | | 22 | (h) | Brighton & HA | W | 1-0 | Hansen | 42,747 |
| 34 | | 29 | (a) | Tottenham H | L | 0-2 | | 32,114 |
| 35 | Apr | 1 | (h) | Stoke C | W | 1-0 | Dalglish | 36,415 |
| 36 | | 5 | (a) | Manchester U | L | 1-2 | Dalglish | 57,342 |
| 37 | | 8 | (h) | Derby C | W | 3-0 | Irwin, Johnson, Osgood (og) | 40,932 |
| 38 | | 19 | (h) | Arsenal | D | 1-1 | Dalglish | 46,878 |
| 39 | | 23 | (a) | Stoke C | W | 2-0 | Johnson, Fairclough | 32,000 |
| 40 | | 26 | (a) | Crystal Palace | D | 0-0 | | 45,583 |
| 41 | May | 3 | (h) | Aston Villa | W | 4-1 | Johnson 2, Cohen, Blake (og) | 51,541 |
| 42 | | 6 | (a) | Middlesbrough | L | 0-1 | | 24,458 |

FINAL LEAGUE POSITION : 1st in Division One

Appearances

Sub. Appearances

Goals

| Clemence | Neal | Kennedy A | Thompson | Kennedy R | Hansen | Dalglish | Case | Johnson | McDermott | Souness | Heighway | Irwin | Cohen | Fairclough | Ogrizovic | Lee | | | | | | | | | | | | | | | | | No. |
|---|---|---|---|---|---|---|---|---|---|---|---|---|---|---|---|---|---|---|---|---|---|---|---|---|---|---|---|---|---|---|---|---|---|
| 1 | 2* | 3 | 4 | 5 | 6 | 7 | 8 | 9 | 10 | 11 | 12 | | | | | | | | | | | | | | | | | | | | | | 1 |
| 1 | 2 | 3 | 4 | 5 | | 7 | 8 | 9 | 10 | 11 | | 6 | | | | | | | | | | | | | | | | | | | | | 2 |
| 1 | 2 | 3 | 4 | 5 | | 7 | 8 | 9 | 10 | 11 | | 6 | | | | | | | | | | | | | | | | | | | | | 3 |
| 1 | 2 | 3 | 4 | 5 | | 7 | 8 | 9 | 10 | 11 | | 6 | | | | | | | | | | | | | | | | | | | | | 4 |
| 1 | 2 | 3 | 4 | | 6 | 7 | 8 | 9 | 10 | 11 | | | 5 | | | | | | | | | | | | | | | | | | | | 5 |
| 1 | 2 | 3 | 4 | | | 7 | 8 | 9* | 10 | 11 | 12 | 6 | | 5 | | | | | | | | | | | | | | | | | | | 6 |
| | 2 | 3* | 4 | 5 | 6 | 7 | 8 | | 10 | 11 | | 12 | | 9 | 1 | | | | | | | | | | | | | | | | | | 7 |
| 1 | 2 | 3 | 4 | 5 | 6 | 7 | 8 | 9 | 10 | 11 | | | | | | | | | | | | | | | | | | | | | | | 8 |
| 1 | 2 | 3 | 4 | 5 | 6 | 7 | 8 | 9 | 10 | 11 | | | | | | | | | | | | | | | | | | | | | | | 9 |
| 1 | 2 | 3 | 4 | 5 | 6 | 7 | 8 | 9 | | 11 | 10 | | | | | | | | | | | | | | | | | | | | | | 10 |
| 1 | 2 | 3 | 4 | 5 | 6 | 7 | 8 | 9 | 10 | 11 | | | | | | | | | | | | | | | | | | | | | | | 11 |
| 1 | 2 | 3 | 4 | 5 | 6 | 7 | 8 | 9 | | 11 | 10 | | | | | | | | | | | | | | | | | | | | | | 12 |
| 1 | 2 | 3 | 4 | 5 | 6 | 7 | 8 | 9 | 10 | 11 | | | | | | | | | | | | | | | | | | | | | | | 13 |
| 1 | 2 | 3 | 4 | 5 | 6 | 7 | 8 | 9* | 10 | 11 | 12 | | | | | | | | | | | | | | | | | | | | | | 14 |
| 1 | 2 | 3 | 4 | 5 | 6 | 7 | 8 | 9 | 10 | 11 | | | | | | | | | | | | | | | | | | | | | | | 15 |
| 1 | 2 | 3 | 4 | 5 | 6 | 7 | 8 | 9 | 10 | 11 | | | | | | | | | | | | | | | | | | | | | | | 16 |
| 1 | 2 | 3 | 4 | 5 | 6 | 7 | 8 | 9 | 10 | 11 | | | | | | | | | | | | | | | | | | | | | | | 17 |
| 1 | 2 | 3 | 4 | 5 | 6 | 7 | 8 | 9 | 10 | 11 | | | | | | | | | | | | | | | | | | | | | | | 18 |
| 1 | 2 | 3 | 4 | 5 | 6 | 7 | 8 | 9 | 10 | 11 | | | | | | | | | | | | | | | | | | | | | | | 19 |
| 1 | 2 | 3 | 4 | 5 | 6 | 7 | 8 | 9 | 10 | 11 | | | | | | | | | | | | | | | | | | | | | | | 20 |
| 1 | 2 | 3 | 4 | 5 | 6 | 7 | 8 | 9 | 10 | 11 | | | | | | | | | | | | | | | | | | | | | | | 21 |
| 1 | 2 | 3 | 4 | 5 | 6 | 7 | 8 | 9* | 10 | 11 | 12 | | | | | | | | | | | | | | | | | | | | | | 22 |
| 1 | 2 | 3 | 4 | 5 | 6 | 7 | 8 | 9 | 10 | 11 | | | | | | | | | | | | | | | | | | | | | | | 23 |
| 1 | 2 | 3 | 4 | 5 | 6 | 7 | 8* | 9 | 10 | 11 | 12 | | | | | | | | | | | | | | | | | | | | | | 24 |
| 1 | 2 | 3 | 4 | 5 | 6 | 7 | 8 | | 10 | | | | | 9 | | 11 | | | | | | | | | | | | | | | | | 25 |
| 1 | 2 | 3 | 4 | 5 | 6 | 7 | 8 | | 10 | 11 | | | | 9 | | | | | | | | | | | | | | | | | | | 26 |
| 1 | 2 | 3 | 4 | 5 | 6 | 7 | 8 | | 10 | 11 | | | | 9 | | | | | | | | | | | | | | | | | | | 27 |
| 1 | 2 | 3 | 4 | 5 | 6 | 7 | 8* | | 10 | 11 | 12 | | | 9 | | | | | | | | | | | | | | | | | | | 28 |
| 1 | 2 | 3 | 4 | 5 | 6 | 7 | 8 | 9* | 10 | 11 | | | | 12 | | | | | | | | | | | | | | | | | | | 29 |
| 1 | 2 | 3 | 4 | 5 | 6 | 7 | 8 | 9 | 10 | 11 | | | | | | | | | | | | | | | | | | | | | | | 30 |
| 1 | 2 | 3 | 4 | 5 | 6 | 7 | 8 | 9 | 10 | 11 | | | | | | | | | | | | | | | | | | | | | | | 31 |
| 1 | 2 | 3 | 4 | 5 | 6 | 7 | 8* | 9 | 10 | 11 | | | | 12 | | | | | | | | | | | | | | | | | | | 32 |
| 1 | 2 | 3 | 4 | 5 | 6 | 7 | 8 | 9 | 10* | 11 | | | | 12 | | | | | | | | | | | | | | | | | | | 33 |
| 1 | 2 | 3 | 4 | 5 | 6 | 7 | 8 | 9 | 10 | 11 | | | | | | | | | | | | | | | | | | | | | | | 34 |
| 1 | 2 | 3 | 4 | 5 | 6 | 7 | 8 | 9 | 10 | 11 | | | | | | | | | | | | | | | | | | | | | | | 35 |
| 1 | 2 | 3* | 4 | 5 | 6 | 7 | 8 | 9 | 10 | 11 | | | | 12 | | | | | | | | | | | | | | | | | | | 36 |
| 1 | 2 | | 4 | 5 | 6 | 7 | 8 | 9 | 10* | 11 | | 3 | | 12 | | | | | | | | | | | | | | | | | | | 37 |
| 1 | 2 | | 4 | 5 | 6 | 7 | | 9* | | 11 | 12 | 3 | | 8 | | 10 | | | | | | | | | | | | | | | | | 38 |
| 1 | 2 | | 4 | 5 | 6 | 7 | | 9 | | 11 | | 3* | 12 | 8 | | 10 | | | | | | | | | | | | | | | | | 39 |
| 1 | 2 | 3 | 4 | 5 | 6 | 7 | | 9 | | 11 | | | | 8 | | 10 | | | | | | | | | | | | | | | | | 40 |
| 1 | 2 | | 4 | 5 | 6 | 7 | | 9 | 10 | 11 | | | 3 | | | 8 | | | | | | | | | | | | | | | | | 41 |
| 1 | 2 | | 4 | 5 | 6 | 7* | | 9 | 10 | 11 | | | 3 | 12 | | 8 | | | | | | | | | | | | | | | | | 42 |
| 41 | 42 | 37 | 42 | 40 | 38 | 42 | 37 | 37 | 37 | 41 | 2 | 7 | 3 | 9 | 1 | 6 | | | | | | | | | | | | | | | | | |
| | | | | | | | | | | | 7 | 1 | 1 | 5 | | 1 | | | | | | | | | | | | | | | | | |
| | 1 | 1 | | 9 | 4 | 16 | 3 | 21 | 11 | 1 | | 2 | 1 | 5 | | | | | | | | | | | | | | | | | | | |

103

# 1980-81

| # | Month | Date | | Opponent | Result | Score | Scorers | Attendance |
|---|---|---|---|---|---|---|---|---|
| 1 | Aug | 16 | (h) | Crystal Palace | W | 3-0 | Dalglish, Kennedy R, Kennedy A | 42,777 |
| 2 | | 19 | (a) | Coventry C | D | 0-0 | | 22,807 |
| 3 | | 23 | (a) | Leicester C | L | 0-2 | | 28,455 |
| 4 | | 30 | (h) | Norwich C | W | 4-1 | Hansen, McDermott, Kennedy A, Johnson | 35,315 |
| 5 | Sep | 6 | (a) | Birmingham C | D | 1-1 | Dalglish | 27,042 |
| 6 | | 13 | (h) | West Brom A | W | 4-0 | McDermott (pen), Souness, Fairclough 2 | 36,792 |
| 7 | | 20 | (a) | Southampton | D | 2-2 | Souness, Fairclough | 24,085 |
| 8 | | 27 | (h) | Brighton & HA | W | 4-1 | Souness, McDermott (pen), Fairclough | 35,836 |
| 9 | Oct | 4 | (a) | Manchester C | W | 3-0 | Dalglish, Souness, Lee | 41,022 |
| 10 | | 7 | (h) | Middlesbrough | W | 4-2 | McDermott 2 (1 pen), Kennedy R, Dalglish | 28,204 |
| 11 | | 11 | (h) | Ipswich T | D | 1-1 | McDermott (pen) | 48,084 |
| 12 | | 18 | (a) | Everton | D | 2-2 | Lee, Dalglish | 52,565 |
| 13 | | 25 | (h) | Arsenal | D | 1-1 | Souness | 40,310 |
| 14 | Nov | 1 | (a) | Stoke C | D | 2-2 | Johnson, Dalglish | 22,864 |
| 15 | | 8 | (h) | Nottingham F | D | 0-0 | | 43,143 |
| 16 | | 11 | (h) | Coventry C | W | 2-1 | Johnson 2 | 26,744 |
| 17 | | 15 | (a) | Crystal Palace | D | 2-2 | Kennedy R, McDermott | 31,154 |
| 18 | | 22 | (h) | Aston Villa | W | 2-1 | Dalglish 2 | 48,114 |
| 19 | | 25 | (a) | Wolverhampton W | L | 1-4 | Neal | 25,497 |
| 20 | | 29 | (a) | Sunderland | W | 4-2 | Johnson, McDermott, Lee 2 | 32,340 |
| 21 | Dec | 6 | (h) | Tottenham H | W | 2-1 | Johnson, Kennedy R | 39,545 |
| 22 | | 13 | (a) | Ipswich T | D | 1-1 | Case | 32,274 |
| 23 | | 20 | (h) | Wolverhampton W | W | 1-0 | Kennedy R | 33,563 |
| 24 | | 26 | (a) | Manchester U | D | 0-0 | | 57,073 |
| 25 | | 27 | (h) | Leeds U | D | 0-0 | | 44,086 |
| 26 | Jan | 10 | (a) | Aston Villa | L | 0-2 | | 47,960 |
| 27 | | 17 | (a) | Norwich C | W | 1-0 | McDermott | 23,829 |
| 28 | | 31 | (h) | Leicester C | L | 1-2 | Young (og) | 35,154 |
| 29 | Feb | 7 | (a) | West Brom A | L | 0-2 | | 27,905 |
| 30 | | 14 | (h) | Birmingham C | D | 2-2 | Johnson, Neal | 32,199 |
| 31 | | 21 | (a) | Brighton & HA | D | 2-2 | Johnson, McDermott | 23,275 |
| 32 | | 28 | (h) | Southampton | W | 2-0 | Kennedy R, McDermott | 41,575 |
| 33 | Mar | 21 | (h) | Everton | W | 1-0 | Bailey (og) | 49,743 |
| 34 | | 28 | (a) | Arsenal | L | 0-1 | | 47,058 |
| 35 | Apr | 3 | (h) | Stoke C | W | 3-0 | Whelan, McDermott 2 | 33,308 |
| 36 | | 11 | (a) | Nottingham F | D | 0-0 | | 27,363 |
| 37 | | 14 | (h) | Manchester U | L | 0-1 | | 31,276 |
| 38 | | 18 | (a) | Leeds U | D | 0-0 | | 39,206 |
| 39 | | 25 | (a) | Tottenham H | D | 1-1 | Gayle | 35,334 |
| 40 | May | 2 | (h) | Sunderland | L | 0-1 | | 40,337 |
| 41 | | 5 | (a) | Middlesbrough | W | 2-1 | Kennedy R, Irwin | 19,102 |
| 42 | | 19 | (h) | Manchester C | W | 1-0 | Kennedy R | 24,462 |

FINAL LEAGUE POSITION : 5th in Division One

Appearances

Sub. Appearances

Goals

| Clemence | Neal | Kennedy A | Thompson | Kennedy R | Hansen | Dalglish | Case | Johnson | McDermott | Souness | Fairclough | Ogrizovic | Lee | Cohen | Money | Irwin | Gayle | Rush | Heighway | Sheedy | Whelan | Russell | |
|---|---|---|---|---|---|---|---|---|---|---|---|---|---|---|---|---|---|---|---|---|---|---|---|
| 1 | 2 | 3 | 4 | 5 | 6 | 7* | 8 | 9 | 10 | 11 | 12 | | | | | | | | | | | | 1 |
| | 2 | 3 | 4 | 5 | 6 | 7 | 8* | 9 | 10 | 11 | 12 | 1 | | | | | | | | | | | 2 |
| 1 | 2 | 3 | 4 | 5 | 6 | 7 | | 9 | 10 | 11 | 12 | | 8* | | | | | | | | | | 3 |
| 1 | 2 | 3 | 4 | 5 | 6 | 7 | 8 | 9 | 10 | 11 | | | | | | | | | | | | | 4 |
| 1 | 2 | 3 | 4 | 5 | 6 | 7 | 8 | 9* | 10 | 11 | | | | 12 | | | | | | | | | 5 |
| 1 | 2 | | 4 | 5 | 6* | 7 | | | 10 | 11 | 9 | | 8 | 3 | 12 | | | | | | | | 6 |
| 1 | 2 | | 4 | 5 | 6 | 7 | | | 10* | 11 | 9 | | 8 | 3 | | 12 | | | | | | | 7 |
| 1 | 2 | | 4 | 5 | 6 | 7 | | | 10 | 11 | 9 | | 8 | 3 | | | | | | | | | 8 |
| 1 | 2 | | 4 | 5 | 6 | 7 | | | 10 | 11 | 9* | | 8 | 3 | | | 12 | | | | | | 9 |
| 1 | 2 | | 4 | 5 | 6 | 7 | 12 | 9* | 10 | 11 | | | 8 | 3 | | | | | | | | | 10 |
| 1 | 2 | | 4 | 5 | 6 | 7 | | 9 | 10 | 11 | | | 8 | 3 | | | | | | | | | 11 |
| 1 | 2 | | 4 | 5 | 6 | 7 | | 9 | 10 | 11 | | | 8 | 3 | | | | | | | | | 12 |
| 1 | 2 | 3 | 4 | 5 | 6 | 7 | 12 | 9* | 10 | 11 | | | 8 | | | | | | | | | | 13 |
| 1 | 2 | 3 | 4 | 5 | 6 | 7 | | 9 | 10 | 11 | | | 8 | | | | | | | | | | 14 |
| 1 | 2 | | 4 | 5 | 6 | 7 | | 9 | 10 | 11 | | | 8 | 3 | | | | | | | | | 15 |
| 1 | 2 | | 4 | 5 | 6 | 7 | | 9 | 10 | 11 | | | 8 | | 3 | | | | | | | | 16 |
| 1 | 2 | 4* | | 5 | 6 | 7 | 12 | 9 | 10 | 11 | | | 8 | 3 | | | | | | | | | 17 |
| 1 | 2 | | | 5 | 6 | 7 | | 9 | 10 | 11 | | | 8 | 3 | | 4 | | | | | | | 18 |
| 1 | 2 | | | 5 | 6 | 7 | 12 | 9 | 10 | 11 | | | 8* | 3 | | 4 | | | | | | | 19 |
| 1 | 2 | 3 | | 5 | 6 | 7 | | 9 | 10 | 11 | | | 8 | | | 4 | | | | | | | 20 |
| 1 | 2 | 3 | | 5 | 6 | 7* | 12 | 9 | 10 | 11 | | | 8 | | | 4 | | | | | | | 21 |
| 1 | 2 | 3 | | 5 | 6 | | 12 | 9* | 10 | 11 | | | 8 | | | 4 | | 7 | | | | | 22 |
| 1 | 2 | 3 | | 5 | 6 | | | 9 | 10 | 11 | | | 8 | | | 4 | | | 7 | | | | 23 |
| 1 | 2 | 3 | | 5 | 6* | 7 | 11 | 9 | 10 | | | | 8 | | 12 | 4 | | | | | | | 24 |
| 1 | 2 | 3 | | 5 | | 7* | 11 | 9 | 10 | | | | 8 | | 6 | 4 | 12 | | | | | | 25 |
| 1 | 2 | 3 | | 5 | | 7 | | 9 | 10 | 11 | | | 8 | | 6 | 4 | | | | | | | 26 |
| 1 | 2 | 3 | 4 | 5 | | 7 | 12 | | 10 | 11 | 9* | | 8 | | | 6 | | | | | | | 27 |
| 1 | 2 | | 4 | 5 | | | 12 | 9 | 10* | 11 | | | 8 | 3 | | 6 | | | 7 | | | | 28 |
| 1 | 2 | | | 5 | 6 | 7 | | 9 | | 11 | 10* | | 8 | 3 | | 4 | | | 12 | | | | 29 |
| 1 | 2 | | | 5 | | 7 | 12 | 9 | 10* | 11 | | | 8 | 3 | | 4 | | 6 | | | | | 30 |
| 1 | 2 | | | 5 | | 7 | 6 | 9 | 10 | 11 | | | 8 | 3 | | 4 | | | | | | | 31 |
| 1 | 2 | 3 | 4 | 5 | 6 | 7 | | 9* | 10 | 11 | | | 8 | | | 12 | | | | | | | 32 |
| 1 | 2 | | | 5 | 6 | 7 | 10 | | | 11 | | | 8 | 3 | | 4 | | | 9 | | | | 33 |
| 1 | 2 | 3 | | 5 | 6 | 7 | 12 | | 10 | 11* | | | 8 | | | 4 | | | 9 | | | | 34 |
| 1 | 2 | 3 | 4 | | 6 | 7 | 11 | | 10 | | | | 8 | | | | | 9 | | 5 | | | 35 |
| 1 | 2 | | 4 | 5 | 6 | 7 | 11 | | 10 | | | | 8 | 3 | | | | 9 | | | | | 36 |
| 1 | 2 | | 4 | 5 | 6 | 7 | 11 | | 10 | | | | 8 | 3 | | | | 9 | | | | | 37 |
| 1 | 2 | | 4 | 5 | 6 | 7 | | 9 | 10 | 11 | | | 8 | 3 | | | | | | | | | 38 |
| 1 | 2 | | | 5 | 6 | | | | 10 | 11 | | | 8 | 3 | | 4 | 7 | 9 | | | | | 39 |
| 1 | 2 | | | 5 | 6 | | | | 10 | 11 | | | 8 | 3 | | 4 | 7* | 9 | | | 12 | | 40 |
| 1 | 2 | | | 5 | 6 | | 7 | | 10 | 11 | | | 8 | 3 | | 4 | | 9 | | | | | 41 |
| 1 | 2 | 3 | 4 | 5 | 6 | | 8 | 9 | 10 | 11 | | | | | | | | 7 | | | | | 42 |
| 41 | 42 | 19 | 25 | 41 | 36 | 34 | 14 | 29 | 40 | 37 | 6 | 1 | 37 | 13 | 12 | 19 | 3 | 7 | 4 | 1 | 1 | | |
| | | | | | | | | | 10 | | 3 | | | 1 | 2 | 2 | 1 | | 2 | | 1 | | |
| | | 2 | 2 | | 8 | 1 | 8 | 1 | 8 | 13 | 6 | 4 | 4 | | | 1 | 1 | | | | 1 | | |

105

# 1981-82

| | | | | | | | | |
|---|---|---|---|---|---|---|---|---|
| 1 | Aug | 29 | (a) | Wolverhampton W | L | 0-1 | | 28,001 |
| 2 | Sep | 1 | (h) | Middlesbrough | D | 1-1 | Neal (pen) | 31,963 |
| 3 | | 5 | (h) | Arsenal | W | 2-0 | McDermott, Johnson | 35,269 |
| 4 | | 12 | (a) | Ipswich T | L | 0-2 | | 26,703 |
| 5 | | 19 | (a) | Aston Villa | D | 0-0 | | 37,474 |
| 6 | | 22 | (a) | Coventry C | W | 2-1 | Kennedy A, McDermott (pen) | 16,731 |
| 7 | | 26 | (a) | West Ham U | D | 1-1 | Johnson | 30,802 |
| 8 | Oct | 3 | (h) | Swansea C | D | 2-2 | McDermott 2 (2 pens) | 48,645 |
| 9 | | 10 | (h) | Leeds U | W | 3-0 | Rush 2, Cherry (og) | 35,840 |
| 10 | | 17 | (a) | Brighton & HA | D | 3-3 | Dalglish, Kennedy R, McDermott | 26,321 |
| 11 | | 24 | (h) | Manchester U | L | 1-2 | McDermott (pen) | 41,438 |
| 12 | | 31 | (a) | Sunderland | W | 2-0 | Souness, McDermott | 27,854 |
| 13 | Nov | 7 | (h) | Everton | W | 3-1 | Dalglish 2, Rush | 48,861 |
| 14 | | 21 | (a) | West Brom A | D | 1-1 | Dalglish | 20,871 |
| 15 | | 28 | (h) | Southampton | L | 0-1 | | 37,189 |
| 16 | Dec | 5 | (a) | Nottingham F | W | 2-0 | Lawrenson, Kennedy R | 24,521 |
| 17 | | 26 | (h) | Manchester C | L | 1-3 | Whelan | 37,929 |
| 18 | Jan | 5 | (h) | West Ham U | W | 3-0 | McDermott, Whelan, Dalglish | 28,427 |
| 19 | | 16 | (h) | Wolverhampton W | W | 2-1 | Whelan, Dalglish | 26,438 |
| 20 | | 26 | (a) | Notts Co | W | 4-0 | Whelan, Rush 3 | 14,407 |
| 21 | | 30 | (a) | Aston Villa | W | 3-0 | Rush, McDermott 2 | 35,947 |
| 22 | Feb | 6 | (h) | Ipswich T | W | 4-0 | McDermott, Rush, Dalglish, Whelan | 41,316 |
| 23 | | 16 | (a) | Swansea C | L | 0-2 | | 22,604 |
| 24 | | 20 | (h) | Coventry C | W | 4-0 | Souness, Lee, Rush, McDermott (pen) | 28,286 |
| 25 | | 27 | (a) | Leeds U | W | 2-0 | Souness, Rush | 33,689 |
| 26 | Mar | 6 | (h) | Brighton & HA | L | 0-1 | | 28,574 |
| 27 | | 9 | (a) | Stoke C | W | 5-1 | McDermott, Dalglish, Souness, Lee, Whelan | 16,758 |
| 28 | | 20 | (h) | Sunderland | W | 1-0 | Rush | 30,344 |
| 29 | | 27 | (a) | Everton | W | 3-1 | Whelan, Souness, Johnston | 51,847 |
| 30 | | 30 | (h) | Birmingham C | W | 3-1 | Rush 2, McDermott | 24,224 |
| 31 | Apr | 2 | (h) | Notts Co | W | 1-0 | Dalglish | 30,126 |
| 32 | | 7 | (a) | Manchester U | W | 1-0 | Johnson | 50,969 |
| 33 | | 10 | (a) | Manchester C | W | 5-0 | Lee, Neal (pen), Johnston, Kennedy A, Rush | 40,112 |
| 34 | | 13 | (h) | Stoke C | W | 2-0 | Kennedy A, Johnston | 30,419 |
| 35 | | 17 | (h) | West Brom A | W | 1-0 | Dalglish | 34,286 |
| 36 | | 24 | (a) | Southampton | W | 3-2 | Rush, Whelan 2 | 24,704 |
| 37 | May | 1 | (h) | Nottingham F | W | 2-0 | Johnston 2 | 34,321 |
| 38 | | 3 | (a) | Tottenham H | D | 2-2 | Dalglish 2 | 38,091 |
| 39 | | 8 | (a) | Birmingham C | W | 1-0 | Rush | 26,381 |
| 40 | | 11 | (a) | Arsenal | D | 1-1 | Rush | 30,932 |
| 41 | | 15 | (h) | Tottenham H | W | 3-1 | Lawrenson, Dalglish, Whelan | 48,122 |
| 42 | | 18 | (a) | Middlesbrough | D | 0-0 | | 17,431 |

FINAL LEAGUE POSITION : 1st in Division One

Appearances

Sub. Appearances

Goals

| Grobbelaar | Neal | Lawrenson | Thompson | Kennedy R | Hansen | Dalglish | Lee | Johnson | McDermott | Souness | Johnston | Kennedy A | Whelan | Sheedy | Rush | |
|---|---|---|---|---|---|---|---|---|---|---|---|---|---|---|---|---|
| 1 | 2 | 3 | 4 | 5* | 6 | 7 | 8 | 9 | 10 | 11 | 12 | | | | | 1 |
| 1 | 2 | 3 | 4 | 5 | 6 | 7 | 8 | 9 | 10 | 11 | | | | | | 2 |
| 1 | 2 | 3 | 4 | 5 | 6 | 7 | 8 | 9 | 10 | 11* | 12 | | | | | 3 |
| 1 | 2 | | 4 | 5 | 6 | 7 | 8 | 9 | 10* | 11 | 12 | 3 | | | | 4 |
| 1 | 2 | | 4 | 5 | 6 | 7 | 8 | 9 | 10 | 11 | | 3 | | | | 5 |
| 1 | 2 | 12 | 4 | 5 | 6 | 7 | 8 | 9* | 10 | 11 | | 3 | | | | 6 |
| 1 | 2 | | 4 | 5 | 6 | 7 | 8 | 9 | 10 | 11 | | 3 | | | | 7 |
| 1 | 2 | 5 | 4 | | | 7 | 8 | 9* | 10 | 11 | | 3 | 6 | 12 | | 8 |
| 1 | 2 | 5 | 4 | | 6 | 7 | 8 | | 10 | 11 | | 3 | | 9 | | 9 |
| 1 | 2 | 12 | 4 | 5 | 6 | 7 | 8 | | 10 | 11 | | 3 | | 9* | | 10 |
| 1 | 2 | 3 | 4 | 5 | 6 | 7 | 8 | 9* | 10 | 11 | | | 12 | | | 11 |
| 1 | 2 | 3 | 4 | 5 | 6 | 7 | | | 10 | 11 | | | 8 | 9 | | 12 |
| 1 | 2 | 3 | 4 | 5* | 6 | 7 | | 12 | 10 | 11 | | | 8 | 9 | | 13 |
| 1 | 2 | 3 | 4 | 5* | 6 | 7 | | 9 | 10 | 11 | | 12 | 8 | | | 14 |
| 1 | 2 | 3 | 4 | 5 | 6 | 7 | | 12 | 10* | 11 | | | 8 | 9 | | 15 |
| 1 | 2 | 3 | 4 | 5 | 6 | 7 | | | 10 | 11 | | | 8 | 9 | | 16 |
| 1 | 2 | 3 | 4 | | 6 | 7 | 8 | | | 11 | 10* | 12 | 5 | | 9 | 17 |
| 1 | 2 | 3 | 4 | | 6 | 7 | | | 10 | 11 | | 8 | 5 | | 9 | 18 |
| 1 | 2 | 3 | 4 | | 6 | 7 | | 12 | 10 | 11 | | 8* | 5 | | 9 | 19 |
| 1 | 2 | 3 | | | 6 | 7 | 8 | | 10 | 11 | | 4 | 5 | | 9 | 20 |
| 1 | 2 | 3 | | | 6 | 7 | 8 | | 10 | 11 | | 4 | 5 | | 9 | 21 |
| 1 | 2 | 3 | | | 6 | 7 | 8 | | 10 | 11 | | 4 | 5 | | 9 | 22 |
| 1 | 2 | 3 | | | 6 | 7 | 8 | | 10 | 11 | | 4 | 5 | | 9 | 23 |
| 1 | 2 | 3 | | | 6 | 7 | 8 | | 10 | 11 | | 4 | 5 | | 9 | 24 |
| 1 | 2 | 3 | | | 6 | 7 | 8 | 12 | 10 | 11 | | 4 | 5 | | 9* | 25 |
| 1 | 2 | 3 | | | 6 | 7 | 8* | | 10 | 11 | | 4 | 5 | 12 | 9 | 26 |
| 1 | 2 | 3 | | | 6 | 7 | 8 | | 10 | 11 | | 4 | 5 | | 9 | 27 |
| 1 | 2 | 3 | 6 | | | 7 | 8 | 12 | | 11 | 10* | 4 | 5 | | 9 | 28 |
| 1 | 2 | 3 | 6 | | | 7 | 8 | | | 11 | 10 | 4 | 5 | | 9 | 29 |
| 1 | 2 | 3 | 6 | | | 7 | 8 | 10 | | 11 | | 4 | 5 | | 9 | 30 |
| 1 | 2 | 3 | 6 | | | 7 | 8 | 10 | | 11 | | 4 | 5 | | 9 | 31 |
| 1 | 2 | 3 | 6 | | | 7 | 8 | 12 | | 11* | 10 | 4 | 5 | | 9 | 32 |
| 1 | 2 | 3 | 6 | | 11 | 7 | 8 | | | 10 | | 4 | 5 | | 9 | 33 |
| 1 | 2 | 3 | 6 | | 11 | 7 | 8 | | | 10 | | 4 | 5 | | 9 | 34 |
| 1 | 2 | 3 | 6 | | 11 | 7 | 8 | | | 10 | | 4 | 5 | | 9 | 35 |
| 1 | 2 | 3 | 6 | | 11 | 7 | 8 | | | 10 | | 4 | 5 | | 9 | 36 |
| 1 | 2 | 3 | 6 | | 11 | 7 | 8 | | | 10 | | 4 | 5 | | 9 | 37 |
| 1 | 2 | 3 | 6 | | 11 | 7 | 8 | | | 12 | 10* | 4 | 5 | | 9 | 38 |
| 1 | 2 | 3 | 6 | | 10 | 7 | 8 | | | 11 | 12 | 4 | 5* | | 9 | 39 |
| 1 | 2 | 3 | 6 | | 10 | 7 | 8* | | | 11 | 12 | 4 | 5 | | 9 | 40 |
| 1 | 2 | 3 | 6 | | 10 | 7 | 8 | | | 11 | | 4 | 5 | | 9 | 41 |
| 1 | 2 | 3 | 6 | | 10 | 7 | 8 | | | 11 | 5 | 4 | | | 9 | 42 |
| 42 | 42 | 37 | 34 | 15 | 35 | 42 | 35 | 10 | 28 | 34 | 13 | 32 | 31 | | 32 | |
| | | 2 | | | | | | 5 | 1 | 1 | 5 | 2 | 1 | 2 | | |
| | 2 | 2 | | 2 | | 13 | 3 | 2 | 14 | 5 | 6 | 3 | 10 | | 17 | |

107

# 1982-83

| # | Month | Date | | Opponent | Res | Score | Scorers | Att |
|---|---|---|---|---|---|---|---|---|
| 1 | Aug | 28 | (h) | West Brom A | W | 2-0 | Lee, Neal (pen) | 35,652 |
| 2 | | 31 | (a) | Birmingham C | D | 0-0 | | 20,176 |
| 3 | Sep | 4 | (a) | Arsenal | W | 2-0 | Hodgson, Neal | 36,429 |
| 4 | | 7 | (h) | Nottingham F | W | 4-3 | Hodgson 2, Souness, Rush | 27,145 |
| 5 | | 11 | (h) | Luton T | D | 3-3 | Souness, Rush, Johnston | 33,694 |
| 6 | | 18 | (a) | Swansea C | W | 3-0 | Rush 2, Johnston | 20,322 |
| 7 | | 25 | (h) | Southampton | W | 5-0 | Whelan 2, Souness, Lawrenson | 32,996 |
| 8 | Oct | 2 | (a) | Ipswich T | L | 0-1 | | 24,342 |
| 9 | | 9 | (a) | West Ham U | L | 1-3 | Souness | 32,500 |
| 10 | | 16 | (h) | Manchester U | D | 0-0 | | 40,853 |
| 11 | | 23 | (a) | Stoke C | D | 1-1 | Lawrenson | 29,411 |
| 12 | | 30 | (h) | Brighton & HA | W | 3-1 | Lawrenson, Dalglish 2 | 27,929 |
| 13 | Nov | 6 | (a) | Everton | W | 5-0 | Rush 4, Lawrenson | 52,741 |
| 14 | | 13 | (h) | Coventry C | W | 4-0 | Dalglish, Rush 3 | 27,870 |
| 15 | | 20 | (a) | Notts Co | W | 2-1 | Johnston, Dalglish | 16,914 |
| 16 | | 27 | (h) | Tottenham H | W | 3-0 | Neal (pen), Dalglish 2 | 40,691 |
| 17 | Dec | 4 | (a) | Norwich C | L | 0-1 | | 22,909 |
| 18 | | 11 | (h) | Watford | W | 3-1 | Rush, Neal 2 (2 pens) | 36,690 |
| 19 | | 18 | (a) | Aston Villa | W | 4-2 | Hodgson, Dalglish, Kennedy, Rush | 34,568 |
| 20 | | 27 | (h) | Manchester C | W | 5-2 | Dalglish 3, Neal, Rush | 44,664 |
| 21 | | 28 | (a) | Sunderland | D | 0-0 | | 35,041 |
| 22 | Jan | 1 | (h) | Notts Co | W | 5-1 | Rush 3, Dalglish 2 | 33,643 |
| 23 | | 3 | (h) | Arsenal | W | 3-1 | Rush, Souness, Dalglish | 37,713 |
| 24 | | 15 | (a) | West Brom A | W | 1-0 | Rush | 24,560 |
| 25 | | 22 | (h) | Birmingham C | W | 1-0 | Neal | 30,986 |
| 26 | Feb | 5 | (a) | Luton T | W | 3-1 | Rush, Kennedy, Souness | 18,434 |
| 27 | | 12 | (h) | Ipswich T | W | 1-0 | Dalglish | 34,976 |
| 28 | | 26 | (a) | Manchester U | D | 1-1 | Dalglish | 57,397 |
| 29 | Mar | 5 | (h) | Stoke C | W | 5-1 | Dalglish 2, Neal, Johnston, Souness | 30,020 |
| 30 | | 12 | (h) | West Ham U | W | 3-0 | Pike (og), Lee, Rush | 28,511 |
| 31 | | 19 | (h) | Everton | D | 0-0 | | 44,737 |
| 32 | | 22 | (a) | Brighton & HA | D | 2-2 | Rush 2 | 25,030 |
| 33 | Apr | 2 | (h) | Sunderland | W | 1-0 | Souness | 35,821 |
| 34 | | 4 | (a) | Manchester C | W | 4-0 | Souness, Fairclough 2, Kennedy | 35,647 |
| 35 | | 9 | (h) | Swansea C | W | 3-0 | Rush, Lee, Fairclough | 30,010 |
| 36 | | 12 | (a) | Coventry C | D | 0-0 | | 14,821 |
| 37 | | 16 | (a) | Southampton | L | 2-3 | Dalglish, Johnston | 25,578 |
| 38 | | 23 | (h) | Norwich C | L | 0-2 | | 37,022 |
| 39 | | 30 | (a) | Tottenham H | L | 0-2 | | 44,907 |
| 40 | May | 2 | (a) | Nottingham F | L | 0-1 | | 25,107 |
| 41 | | 7 | (h) | Aston Villa | D | 1-1 | Johnston | 39,939 |
| 42 | | 14 | (a) | Watford | L | 1-2 | Johnston | 27,173 |

FINAL LEAGUE POSITION : 1st in Division One

Appearances

Sub. Appearances

Goals

| Grobbelaar | Neal | Kennedy | Thompson | Whelan | Lawrenson | Dalglish | Lee | Rush | Hodgson | Souness | Johnston | Nicol | McDermott | Hansen | Fairclough | # |
|---|---|---|---|---|---|---|---|---|---|---|---|---|---|---|---|---|
| 1 | 2 | 3 | 4 | 5 | 6 | 7 | 8 | 9 | 10 | 11 | 12 |  |  |  |  | 1 |
| 1 | 6 | 3 | 4 | 5 |  | 7 | 8 | 9 | 10 | 11 |  | 2 |  |  |  | 2 |
| 1 | 2 | 3 | 4 | 6 | 5 | 7 | 8 | 9 | 10 | 11 |  |  |  |  |  | 3 |
| 1 | 2 | 3 | 4 | 6 | 5 | 7 | 8 | 9 | 10 | 11 |  |  |  |  |  | 4 |
| 1 | 2 | 3 | 4 | 6 | 5 | 7* | 8 | 9 | 10 | 11 | 12 |  |  |  |  | 5 |
| 1 | 2 | 3 | 4 |  | 5 | 7 | 8 | 9 | 10* | 11 |  |  |  | 6 | 12 | 6 |
| 1 | 2 | 3 | 4 | 5 | 6 | 7 | 8 | 9* |  | 11 | 10 |  |  |  | 12 | 7 |
| 1 | 2 | 3 | 4 | 5 | 10 | 7 | 8* |  |  | 11 | 9 |  |  | 6 | 12 | 8 |
| 1 | 2 | 3* | 4 | 5 | 10 | 7 | 8 | 9 |  | 11 | 12 |  |  | 6 |  | 9 |
| 1 | 2 | 3 | 4 | 5 | 10 | 7 | 8 | 9 |  | 11 |  |  |  | 6 |  | 10 |
| 1 | 2 | 3 | 4 | 5 | 10 | 7 | 8 | 9 |  | 11 |  |  |  | 6 |  | 11 |
| 1 | 2 | 3 | 4 | 5 | 10 | 7 | 8 | 9 |  | 11 |  |  |  | 6 |  | 12 |
| 1 | 2 | 3 | 4 |  | 10 | 7* | 8 | 9 | 12 | 11 | 5 |  |  | 6 |  | 13 |
| 1 | 2 | 3 | 4 |  | 10 | 7 | 8 | 9 |  | 11 | 5 |  |  | 6 |  | 14 |
| 1 | 2 | 3 | 4 |  | 10 | 7 | 8 | 9 |  | 11 | 5 |  |  | 6 |  | 15 |
| 1 | 2 | 3 | 4 |  | 10 | 7 | 8 | 9 |  | 11 | 5 |  |  | 6 |  | 16 |
| 1 | 2 | 3 | 4 |  | 10 | 7 | 8 | 9 |  | 11 | 5 |  |  | 6 |  | 17 |
| 1 | 2 | 3 | 4* |  | 5 | 7 | 8 | 9 |  | 11 | 10 |  |  | 6 | 12 | 18 |
| 1 | 2 | 3 |  | 5 | 4 | 7 | 8 | 9 | 10 | 11 |  |  |  | 6 |  | 19 |
| 1 | 2 | 3 |  | 5* | 4 | 7 | 8 | 9 | 10 | 11 |  |  |  | 6 | 12 | 20 |
| 1 | 2 | 3 |  |  | 4 | 7 | 8 | 9 | 10 | 11 | 5 |  |  | 6 |  | 21 |
| 1 | 2 | 3 |  |  | 4 | 7 | 8 | 9 | 10 | 11 | 5 |  |  | 6 |  | 22 |
| 1 | 2 | 3 |  |  | 4 | 7 | 8 | 9 | 10 | 11 | 5 |  |  | 6 |  | 23 |
| 1 | 2 | 3 |  |  | 4 | 7 | 8 | 9 | 10 | 11 | 5 |  |  | 6 |  | 24 |
| 1 | 2 | 3 |  | 5 | 4 | 7 | 8 |  | 10 | 11 | 9 |  |  | 6 |  | 25 |
| 1 | 2 | 3 |  | 12 | 4 | 7 | 8 | 9 | 10 | 11 | 5* |  |  | 6 |  | 26 |
| 1 | 2 | 3 |  | 12 | 4 | 7 | 8 | 9 | 10 | 11 | 5* |  |  | 6 |  | 27 |
| 1 | 2 | 3 | 4 | 5 |  | 7 | 8 | 9 |  | 11 | 10 |  |  |  |  | 28 |
| 1 | 2 | 3 |  | 5 | 4 | 7 | 8 | 9 |  | 11 | 10 |  |  | 6 |  | 29 |
| 1 | 2 | 3 |  | 5 | 4 | 7 | 8 | 9 |  | 11 | 10 |  |  | 6 |  | 30 |
| 1 | 2 | 3 |  | 5 | 4 | 7 | 8 | 9 | 12 | 11* | 10 |  |  | 6 |  | 31 |
| 1 | 2 | 3 | 4* | 5 | 11 | 7 | 8 | 9 |  | 10 |  |  |  | 6 | 12 | 32 |
| 1 | 2 | 3 |  | 5 | 4 | 7 | 8 |  |  | 11 | 10 |  |  | 6 | 9 | 33 |
| 1 | 2 | 3 |  | 5 | 4 | 7 | 8 |  |  | 11 | 10 |  |  | 6 | 9 | 34 |
| 1 | 2 | 3 |  | 5 | 4 | 7 | 8 | 9 |  | 11 | 10* |  |  | 6 | 12 | 35 |
| 1 | 2 | 3 |  | 5 | 4 | 7 | 8 | 9 |  | 11 | 10 |  |  | 6 |  | 36 |
| 1 | 2 | 3 |  | 5 | 4 | 7 | 8 |  | 12 | 11 | 10 |  |  | 6 | 9* | 37 |
| 1 | 2 | 3 |  | 5 | 4 | 7 | 8 |  | 9 | 11 | 10 |  |  | 6 |  | 38 |
| 1 | 2 | 3 | 4 |  | 5 | 7 |  | 9 | 10 | 11 | 8 |  |  | 6 |  | 39 |
| 1 | 2 | 3 | 4 |  | 5 | 7 |  | 9* | 10 | 11 | 8 |  | 12 | 6 |  | 40 |
| 1 | 2 | 3 | 4 |  | 5 | 7 | 8 |  | 10 | 11 | 9 |  |  | 6 |  | 41 |
| 1 | 2 | 3 | 4 |  | 5* | 7 | 8 |  | 9 | 11 | 10 |  | 12 | 6 |  | 42 |
| 42 | 42 | 42 | 24 | 26 | 40 | 42 | 40 | 34 | 20 | 41 | 30 | 2 |  | 34 | 3 |  |
|  |  |  | 2 |  |  |  |  |  |  | 3 |  | 3 | 2 | 2 | 5 |  |
|  | 8 | 3 |  | 2 | 5 | 18 | 3 | 24 | 4 | 9 | 7 |  |  |  | 3 |  |

# 1983-84

| | | | | | | | | | |
|---|---|---|---|---|---|---|---|---|---|
| 1 | Aug | 27 | (a) | Wolves | D | 1-1 | Rush | | 26,249 |
| 2 | | 31 | (a) | Norwich C | W | 1-0 | Souness | | 23,859 |
| 3 | Sep | 3 | (h) | Nottingham F | W | 1-0 | Rush | | 31,376 |
| 4 | | 6 | (h) | Southampton | D | 1-1 | Rush | | 26,331 |
| 5 | | 10 | (a) | Arsenal | W | 2-0 | Johnston, Dalglish | | 47,896 |
| 6 | | 17 | (h) | Aston Villa | W | 2-1 | Dalglish, Rush | | 34,246 |
| 7 | | 24 | (a) | Manchester U | L | 0-1 | | | 56,121 |
| 8 | Oct | 1 | (h) | Sunderland | L | 0-1 | | | 29,534 |
| 9 | | 15 | (a) | West Ham U | W | 3-1 | Robinson 3 | | 32,555 |
| 10 | | 22 | (a) | Queen's Park R | W | 1-0 | Nicol | | 27,140 |
| 11 | | 29 | (h) | Luton T | W | 6-0 | Rush 5, Dalglish | | 31,940 |
| 12 | Nov | 6 | (h) | Everton | W | 3-0 | Rush, Robinson, Nicol | | 40,875 |
| 13 | | 12 | (a) | Tottenham H | D | 2-2 | Robinson, Rush | | 45,032 |
| 14 | | 19 | (h) | Stoke C | W | 1-0 | Rush | | 26,529 |
| 15 | | 26 | (a) | Ipswich T | D | 1-1 | Dalglish | | 23,826 |
| 16 | Dec | 3 | (h) | Birmingham C | W | 1-0 | Rush | | 24,791 |
| 17 | | 10 | (a) | Coventry C | L | 0-4 | | | 20,586 |
| 18 | | 17 | (h) | Notts C | W | 5-0 | Nicol, Souness 2 (1 pen), Hunt (og), Rush | | 22,436 |
| 19 | | 26 | (a) | West Brom A | W | 2-1 | Nicol, Souness | | 25,139 |
| 20 | | 27 | (h) | Leicester C | D | 2-2 | Lee, Rush | | 33,664 |
| 21 | | 31 | (a) | Nottingham F | W | 1-0 | Rush | | 29,692 |
| 22 | Jan | 2 | (h) | Manchester U | D | 1-1 | Johnston | | 45,122 |
| 23 | | 14 | (h) | Wolves | L | 0-1 | | | 23,325 |
| 24 | | 20 | (a) | Aston Villa | W | 3-1 | Rush 3 | | 19,566 |
| 25 | Feb | 1 | (h) | Watford | W | 3-0 | Rush, Nicol, Whelan | | 20,746 |
| 26 | | 4 | (a) | Sunderland | D | 0-0 | | | 25,646 |
| 27 | | 11 | (h) | Arsenal | W | 2-1 | Kennedy, Neal | | 34,642 |
| 28 | | 18 | (a) | Luton T | D | 0-0 | | | 14,877 |
| 29 | | 25 | (h) | Queen's Park R | W | 2-0 | Rush, Robinson | | 32,206 |
| 30 | Mar | 3 | (a) | Everton | D | 1-1 | Rush | | 51,245 |
| 31 | | 10 | (h) | Tottenham H | W | 3-1 | Dalglish, Whelan, Lee | | 36,718 |
| 32 | | 16 | (a) | Southampton | L | 0-2 | | | 19,698 |
| 33 | | 31 | (a) | Watford | W | 2-0 | Wark, Rush | | 21,293 |
| 34 | Apr | 7 | (h) | West Ham U | W | 6-0 | Rush 2, Dalglish, Whelan, Souness 2 | | 38,359 |
| 35 | | 14 | (a) | Stoke C | L | 0-2 | | | 24,372 |
| 36 | | 18 | (a) | Leicester C | D | 3-3 | Whelan, Rush, Wark | | 26,553 |
| 37 | | 21 | (h) | West Brom A | W | 3-0 | McNaught (og), Souness, Dalglish | | 35,320 |
| 38 | | 28 | (h) | Ipswich T | D | 2-2 | Kennedy, Rush | | 32,069 |
| 39 | May | 5 | (a) | Birmingham C | D | 0-0 | | | 18,809 |
| 40 | | 7 | (h) | Coventry C | W | 5-0 | Rush 4 (1 pen), Hansen | | 33,393 |
| 41 | | 12 | (a) | Notts C | D | 0-0 | | | 18,745 |
| 42 | | 15 | (h) | Norwich C | D | 1-1 | Rush | | 28,837 |

FINAL LEAGUE POSITION : 1st in Division One

Appearances

Sub. Appearances

Goals

| Grobbelaar | Neal | Kennedy | Lawrenson | Johnston | Hansen | Dalglish | Lee | Rush | Robinson | Souness | Hodgson | Nicol | Whelan | Wark | # |
|---|---|---|---|---|---|---|---|---|---|---|---|---|---|---|---|
| 1 | 2 | 3 | 4 | 5 | 6 | 7 | 8 | 9 | 10 | 11 | | | | | 1 |
| 1 | 2 | 3 | 4 | 5 | 6 | 7 | 8 | 9 | 10 | 11 | | | | | 2 |
| 1 | 2 | 3 | 4 | 5 | 6 | 7 | 8 | 9 | 10* | 11 | 12 | | | | 3 |
| 1 | 2 | 3 | 4 | 5 | 6 | 7 | 8 | 9 | 10 | 11 | | | | | 4 |
| 1 | 2 | 3 | 4 | 5 | 6 | 7 | 8 | 9 | 10 | 11 | | | | | 5 |
| 1 | 2 | 3 | 4 | 5 | 6 | 7 | 8 | 9 | 10 | 11 | | | | | 6 |
| 1 | 2* | 3 | 4 | 5 | 6 | 7 | 8 | 9 | 10 | 11 | | 12 | | | 7 |
| 1 | | 3 | 4 | 5 | 6 | 7 | 8 | 9 | 10 | 11 | | 2 | | | 8 |
| 1 | 2 | 3 | 4 | 5 | 6 | 7 | 8 | 9* | io | 11 | 12 | | | | 9 |
| 1 | 2 | 3 | 4 | 5* | 6 | 7 | 8 | 9 | 10 | 11 | | 12 | | | 10 |
| 1 | 2 | 3 | 4 | | 6 | 7 | 8 | 9 | 10 | 11 | | 5 | | | 11 |
| 1 | 2 | 3 | 4 | | 6 | 7 | 8 | 9 | 10 | 11 | | 5 | | | 12 |
| 1 | 2 | 3 | 4 | | 6 | 7 | 8 | 9 | 10 | 11 | | 5 | | | 13 |
| 1 | 2 | 3 | 4 | | 6 | 7 | 8 | 9 | 10 | 11 | | 5 | | | 14 |
| 1 | 2 | 3 | 4 | | 6 | 7 | 8 | 9 | | 11 | | 5 | 10 | | 15 |
| 1 | 2 | 3 | 4 | 7 | 6 | | 8 | 9 | 10* | 11 | | 5 | 12 | | 16 |
| 1 | 2 | 3 | 4 | | 6 | 7 | 8 | 9 | | 11 | | 5 | 10 | | 17 |
| 1 | 2 | 3 | 4 | 10 | 6 | 7 | 8 | 9 | | 11 | | 5 | | | 18 |
| 1 | 2 | 3 | 4 | 10 | 6 | 7 | 8 | 9 | | 11 | | 5 | | | 19 |
| 1 | 2 | 3 | 4 | 10* | 6 | 7 | 8 | 9 | | 11 | 12 | 5 | | | 20 |
| 1 | 2 | 3 | 4 | 10 | 6 | 7* | 8 | 9 | | 11 | | 5 | 12 | | 21 |
| 1 | 2 | 3 | 4 | 10 | 6 | 7* | 8 | 9 | | 11 | 12 | 5 | | | 22 |
| 1 | 2 | 3 | 4 | 10 | 6 | | 8 | 9 | 7 | 11 | | 5* | 12 | | 23 |
| 1 | 2 | 3 | 4 | 10 | 6 | | 8 | 9 | 7 | 11 | | 5 | | | 24 |
| 1 | 2 | 3 | 4 | 10 | 6 | | 8 | 9 | 7 | | | 5 | 11 | | 25 |
| 1 | 2 | 3 | 4 | 10 | 6 | | 8 | 9 | 7 | | | 5 | 11 | | 26 |
| 1 | 2 | 3 | 4 | 10 | 6 | | 8 | 9 | 7 | | | 5 | 11 | | 27 |
| 1 | 2 | 3 | 4 | 10 | 6 | | 8 | 9 | | 11 | 7 | 5 | | | 28 |
| 1 | 2 | 3 | 4 | 10 | 6 | | 8 | 9 | 7 | 11 | | 5 | | | 29 |
| 1 | 2 | 3 | 4 | 10 | 6 | | 8* | 9 | 7 | 11 | 12 | 5 | | | 30 |
| 1 | 2 | 3 | 4 | 10 | 6 | 7 | 8 | 9 | | 11 | | 5 | | | 31 |
| 1 | 2 | 3 | 4 | 10 | 6 | 7 | 8 | 9 | 12 | | 11* | 5 | | | 32 |
| 1 | 2 | 3 | 4 | | 6 | 7 | 8 | 9 | | 11 | | 5 | 10 | | 33 |
| 1 | 2 | 3 | 4 | | 6 | 7 | 8 | 9 | | 11 | | 5 | 10 | | 34 |
| 1 | 2 | 3 | 4 | 12 | 6 | 7* | 8 | 9 | | 11 | | 5 | 10 | | 35 |
| 1 | 2 | 3 | 4 | | 6 | 7 | 8 | 9 | | 11 | | 5 | 10 | | 36 |
| 1 | 2 | 3 | 4 | | 6 | 7 | 8 | 9 | | 11 | | 5 | 10 | | 37 |
| 1 | 2 | 3 | 4* | 11 | 6 | 7 | 8 | 9 | | | 12 | 5 | 10 | | 38 |
| 1 | 2 | 3 | 4 | | 6 | 7 | 8 | 9 | | 11 | | 5 | 10 | | 39 |
| 1 | 2 | 3 | 4 | | 6 | 7 | 8 | 9 | | 11 | | 5 | 10 | | 40 |
| 1 | 2 | 3 | 4 | | 6 | 7 | 8 | 9 | | 11 | | 5 | 10 | | 41 |
| 1 | 2 | 3 | 4 | 10 | 6 | 7 | 8 | 9 | | 11 | | 5 | | | 42 |
| 42 | 41 | 42 | 42 | 28 | 42 | 33 | 42 | 41 | 23 | 37 | 1 | 19 | 20 | 9 | |
| | | | 1 | | | | | | | 1 | 4 | 3 | 3 | | |
| | 1 | 2 | | 2 | 1 | 7 | 2 | 32 | 6 | 7 | | 6 | 4 | 2 | |

111

# 1984-85

| | | | | | | | | |
|---|---|---|---|---|---|---|---|---|
| 1 | Aug | 25 | (a) | Norwich C | D | 3-3 | Bruce (og), Dalglish, Neal (pen) | 22,005 |
| 2 | | 27 | (h) | West Ham U | W | 3-0 | Walsh, Wark 2 | 32,633 |
| 3 | Sep | 1 | (h) | QPR | D | 1-1 | Whelan | 33,982 |
| 4 | | 4 | (a) | Luton T | W | 2-1 | Dalglish, Neal (pen) | 14,127 |
| 5 | | 8 | (a) | Arsenal | L | 1-3 | Kennedy | 50,006 |
| 6 | | 15 | (h) | Sunderland | D | 1-1 | Walsh | 34,044 |
| 7 | | 22 | (a) | Manchester U | D | 1-1 | Walsh | 56,638 |
| 8 | | 29 | (h) | Sheffield W | L | 0-2 | | 40,196 |
| 9 | Oct | 6 | (h) | West Brom A | D | 0-0 | | 29,346 |
| 10 | | 12 | (a) | Tottenham H | L | 0-1 | | 28,599 |
| 11 | | 20 | (h) | Everton | L | 0-1 | | 45,545 |
| 12 | | 28 | (a) | Nottingham F | W | 2-0 | Rush, Whelan | 19,838 |
| 13 | Nov | 3 | (a) | Stoke C | W | 1-0 | Whelan | 20,576 |
| 14 | | 10 | (h) | Southampton | D | 1-1 | Rush | 36,382 |
| 15 | | 18 | (a) | Newcastle U | W | 2-0 | Nicol, Wark | 28,003 |
| 16 | | 24 | (h) | Ipswich T | W | 2-0 | Wark 2 | 34,918 |
| 17 | Dec | 1 | (a) | Chelsea | L | 1-3 | Molby | 40,972 |
| 18 | | 4 | (h) | Coventry C | W | 3-1 | Rush (pen), Wark 2 | 27,237 |
| 19 | | 15 | (a) | Aston Villa | D | 0-0 | | 24,007 |
| 20 | | 21 | (a) | QPR | W | 2-0 | Rush, Wark | 11,007 |
| 21 | | 26 | (h) | Leicester C | L | 1-2 | Neal (pen) | 38,419 |
| 22 | | 29 | (h) | Luton T | W | 1-0 | Wark | 35,403 |
| 23 | Jan | 1 | (a) | Watford | D | 1-1 | Rush | 27,073 |
| 24 | | 19 | (h) | Norwich C | W | 4-0 | Dalglish, Rush 2, Wark | 30,627 |
| 25 | Feb | 2 | (a) | Sheffield W | D | 1-1 | Lawrenson | 48,246 |
| 26 | | 12 | (h) | Arsenal | W | 3-0 | Neal, Rush, Whelan | 28,645 |
| 27 | | 23 | (h) | Stoke C | W | 2-0 | Dalglish, Nicol | 31,368 |
| 28 | Mar | 2 | (h) | Nottingham F | W | 1-0 | Wark (pen) | 35,696 |
| 29 | | 16 | (h) | Tottenham H | L | 0-1 | | 43,852 |
| 30 | | 23 | (a) | West Brom A | W | 5-0 | Dalglish, Nicol, Wark 3 | 20,500 |
| 31 | | 31 | (h) | Manchester U | L | 0-1 | | 34,886 |
| 32 | Apr | 3 | (a) | Sunderland | W | 3-0 | Rush 2, Wark | 24,096 |
| 33 | | 6 | (a) | Leicester C | W | 1-0 | Whelan | 22,942 |
| 34 | | 20 | (h) | Newcastle U | W | 3-1 | Gillespie, Walsh, Wark | 34,733 |
| 35 | | 27 | (a) | Ipswich T | D | 0-0 | | 24,484 |
| 36 | May | 4 | (h) | Chelsea | W | 4-3 | Nicol 2, Rush, Whelan | 33,733 |
| 37 | | 6 | (a) | Coventry C | W | 2-0 | Walsh 2 | 18,951 |
| 38 | | 11 | (h) | Aston Villa | W | 2-1 | Rush, Whelan | 33,001 |
| 39 | | 14 | (a) | Southampton | D | 1-1 | Wark | 23,001 |
| 40 | | 17 | (h) | Watford | W | 4-3 | Dalglish, Rush 2, Wark (pen) | 29,130 |
| 41 | | 20 | (a) | West Ham U | W | 3-0 | Beglin, Walsh 2 | 22,408 |
| 42 | | 23 | (a) | Everton | L | 0-1 | | 15,045 |

FINAL LEAGUE POSITION : 2nd in Division One

Appearances

Sub. Appearances

Goals

112

Liverpool — League appearances grid (shirt numbers worn; * = substituted/substitute). Player columns left to right, match number at right.

| Grobbelaar | Neal | Kennedy | Lawrenson | Whelan | Hansen | Dalglish | Lee | Walsh | Wark | Molby | Robinson | Nicol | Gillespie | Rush | Johnston | Beglin | MacDonald | # |
|---|---|---|---|---|---|---|---|---|---|---|---|---|---|---|---|---|---|---|
| 1 | 2 | 3 | 4 | 5 | 6 | 7* | 8 | 9 | 10 | 11 | 12 | | | | | | | 1 |
| 1 | 2 | 3 | 4 | 5 | 6 | 7 | 8 | 9 | 10 | 11 | | | | | | | | 2 |
| 1 | 2 | 3 | 4 | 5 | 6 | 7 | 8 | 9 | 10 | 11 | | | | | | | | 3 |
| 1 | 2 | 3 | 4 | 5 | 6 | 7* | 8 | 9 | 10 | 11 | 12 | | | | | | | 4 |
| 1 | 2 | 3 | 4 | 5 | 6 | 7 | 8 | 9 | 10 | 11 | | | | | | | | 5 |
| 1 | 2 | 3 | 4* | 5 | 6 | 7 | 8 | 9 | 10 | 11 | 12 | | | | | | | 6 |
| 1 | 2 | 3 | 4 | 5 | 6 | 7 | 8 | 9 | 10 | | | 11 | | | | | | 7 |
| 1 | 2 | 3 | 4 | 5 | 6 | 7 | 8 | 9 | 10* | 12 | | 11 | | | | | | 8 |
| 1 | 2 | 3 | 4 | 5 | 6 | 7 | 8* | 9 | 10 | | | 11 | 12 | | | | | 9 |
| 1 | 2 | 3 | 4 | 5 | 6 | | 9* | 10 | 7 | 11 | | 8 | 12 | | | | | 10 |
| 1 | 2 | 3 | 4 | 5 | 6 | 7 | | | 10 | 11 | | 8 | | 9 | | | | 11 |
| 1 | 2 | 3 | 4 | 5 | 6 | 7 | 8 | | | 11 | | | | 9 | 10 | | | 12 |
| 1 | 2 | 3 | 4 | 5 | 6 | 7 | 8 | | | 11 | | | | 9 | 10 | | | 13 |
| 1 | 2* | 3 | 4 | | 6 | 7 | | | 11 | 8 | | 12 | | 9 | 10 | 5 | | 14 |
| 1 | 2 | 3 | 4 | | 6 | 7 | | | 11 | 8 | | 5 | | 9 | 10 | | | 15 |
| 1 | 2 | 3 | 4 | 12 | 6 | 7 | | | 11 | 8 | | 5 | | 9* | 10 | | | 16 |
| 1 | 2 | 3 | 4 | | 6 | 7 | | | 11 | 8 | | 5 | | 9 | 10 | | | 17 |
| 1 | 2 | 3 | 4* | 12 | 6 | 7 | | | 11 | 8 | | 5 | | 9 | 10 | | | 18 |
| 1 | 2 | 3 | | | 6 | 7 | | | 11 | 8 | | 5 | 4 | 9 | 10 | | | 19 |
| 1 | 2 | 3 | 4 | | 6 | 7 | | | 11 | 8 | | 5 | 12 | 9* | 10 | | | 20 |
| 1 | 2 | 3 | | 9 | 6 | 7 | | | 11 | 8 | | 5 | 4 | | 10 | | | 21 |
| 1 | 2 | 3 | | 8 | 6 | 7 | | 9 | 11 | | | 5 | 4 | | | | 10 | 22 |
| 1 | 2 | 3 | 4 | 8 | | 7 | | | 11 | | | 5 | 5 | 9 | | | 10 | 23 |
| 1 | 2 | 3 | | 8 | 6 | 7 | | | 11 | | | 5 | 4 | 9 | | | 10 | 24 |
| 1 | 2 | 3 | 4 | 8 | 6 | 7 | | 12 | 11* | | | 5 | | 9 | | | 10 | 25 |
| 1 | 2 | 3 | | 8 | 6 | 7 | | | 11 | | | 5 | 4 | 9 | | | 10 | 26 |
| 1 | 2 | 3 | | 8 | 6 | 7 | | | 11 | | | 5 | 4 | 9 | | | 10 | 27 |
| 1 | 2 | 3 | 4 | 8 | 6 | 7* | | 12 | 11 | | | | | 9 | 5 | | 10 | 28 |
| 1 | 2 | 3 | 4 | 8 | 6 | 7 | | 12 | 11* | | | 5 | | 9 | | | 10 | 29 |
| 1 | 2 | 3 | 4 | 8 | 6 | 7 | | | 11 | | | 5 | | 9 | | | 10 | 30 |
| 1 | 2 | 3* | 4 | 8 | 6 | 7 | | 12 | 11 | | | 5 | | 9 | | | 10 | 31 |
| 1 | 2 | | 4 | 8 | 6 | 7 | | | 11 | | | 5 | | 9 | | 3 | 10 | 32 |
| 1 | 2 | | 4 | 8 | 6 | 7 | 5 | | 11 | | | | | 9 | | 3 | 10 | 33 |
| 1 | 2 | | 4 | 8 | 6 | 7 | 10 | 9 | 11 | | | 5 | | | | 3 | | 34 |
| 1 | 2 | | 4 | 8 | 6 | 7 | | 9 | 11 | | | 5 | | | 10 | 3 | | 35 |
| 1 | 2 | | 4 | 8 | 6 | 7 | | 10 | 11 | | | 5 | | 9 | | 3 | | 36 |
| 1 | 2 | | 4 | 8 | 6 | | 7 | 10 | 11 | | | 5 | | 9 | | 3 | | 37 |
| 1 | 2 | 3 | 4 | 8 | 6 | 7 | | 10 | 11 | | | 5 | | 9 | | | | 38 |
| 1 | 2 | | 4* | 8 | 6 | | 7 | 10 | 11 | 12 | | 5 | | 9 | | 3 | | 39 |
| 1 | 2 | | | 8 | 6 | 7* | | 10 | 11 | 12 | | 5 | | 9 | | 3 | 4 | 40 |
| 1 | 2 | | | 8 | 6 | 7 | 12 | 10 | 11 | 4* | | 5 | | 9 | | 3 | | 41 |
| 1 | 2 | | | 8 | 6 | 7 | 10 | | 11 | 4* | | 5 | | 9 | | 3 | | 42 |
| 42 | 42 | 32 | 33 | 35 | 41 | 36 | 16 | 22 | 40 | 19 | 3 | 29 | 10 | 28 | 11 | 10 | 13 | |
| | | | 2 | | | | 1 | 4 | | 3 | 3 | 2 | 2 | | | | | |
| | 4 | 1 | 1 | 7 | | 6 | | 8 | 18 | 1 | | 5 | 1 | 14 | | 1 | | |

# 1985-86

| 1 | Aug | 17 | (h) | Arsenal | W | 2-0 | Whelan, Nicol | 38,261 |
|---|---|---|---|---|---|---|---|---|
| 2 | | 21 | (a) | Aston Villa | D | 2-2 | Rush, Molby | 20,197 |
| 3 | | 24 | (a) | Newcastle U | L | 0-1 | | 29,670 |
| 4 | | 26 | (h) | Ipswich T | W | 5-0 | Nicol, Rush 2, Molby, Johnston | 29,383 |
| 5 | | 31 | (a) | West Ham U | D | 2-2 | Johnston, Whelan | 19,762 |
| 6 | Sep | 3 | (h) | Nottingham F | W | 2-0 | Whelan 2 | 27,135 |
| 7 | | 7 | (h) | Watford | W | 3-1 | Neal (pen), Johnston, Rush | 31,395 |
| 8 | | 14 | (a) | Oxford U | D | 2-2 | Rush, Johnston | 11,474 |
| 9 | | 21 | (a) | Everton | W | 3-2 | Dalglish, Rush, McMahon | 51,509 |
| 10 | | 28 | (h) | Tottenham H | W | 4-1 | Lawrenson, Rush, Molby 2 (2 pens) | 41,521 |
| 11 | Oct | 5 | (a) | QPR | L | 1-2 | Walsh | 24,621 |
| 12 | | 12 | (h) | Southampton | W | 1-0 | McMahon | 31,070 |
| 13 | | 19 | (a) | Manchester U | D | 1-1 | Johnston | 54,492 |
| 14 | | 26 | (h) | Luton T | W | 3-2 | Walsh 2, Molby | 31,488 |
| 15 | Nov | 2 | (h) | Leicester C | W | 1-0 | Rush | 31,718 |
| 16 | | 9 | (a) | Coventry C | W | 3-0 | Beglin, Walsh, Rush | 16,497 |
| 17 | | 16 | (h) | West Brom A | W | 4-1 | Nicol, Molby, Lawrenson, Walsh | 28,407 |
| 18 | | 23 | (a) | Birmingham C | W | 2-0 | Rush, Walsh | 15,062 |
| 19 | | 30 | (h) | Chelsea | D | 1-1 | Molby (pen) | 38,482 |
| 20 | Dec | 7 | (h) | Aston Villa | W | 3-0 | Molby, Walsh, Johnston | 29,418 |
| 21 | | 14 | (a) | Arsenal | L | 0-2 | | 35,048 |
| 22 | | 21 | (h) | Newcastle U | D | 1-1 | Nicol | 30,746 |
| 23 | | 26 | (a) | Manchester C | L | 0-1 | | 35,584 |
| 24 | | 28 | (a) | Nottingham F | D | 1-1 | MacDonald | 27,141 |
| 25 | Jan | 1 | (h) | Sheffield W | D | 2-2 | Rush, Walsh | 38,964 |
| 26 | | 12 | (a) | Watford | W | 3-2 | Walsh 2, Rush | 16,697 |
| 27 | | 18 | (h) | West Ham U | W | 3-1 | Molby (pen), Rush, Walsh | 41,056 |
| 28 | Feb | 1 | (a) | Ipswich T | L | 1-2 | Whelan | 20,551 |
| 29 | | 9 | (h) | Manchester U | D | 1-1 | Wark | 35,064 |
| 30 | | 22 | (h) | Everton | L | 0-2 | | 45,445 |
| 31 | Mar | 2 | (a) | Tottenham H | W | 2-1 | Molby, Rush | 16,436 |
| 32 | | 8 | (h) | QPR | W | 4-1 | McMahon 2, Rush, Wark | 26,219 |
| 33 | | 15 | (a) | Southampton | W | 2-1 | Wark, Rush | 19,784 |
| 34 | | 22 | (h) | Oxford U | W | 6-0 | Rush 2, Lawrenson, Whelan, Molby 2 (1 pen) | 37,861 |
| 35 | | 29 | (a) | Sheffield W | D | 0-0 | | 37,946 |
| 36 | | 31 | (h) | Manchester C | W | 2-0 | McMahon 2 | 43,316 |
| 37 | Apr | 12 | (h) | Coventry C | W | 5-0 | Whelan 3, Molby, Rush | 42,729 |
| 38 | | 16 | (a) | Luton T | W | 1-0 | Johnston | 15,390 |
| 39 | | 19 | (a) | West Brom A | W | 2-1 | Dalglish, Rush | 22,010 |
| 40 | | 26 | (h) | Birmingham C | W | 5-0 | Rush, Gillespie 3 (1 pen), Molby | 42,021 |
| 41 | | 30 | (a) | Leicester C | W | 2-0 | Rush, Whelan | 27,797 |
| 42 | May | 3 | (a) | Chelsea | W | 1-0 | Dalglish | 43,900 |

FINAL LEAGUE POSITION : 1st in Division One

Appearances

Sub. Appearances

Goals

| Grobbelaar | Neal | Kennedy | Lawrenson | Whelan | Hansen | Dalglish | Nicol | Rush | Molby | Beglin | Walsh | Johnston | Lee | McMahon | MacDonald | Wark | Gillespie | |
|---|---|---|---|---|---|---|---|---|---|---|---|---|---|---|---|---|---|---|
| 1 | 2 | 3 | 4 | 5 | 6 | 7 | 8 | 9 | 10 | 11 | | | | | | | | 1 |
| 1 | 2 | 3 | 4 | 5 | 6 | | 8 | 9 | 10 | 11 | 7* | 12 | | | | | | 2 |
| 1 | 2 | 3 | 4 | 5 | 6 | 7* | 8 | 9 | 10 | 11 | | 12 | | | | | | 3 |
| 1 | 2* | 3 | 4 | 5 | 6 | | 8 | 9 | 10 | | 12 | 7 | 11 | | | | | 4 |
| 1 | 2 | 3 | 4 | 5 | 6 | | 8 | 9 | 10 | | | 7 | 11 | | | | | 5 |
| 1 | 2 | 3 | 4 | 5 | 6 | | 8 | 9 | 10 | | | 7 | 11 | | | | | 6 |
| 1 | 2 | 3 | 4 | 5 | 6 | | 8 | 9 | 10 | | | 7 | 11 | | | | | 7 |
| 1 | 2 | 3 | 4 | 5* | 6 | | 8 | 9 | 10 | | 12 | 7 | | 11 | | | | 8 |
| 1 | 12 | | 4 | 5 | 6 | 7 | 2* | 9 | 10 | 3 | | 8 | | 11 | | | | 9 |
| 1 | 2 | | 4 | 5 | 6 | 7 | | 9 | 10 | 3 | | 8 | | 11* | 12 | | | 10 |
| 1 | 2 | | 4 | 5 | 6 | | | 9 | 10 | 3 | 7 | 8 | | 11 | | | | 11 |
| 1 | 2 | | 4 | 5 | | 7 | | 9 | 10 | 3 | | 8 | | 11 | 12 | 6* | | 12 |
| 1 | | | 4 | 5 | 6 | | 2 | 9 | 10 | 3 | | 8 | | 11 | 12 | 7* | | 13 |
| 1 | | | 4 | 5 | 6 | 7 | 2 | | 10 | 3 | 9 | 8 | | 11 | | | | 14 |
| 1 | | | 4 | 5 | 6 | 12 | 2 | 9 | 10 | 3 | 7 | 8* | | 11 | | | | 15 |
| 1 | 12 | | 4 | 5 | 6 | | 2 | 9 | 10 | 3 | 7 | 8 | | 11* | | | | 16 |
| 1 | | | 4 | 5* | 6 | 12 | 2 | 9 | 10 | 3 | 7 | 8 | | 11 | | | | 17 |
| 1 | | | 4 | 5 | 6 | | 2 | 9 | 10 | 3 | 7 | 8 | | 11 | | | | 18 |
| 1 | | | 4 | 5 | 6 | | 2 | 9 | 10 | 3 | 7 | 8 | | 11 | | | | 19 |
| 1 | | | 4 | | 6 | | 2 | 9 | 10 | 3 | 7 | 8 | 5 | 11 | | | | 20 |
| 1 | | | 4 | | 6 | | 2 | 9 | 10 | 3 | 7 | 8 | 5* | 11 | 12 | | | 21 |
| 1 | | | 4 | | 6 | 12 | 2 | 9 | | 3 | 7 | 8 | 5 | 11 | | 10* | | 22 |
| 1 | | | 4 | 5 | 6 | 12 | 2 | 9 | | 3 | 7* | 8 | | 11 | 10 | | | 23 |
| 1 | | | 4 | 5 | 6 | 7 | 2 | 9 | 10 | 3 | | 8* | 12 | 11 | | | | 24 |
| 1 | | | 4 | 5 | 6 | 7* | 2 | 9 | 10 | | 12 | 8 | | 11 | 3 | | | 25 |
| 1 | | | 4 | 5 | 6 | | 2 | 9 | 10 | | 7 | 8 | | 11 | 3 | | | 26 |
| 1 | | | 4 | 5 | 6 | | 2 | 9 | 10 | | 7 | 8 | | | 11 | 3 | | 27 |
| 1 | | | 4 | 5 | 6 | | 2 | | 10 | 3 | 7 | 8* | 9 | | | 12 | 11 | 28 |
| 1 | | | 4 | 5 | 6 | | | 9 | 10 | 3 | 7* | 8 | 2 | | | 12 | 11 | 29 |
| 1 | | | 4 | 5 | 6 | | | 9 | 10* | 3 | | 8 | 2 | 11 | 12 | | 7 | 30 |
| 1 | | | 4 | 5 | 6 | | | 9 | 10 | 3 | | 8 | 2 | 11 | | | 7 | 31 |
| 1 | | | 4 | 5 | 6 | 7 | | 9 | 10 | 3 | | 12 | 2 | 11 | 8* | | | 32 |
| 1 | | | 4 | 5 | 6 | | | 9 | 10 | 3 | | 7 | 2 | | 11 | 8 | | 33 |
| 1 | | | 4* | 5 | 6 | 7 | 12 | 9 | 10 | 3 | | 8 | | 11 | | | 2 | 34 |
| 1 | | | | 5 | 6 | | 4 | 9 | 10 | 3 | 7* | 8 | | 11 | 12 | | 2 | 35 |
| 1 | | | | 5 | 6 | 7 | 4 | 9 | 10 | 3 | | 8 | | 11 | | | 2 | 36 |
| 1 | | | | 5 | 6 | 7 | 4 | 9* | 10 | 3 | | 8 | | | 12 | 11 | 2 | 37 |
| 1 | | | | 5 | 6 | 7 | 4 | 9 | 10 | 3 | | 8 | 12 | | 11 | | 2* | 38 |
| 1 | 2 | | | 5 | 6 | 7 | 4 | 9 | 10 | 3 | | 8 | | | 11 | | 2 | 39 |
| 1 | | | 12 | 5* | 6 | 7 | 4 | 9 | 10 | 3 | | 8 | | | 11 | | 2 | 40 |
| 1 | | | 12 | 5 | 6 | 7 | 4 | 9* | 10 | 3 | | 8 | | | 11 | | 2 | 41 |
| 1 | | | 10 | 5 | 6 | 7 | 4 | 9 | | 3 | | 8 | | | 11 | | 2 | 42 |
| 42 | 11 | 8 | 36 | 39 | 41 | 17 | 33 | 40 | 39 | 34 | 17 | 38 | 13 | 23 | 10 | 7 | 14 | |
| | 2 | 2 | | 4 | 1 | | | | | 3 | 3 | 2 | | 7 | 2 | | | |
| | 1 | | 3 | 10 | | 3 | 4 | 22 | 14 | 1 | 11 | 7 | | 6 | 1 | 3 | 3 | |

115

# 1986-87

| | | | | | | | | |
|---|---|---|---|---|---|---|---|---|
| 1 | Aug | 23 | (a) | Newcastle U | W | 2-0 | Rush 2 | 33,306 |
| 2 | | 25 | (h) | Manchester C | D | 0-0 | | 39,989 |
| 3 | | 30 | (h) | Arsenal | W | 2-1 | Molby (pen), Rush | 38,637 |
| 4 | Sep | 3 | (a) | Leicester C | L | 1-2 | Dalglish | 16,344 |
| 5 | | 6 | (a) | West Ham U | W | 5-2 | Whelan, Johnston, Dalglish 2, Rush | 29,807 |
| 6 | | 13 | (h) | Charlton A | W | 2-0 | Molby (pen), Rush | 37,413 |
| 7 | | 20 | (a) | Southampton | L | 1-2 | McMahon | 20,452 |
| 8 | | 27 | (h) | Aston Villa | D | 3-3 | Wark 2 (1 pen), McMahon | 38,298 |
| 9 | Oct | 4 | (a) | Wimbledon | W | 3-1 | Molby, Rush 2 | 15,978 |
| 10 | | 11 | (h) | Tottenham H | L | 0-1 | | 43,139 |
| 11 | | 18 | (h) | Oxford U | W | 4-0 | Rush 2, Dalglish, Molby (pen) | 34,512 |
| 12 | | 25 | (a) | Luton T | L | 1-4 | Molby (pen) | 13,140 |
| 13 | Nov | 1 | (h) | Norwich C | W | 6-2 | Nicol, Walsh 3, Rush 2 | 36,916 |
| 14 | | 8 | (a) | QPR | W | 3-1 | Rush, Nicol, Johnston | 24,045 |
| 15 | | 16 | (h) | Sheffield W | D | 1-1 | Rush | 28,020 |
| 16 | | 23 | (a) | Everton | D | 0-0 | | 48,247 |
| 17 | | 29 | (h) | Coventry C | W | 2-0 | Molby (pen), Wark | 31,614 |
| 18 | Dec | 6 | (a) | Watford | L | 0-2 | | 23,954 |
| 19 | | 14 | (h) | Chelsea | W | 3-0 | Whelan, Rush, Nicol | 25,856 |
| 20 | | 20 | (a) | Charlton A | D | 0-0 | | 16,564 |
| 21 | | 26 | (h) | Manchester U | L | 0-1 | | 40,663 |
| 22 | | 27 | (a) | Sheffield W | W | 1-0 | Rush | 40,959 |
| 23 | Jan | 1 | (a) | Nottingham F | D | 1-1 | Rush | 32,854 |
| 24 | | 3 | (h) | West Ham U | W | 1-0 | McMahon | 41,286 |
| 25 | | 17 | (a) | Manchester C | W | 1-0 | Rush | 35,336 |
| 26 | | 24 | (h) | Newcastle U | W | 2-0 | Walsh, Rush | 38,054 |
| 27 | Feb | 14 | (h) | Leicester C | W | 4-3 | Walsh, Rush 3 | 34,259 |
| 28 | | 21 | (a) | Aston Villa | D | 2-2 | Johnston, Walsh | 32,093 |
| 29 | | 28 | (h) | Southampton | W | 1-0 | Aldridge | 33,133 |
| 30 | Mar | 7 | (h) | Luton T | W | 2-0 | Molby (pen), Donaghy (og) | 32,433 |
| 31 | | 10 | (a) | Arsenal | W | 1-0 | Rush | 47,777 |
| 32 | | 14 | (a) | Oxford U | W | 3-1 | Wark 2, Rush | 14,211 |
| 33 | | 18 | (h) | QPR | W | 2-1 | Rush 2 | 28,988 |
| 34 | | 22 | (a) | Tottenham H | L | 0-1 | | 32,763 |
| 35 | | 28 | (h) | Wimbledon | L | 1-2 | Dalglish | 36,409 |
| 36 | Apr | 11 | (a) | Norwich C | L | 1-2 | Rush | 22,878 |
| 37 | | 18 | (h) | Nottingham F | W | 3-0 | Dalglish, Whelan, Ablett | 37,359 |
| 38 | | 20 | (a) | Manchester U | L | 0-1 | | 54,103 |
| 39 | | 25 | (h) | Everton | W | 3-1 | McMahon, Rush 2 | 44,827 |
| 40 | May | 2 | (a) | Coventry C | L | 0-1 | | 26,700 |
| 41 | | 4 | (h) | Watford | W | 1-0 | Rush | 40,150 |
| 42 | | 9 | (a) | Chelsea | D | 3-3 | Rush, McMahon, Aldridge | 29,245 |

FINAL LEAGUE POSITION : 2nd in Division One

Appearances

Sub. Appearances

Goals

Chart of player appearances (shirt numbers by match). Column headers are rotated in the original. Match number shown at right.

| Hooper | Venison | Gillespie | Lawrenson | Whelan | Hansen | McMahon | Johnston | Rush | Molby | MacDonald | Dalglish | Beglin | Nicol | Grobbelaar | Wark | Walsh | Ablett | Irvine | Aldridge | Spackman | No. |
|---|---|---|---|---|---|---|---|---|---|---|---|---|---|---|---|---|---|---|---|---|---|
| 1 | 2 | 3 | 4 | 5 | 6 | 7 | 8* | 9 | 10 | 11 | 12 |  |  |  |  |  |  |  |  |  | 1 |
| 1 | 2 | 3 | 4 | 5 | 6 | 11* | 8 | 9 | 10 | 12 | 7 |  |  |  |  |  |  |  |  |  | 2 |
| 1 | 2 | 3 | 4 | 5 | 6 | 11 | 8 | 9 | 10 |  | 7 |  |  |  |  |  |  |  |  |  | 3 |
| 1 | 2 | 3 | 4 | 5 | 6 | 11* | 8 | 9 | 10 | 7 | 12 |  |  |  |  |  |  |  |  |  | 4 |
| 1 | 2 | 4 | 10 | 5 | 6* | 11 | 8 | 9 |  | 7 | 12 | 3 |  |  |  |  |  |  |  |  | 5 |
| 1 | 2 | 6 | 4 | 5 |  | 11 | 8 | 9 | 10* | 12 | 7 | 3 |  |  |  |  |  |  |  |  | 6 |
| 1 | 2 | 6 | 4 | 5 |  | 11 |  | 9 | 10 | 12 | 7 | 3 | 8* |  |  |  |  |  |  |  | 7 |
|  | 12 | 2 | 4 | 5 | 6 | 11 |  | 9 |  |  | 7 | 3 | 8* | 1 | 10 |  |  |  |  |  | 8 |
|  | 2 |  | 4 | 5 | 6 | 11 |  | 9 | 10 |  |  | 3 | 8 | 1 |  | 7 |  |  |  |  | 9 |
|  | 5 | 2 | 4* |  | 6 | 11 |  | 9 | 10 |  | 7 | 3 | 8 | 1 | 12 |  |  |  |  |  | 10 |
|  | 3 | 2 | 4 | 5 | 6 | 11 |  | 9 | 10 |  | 7 |  | 8* | 1 | 12 |  |  |  |  |  | 11 |
|  | 2* |  | 4 | 5 | 6 | 11 | 12 | 9 | 10 |  |  | 3 | 8 | 1 |  | 7 |  |  |  |  | 12 |
|  |  | 2 | 4 | 5 | 6 | 11 |  | 9 | 10 |  | 12 | 3 | 8* | 1 |  | 7 |  |  |  |  | 13 |
|  |  | 2 | 4 |  | 6 | 11 | 5 | 9 | 10 |  |  | 3 | 8 | 1 |  | 7 |  |  |  |  | 14 |
|  |  | 2 | 4 |  | 6 | 11 | 5 | 9 | 10 |  |  | 3 | 8 | 1 |  | 7 |  |  |  |  | 15 |
|  |  | 2 | 4 | 5 | 6 | 11 |  | 9 | 10 |  |  | 3 | 8 | 1 |  | 7 |  |  |  |  | 16 |
|  |  | 2 | 4 | 5 | 6 | 11 |  | 9 | 10* |  |  | 3 | 8 | 1 | 12 | 7 |  |  |  |  | 17 |
|  | 12 | 2 | 4 | 5 | 6 | 11* |  | 9 |  |  |  | 3 | 8 | 1 | 10 | 7 |  |  |  |  | 18 |
|  | 10 | 2 | 4 | 5 | 6 | 11 |  | 9 |  |  | 12 | 3 | 8 | 1 |  | 7* |  |  |  |  | 19 |
|  |  | 2 | 4 | 5 |  | 11 |  | 9 |  |  |  | 3 | 8 | 1 | 10 | 7* | 6 | 12 |  |  | 20 |
|  | 8 | 2 | 4 | 5 | 6 | 11 |  | 9 | 10 |  | 7 | 3 |  | 1 |  |  |  |  |  |  | 21 |
|  | 8 | 2 | 4 | 5 | 6 | 11 |  | 9 | 10 |  |  | 3 |  | 1 |  | 7 |  |  |  |  | 22 |
|  | 8 | 2 | 4 | 5 | 6 | 11 |  | 9 | 10 |  |  | 3 |  | 1 |  | 7 |  |  |  |  | 23 |
|  |  | 2 | 4 | 5 | 6 | 11 | 8 | 9 | 10 |  |  | 3 |  | 1 |  | 7 |  |  |  |  | 24 |
|  |  | 2 | 4 | 5 | 6 | 11 | 8 | 9 | 10 |  |  | 3 |  | 1 |  | 7 |  |  |  |  | 25 |
|  | 3 | 2 | 4 | 5 | 6 |  | 8 | 9 | 10 |  |  |  |  | 1 | 11 | 7 |  |  |  |  | 26 |
|  | 3 | 2 | 4 | 5 | 6 | 11* | 8 | 9 | 10 | 12 |  |  |  | 1 |  | 7 |  |  |  |  | 27 |
|  | 3 | 2 | 4 | 5 | 6 | 11 | 8* | 9 | 10 |  |  |  |  | 1 |  | 7 |  |  | 12 |  | 28 |
|  | 3 | 2* | 4 | 5 | 6 |  | 8 | 9 | 10 |  |  |  |  | 1 |  |  | 12 | 11 | 7 |  | 29 |
|  | 3 |  | 4 | 5 | 6 | 11 | 8 | 9 | 10 |  |  |  |  | 1 |  | 7 |  |  | 2 |  | 30 |
|  | 3 |  | 4 | 5 | 6 | 11 | 8 | 9 | 10 |  |  |  |  | 1 |  | 7* |  |  | 12 | 2 | 31 |
|  | 3 |  | 4 | 5 | 6 |  | 8 | 9 | 10 |  | 7 |  |  | 1 | 11 |  |  |  | 2 |  | 32 |
|  | 3 |  | 4 | 5 | 6 |  | 8 | 9 | 10 |  |  |  |  | 1 | 11* | 7 |  |  | 12 | 2 | 33 |
|  | 3 | 11 | 4 | 5 | 6 |  | 8 | 9 | 10* |  |  |  |  | 1 |  | 7 |  |  | 12 | 2 | 34 |
|  | 3 | 2 | 4* | 5 | 6 | 11 | 8 | 9 |  |  | 7 |  |  | 1 |  |  |  |  | 12 | 10 | 35 |
|  | 3 | 2 |  | 5 | 6 | 11 | 8 | 9 | 10 |  |  |  |  | 1 | 4 | 7 |  |  |  |  | 36 |
|  | 3 | 2 |  | 5 | 6 | 11 | 8 | 9* |  |  | 7 |  |  | 1 | 10 | 4 |  |  | 12 |  | 37 |
|  | 3 | 2 |  | 5 | 6 | 11 | 8 | 9 |  |  |  |  |  | 1 | 7 | 10 |  |  | 4 |  | 38 |
| 1 | 3 | 2 |  | 5 | 6 | 11 | 8 | 9 | 10 |  |  |  |  |  |  | 7 |  |  | 4 |  | 39 |
| 1 | 3 | 2 |  | 5 | 6 | 11 | 8 | 9 | 10 |  |  |  |  |  |  | 7* |  |  | 12 | 4 | 40 |
| 1 | 3 | 2 |  | 5 | 6 | 11 | 8 | 9 | 10* |  | 7 |  |  |  |  |  |  |  | 12 | 4 | 41 |
| 1 | 3 | 2 |  | 5 | 6 | 11 | 8 | 9 | 10 |  |  |  |  |  |  | 7 |  |  |  | 4 | 42 |
| 11 | 31 | 37 | 35 | 39 | 39 | 37 | 27 | 42 | 34 | 3 | 12 | 20 | 14 | 31 | 8 | 23 | 5 |  | 2 | 12 |  |
|  | 2 |  |  |  |  |  | 1 |  |  | 3 | 6 |  |  | 3 |  |  | 2 | 8 |  |  |  |
|  |  |  | 3 |  | 5 | 3 | 30 | 7 |  | 6 |  | 3 |  | 5 | 6 | 1 |  | 2 |  |  |  |

117

# 1987-88

| | | | | | | | | |
|---|---|---|---|---|---|---|---|---|
| 1 | Aug | 15 | (a) | Arsenal | W | 2-1 | Aldridge, Nicol | 54703 |
| 2 | | 29 | (a) | Coventry C | W | 4-1 | Nicol 2, Aldridge (pen), Beardsley | 27637 |
| 3 | Sep | 5 | (a) | West Ham U | D | 1-1 | Aldridge (pen) | 29865 |
| 4 | | 12 | (h) | Oxford U | W | 2-0 | Aldridge, Barnes | 42266 |
| 5 | | 15 | (h) | Charlton Ath | W | 3-2 | Aldridge (pen), Hansen, McMahon | 36637 |
| 6 | | 20 | (a) | Newcastle U | W | 4-1 | Nicol 3, Aldridge | 24141 |
| 7 | | 29 | (h) | Derby Co | W | 4-0 | Aldridge 3 (2 pens), Beardsley | 43405 |
| 8 | Oct | 3 | (h) | Portsmouth | W | 4-0 | Beardsley, McMahon, Aldridge, Whelan (pen) | 44366 |
| 9 | | 17 | (h) | QPR | W | 4-0 | Johnston, Aldridge (pen), Barnes 2 | 43735 |
| 10 | | 24 | (a) | Luton T | W | 1-0 | Gillespie | 12452 |
| 11 | Nov | 1 | (h) | Everton | W | 2-0 | McMahon, Beardsley | 44760 |
| 12 | | 4 | (a) | Wimbledon | D | 1-1 | Houghton | 13454 |
| 13 | | 15 | (a) | Manchester U | D | 1-1 | Aldridge | 47106 |
| 14 | | 21 | (h) | Norwich C | D | 0-0 | | 37446 |
| 15 | | 24 | (h) | Watford | W | 4-0 | McMahon, Houghton, Aldridge, Barnes | 32396 |
| 16 | | 28 | (a) | Tottenham H | W | 2-0 | McMahon, Johnston | 47362 |
| 17 | Dec | 6 | (h) | Chelsea | W | 2-1 | Aldridge (pen), McMahon | 31211 |
| 18 | | 12 | (a) | Southampton | D | 2-2 | Barnes 2 | 19507 |
| 19 | | 19 | (h) | Sheffield W | W | 1-0 | Gillespie | 35383 |
| 20 | | 26 | (a) | Oxford U | W | 3-0 | Aldridge, Barnes, McMahon | 13680 |
| 21 | | 28 | (h) | Newcastle U | W | 4-0 | McMahon, Aldridge 2 (1 pen), Houghton | 44637 |
| 22 | Jan | 1 | (h) | Coventry C | W | 4-0 | Beardsley 2, Aldridge, Houghton | 38790 |
| 23 | | 4 | (h) | Arsenal | W | 2-0 | Aldridge, Beardsley | 44294 |
| 24 | | 23 | (a) | Charlton A | W | 2-0 | Beardsley, Barnes | 28095 |
| 25 | Feb | 6 | (h) | West Ham U | D | 0-0 | | 42049 |
| 26 | | 13 | (a) | Watford | W | 4-1 | Beardsley 2, Aldridge, Barnes | 23838 |
| 27 | | 27 | (a) | Portsmouth | W | 2-0 | Barnes 2 | 28197 |
| 28 | Mar | 5 | (a) | QPR | W | 1-0 | Barnes | 23171 |
| 29 | | 16 | (a) | Derby Co | D | 1-1 | Johnston | 26356 |
| 30 | | 20 | (a) | Everton | L | 0-1 | | 44162 |
| 31 | | 26 | (h) | Wimbledon | W | 2-1 | Aldridge, Barnes | 36464 |
| 32 | Apr | 2 | (a) | Nottingham F | L | 1-2 | Aldridge (pen) | 29188 |
| 33 | | 4 | (h) | Manchester U | D | 3-3 | Beardsley, Gillespie, McMahon | 43497 |
| 34 | | 13 | (h) | Nottingham F | W | 5-0 | Houghton, Aldridge 2, Beardsley, Gillespie | 39535 |
| 35 | | 20 | (a) | Norwich C | D | 0-0 | | 22509 |
| 36 | | 23 | (h) | Tottenham H | W | 1-0 | Beardsley | 44798 |
| 37 | | 30 | (a) | Chelsea | D | 1-1 | Barnes | 35625 |
| 38 | May | 2 | (h) | Southampton | D | 1-1 | Aldridge | 37610 |
| 39 | | 7 | (a) | Sheffield W | W | 5-1 | Johnston 2, Barnes, Beardsley | 35893 |
| 40 | | 9 | (h) | Luton T | D | 1-1 | Aldridge | 30374 |

FINAL LEAGUE POSITION : 1st in Division One

Appearances

Sub. Appearances

Goals

118

| Grobbelaar | Gillespie | Venison | Nicol | Whelan | Hansen | Beardsley | Aldridge | Johnston | Barnes | McMahon | Walsh | Spackman | Wark | Lawrenson | Houghton | Ablett | Hooper | Molby | Watson | Dalglish | MacDonald | No. |
|---|---|---|---|---|---|---|---|---|---|---|---|---|---|---|---|---|---|---|---|---|---|---|
| 1 | 2 | 3 | 4 | 5 | 6 | 7* | 8 | 9 | 10 | 11 | 12 |  |  |  |  |  |  |  |  |  |  | 1 |
| 1 | 2 | 3 | 4 | 5 | 6 | 7 | 8* | 9 | 10 | 11 | 12 |  |  |  |  |  |  |  |  |  |  | 2 |
| 1 | 2 | 3 | 4 | 5 | 6 | 7 | 8 |  | 10 | 11 |  | 9 |  |  |  |  |  |  |  |  |  | 3 |
| 1 | 2 | 3 | 4 | 5 | 6 | 7 | 8* |  | 10 | 11† | 12 | 9 | 14 |  |  |  |  |  |  |  |  | 4 |
| 1 | 2 | 3 | 4 | 5 | 6 | 7 | 8 |  | 10 | 11 |  | 9* |  | 12 |  |  |  |  |  |  |  | 5 |
| 1 | 2* | 3 | 4 | 5 | 6 | 7 | 8 |  | 10 | 11 |  | 12 |  | 9 |  |  |  |  |  |  |  | 6 |
| 1 | 2 | 3 | 4† | 5 | 6 | 7 | 8 | 9* | 10 | 11 | 12 |  | 14 |  |  |  |  |  |  |  |  | 7 |
| 1 | 2 | 3 | 4 | 5 | 6 | 7 | 8 | 9* | 10 | 11† | 12 |  | 14 |  |  |  |  |  |  |  |  | 8 |
| 1 | 2 | 3 | 4 | 5 | 6 | 7 | 8 | 9† | 10 | 11* | 12 |  | 14 |  |  |  |  |  |  |  |  | 9 |
| 1 | 2 | 3 | 4 | 5 | 6 | 7 | 8 |  | 10 | 11 |  |  |  |  | 9 |  |  |  |  |  |  | 10 |
| 1 | 2 |  | 4 | 5 | 6 | 7 | 8 | 9 | 10 | 11 |  |  |  | 3 |  |  |  |  |  |  |  | 11 |
| 1 | 2 |  | 4 | 5 | 6 | 7 | 8 | 9* | 10 | 11 |  |  |  | 3 | 12 |  |  |  |  |  |  | 12 |
| 1 | 2 |  | 4 | 5 | 6 | 7 | 8 | 9 | 10 | 11 |  |  |  | 3 |  |  |  |  |  |  |  | 13 |
| 1 | 2 |  | 4 | 5 | 6 | 7* | 8 | 12 | 10 | 11 |  |  |  | 3 | 9 |  |  |  |  |  |  | 14 |
| 1 | 2* |  | 4 | 5 | 6 | 7 | 8† |  | 10 | 11 | 14 | 12 |  | 3 | 9 |  |  |  |  |  |  | 15 |
| 1 | 2* |  | 4 | 5 | 6 |  | 8 | 14 | 10 | 11 | 7† | 12 |  | 3 | 9 |  |  |  |  |  |  | 16 |
| 1 | 2 |  | 4 | 5 | 6 | 7 | 8* | 12 | 10 | 11 |  |  |  | 3 | 9 |  |  |  |  |  |  | 17 |
| 1 | 2 |  | 4 | 5 | 6 | 7 | 8 |  | 10 | 11 |  |  |  | 3* | 9 | 12 |  |  |  |  |  | 18 |
| 1 | 2 | 3 | 4 | 5 | 6 | 7* | 8 | 12 | 10 | 11 |  |  |  |  | 9 |  |  |  |  |  |  | 19 |
| 1 | 2 | 3 | 4 | 5 | 6 | 7 | 8 | 12 | 10† | 11* |  |  |  | 14 | 9 |  |  |  |  |  |  | 20 |
| 1 | 2 | 3 | 4 | 5* | 6 | 7 | 8 | 12 | 10† | 11 |  |  |  | 14 | 9 |  |  |  |  |  |  | 21 |
| 1 | 2 | 3* | 4 | 5 | 6 | 7 | 8 |  | 10 | 11† |  |  |  | 14 | 9 | 12 |  |  |  |  |  | 22 |
|  | 2 |  | 4 | 5 | 6 | 7 | 8 |  | 10 | 11 |  | 12 |  | 3* | 9 |  | 1 |  |  |  |  | 23 |
|  | 2 | 3† | 4 | 5 | 6 | 7 | 8* | 12 | 10 | 11 |  |  |  | 14 | 9 |  | 1 |  |  |  |  | 24 |
| 1 |  | 3 | 4 |  | 6 | 7 | 8* | 12 | 10 | 11 |  |  |  | 5 | 9 | 2 |  |  |  |  |  | 25 |
| 1 |  | 3 | 4 |  | 6 | 7 | 8 | 12 | 10* | 11† |  |  |  | 5 | 9 | 2 |  | 14 |  |  |  | 26 |
| 1 |  | 3 | 4 |  | 6 | 7 | 8 |  | 10 | 11 |  |  |  | 5 | 9 | 2 |  |  |  |  |  | 27 |
| 1 |  |  | 4 |  | 6 | 7 |  | 8 | 10 | 11 |  |  |  | 5 | 9 | 2 |  |  | 3 |  |  | 28 |
| 1 | 2 |  | 4 |  | 6 | 7 |  | 8 | 10 | 11* |  |  |  | 5 | 9 | 3 |  | 12 |  |  |  | 29 |
| 1 | 2 |  | 4 |  | 6 | 7 |  | 8 | 10 | 11 |  |  |  | 5* | 9 | 3 |  | 12 |  |  |  | 30 |
| 1 | 2 |  | 4 |  | 6 | 7 | 8* | 9 | 10 | 11† |  |  |  | 5 |  | 3 |  | 14 |  | 12 |  | 31 |
| 1 | 2 |  | 4 |  | 6 | 12 | 8† | 9 | 10 | 11 |  |  |  | 5 | 14 | 3 |  | 7* |  |  |  | 32 |
| 1 | 2 |  | 4 |  | 6 | 7 | 8* | 12 | 10 | 11 |  |  |  | 5 | 9 | 3 |  |  |  |  |  | 33 |
| 1 | 2 |  | 4 |  | 6 | 7 | 8 | 12 | 10 | 11† |  |  |  | 5 | 9* | 3 |  | 14 |  |  |  | 34 |
| 1 | 2 |  | 4 |  | 6 | 7 | 8 | 10 |  | 11 |  |  |  | 5 | 9 | 3 |  |  |  |  |  | 35 |
| 1 | 2 |  | 4 |  | 6 | 7 | 8 | 10 |  | 11 |  |  |  | 5 | 9 | 3 |  |  |  |  |  | 36 |
| 1 |  |  | 4 | 3 | 6 | 12 | 8* | 7 | 10 | 11 |  |  |  | 5 | 9 |  |  |  | 2 |  |  | 37 |
| 1 | 2 |  | 4 | 14 | 6 | 7 | 8 | 12 | 10 | 11* |  |  |  | 5† | 9 | 3 |  |  |  |  |  | 38 |
| 1 | 2 |  | 4 | 12 | 6† | 7 |  | 8 | 10 | 11* |  |  |  | 5 | 9 | 3 |  |  |  | 14 |  | 39 |
| 1 | 2 |  | 4 |  | 6 |  | 8 | 7* | 10 | 11 |  |  |  | 5* | 9 | 3 |  |  |  |  | 14 | 40 |
| 38 | 35 | 18 | 40 | 26 | 39 | 36 | 36 | 18 | 38 | 40 | 1 | 19 |  | 10 | 26 | 15 | 2 | 1 | 2 |  |  |  |
|  |  |  | 2 |  | 2 |  | 1 |  |  |  | 7 | 8 | 1 | 4 | 2 | 2 |  | 6 |  | 2 | 1 |  |
|  | 4 |  | 6 | 1 | 1 | 15 | 26 | 5 | 15 | 9 |  |  |  | 5 |  |  |  |  |  |  |  |  |

119

# 1988-89

| | | | | | | | | |
|---|---|---|---|---|---|---|---|---|
| 1 | Aug | 27 | (a) | Charlton A | W | 3-0 | Aldridge 3 | 21,389 |
| 2 | Sep | 3 | (h) | Manchester U | W | 1-0 | Molby (pen) | 42,026 |
| 3 | | 10 | (a) | Aston Villa | D | 1-1 | Houghton | 41,409 |
| 4 | | 17 | (h) | Tottenham H | D | 1-1 | Beardsley | 40,929 |
| 5 | | 24 | (a) | Southampton | W | 3-1 | Aldridge, Beardsley, Molby (pen) | 21,046 |
| 6 | Oct | 1 | (h) | Newcastle U | L | 1-2 | Gillespie | 39,139 |
| 7 | | 8 | (a) | Luton T | L | 0-1 | | 12,117 |
| 8 | | 22 | (h) | Coventry C | D | 0-0 | | 38,742 |
| 9 | | 26 | (a) | Nottingham F | L | 1-2 | Rush | 29,755 |
| 10 | | 29 | (a) | West Ham U | W | 2-0 | Rush, Beardsley | 30,198 |
| 11 | Nov | 5 | (h) | Middlesbrough | W | 3-0 | Rush, Aldridge, Beardsley | 39,489 |
| 12 | | 12 | (h) | Millwall | D | 1-1 | Nicol | 41,966 |
| 13 | | 19 | (a) | QPR | W | 1-0 | Aldridge | 20,063 |
| 14 | | 26 | (h) | Wimbledon | D | 1-1 | Houghton | 36,189 |
| 15 | Dec | 4 | (a) | Arsenal | D | 1-1 | Barnes | 31,863 |
| 16 | | 11 | (h) | Everton | D | 1-1 | Houghton | 42,372 |
| 17 | | 17 | (h) | Norwich C | L | 0-1 | | 34,325 |
| 18 | | 26 | (a) | Derby Co | W | 1-0 | Rush | 25,213 |
| 19 | Jan | 1 | (a) | Manchester U | L | 1-3 | Barnes | 44,745 |
| 20 | | 3 | (h) | Aston Villa | W | 1-0 | Whelan | 39,014 |
| 21 | | 14 | (a) | Sheffield W | D | 2-2 | Nicol, Aldridge | 31,524 |
| 22 | | 21 | (h) | Southampton | W | 2-0 | Aldridge, Rush | 35,565 |
| 23 | Feb | 4 | (a) | Newcastle U | D | 2-2 | Rush, Aldridge | 30,966 |
| 24 | Mar | 1 | (h) | Charlton A | W | 2-0 | Beardsley, Aldridge (pen) | 30,283 |
| 25 | | 11 | (a) | Middlesbrough | W | 4-0 | Beardsley, Houghton, Aldridge, McMahon | 25,197 |
| 26 | | 14 | (h) | Luton T | W | 5-0 | Aldridge 3 (1 pen), Beardsley, McMahon | 31,447 |
| 27 | | 22 | (a) | Coventry C | W | 3-1 | Barnes, Aldridge, Whelan | 23,807 |
| 28 | | 26 | (a) | Tottenham H | W | 2-1 | Aldridge (pen), Beardsley | 30,012 |
| 29 | | 29 | (h) | Derby Co | W | 1-0 | Barnes | 42,518 |
| 30 | Apr | 1 | (a) | Norwich C | W | 1-0 | Whelan | 26,338 |
| 31 | | 8 | (h) | Sheffield W | W | 5-1 | McMahon, Beardsley 2, Houghton, Barnes | 39,672 |
| 32 | | 11 | (a) | Millwall | W | 2-1 | Barnes, Aldridge | 22,130 |
| 33 | May | 3 | (a) | Everton | D | 0-0 | | 45,994 |
| 34 | | 10 | (h) | Nottingham F | W | 1-0 | Aldridge (pen) | 39,793 |
| 35 | | 13 | (a) | Wimbledon | W | 2-1 | Aldridge, Barnes | 14,730 |
| 36 | | 16 | (h) | QPR | W | 2-0 | Aldridge, Whelan | 38,368 |
| 37 | | 23 | (h) | West Ham U | W | 5-1 | Aldridge, Houghton 2, Rush, Barnes | 41,855 |
| 38 | | 26 | (h) | Arsenal | L | 0-2 | | 41,783 |

FINAL LEAGUE POSITION : 2nd in Division One

Appearances

Sub. Appearances

Goals

| Grobbelaar | Gillespie | Venison | Nicol | Whelan | Molby | Beardsley | Aldridge | Houghton | Barnes | McMahon | Rush | Spackman | Ablett | Staunton | Hooper | MacDonald | Burrows | Marsh | Watson | Hansen | |
|---|---|---|---|---|---|---|---|---|---|---|---|---|---|---|---|---|---|---|---|---|---|
| 1 | 2 | 3 | 4 | 5 | 6 | 7* | 8 | 9 | 10 | 11 | 12 | | | | | | | | | | 1 |
| 1 | 2 | 3 | 4 | 5 | 6 | 7 | 8* | 9 | 10 | 11† | 12 | 14 | | | | | | | | | 2 |
| 1 | 2 | 3 | 4 | 5 | 6 | 12 | 8 | 7 | 10* | | 9 | 11 | | | | | | | | | 3 |
| 1 | 2 | | 4 | 5 | 6* | 7 | 8 | 10 | | | 9 | 11 | 3 | 12 | | | | | | | 4 |
| | 2 | 3* | 4 | 5 | 10 | 7 | 8 | 9 | | | | | 11 | 12 | 1 | 6 | | | | | 5 |
| | 2 | | 4 | 5 | 10 | 7 | 8 | 9 | | | 12 | 6 | 3 | 11* | 1 | | | | | | 6 |
| | 2* | 3 | 4 | 5 | 6 | 7 | | 8 | 10 | | 9 | | 12 | | 1 | 11 | | | | | 7 |
| | | 3 | 4 | 5 | | 7 | 12 | 8 | 10 | | 9 | | 2 | | 1 | 11* | 6 | | | | 8 |
| | | 3 | 4 | 5 | | 7 | 12 | 8 | 10 | | 9 | 11* | 2 | | 1 | | 6 | | | | 9 |
| | | 3 | 4 | 5* | | 7 | 8 | 11 | 10 | | 9 | 12 | 2 | | 1 | | 6 | | | | 10 |
| | | 3† | 4 | 5 | | 7 | 8 | 11 | 10 | 12 | 9* | 14 | 2 | | 1 | | 6 | | | | 11 |
| | | | 4 | 5* | | 7 | 8 | 9 | 10 | 11 | | 6 | 2 | 12 | 1 | | 3 | | | | 12 |
| | | | 4 | 5 | | 7 | 8* | 10 | | 11 | 9 | 6 | 2 | 12 | 1 | | 3 | | | | 13 |
| | | 3 | 4 | 5 | | 7 | 12 | 10 | | 11 | 9* | 6 | 2 | 8 | 1 | | | | | | 14 |
| | | | 4 | 5 | | 7 | 8 | 9 | 10 | 11 | 6 | | 2 | 3* | 1 | | 12 | | | | 15 |
| | | 3 | 4 | 5 | | 7 | 8* | 9 | 10 | 11 | 12 | | 2 | | 1 | | 6 | | | | 16 |
| | | 3* | 4 | 5 | | 7 | | 8 | 10 | 11 | 9 | 12 | 2 | | 1 | | 6 | | | | 17 |
| | | | 4 | 5 | | 7 | | 8 | 10 | 11 | 9 | | 2 | 3 | 1 | | 6 | | | | 18 |
| | | | 4 | 5 | 12 | 7 | 8 | 9 | 10 | 11 | | | 2 | 3* | 1 | | 6 | | | | 19 |
| | | | 4 | 5 | 6 | 7 | 8 | 9 | 10 | 11 | | | 2 | | 1 | | 3 | | | | 20 |
| | | | 4 | 5 | 6 | 7 | 12 | 8 | 10 | 11* | 9 | | 2 | | 1 | | 3 | | | | 21 |
| 1 | | | 4 | 5 | 6 | 7 | 8 | 11 | 10 | | 9 | | 2 | | | | 3 | | | | 22 |
| 1 | | | 4 | 5 | 6 | 12 | 8 | 7 | 10 | 11* | 9 | | 2 | | | | 3 | | | | 23 |
| 1 | 5 | | 4 | | 6* | 7 | 8 | 9 | 10 | 11 | | | 2 | | | | 3 | 12 | | | 24 |
| 1 | 6 | | 4 | 5 | | 7 | 8 | 9 | 10 | 11 | | | 2 | 3 | | | | | | | 25 |
| 1 | 6† | | 4 | 5 | | 7 | 8 | 9 | 10* | 11 | | | 2 | 3 | | | 12 | 14 | | | 26 |
| 1 | 6 | | 4 | 5 | | 7 | 8 | 9 | 10 | 11 | | | 2 | 3 | | | | | | | 27 |
| 1 | 6 | | 4 | 5 | | 7 | 8 | 9 | 10 | 11 | | | 2 | 3 | | | | | | | 28 |
| 1 | 6 | | 4 | 5 | | 7 | 8 | 9 | 10 | 11 | | | 2 | 3 | | | | | | | 29 |
| 1 | 6 | | 4 | 5 | | 7 | 8 | 9 | 10 | 11 | | | 2 | 3 | | | | | | | 30 |
| 1 | 6† | 14 | 4 | 5 | | 7 | 8 | 9 | 10 | 11 | | | 2 | 3* | | | 12 | | | | 31 |
| 1 | 6 | | 4 | 5 | | 7 | 8 | 9 | 10 | 11 | | | 2 | 3 | | | | | | | 32 |
| 1 | | | 4 | 5 | | 7 | 8* | 9 | 10 | 11 | 12 | | 2 | 3 | | | | | | 6 | 33 |
| 1 | | | 4 | 5 | | 7* | 8 | 9 | 10 | 11 | 12 | | 2 | | | | 3 | | | 6 | 34 |
| 1 | | | 4 | 5 | | | 8 | 9 | 10 | 11 | 12 | | 2 | 3 | | | | | 7* | 6 | 35 |
| 1 | | | 4 | 5 | | 7 | 8† | 9 | 10 | 11 | 14 | | 2 | 3* | | | 12 | | | 6 | 36 |
| 1 | | 3 | 4 | 5 | | 12 | 8* | 7 | 10 | 11 | 9 | | 2 | | | | 14 | | 6† | 6 | 37 |
| 1 | | | 4 | 5 | | 12 | 8 | 7 | 10 | 11 | 9* | | 2 | 3 | | | | | | 6 | 38 |
| 21 | 15 | 14 | 38 | 37 | 12 | 33 | 31 | 38 | 33 | 28 | 16 | 8 | 34 | 17 | 17 | 3 | 16 | | 1 | 6 | |
| | | 1 | | 1 | 4 | 4 | | | 1 | 8 | 4 | 1 | 4 | | | | 5 | 1 | 1 | | |
| | 1 | | 2 | 4 | 2 | 10 | 21 | 7 | 8 | 3 | 7 | | | | | | | | | | |

# 1989-90

| | | | | | | | | |
|---|---|---|---|---|---|---|---|---|
| 1 | Aug | 19 | (h) | Manchester C | W | 3-1 | Barnes (pen), Beardsley, Nicol | 37,628 |
| 2 | | 23 | (a) | Aston Villa | D | 1-1 | Barnes | 35,796 |
| 3 | | 26 | (a) | Luton T | D | 0-0 | | 11,124 |
| 4 | Sep | 9 | (a) | Derby Co | W | 3-0 | Rush, Barnes (pen), Beardsley | 20,034 |
| 5 | | 12 | (h) | Crystal Palace | W | 9-0 | Nicol 2, McMahon, Rush, Gillespie, Beardsley, Aldridge (pen), Barnes, Hysen | 35,779 |
| 6 | | 16 | (h) | Norwich C | D | 0-0 | | 36,885 |
| 7 | | 23 | (a) | Everton | W | 3-1 | Barnes, Rush 2 | 42,453 |
| 8 | Oct | 14 | (a) | Wimbledon | W | 2-1 | Beardsley, Whelan | 13,510 |
| 9 | | 21 | (a) | Southampton | L | 1-4 | Beardsley (pen) | 20,501 |
| 10 | | 29 | (h) | Tottenham H | W | 1-0 | Barnes | 36,550 |
| 11 | Nov | 4 | (h) | Coventry C | L | 0-1 | | 36,433 |
| 12 | | 11 | (a) | QPR | L | 2-3 | Barnes 2 (1 pen) | 18,804 |
| 13 | | 19 | (a) | Millwall | W | 2-1 | Barnes, Rush | 13,547 |
| 14 | | 26 | (h) | Arsenal | W | 2-1 | McMahon, Barnes | 35,983 |
| 15 | | 29 | (a) | Sheffield W | L | 0-2 | | 32,732 |
| 16 | Dec | 2 | (a) | Manchester C | W | 4-1 | Rush 2, Beardsley, McMahon | 31,641 |
| 17 | | 9 | (h) | Aston Villa | D | 1-1 | Beardsley | 37,435 |
| 18 | | 16 | (a) | Chelsea | W | 5-2 | Beardsley, Rush 2, Houghton, McMahon | 31,005 |
| 19 | | 23 | (h) | Manchester U | D | 0-0 | | 37,426 |
| 20 | | 26 | (h) | Sheffield W | W | 2-1 | Molby, Rush | 37,488 |
| 21 | | 30 | (h) | Charlton A | W | 1-0 | Barnes | 36,678 |
| 22 | Jan | 1 | (a) | Nottingham F | D | 2-2 | Rush 2 | 24,518 |
| 23 | | 13 | (h) | Luton T | D | 2-2 | Barnes, Nicol | 35,312 |
| 24 | | 20 | (a) | Crystal Palace | W | 2-0 | Rush, Beardsley | 29,807 |
| 25 | Feb | 3 | (h) | Everton | W | 2-1 | Barnes, Beardsley (pen) | 38,730 |
| 26 | | 10 | (a) | Norwich C | D | 0-0 | | 20,210 |
| 27 | Mar | 3 | (h) | Millwall | W | 1-0 | Gillespie | 36,427 |
| 28 | | 18 | (a) | Manchester U | W | 2-1 | Barnes 2 (1 pen) | 46,629 |
| 29 | | 21 | (a) | Tottenham H | L | 0-1 | | 25,656 |
| 30 | | 31 | (h) | Southampton | W | 3-2 | Barnes, Osman (og), Rush | 37,027 |
| 31 | Apr | 3 | (h) | Wimbledon | W | 2-1 | Rush, Gillespie | 33,319 |
| 32 | | 11 | (a) | Charlton A | W | 4-0 | Rosenthal 3, Barnes | 13,982 |
| 33 | | 14 | (h) | Nottingham F | D | 2-2 | Rosenthal, McMahon | 37,265 |
| 34 | | 18 | (a) | Arsenal | D | 1-1 | Barnes | 33,395 |
| 35 | | 21 | (h) | Chelsea | W | 4-1 | Rosenthal, Nicol 2, Rush | 38,431 |
| 36 | | 28 | (h) | QPR | W | 2-1 | Rush, Barnes (pen) | 37,758 |
| 37 | May | 1 | (h) | Derby Co | W | 1-0 | Gillespie | 38,038 |
| 38 | | 5 | (a) | Coventry C | W | 6-1 | Rush, Barnes 3, Rosenthal 2 | 23,204 |

FINAL LEAGUE POSITION : 1st in Division One

Appearances

Sub Appearances

Goals

122

| Grobbelaar | Hysen | Burrows | Nicol | Whelan | Hansen | Beardsley | Venison | Rush | Barnes | McMahon | Aldridge | Gillespie | Molby | Staunton | Houghton | Ablett | Marsh | Tanner | Rosenthal | Dalglish | |
|---|---|---|---|---|---|---|---|---|---|---|---|---|---|---|---|---|---|---|---|---|---|
| 1 | 2 | 3 | 4 | 5 | 6 | 7 | 8 | 9 | 10 | 11 | | | | | | | | | | | 1 |
| 1 | 2 | 3 | 4 | 5 | 6 | 7 | 8 | 9 | 10 | 11 | | | | | | | | | | | 2 |
| 1 | 2 | 3 | 4 | 5 | 6 | 7* | | 9 | 10 | 11 | 12 | 8 | | | | | | | | | 3 |
| 1 | 2 | 3 | 4 | 5 | 6 | 7 | | 9 | 10 | 11 | | 8 | | | | | | | | | 4 |
| 1 | 2 | 3 | 4 | 5 | 6 | 7* | | 9 | 10 | 11† | 12 | 8 | 14 | | | | | | | | 5 |
| 1 | 2 | 3 | 4 | 5 | 6 | 7 | | 9 | 10 | 11 | | 8 | | | | | | | | | 6 |
| 1 | 2 | 3 | 4 | 5 | 6 | 7 | 8 | 9 | 10 | 11 | | | | | | | | | | | 7 |
| 1 | 2 | 3 | 4 | 5 | 6 | 7 | 8 | | 10 | 11 | | | | 9 | | | | | | | 8 |
| 1 | 2 | 3 | 4 | 5 | 6 | 7 | 8* | 9 | 10 | 11 | | | | | 12 | | | | | | 9 |
| 1 | 2 | 3 | | 5 | | 7 | 4* | 9 | 10 | 11 | | | | | 12 | 8 | 6 | | | | 10 |
| 1 | 2 | 3 | | 5 | 6 | 7 | | 9 | 10 | 11* | | | | | 12 | 8 | 4 | | | | 11 |
| 1 | 2 | 3 | 4* | 5 | 6 | 7 | | 9 | 10 | 11 | | | | | 12 | 8 | | | | | 12 |
| 1 | 2 | | | 5 | 6 | 7 | | 9 | 10 | 11 | | | | 4 | 3 | 8 | | | | | 13 |
| 1 | 2 | 4 | | 5 | 6 | 12 | 7* | 9 | 10 | 11 | | | | | 3 | 8 | | | | | 14 |
| 1 | | 12 | | 5 | | 7 | | 9 | 10* | 11 | | 2 | 6 | 3 | 8 | 4 | | | | | 15 |
| 1 | 2 | | | 5 | | 7 | | 9 | | 11 | | 6† | 10 | 3* | 8 | 4 | 12 | 14 | | | 16 |
| 1 | 2 | | | 5 | | 7 | | 9 | 10* | 11 | | 6 | 3 | 8 | 4 | | 12 | | | | 17 |
| 1 | 2 | 12 | | 5 | 6 | 7 | 3 | 9 | | 11 | | 10* | | 8 | 4 | | | | | | 18 |
| 1 | 2 | 12 | | 5 | 6* | 7 | 3 | 9 | | 11 | | 10 | | 8 | 4 | | | | | | 19 |
| 1 | 2 | 12 | 4 | 5 | | 7 | 3* | 9 | | 11† | | 10 | 14 | 8 | 6 | | | | | | 20 |
| 1 | 2 | | 4 | 5 | 6 | 12 | 3 | 9 | 10 | 14 | | 11† | | 8 | | 7* | | | | | 21 |
| 1 | 2 | 8 | 4 | 5 | 6 | 7 | 3 | 9 | 10 | 11 | | | | | | | | | | | 22 |
| 1 | 2 | 12 | 4 | 5 | 6 | 7 | 3 | 9 | 10 | 11 | | | | 8* | | | | | | | 23 |
| 1 | 2 | | 4 | 5 | 6 | 7 | 3 | 9 | 10 | 11 | | | | 8 | | | | | | | 24 |
| 1 | 2 | 8 | 4 | 5 | 6 | 7 | 3 | 9 | 10 | 11 | | | | | | | | | | | 25 |
| 1 | 2 | 8 | 4 | 5 | 6 | 7 | 3 | 9 | 10 | 11 | | | | | | | | | | | 26 |
| 1 | | 8* | 4 | 5 | 6 | 7 | 3 | 9 | 10 | 11 | | 2 | | | 12 | | | | | | 27 |
| 1 | 2 | | | 5 | 6 | 7 | 3 | 9 | 10 | 11 | | | | 4 | 8 | | | | | | 28 |
| 1 | 2 | | | 5 | 6 | 7 | 3 | 9 | 10 | 11 | | | | 4 | 8 | | | | | | 29 |
| 1 | 2 | | | 5 | 6 | 7 | 3* | 9 | 10 | 11† | | 12 | | 4 | 8 | | | | 14 | | 30 |
| 1 | 2 | 3 | | 5 | 6 | | | 9 | 10 | 11 | | 4 | | 7 | 8 | | | | | | 31 |
| 1 | | 3 | | 5 | 6 | 2* | | | 10 | 11† | | 12 | 7 | | | 4 | 14 | 8 | 9 | | 32 |
| 1 | 2 | 3 | | 5 | 6 | | | 9 | 10 | 11 | | | | 4 | 12 | | 7* | | 8 | | 33 |
| 1 | 2 | 3 | 4 | 5* | 6 | | | 9 | 10 | 11 | | | 12 | 8† | 7 | | | | 14 | | 34 |
| 1 | 2 | 3 | 4 | | 6 | | | 9 | 10 | 11 | | 5* | | 7 | 12 | | | | 8 | | 35 |
| 1 | 2 | 3* | 4 | | 6† | | 5 | 9 | 10 | 11 | | 14 | | 7 | 12 | | | | 8 | | 36 |
| 1 | 2 | | | | | | 3 | 9 | 10 | 11 | | 5 | 7† | 6* | 8 | 4 | | | 12 | 14 | 37 |
| 1 | 2 | | | | | | 3 | 9 | 10 | 11 | | 5 | 7 | 6 | | 4 | | | 8 | | 38 |
| 38 | 25 | 23 | 21 | 34 | 31 | 27 | 25 | 36 | 34 | 37 | | 11 | 12 | 18 | 16 | 13 | | 2 | 5 | | |
| | | 3 | 2 | | | | 2 | | | | 1 | 2 | 2 | 5 | 2 | 3 | 2 | 2 | 2 | 3 | 1 |
| | | 1 | 6 | | 1 | 10 | | 18 | 22 | 5 | 1 | | 4 | 1 | 1 | | | | 7 | | |

123

# 1990-91

| 1 | Aug | 25 | (a) | Sheffield U | W | 3-1 | Barnes, Houghton, Rush | 27,009 |
|---|-----|-----|-----|-------------|---|-----|------------------------|--------|
| 2 | | 28 | (h) | Nottingham F | W | 2-0 | Rush, Beardsley | 33,663 |
| 3 | Sep | 1 | (h) | Aston Villa | W | 2-1 | Beardsley, Barnes | 38,061 |
| 4 | | 8 | (a) | Wimbledon | W | 2-1 | Barnes, Whelan | 12,364 |
| 5 | | 16 | (h) | Manchester U | W | 4-0 | Beardsley 3, Barnes | 35,726 |
| 6 | | 22 | (a) | Everton | W | 3-2 | Beardsley 2, Barnes | 39,847 |
| 7 | | 29 | (a) | Sunderland | W | 1-0 | Houghton | 31,107 |
| 8 | Oct | 6 | (h) | Derby Co | W | 2-0 | Houghton, Beardsley | 37,076 |
| 9 | | 20 | (a) | Norwich C | D | 1-1 | Gillespie | 21,275 |
| 10 | | 27 | (h) | Chelsea | W | 2-0 | Rush, Nicol | 38,463 |
| 11 | Nov | 4 | (a) | Tottenham H | W | 3-1 | Rush 2, Beardsley | 35,003 |
| 12 | | 10 | (h) | Luton T | W | 4-0 | Rush 2, Molby (pen), Beardsley | 35,207 |
| 13 | | 17 | (a) | Coventry C | W | 1-0 | Beardsley | 22,571 |
| 14 | | 24 | (h) | Manchester C | D | 2-2 | Rush, Rosenthal | 37,849 |
| 15 | Dec | 2 | (a) | Arsenal | L | 0-3 | | 40,419 |
| 16 | | 15 | (h) | Sheffield U | W | 2-0 | Barnes, Rush | 33,516 |
| 17 | | 22 | (h) | Southampton | W | 3-2 | Rosenthal 2, Houghton | 31,894 |
| 18 | | 26 | (a) | QPR | D | 1-1 | Barnes | 17,848 |
| 19 | | 30 | (a) | Crystal Palace | L | 0-1 | | 26,280 |
| 20 | Jan | 1 | (h) | Leeds U | W | 3-0 | Barnes, Rosenthal, Rush | 36,975 |
| 21 | | 12 | (a) | Aston Villa | D | 0-0 | | 40,026 |
| 22 | | 19 | (h) | Wimbledon | D | 1-1 | Barnes | 35,030 |
| 23 | Feb | 3 | (a) | Manchester U | D | 1-1 | Speedie | 43,690 |
| 24 | | 9 | (h) | Everton | W | 3-1 | Molby, Speedie 2 | 38,127 |
| 25 | | 23 | (a) | Luton T | L | 1-3 | Molby (pen) | 12,032 |
| 26 | Mar | 3 | (h) | Arsenal | L | 0-1 | | 37,221 |
| 27 | | 9 | (a) | Manchester C | W | 3-0 | Molby 2 (2 pens), Barnes | 35,150 |
| 28 | | 16 | (h) | Sunderland | W | 2-1 | Rush, Owers (og) | 37,582 |
| 29 | | 23 | (a) | Derby Co | W | 7-1 | Molby (pen), Barnes 2, Rush, Nicol 2, Houghton | 20,531 |
| 30 | | 30 | (h) | QPR | L | 1-3 | Molby (pen) | 37,251 |
| 31 | Apr | 1 | (a) | Southampton | L | 0-1 | | 20,255 |
| 32 | | 9 | (h) | Coventry C | D | 1-1 | Rush | 31,063 |
| 33 | | 13 | (a) | Leeds U | W | 5-4 | Houghton, Molby (pen), Speedie, Barnes 2 | 31,460 |
| 34 | | 20 | (h) | Norwich C | W | 3-0 | Barnes, Houghton, Rush | 37,065 |
| 35 | | 23 | (h) | Crystal Palace | W | 3-0 | Rush, Barnes, McGoldrick (og) | 36,767 |
| 36 | May | 4 | (a) | Chelsea | L | 2-4 | Speedie, Rosenthal | 32,266 |
| 37 | | 6 | (a) | Nottingham F | L | 1-2 | Molby (pen) | 26,151 |
| 38 | | 11 | (h) | Tottenham H | W | 2-0 | Rush, Speedie | 36,192 |

FINAL LEAGUE POSITION : 2nd in Division One

Appearances

Sub. Appearances

Goals

| Grobbelaar | Hysen | Burrows | Nicol | Whelan | Molby | Gillespie | Houghton | Rush | Barnes | McMahon | Rosenthal | Venison | Beardsley | Ablett | Staunton | McManaman | Carter | Speedie | Hooper | Marsh | |
|---|---|---|---|---|---|---|---|---|---|---|---|---|---|---|---|---|---|---|---|---|---|
| 1 | 2 | 3 | 4 | 5 | 6* | 7 | 8 | 9 | 10 | 11 | 12 | | | | | | | | | | 1 |
| 1 | 2 | 3 | | 5 | | 6 | 8 | 9 | 10 | 11 | 12 | 4 | 7* | | | | | | | | 2 |
| 1 | 2 | | 4 | 5 | | 6 | 8 | 9 | 10 | 11 | | | 7 | 3 | | | | | | | 3 |
| 1 | 2 | 3 | 4 | 5 | 8 | 6 | | 9 | 10 | 11 | | | 7 | | | | | | | | 4 |
| 1 | 2 | 3 | 4 | 5 | 6 | | 8 | 9 | 10 | 11 | | | 7 | | | | | | | | 5 |
| 1 | 2 | 3 | | 5 | | 6 | 8 | 9 | 10 | 11 | | 4 | 7 | | | | | | | | 6 |
| 1 | 2 | 3 | 4 | 5 | | 6 | 8 | 9 | 10 | 11 | | | 7 | | | | | | | | 7 |
| 1 | | 3 | 4 | 5 | | 6 | 8 | 9 | 10 | 11 | | | 7 | 2 | | | | | | | 8 |
| 1 | 2 | 3 | 4 | | | 6 | 8 | 9 | 10 | 11 | | | 5* | 7 | 12 | | | | | | 9 |
| 1 | 2 | 3 | 4 | 14 | 6† | | 8 | 9 | 10* | 11† | 12 | | 7 | 5 | | | | | | | 10 |
| 1 | 2 | 3 | 4 | 7 | 6 | | | 9 | 10* | 11 | 12 | 8 | 5 | | | | | | | | 11 |
| 1 | 2 | 3 | 4† | 10 | 6 | | 8 | 9 | | 11 | 12 | | 7* | 5 | 14 | | | | | | 12 |
| 1 | 2 | 3 | 4 | 5 | 6 | | 8 | 9 | | 11 | | | 7 | 10 | | | | | | | 13 |
| 1 | 2 | 3 | | 5 | 14 | 6 | 8 | 9 | 10 | 11* | | | 7 | 4 | | | | | | | 14 |
| 1 | 2 | 3 | 4 | 5 | 11* | 6 | 14 | 9 | 10 | | 12 | 8† | 7 | | | | | | | | 15 |
| 1 | 2 | 3 | 4 | 5 | | 6 | 8 | 9 | 10 | 11 | | | 7* | | 12 | | | | | | 16 |
| 1 | 2 | 3 | 4 | | | 6 | 8 | 9 | 10 | 11 | | | 7 | 5 | | | | | | | 17 |
| 1 | 2 | 3 | 4 | | | 6 | 8 | 9 | 10 | 11 | | | 7 | 5 | | | | | | | 18 |
| 1 | 2 | 3 | 4 | 5 | | 6 | 8* | 9 | 10 | 11 | 12 | | 7 | | | | | | | | 19 |
| 1 | 2 | 3 | 4 | | | 6 | 8 | 9 | 10 | 11 | | | 7 | 5 | | | | | | | 20 |
| 1 | 2 | 3 | 4 | 8 | | 6 | | 9 | 10 | 11 | 12 | | | 5 | | 7* | | | | | 21 |
| 1 | | 3 | 4 | 8* | | 6 | | 9 | 10 | 11 | 12 | | | 2 | 5 | 7 | | | | | 22 |
| 1 | 2 | 3 | 4 | 5 | 12 | | | 9 | 10 | 11* | | | 6 | 8 | | | 7 | | | | 23 |
| 1 | 2 | 3 | 4 | 5† | 11 | | 10 | | | 9 | 12 | | 6 | 8 | | 14 | 7* | | | | 24 |
| | 2 | | 4 | | 5 | | 8 | 9 | 10 | | | 3 | 7 | 6 | 11* | | 12 | | 1 | | 25 |
| 1 | 2 | 3 | 4 | 5 | 11* | | 8 | 9 | 10 | | | | 7 | 6 | | 12 | | | | | 26 |
| 1 | 2 | 3 | 4 | 5 | | | 8 | 9* | 10 | | 12 | | 7 | 6 | | | | 11 | | | 27 |
| | 2 | 3 | 4 | | 5 | | 8 | 9 | 10 | | | | 7* | 6 | | 12 | | 11 | 1 | | 28 |
| | 2 | 3 | 4 | | 5* | 11 | 8 | 9 | 10 | | | | 7 | 6 | | 12 | | | 1 | | 29 |
| | 2 | 3 | 4 | | 5 | 11 | 8 | 9 | | | 12 | | 7 | 6 | | 10* | | | 1 | | 30 |
| | 2 | 14 | 4 | | 5 | 11† | 8 | 9 | 10 | | | | 7 | 6 | | 3* | | 12 | 1 | | 31 |
| | 2 | | 4 | | 5 | 11 | 8† | 9 | 10 | | | | 7 | 6 | | 3* | 14 | 12 | 1 | | 32 |
| | 2 | 6 | 4 | | 5 | | 8 | 9 | 10 | | | | 7 | | | 3 | | 11 | 1 | | 33 |
| 1 | | 3 | 4 | | 5 | 11 | 8 | 9 | 10 | | | | 7 | 2 | 6 | | | | | | 34 |
| 1 | | 3 | 4 | | 5 | 11 | 8 | 9 | 10 | | | | 7 | 2 | 6 | | | | | | 35 |
| 1 | | 3 | 4 | | 5 | 2† | 8 | 9 | 10 | | 12 | | 7 | 6 | | | 14* | 11 | | | 36 |
| 1 | | 3 | 4 | | 5 | | 8 | 9 | 10 | | | | 7* | 2 | 6 | 12 | | 11 | | | 37 |
| 1 | 5 | 3† | 4 | | | | 8 | 9 | 10* | | 12 | | | 2 | 6 | 14 | | 11 | | 7 | 38 |
| 31 | 32 | 34 | 35 | 14 | 22 | 30 | 31 | 37 | 35 | 22 | 4 | 6 | 24 | 23 | 20 | | 2 | 8 | 7 | 1 | |
| | | 1 | | 3 | | 1 | | | | | 12 | 3 | | 4 | 2 | 3 | 4 | | | 1 | |
| | | | 3 | 1 | 9 | 1 | 7 | 16 | 16 | | | | 5 | | | | | 11 | 6 | | |

# 1991-92

| 1 | Aug | 17 | (h) | Oldham A | W | 2-1 | Houghton, Barnes | 38,841 |
|---|---|---|---|---|---|---|---|---|
| 2 | | 21 | (a) | Manchester C | L | 1-2 | McManaman | 37,322 |
| 3 | | 24 | (a) | Luton T | D | 0-0 | | 11,132 |
| 4 | | 27 | (h) | QPR | W | 1-0 | Saunders | 32,700 |
| 5 | | 31 | (h) | Everton | W | 3-1 | Burrows, Saunders, Houghton | 39,072 |
| 6 | Sep | 7 | (a) | Notts Co | W | 2-1 | Rosenthal, Walters (pen) | 16,051 |
| 7 | | 14 | (h) | Aston Villa | D | 1-1 | Walters (pen) | 38,400 |
| 8 | | 21 | (a) | Leeds U | L | 0-1 | | 32,917 |
| 9 | | 28 | (h) | Sheffield W | D | 1-1 | Houghton | 37,071 |
| 10 | Oct | 6 | (a) | Manchester U | D | 0-0 | | 44,997 |
| 11 | | 19 | (a) | Chelsea | D | 2-2 | McManaman, Elliott (og) | 30,230 |
| 12 | | 26 | (h) | Coventry C | W | 1-0 | Houghton | 33,339 |
| 13 | Nov | 2 | (h) | Crystal Palace | L | 1-2 | Hysen | 34,231 |
| 14 | | 17 | (a) | West Ham U | D | 0-0 | | 23,569 |
| 15 | | 23 | (a) | Wimbledon | D | 0-0 | | 13,373 |
| 16 | | 30 | (h) | Norwich C | W | 2-1 | Molby, Houghton | 34,881 |
| 17 | Dec | 7 | (a) | Southampton | D | 1-1 | Redknapp | 10,053 |
| 18 | | 13 | (h) | Nottingham F | W | 2-0 | McMahon, Molby | 35,285 |
| 19 | | 18 | (a) | Tottenham H | W | 2-1 | Saunders, Houghton | 27,434 |
| 20 | | 20 | (h) | Manchester C | D | 2-2 | Saunders, Nicol | 36,743 |
| 21 | | 26 | (a) | QPR | D | 0-0 | | 21,693 |
| 22 | | 28 | (a) | Everton | D | 1-1 | Tanner | 37,681 |
| 23 | Jan | 1 | (h) | Sheffield U | W | 2-1 | Houghton, Saunders | 35,993 |
| 24 | | 11 | (h) | Luton T | W | 2-1 | McManaman, Saunders | 35,095 |
| 25 | | 18 | (a) | Oldham A | W | 3-2 | McManaman, Saunders, Thomas | 18,952 |
| 26 | | 29 | (h) | Arsenal | W | 2-0 | Molby (pen), Houghton | 33,753 |
| 27 | Feb | 1 | (h) | Chelsea | L | 1-2 | Rosenthal | 38,681 |
| 28 | | 8 | (a) | Coventry C | D | 0-0 | | 21,540 |
| 29 | | 22 | (a) | Norwich C | L | 0-3 | | 20,411 |
| 30 | | 29 | (h) | Southampton | D | 0-0 | | 34,449 |
| 31 | Mar | 11 | (h) | West Ham U | W | 1-0 | Saunders | 30,821 |
| 32 | | 14 | (a) | Crystal Palace | L | 0-1 | | 23,680 |
| 33 | | 21 | (h) | Tottenham H | W | 2-1 | Saunders 2 | 36,968 |
| 34 | | 28 | (a) | Sheffield U | L | 0-2 | | 26,943 |
| 35 | | 31 | (h) | Notts Co | W | 4-0 | Thomas, McManaman, Rush, Venison | 25,457 |
| 36 | Apr | 8 | (h) | Wimbledon | L | 2-3 | Thomas, Rosenthal | 26,134 |
| 37 | | 11 | (a) | Aston Villa | L | 0-1 | | 35,755 |
| 38 | | 18 | (h) | Leeds U | D | 0-0 | | 37,186 |
| 39 | | 20 | (a) | Arsenal | L | 0-4 | | 38,517 |
| 40 | | 22 | (a) | NottinghamF | D | 1-1 | Rush | 23,787 |
| 41 | | 26 | (h) | Manchester U | W | 2-0 | Rush, Walters | 38,669 |
| 42 | May | 2 | (a) | Sheffield W | D | 0-0 | | 34,861 |

FINAL LEAGUE POSITION : 6th in Division One

Appearances

Sub. Appearances

Goals

| Grobbelaar | Ablett | Burrows | Nicol | Whelan | Wright | Saunders | Houghton | McManaman | Barnes | McMahon | Walters | Marsh | Tanner | Rosenthal | Harkness | Rush | Hooper | Jones R | Hysen | Molby | Redknapp | Thomas | Venison | Kozma | Hutchison | # |
|---|---|---|---|---|---|---|---|---|---|---|---|---|---|---|---|---|---|---|---|---|---|---|---|---|---|---|
| 1 | 2 | 3 | 4 | 5 | 6 | 7 | 8 | 9 | 10 | 11* | 12 | | | | | | | | | | | | | | | 1 |
| 1 | 2 | 3 | 4 | 5 | 6† | 7 | 8 | 9 | 10* | 11 | 12 | 14 | | | | | | | | | | | | | | 2 |
| 1 | 2 | 3 | 4 | 5† | | 7 | 8 | 9 | | 11 | 10* | 14 | 6 | 12 | | | | | | | | | | | | 3 |
| 1 | | 3 | 4 | | | 7 | 8 | 9 | | 11 | 10* | 5 | 2 | 12 | 6 | | | | | | | | | | | 4 |
| 1 | 2 | 3 | 4 | 5† | | 7 | 8 | 9 | | 11 | 10* | 14 | 6 | 12 | | | | | | | | | | | | 5 |
| 1 | 2 | 3 | 4 | | | 7 | 8 | 9 | | 10 | | 5 | 6 | 12 | 11* | | | | | | | | | | | 6 |
| 1 | 2 | 3 | 4 | | | 7* | 8 | 9 | | 10 | | 5 | 6 | 11† | 14 | 12 | | | | | | | | | | 7 |
| 1 | 2 | 3 | 4 | | | 7 | 8 | 11 | | 10* | | 5 | 6† | 12 | 14 | 9 | | | | | | | | | | 8 |
| 1 | 14 | 3 | 4 | | | 7 | 8 | 10 | | 11 | 12 | 5* | 6† | 2 | 9 | | | | | | | | | | | 9 |
| | 2 | 3 | 4 | | | 7* | 8 | 12 | | 11 | 10 | 14 | 6 | | | 9 | 1 | | | 5† | | | | | | 10 |
| 1 | | 3 | 4 | | | 7 | 8 | 5 | | 11 | 10 | | 6 | | | 9 | | 2 | | | | | | | | 11 |
| 1 | | 3 | | | | 7* | 8 | 11 | | | 10 | | 6 | 12 | 14 | 9 | | 2 | 4 | 5† | | | | | | 12 |
| 1 | 10 | 3 | | | | 7 | 8 | 11 | | | | | 6 | 12 | | 9 | | 2 | 4 | 5* | | | | | | 13 |
| 1 | | 3 | 4 | | | 7 | | 11 | | | 10 | 8 | 6 | | | 9 | | 2 | | 5 | | | | | | 14 |
| 1 | 10 | 3 | 4 | | | 7 | | 11 | | | 8 | | 6 | | | 9* | | 2 | 12 | 5 | | | | | | 15 |
| 1 | 2 | 3 | 4 | 5 | | 7 | 8 | 9 | | 11* | 12 | | 6 | | | | | | | 10 | | | | | | 16 |
| 1 | | 3 | 4 | 5 | | 7 | 8 | 9 | | 11 | | | 6 | | 2† | | | 14 | | 10* | 12 | | | | | 17 |
| 1 | | 3 | 4 | 5 | | 7 | 8 | 9 | | 11 | | | 6 | | | | | 2 | | 10 | | | | | | 18 |
| 1 | | 3 | 4 | 5 | | 7 | 8 | 9 | | 11† | 14 | | 6 | | | | | 2 | | 10* | | 12 | | | | 19 |
| 1 | | 3 | 4 | 5 | | 7 | 8 | 9† | | 11* | 12 | 14 | 6 | | | | | 2 | | 10 | | | | | | 20 |
| 1 | | 3* | 4 | 5 | | 7 | 8 | 9 | | | | | 6 | | | | | 2 | | 10 | | 11 | 12 | | | 21 |
| 1 | | 3 | 4 | 5* | | 7 | 8 | 12 | | 9 | | | 6 | | | | | 2 | | 10 | | 11 | | | | 22 |
| 1 | | 3 | 4 | 5 | | 7 | 8 | 12 | | 9* | | | 6 | | | | | 2 | | 10 | | 11 | | | | 23 |
| 1 | | | 4 | 5 | | 7 | 8 | 9 | 10 | | | | 6 | 12 | | | | 2 | | | 3* | 11 | | | | 24 |
| 1 | | | 4 | 5 | | 7 | 8 | 9 | 10* | | 12 | | 6 | 3 | | | | 2 | | | | 11 | | | | 25 |
| 1 | | | 4 | 5 | | 7 | 8 | 9 | | | 12 | | 6 | 3 | | | | 2 | | 10 | | 11* | | | | 26 |
| 1 | | 3 | 5† | | | 7 | 8 | 11 | | 9* | 12 | | 6 | 4 | | | | 2 | | 10 | | | 14 | | | 27 |
| 1 | | 3 | 5 | | | 7 | 8 | 11 | | 9* | 4 | | 6† | 12 | 14 | | | 2 | | 10 | | | | | | 28 |
| 1 | | | 5 | | | 7† | 8 | 11 | 14 | 4 | 12 | 3 | | | | 9 | | 2 | | 10 | | 6* | | | | 29 |
| 1 | | 3 | 4 | 5 | | 7 | | 11* | | | | | 6 | 12 | | | | 2† | | 10 | | 9 | 14 | 8 | | 30 |
| 1 | | | 4 | | 6 | 7 | 8† | 11 | 10* | | | 14 | | 12 | | | | 2 | | 5 | | 9 | 3 | | | 31 |
| 1 | | | 4 | | 6 | 7* | | 11 | 10 | | 12 | 14 | | | | | | 2 | | 5† | | 9 | 3 | 8 | | 32 |
| 1 | | 3 | 4 | 14 | | 7 | | 12 | 10 | 8* | | | 6 | | | 9 | | 2 | | 5† | | 11 | | | | 33 |
| 1 | | 3 | 4 | 5 | | 7 | 8 | 12 | | 9 | | | | | | | | 2 | | 10 | | 11* | 6 | | | 34 |
| 1 | | 3 | 5 | | | 7* | 8 | | | | | | 6 | | 9† | | | 2 | | 10 | | 11 | 4 | 12 | 14 | 35 |
| 1 | | | 5 | | | 7 | 8 | 9 | | | 12 | | 4 | | 6* | | | 2 | | 10 | | 11 | 3 | | | 36 |
| 1 | | | 4 | 5 | | 7 | 8 | 9† | | | 12 | | 6 | | | 2* | | | | 10 | | 11 | 3 | | 14 | 37 |
| 1 | | 3 | 4 | | | 7 | 8 | | 10 | | 12 | | | | | 9 | | 2 | | 5 | | 11* | 6 | | | 38 |
| | | | 4 | | | 7† | 8 | | 10 | 11 | 12 | 3 | | | | 9 | 1 | 2* | | 5 | | 6 | | | 14 | 39 |
| | | | 4 | | | | 8 | | 10 | 11 | 7 | 3 | 2 | | | 9 | 1 | | | 5 | | 6 | | | | 40 |
| | | 3 | | | 6 | 7 | 8 | | 10 | | 12 | | 4† | | | 9* | 1 | 2 | | 5 | | 11 | 14 | | | 41 |
| | | 3 | 4 | 5† | 6 | 7 | 8 | | 10* | | 12 | | | | | 9 | 1 | 2 | | | | 11 | 14 | | | 42 |
| 37 | 13 | 30 | 34 | 9 | 21 | 36 | 36 | 26 | 12 | 15 | 18 | 19 | 32 | 7 | 7 | 16 | 5 | 28 | 3 | 25 | 5 | 16 | 9 | 3 | | |
| | 1 | | 1 | | | | | 4 | | | | 7 | 15 | | 13 | 4 | 2 | | 2 | 1 | 1 | 1 | 4 | 2 | 3 | |
| | | 1 | 1 | | | | | 10 | 8 | 5 | 1 | 1 | 3 | | | 1 | | 3 | | 3 | | 1 | 3 | 1 | 3 | |

127

# 1992-93

| | | | | | | | | |
|---|---|---|---|---|---|---|---|---|
| 1 | Aug | 16 | (a) | Nottingham F | L | 0-1 | | 20,038 |
| 2 | | 19 | (h) | Sheffield U | W | 2-1 | Walters, Stewart | 33,107 |
| 3 | | 23 | (h) | Arsenal | L | 0-2 | | 34,961 |
| 4 | | 25 | (a) | Ipswich T | D | 2-2 | Walters, Molby (pen) | 20,109 |
| 5 | | 29 | (a) | Leeds U | D | 2-2 | Whelan, Molby (pen) | 29,597 |
| 6 | Sep | 1 | (h) | Southampton | D | 1-1 | Wright | 30,024 |
| 7 | | 5 | (h) | Chelsea | W | 2-1 | Saunders, Redknapp | 34,199 |
| 8 | | 12 | (a) | Sheffield U | L | 0-1 | | 20,632 |
| 9 | | 19 | (a) | Aston Villa | L | 2-4 | Walters, Rosenthal | 37,863 |
| 10 | | 26 | (h) | Wimbledon | L | 2-3 | Molby (pen), McManaman | 29,574 |
| 11 | Oct | 3 | (h) | Sheffield W | W | 1-0 | Hutchison | 35,785 |
| 12 | | 18 | (a) | Manchester U | D | 2-2 | Hutchison, Rush | 33,243 |
| 13 | | 25 | (h) | Norwich C | W | 4-1 | Thomas, Hutchison, Burrows, Walters (pen) | 36,318 |
| 14 | | 31 | (a) | Tottenham H | L | 0-2 | | 32,917 |
| 15 | Nov | 7 | (h) | Middlesbrough | W | 4-1 | Rosenthal 2, McManaman, Rush | 34,974 |
| 16 | | 23 | (a) | QPR | W | 1-0 | Rosenthal | 21,056 |
| 17 | | 28 | (h) | Crystal Palace | W | 5-0 | McManaman 2, Marsh, Rosenthal, Hutchison | 36,380 |
| 18 | Dec | 7 | (a) | Everton | L | 1-2 | Wright | 35,826 |
| 19 | | 13 | (h) | Blackburn R | W | 2-1 | Walters 2 | 43,668 |
| 20 | | 19 | (a) | Coventry C | L | 1-5 | Redknapp | 19,779 |
| 21 | | 28 | (h) | Manchester C | D | 1-1 | Rush | 43,037 |
| 22 | Jan | 9 | (h) | Aston Villa | L | 1-2 | Barnes | 40,826 |
| 23 | | 16 | (a) | Wimbledon | L | 0-2 | | 11,294 |
| 24 | | 31 | (a) | Arsenal | W | 1-0 | Barnes (pen) | 27,580 |
| 25 | Feb | 6 | (h) | Nottingham F | D | 0-0 | | 40,463 |
| 26 | | 10 | (a) | Chelsea | D | 0-0 | | 20,981 |
| 27 | | 13 | (a) | Southampton | L | 1-2 | Hutchison | 17,216 |
| 28 | | 20 | (h) | Ipswich T | D | 0-0 | | 36,680 |
| 29 | | 27 | (a) | Sheffield W | D | 1-1 | Hutchison | 33,964 |
| 30 | Mar | 6 | (h) | Manchester U | L | 1-2 | Rush | 44,374 |
| 31 | | 10 | (h) | QPR | W | 1-0 | Rush | 30,370 |
| 32 | | 13 | (a) | Middlesbrough | W | 2-1 | Hutchison, Rush | 22,463 |
| 33 | | 20 | (h) | Everton | W | 1-0 | Rosenthal | 44,619 |
| 34 | | 23 | (a) | Crystal Palace | D | 1-1 | Rush | 18,688 |
| 35 | Apr | 3 | (a) | Blackburn R | L | 1-4 | Rush | 15,032 |
| 36 | | 10 | (h) | Oldham A | W | 1-0 | Rush | 36,129 |
| 37 | | 12 | (a) | Manchester C | D | 1-1 | Rush | 28,098 |
| 38 | | 17 | (h) | Coventry C | W | 4-0 | Walters 3 (1 pen), Burrows | 33,328 |
| 39 | | 21 | (h) | Leeds U | W | 2-0 | Barnes, Walters (pen) | 34,992 |
| 40 | May | 1 | (a) | Norwich C | L | 0-1 | | 20,610 |
| 41 | | 5 | (a) | Oldham A | L | 2-3 | Rush 2 | 15,381 |
| 42 | | 8 | (h) | Tottenham H | W | 6-2 | Rush 2, Barnes 2, Harkness, Walters (pen) | 43,385 |

FINAL LEAGUE POSITION : 6th in Premier League

Appearances

Sub Appearances

Goals

| James | Tanner | Burrows | Nicol | Whelan | Wright | Saunders | Stewart | Rush | Walters | Thomas | McManaman | Rosenthal | Jones | Molby | Marsh | Harkness | Redknapp | Piechnik | Hutchison | Grobbelaar | Kozma | Hooper | Barnes | Bjornebye | No. |
|---|---|---|---|---|---|---|---|---|---|---|---|---|---|---|---|---|---|---|---|---|---|---|---|---|---|
| 1 | 2 | 3 | 4 | 5 | 6 | 7 | 8 | 9* | 10† | 11 | 12 | 14 |  |  |  |  |  |  |  |  |  |  |  |  | 1 |
| 1 |  | 3 | 4 | 5 | 6 | 7* | 8 |  | 10 | 11 | 9 | 12 | 2 |  |  |  |  |  |  |  |  |  |  |  | 2 |
| 1 | 8 | 3 |  | 5 | 6 | 7 |  |  | 10 | 11† | 9 | 12 | 2* | 4 | 14 |  |  |  |  |  |  |  |  |  | 3 |
| 1 |  | 3 |  | 5 | 6 | 7* | 8 | 9 | 11 |  | 12 |  | 2 | 10 |  | 4 |  |  |  |  |  |  |  |  | 4 |
| 1 |  | 3 |  | 5 | 6 | 7* | 8† | 9 | 12 |  |  |  | 2 | 10 | 14 | 4 | 11 |  |  |  |  |  |  |  | 5 |
| 1 |  | 3 |  | 5 | 6 |  |  | 9 | 11 | 12 | 7 |  | 2 | 10 |  | 4 | 8* |  |  |  |  |  |  |  | 6 |
| 1 |  | 3 |  | 5 | 6 | 7 |  | 9 | 12 |  | 11* |  | 2 | 10 |  | 4 | 8 |  |  |  |  |  |  |  | 7 |
| 1 |  | 3 | 4 | 5* | 6 |  | 8 | 9 | 11 |  |  | 7 |  | 12 | 14 | 2 | 10† |  |  |  |  |  |  |  | 8 |
| 1 |  | 3 | 4 |  | 6 |  |  |  | 11 |  |  | 7 |  | 10 | 8 |  | 5 | 2 | 9 |  |  |  |  |  | 9 |
|  |  | 3 |  |  | 6 |  |  |  | 11* |  | 8 | 7 |  | 10 | 2 |  | 5 | 4 | 9 | 1 | 12 |  |  |  | 10 |
|  |  | 3 | 4 |  |  |  | 8* | 9 | 11 |  |  | 7 | 12 |  | 2 |  | 10 | 5 | 6 | 1 |  |  |  |  | 11 |
|  | 14 | 3 | 4 |  |  |  |  | 9 | 12 | 7 | 11 |  |  | 10† | 2 |  | 8* | 5 | 6 | 1 |  |  |  |  | 12 |
|  |  | 3 | 4 |  |  |  | 8 | 9 | 12 | 11 |  | 7 |  |  | 2* |  | 10 | 5 | 6 | 1 |  |  |  |  | 13 |
| 1 | 14 | 3 |  | 5 |  |  | 8† | 9 | 12 |  | 11 | 7 |  |  | 2 |  | 10* | 4 | 6 |  |  |  |  |  | 14 |
|  |  | 3 | 4 |  |  |  |  | 9 | 11 |  |  | 7 |  | 10 | 2 |  | 8 | 5 | 6 | 1 |  |  |  |  | 15 |
|  |  | 3 | 4 |  |  |  |  | 9* | 11 |  |  | 7 |  | 10 | 2 |  | 8 | 5 | 6 | 1 | 12 |  |  |  | 16 |
|  |  | 3 | 4 |  |  |  |  | 9* | 12 |  | 11 | 7 |  |  | 2 |  | 8 | 5 | 6 | 1 |  |  | 10 |  | 17 |
|  |  | 3 | 4 |  |  |  |  | 9† | 12 | 14 | 11 | 7 |  |  | 2 |  | 8 | 5 | 6* | 1 |  |  | 10 |  | 18 |
|  |  | 3 | 4 |  |  |  |  | 9 | 12 |  | 11 | 7 |  |  | 2 |  | 8 | 5 | 6* | 1 |  |  | 10 |  | 19 |
|  |  |  |  |  | 6 | 7 |  | 9 | 11 |  |  | 3* |  |  | 2 |  | 8 | 5 | 12 | 1 |  |  | 10 | 4 | 20 |
|  |  |  | 4 |  |  |  |  | 9 | 11 |  |  | 7 | 3 |  | 2 |  | 8 | 5 |  | 1 |  |  | 10 | 6 | 21 |
|  |  |  | 4 |  |  |  |  | 9† |  | 14 | 11 | 7 | 3 |  | 2 |  | 8* | 5 | 12 | 1 |  |  | 10 | 6 | 22 |
| 1 |  | 6 | 4 |  |  | 7* |  |  |  |  | 12 | 3 | 2 | 14 | 8 | 5† |  |  | 9 |  |  |  | 10 | 11 | 23 |
| 1 |  |  | 4 | 5 |  |  |  | 9 | 11 |  |  | 7 | 3 |  | 2* |  | 8 |  |  |  |  |  | 10 | 6 | 24 |
| 1 |  |  | 4 | 5 |  |  |  | 9 | 11 | 12 |  | 7 | 3 |  | 2* |  | 8 |  |  |  |  |  | 10 | 6 | 25 |
| 1 |  |  | 4 | 5 |  |  |  | 9 | 11 |  |  | 7 | 8* |  | 2 | 3 |  |  | 12 |  |  |  | 10 | 6 | 26 |
| 1 |  |  | 4 | 5 |  |  |  | 9 | 11 |  |  | 7 | 3 |  | 2* |  | 12 | 8 |  |  |  |  | 10 | 6 | 27 |
| 1 |  |  | 4 | 5 |  |  |  | 9 | 11 | 12 |  | 7 | 3 | 14 | 2 |  | 8* |  |  |  |  |  | 10 | 6† | 28 |
| 1 |  |  | 4 | 5 |  |  |  | 9 | 11 |  |  | 7 | 3 | 12 | 2 |  | 8 |  |  |  |  |  | 10 | 6* | 29 |
| 1 | 14 |  | 4 | 5 |  |  |  | 9† | 11* | 12 |  | 7 | 3 |  | 2 |  | 8 |  |  |  |  |  | 10 | 6 | 30 |
| 1 | 11 |  | 4 | 5 | 6 |  |  | 9 |  |  |  | 7 | 12 |  | 3 | 2* | 8 |  |  |  |  |  | 10 |  | 31 |
| 1 | 2 |  | 4 | 5 | 6 |  |  | 9 | 12 | 11* | 7† |  | 3 |  |  | 14 | 8 |  |  |  |  |  | 10 |  | 32 |
| 1 | 2 |  | 4 | 5† | 6 |  |  | 9 | 11 |  | 7* |  | 12 | 14 |  | 3 | 8 |  |  |  |  |  |  |  | 33 |
| 1 | 2 |  | 4 |  | 6 |  |  | 9 | 11 | 12 | 7* |  |  | 5 |  | 3 | 8 |  |  |  |  |  |  |  | 34 |
| 1 | 3 |  | 4 |  | 6 |  |  | 9 | 11 | 12 | 7* |  |  |  | 2 | 5 | 8 |  |  |  |  |  |  |  | 35 |
| 1 | 3 |  | 4 | 5 | 6 |  |  | 9 | 11 |  | 7* |  | 12 |  | 2 |  | 8 |  |  |  |  |  |  |  | 36 |
| 1 | 3 |  | 4 | 5 | 6 |  |  | 9 | 11 |  | 7* |  | 2 | 12 |  |  | 8 |  |  |  |  |  |  |  | 37 |
| 1 | 3 |  | 4 | 5 | 6 | 7* |  | 9 | 11 | 12 |  |  |  |  | 2 |  | 8 |  |  |  |  |  |  |  | 38 |
| 1 | 3 |  | 4 | 5 | 6 | 7 |  | 9 | 11 |  |  |  |  |  | 2 |  | 8 |  |  |  |  |  |  |  | 39 |
| 1 | 3 |  | 4 | 5 |  | 7* |  | 9 | 11 |  |  |  |  |  | 2 |  | 6† | 8 |  |  |  | 14 | 10 |  | 40 |
| 1 | 3 |  | 4 | 5† |  | 7* |  | 9 | 11 |  |  |  |  |  | 2 |  | 6 | 14 | 8 |  |  |  | 10 |  | 41 |
|  | 3 |  | 4 | 5 |  |  |  | 9 | 11 |  |  |  |  |  | 2 |  | 7 | 6 | 8 | 1 |  |  | 10 |  | 42 |
| 29 | 2 | 29 | 32 | 17 | 32 | 6 | 21 | 31 | 26 | 6 | 27 | 16 | 30 | 8 | 22 | 9 | 27 | 15 | 27 | 5 |  | 8 | 26 | 11 |  |
|  | 2 | 1 |  | 1 |  | 3 | 1 | 8 | 2 | 4 | 11 |  | 2 | 6 | 1 |  | 2 | 1 | 4 |  | 1 | 1 | 1 |  |  |
|  | 2 |  | 1 | 2 | 1 | 1 |  | 14 | 11 | 1 | 4 | 6 |  | 3 | 1 | 1 | 2 |  | 7 |  |  |  | 5 |  |  |

# 1993-94

| 1 | Aug | 14 | (h) | Sheffield W | W | 2-0 | Clough 2 | 44,004 |
|---|---|---|---|---|---|---|---|---|
| 2 | | 18 | (a) | Q.P.R. | W | 3-1 | Nicol, Clough, Rush | 19,635 |
| 3 | | 22 | (a) | Swindon T | W | 5-0 | Ruddock, Whelan, McManaman 2, Marsh | 17,017 |
| 4 | | 25 | (h) | Tottenham H | L | 1-2 | Clough | 42,456 |
| 5 | | 28 | (h) | Leeds U | W | 2-0 | Molby (pen), Rush | 44,068 |
| 6 | Sep | 1 | (a) | Coventry C | L | 0-1 | | 16,740 |
| 7 | | 12 | (h) | Blackburn R | L | 0-1 | | 37,355 |
| 8 | | 18 | (a) | Everton | L | 0-2 | | 38,157 |
| 9 | | 25 | (a) | Chelsea | L | 0-1 | | 31,271 |
| 10 | Oct | 2 | (h) | Arsenal | D | 0-0 | | 42,750 |
| 11 | | 16 | (h) | Oldham Ath | W | 2-1 | Fowler, Barlow (og) | 32,661 |
| 12 | | 23 | (a) | Manchester C | D | 1-1 | Rush | 30,403 |
| 13 | | 30 | (h) | Southampton | W | 4-2 | Rush, Fowler 3 | 32,818 |
| 14 | Nov | 6 | (h) | West Ham U | W | 2-0 | Clough, Martin (og) | 42,254 |
| 15 | | 21 | (a) | Newcastle U | L | 0-3 | | 36,374 |
| 16 | | 28 | (h) | Aston Villa | W | 2-1 | Redknapp, Fowler | 38,484 |
| 17 | Dec | 4 | (a) | Sheffield W | L | 1-3 | Fowler | 32,177 |
| 18 | | 8 | (h) | Q.P.R. | W | 3-2 | Molby (pen), Barnes, Rush | 24,561 |
| 19 | | 11 | (h) | Swindon T | D | 2-2 | Wright, Barnes | 32,739 |
| 20 | | 18 | (a) | Tottenham H | D | 3-3 | Redknapp, Fowler 2 | 31,394 |
| 21 | | 26 | (a) | Sheffield U | D | 0-0 | | 22,932 |
| 22 | | 28 | (h) | Wimbledon | D | 1-1 | Scales (og) | 32,232 |
| 23 | Jan | 1 | (a) | Ipswich T | W | 2-1 | Ruddock, Rush | 22,355 |
| 24 | | 4 | (h) | Manchester U | D | 3-3 | Ruddock, Clough 2 | 42,795 |
| 25 | | 15 | (a) | Oldham Ath | W | 3-0 | Dicks, Redknapp, Fowler | 14,573 |
| 26 | | 22 | (h) | Manchester C | W | 2-1 | Rush 2 | 41,872 |
| 27 | Feb | 5 | (a) | Norwich C | D | 2-2 | Barnes, Culverhouse (og) | 19,746 |
| 28 | | 14 | (a) | Southampton | L | 2-4 | Dicks (pen), Rush | 18,306 |
| 29 | | 19 | (a) | Leeds U | L | 0-2 | | 40,053 |
| 30 | | 26 | (h) | Coventry C | W | 1-0 | Rush | 38,547 |
| 31 | Mar | 5 | (a) | Blackburn R | L | 0-2 | | 20,831 |
| 32 | | 13 | (h) | Everton | W | 2-1 | Rush, Fowler | 44,281 |
| 33 | | 19 | (h) | Chelsea | W | 2-1 | Rush, Burley (og) | 38,629 |
| 34 | | 26 | (a) | Arsenal | L | 0-1 | | 35,556 |
| 35 | | 30 | (a) | Manchester U | L | 0-1 | | 44,751 |
| 36 | Apr | 2 | (h) | Sheffield U | L | 1-2 | Rush | 36,642 |
| 37 | | 4 | (a) | Wimbledon | D | 1-1 | Redknapp | 13,819 |
| 38 | | 9 | (h) | Ipswich T | W | 1-0 | Dicks (pen) | 30,485 |
| 39 | | 16 | (h) | Newcastle U | L | 0-2 | | 44,601 |
| 40 | | 23 | (a) | West Ham U | W | 2-1 | Rush, Fowler | 26,096 |
| 41 | | 30 | (h) | Norwich C | L | 0-1 | | 44,339 |
| 42 | May | 7 | (a) | Aston Villa | L | 1-2 | Fowler | 45,347 |

FINAL LEAGUE POSITION: 8th in F.A. Premiership

Appearances

Sub. Appearances

Goals

| Grobbelaar | Jones | Bjørnebye | Nicol | Wright | Ruddock | Clough | Molby | Rush | Whelan | Walters | Redknapp | McManaman | Burrows | Marsh | Hutchison | Rosenthal | Dicks | Stewart | Fowler | Matteo | Harkness | Piechnik | Barnes | Thomas | James | No. |
|---|---|---|---|---|---|---|---|---|---|---|---|---|---|---|---|---|---|---|---|---|---|---|---|---|---|---|
| 1 | 2 | 3 | 4 | 5 | 6 | 7 | 8* | 9 | 10 | 11 | 12 | | | | | | | | | | | | | | | 1 |
| 1 | 2 | 3 | 4 | 5 | 6 | 7* | 8 | 9 | 10 | | 12 | 11 | | | | | | | | | | | | | | 2 |
| 1 | 2 | 3* | 4 | 5 | 6† | 7 | 8 | 9 | 10 | | | 11 | 12 | 14 | | | | | | | | | | | | 3 |
| 1 | 2 | | 4 | 5 | 6 | 7 | 8 | 9 | 10 | 12 | | 11 | 3* | | | | | | | | | | | | | 4 |
| 1 | 2 | | | 5 | 6 | 7 | 8 | 9 | 10 | | | 11 | 3 | 12 | 4* | | | | | | | | | | | 5 |
| 1 | 2 | | 4 | 5 | 6 | 7 | 8 | 9 | 10 | 12 | | 11 | 3* | | | | | | | | | | | | | 6 |
| 1 | 2 | 3* | 4 | 5 | 6 | 7 | 8 | 9† | 10 | 14 | 11 | | | | | 12 | | | | | | | | | | 7 |
| 1 | | | 2 | 5 | 6 | 7 | | 9 | 10 | 11* | 4 | 8† | | | | 12 | 3 | 14 | | | | | | | | 8 |
| 1 | 2 | | | 5 | 6 | 7 | | 9 | 4 | | 12 | | | | 10* | | 3 | 8 | 11 | | | | | | | 9 |
| 1 | 2 | | | 5 | 6 | 7 | | 9 | 4 | | | | | | 10 | | 3 | 8 | 11 | | | | | | | 10 |
| 1 | 2 | 12 | | 5 | 6 | 7 | | 9 | 14 | 4 | | | | | 10* | | 3† | 8 | 11 | | | | | | | 11 |
| 1 | 2 | 3 | 4 | 5 | 6 | | | 9 | 7* | 12 | | | | | 14 | | | 8† | 11 | 10 | | | | | | 12 |
| 1 | 2 | 3* | 4 | 5 | 6 | | | 9 | | | | | | | | 12 | | 8 | 11 | 10 | 7 | | | | | 13 |
| 1 | 2* | 14 | 4† | 5 | 6 | 7 | | 9 | | | 12 | | | | | | | 8 | 11 | 10 | 3 | | | | | 14 |
| 1 | | 2 | | | 6 | 7 | | 9 | 4 | | | | | | | | 8 | 11 | 10 | 3 | 5* | 12 | | | | 15 |
| 1 | | 2 | | 5 | 6 | 7* | | 9 | 12 | 4 | | | | | | | | | 11 | 10 | 3 | | 8 | | | 16 |
| 1 | 2 | | 4† | 5 | 6 | | | 9 | | | 7 | | 12 | 14 | | | | | 11 | 10* | 3 | | 8 | | | 17 |
| 1 | 2 | 12 | | 5 | 6 | 7 | | 9 | 4 | | | 10 | | | | | 3 | | 11 | | | | 8* | | | 18 |
| 1 | 2 | 12 | | 5 | 6 | 7 | | 9 | 4 | | | 10 | | | | | 3* | | 11 | | | | 8 | | | 19 |
| 1 | 2 | | 6 | 5 | | | | 9 | 14 | 4 | 12 | 10 | | | | | 3 | | 11 | 7† | | | 8* | | | 20 |
| 1 | 2 | | 4 | 5 | 6 | 7 | | 9* | | | 12 | 10 | | | | | 3 | | 11 | | | | 8 | | | 21 |
| 1 | 2 | 3* | | 5 | 6 | 7 | | 9 | 4 | | 12 | 10 | | | | | | | 11 | | | | 8 | | | 22 |
| 1 | 2 | 12 | | 5 | 6 | 7 | | 9 | 4* | | | 10† | | 14 | | | 3 | | 11 | | | | 8 | | | 23 |
| 1 | 2 | 12 | | 5 | 6 | 7 | | 9 | 4 | | | 10* | | | | | 3 | | 11 | | | | 8 | | | 24 |
| 1 | 2 | | | 5 | 6 | 7 | | 9 | 4 | | | 10 | | | | | 3 | | 11 | | | | 8* | 12 | | 25 |
| 1 | 2 | | | 5 | 6 | 7 | | 9 | 4 | | | 10 | | | | | 3 | | 11 | | | | 8 | | | 26 |
| 1 | 2 | | | 5 | 6 | 7 | | 9 | 4 | | | 10 | | | | | 3 | | 11 | | | | 8 | | | 27 |
| 1 | 2 | | 4 | 5 | 6 | 7* | | 9 | | | 12 | 10 | | | | | 3 | | 11 | | | | 8 | | | 28 |
| 1† | 2 | | | 5 | 6 | | | 9 | 4 | | 12 | 7 | | | | 10 | 3 | | 11* | | | | 8 | 14 | | 29 |
| | 2 | | | 5 | 6 | | | 9 | 4 | | 7 | 10 | | | | | 3 | | | | | | 8 | | 1 | 30 |
| | 2 | | | 5 | 6 | 11* | | 9 | 4 | | 12 | 7 | | | | 10 | 3 | | | | | | 8 | | 1 | 31 |
| | 2 | | | 5 | 6 | | | 9 | 4 | | 7 | 10 | | | | | 3 | | 11 | | | | 8* | 12 | 1 | 32 |
| | 2 | | | 5 | 6 | | | 9 | 4 | | 7 | 10 | | | | | 3 | | 11 | | | | 8* | 12 | 1 | 33 |
| | 2 | 12 | | 5* | 6 | | | 9 | 4 | | 7 | 10 | | | | | 3 | | 11† | | | | 8 | 14 | 1 | 34 |
| | 2 | | | 5 | 6 | | | 9 | 4 | | 7 | 10 | | | | | 3 | | 11* | 12 | | | 8 | | 1 | 35 |
| | 2 | | | 5 | 6 | | | 9 | 4* | | 7 | 10 | | 14 | | | 3 | | 11 | | | | 8† | 12 | 1 | 36 |
| | 2 | | | 5 | 6 | | | 9 | 4 | | 7 | 10 | | | | | 3 | | 11 | | | | 8 | | 1 | 37 |
| | 2 | | | 5 | 6 | | | 9 | 4 | | 7 | 10 | | | | 12 | 3 | | 11* | | | | 8 | | 1 | 38 |
| | 2 | | | 5 | 6 | | | 9 | 4 | | 7 | 10* | | 14 | | | 3 | | 11† | | | | 8 | 14 | 1 | 39 |
| | | | | 5 | 6 | | 10 | 9 | 4 | | 7 | | | | | | 3 | | 11 | | 3 | | 8 | | 1 | 40 |
| | 2 | | | 5 | 6 | | 10* | 9 | 4 | | 7 | | | | | 12 | 3 | | 11 | | | | 8 | | 1 | 41 |
| | 2 | | | 5 | 6 | | | 9 | 4 | | 7 | 10 | | | | | 3 | | 11 | | | | 8 | | 1 | 42 |
| 29 | 38 | 6 | 27 | 31 | 39 | 25 | 11 | 41 | 23 | 7 | 29 | 29 | 3 | - | 6 | - | 24 | 7 | 27 | 11 | 10 | 1 | 24 | 1 | 13 | |
| | 3 | 4 | | 1 | | | 10 | | 6 | 1 | 1 | 2 | 5 | 3 | | | 1 | 1 | | | | | 2 | 6 | 1 | |
| | | | 1 | 1 | 3 | 7 | 2 | 14 | 1 | | 4 | 2 | | | 1 | | | | 3 | | | | 12 | | 3 | |

131

# 1994-95

| | | | | | | | | |
|---|---|---|---|---|---|---|---|---|
| 1 | Aug | 20 | (a) | Crystal Palace | W | 6-1 | Molby (pen), McManaman 2, Fowler, Rush 2 | 18,084 |
| 2 | | 28 | (h) | Arsenal | W | 3-0 | Fowler 3 | 30,017 |
| 3 | | 31 | (a) | Southampton | W | 2-0 | Fowler, Barnes | 15,190 |
| 4 | Sep | 10 | (h) | West Ham U | D | 0-0 | | 30,907 |
| 5 | | 17 | (a) | Manchester U | L | 0-2 | | 43,740 |
| 6 | | 24 | (a) | Newcastle U | D | 1-1 | Rush | 34,435 |
| 7 | Oct | 1 | (h) | Sheffield W | W | 4-1 | McManaman 2, Walker (og), Rush | 31,493 |
| 8 | | 8 | (h) | Aston Villa | W | 3-2 | Ruddock, Fowler 2 | 32,158 |
| 9 | | 15 | (a) | Blackburn R | L | 2-3 | Fowler, Barnes | 30,263 |
| 10 | | 22 | (h) | Wimbledon | W | 3-0 | McManaman, Fowler, Barnes | 31,139 |
| 11 | | 29 | (a) | Ipswich T | W | 3-1 | Barnes, Fowler 2 | 22,379 |
| 12 | | 31 | (a) | QPR | L | 1-2 | Barnes | 18,295 |
| 13 | Nov | 5 | (h) | Nottingham F | W | 1-0 | Fowler | 33,329 |
| 14 | | 9 | (h) | Chelsea | W | 3-1 | Fowler 2, Ruddock | 32,885 |
| 15 | | 21 | (a) | Everton | L | 0-2 | | 39,866 |
| 16 | | 26 | (h) | Tottenham H | D | 1-1 | Fowler (pen) | 35,007 |
| 17 | Dec | 3 | (a) | Coventry C | D | 1-1 | Rush | 21,032 |
| 18 | | 11 | (h) | Crystal Palace | D | 0-0 | | 30,972 |
| 19 | | 18 | (a) | Chelsea | D | 0-0 | | 27,050 |
| 20 | | 26 | (a) | Leicester C | W | 2-1 | Fowler (pen), Rush | 21,393 |
| 21 | | 28 | (h) | Manchester C | W | 2-0 | Phelan (og), Fowler | 38,122 |
| 22 | | 31 | (a) | Leeds U | W | 2-0 | Redknapp, Fowler | 38,468 |
| 23 | Jan | 2 | (h) | Norwich C | W | 4-0 | Scales, Fowler 2, Rush | 34,709 |
| 24 | | 14 | (h) | Ipswich T | L | 0-1 | | 32,733 |
| 25 | | 24 | (h) | Everton | D | 0-0 | | 39,505 |
| 26 | Feb | 4 | (a) | Nottingham F | D | 1-1 | Fowler | 25,418 |
| 27 | | 11 | (h) | QPR | D | 1-1 | Scales | 35,996 |
| 28 | | 25 | (a) | Sheffield W | W | 2-1 | Barnes, McManaman | 31,964 |
| 29 | Mar | 4 | (h) | Newcastle U | W | 2-0 | Fowler, Rush | 39,300 |
| 30 | | 14 | (a) | Coventry C | L | 2-3 | Molby (pen), Burrows (og) | 27,183 |
| 31 | | 19 | (h) | Manchester U | W | 2-0 | Bruce (og), Redknapp | 38,906 |
| 32 | | 22 | (a) | Tottenham H | D | 0-0 | | 31,988 |
| 33 | Apr | 5 | (h) | Southampton | W | 3-1 | Rush 2, Fowler (pen) | 29,881 |
| 34 | | 9 | (h) | Leeds U | L | 0-1 | | 37,454 |
| 35 | | 12 | (a) | Arsenal | W | 1-0 | Fowler | 38,036 |
| 36 | | 14 | (a) | Manchester C | L | 1-2 | McManaman | 27,055 |
| 37 | | 17 | (h) | Leicester C | W | 2-0 | Fowler, Rush | 36,012 |
| 38 | | 29 | (a) | Norwich C | W | 2-1 | Harkness, Rush | 21,843 |
| 39 | May | 2 | (a) | Wimbledon | D | 0-0 | | 12,041 |
| 40 | | 6 | (a) | Aston Villa | L | 0-2 | | 40,154 |
| 41 | | 10 | (a) | West Ham U | L | 0-3 | | 22,446 |
| 42 | | 14 | (h) | Blackburn R | W | 2-1 | Barnes, Redknapp | 40,014 |

FINAL LEAGUE POSITION : 4th in F.A. Carling Premiership

Appearances

Sub. Appearances

Goals

| James | Jones R | Bjornebye | Nicol | Molby | Ruddock | McManaman | Redknapp | Rush | Barnes | Fowler | Thomas | Scales | Babb | Clough | Jones P | Harkness | Walters | Matteo | Wright | Kennedy | No. |
|---|---|---|---|---|---|---|---|---|---|---|---|---|---|---|---|---|---|---|---|---|---|
| 1 | 2 | 3 | 4 | 5* | 6 | 7 | 8 | 9 | 10 | 11 | 12 | | | | | | | | | | 1 |
| 1 | 2 | 3 | 4 | 5* | 6 | 7 | 8 | 9 | 10 | 11 | 12 | | | | | | | | | | 2 |
| 1 | 2 | 3 | 4 | 5 | 6 | 7 | 8 | 9 | 10 | 11 | | | | | | | | | | | 3 |
| 1 | 2 | 3 | | 5 | 6 | 7 | 8 | 9 | 10 | 11 | | 4 | | | | | | | | | 4 |
| 1 | 2 | 3 | | 5* | 6 | 7 | 8 | 9 | 10 | 11 | | 4 | 12 | | | | | | | | 5 |
| 1 | 2 | 3 | | 8 | 6 | 7 | | 9* | 10 | 11 | | 4 | 5 | 12 | | | | | | | 6 |
| 1 | 2 | 3 | 4 | 8 | 6 | 7 | 12 | 9 | 10 | 11* | | | 5 | | | | | | | | 7 |
| 1 | 2 | 3 | | 8 | 6 | 7 | 12 | 9* | 10 | 11 | | 4 | 5 | | | | | | | | 8 |
| 1 | 2 | 3* | | 8 | 6 | 7 | 12 | 9 | 10 | 11 | | 4 | 5 | | | | | | | | 9 |
| 1 | 2 | 3 | | | 6 | 7 | 8 | 9* | 10 | 11† | | 4 | 5 | 12 | 14 | | | | | | 10 |
| 1 | 2 | 3 | | | 6 | 7 | 8 | 9 | 10 | 11 | | 4 | 5 | | | | | | | | 11 |
| 1 | 2 | 3 | | 12 | 6 | 7 | 8 | 9 | 10 | 11 | | 4 | 5* | | | | | | | | 12 |
| 1 | 2 | 3 | | 12 | 6 | 7 | 8 | 9 | 10 | 11 | | 4* | 5 | | | | | | | | 13 |
| 1 | 2 | 3 | 4 | | 6 | 7 | 8 | 9 | 10 | 11 | | | 5 | | | | | | | | 14 |
| 1 | 2 | 3* | | 8 | 6 | 7 | 12 | 9 | 10 | 11 | | 4 | 5 | | | | | | | | 15 |
| 1 | 2 | 3 | | | 6 | 7 | 8 | 9 | 10* | 11 | 12 | 4 | 5 | | | | | | | | 16 |
| 1 | 2* | | | | 6 | 7 | 8 | 9 | | 11 | 10 | 4 | 5 | | | 3 | 12 | | | | 17 |
| 1 | 2* | | | | 6 | | 8 | | 10 | 11 | 7 | 4 | 5 | 9 | | 3 | 12 | | | | 18 |
| 1 | | 3 | | | 6 | | 8 | 9 | 10 | 11 | 2 | 4 | 5 | | | 7 | | | | | 19 |
| 1 | 2* | 3 | | | 6 | 7 | 8 | 9 | 10 | 11 | 12 | 4 | 5 | | | | | | | | 20 |
| 1 | 2 | 3 | | | 6 | 7 | 8 | 9 | 10 | 11 | | 4 | 5 | | | | | | | | 21 |
| 1 | 2 | 3 | | | 6 | 7 | 8 | 9 | 10 | 11 | | 4 | 5 | | | | | | | | 22 |
| 1 | 2 | 3* | | | 6 | 7 | 8 | 9 | 10 | 11 | | 4 | 5 | | | | | | | | 23 |
| 1 | 2 | 3 | | | 6 | 7 | 8 | 9 | | 11 | 10 | 4 | 5 | | | | 12 | | | | 24 |
| 1 | 2 | | | | 6 | 7 | 8 | 9 | 10 | 11 | | 4 | 5 | | | | | | | | 25 |
| 1 | 2 | 3† | | | 6 | 7 | 8* | 9 | 10 | 11 | 12 | 4 | 5 | | | | 14 | 3† | | | 26 |
| 1 | 2 | 3 | | | 6 | 7 | 12 | 9 | 10 | 11 | 8* | 4 | 5 | | | | 14 | | | | 27 |
| 1 | 2 | | | | | 7 | 6 | | 10 | 9 | 8 | 4 | 5 | | | | 11* | 12 | | | 28 |
| 1 | 2 | 3* | | 5 | 6 | 7 | 4 | 9 | 10 | 11 | 12 | 5 | 3 | | | | 8* | | | | 29 |
| 1 | 2 | 3 | | | 6 | 7 | 8 | 9 | | 11 | 10 | 4 | | | | | 12 | | | | 30 |
| 1 | | 3 | | | 6 | 7 | 8 | 9* | 10† | 11 | 14 | 4 | 5 | | | | 12 | 2 | | | 31 |
| 1 | 2 | 3* | | | 6 | 7 | 8 | | | 11 | 9 | 4 | 5 | 12 | | | 10* | | | | 32 |
| 1 | 2 | | | | 6 | 7 | 8 | 9 | 10 | 11 | | 4 | 5 | | | | 12 | | | | 33 |
| 1 | 2 | | | | 6 | 7 | 4 | 9 | 10 | 11 | | 5 | 3 | | | | 8* | | 12 | | 34 |
| 1 | 2† | | | | 6 | 7 | 4 | | 10 | 8 | 9 | 5* | 3 | | | | 12 | 14 | 11 | | 35 |
| 1 | | | | | 6 | 7† | 4 | 9 | 10 | 8 | | 5 | 3 | 12 | | | | 14* | 2 | 11 | 36 |
| 1 | | | | | 6 | 7 | 4 | 9 | 10 | 8 | 2 | | | 12 | 3 | | | | 5 | 11* | 37 |
| 1 | | | | | | 7 | 8 | 9 | 10* | 11† | 2 | 4 | 5 | 12 | 3 | | 14 | | 6 | | 38 |
| 1 | | | | | 6* | 7 | 4 | 9 | 10 | 11 | 2 | 5 | | | 3 | | 8 | 12 | | | 39 |
| 1 | | | | | | 7 | 4 | 9* | 10 | 11 | 2 | 5 | | 12 | 3 | | 8† | 14 | 6 | | 40 |
| 1 | | | | | | 7 | 8 | | 10 | 11* | 2 | 4 | 5 | 9 | | 6 | 12 | 3† | | 14 | 41 |
| 1 | | | | | | 7 | 6 | | 10 | 8 | 2 | 4* | 5 | 9 | | 3 | 12 | | | 11 | 42 |
| 42 | 31 | 31 | 4 | 12 | 37 | 40 | 36 | 36 | 38 | 42 | 16 | 35 | 33 | 3 | | 8 | 7 | 2 | 5 | 4 | |
| | | | | 2 | | | | 5 | | | 7 | | | 1 | 7 | 1 | 11 | 5 | 1 | 2 | |
| | | | | 2 | 2 | 7 | 3 | 12 | 7 | 25 | | 2 | | | 1 | | | | | | |

# 1995-96

| 1 | Aug | 19 | (h) | Sheffield W | W | 1-0 | Collymore | 40,535 |
|---|---|---|---|---|---|---|---|---|
| 2 | | 21 | (a) | Leeds U | L | 0-1 | | 36,007 |
| 3 | | 26 | (a) | Tottenham H | W | 3-1 | Barnes 2, Fowler | 31,254 |
| 4 | | 30 | (h) | QPR | W | 1-0 | Ruddock | 37,548 |
| 5 | Sep | 9 | (a) | Wimbledon | L | 0-1 | | 19,530 |
| 6 | | 16 | (h) | Blackburn R | W | 3-0 | Redknapp, Fowler, Collymore | 39,502 |
| 7 | | 23 | (h) | Bolton W | W | 5-2 | Fowler 4, Harkness | 40,104 |
| 8 | Oct | 1 | (a) | Manchester U | D | 2-2 | Fowler 2 | 34,934 |
| 9 | | 14 | (h) | Coventry C | D | 0-0 | | 39,079 |
| 10 | | 22 | (a) | Southampton | W | 3-1 | McManaman 2, Redknapp | 15,245 |
| 11 | | 28 | (h) | Manchester C | W | 6-0 | Rush 2, Redknapp, Fowler 2, Ruddock | 39,267 |
| 12 | Nov | 4 | (a) | Newcastle U | L | 1-2 | Rush | 36,547 |
| 13 | | 18 | (h) | Everton | L | 1-2 | Fowler | 40,818 |
| 14 | | 22 | (a) | West Ham U | D | 0-0 | | 24,324 |
| 15 | | 25 | (a) | Middlesbrough | L | 1-2 | Ruddock | 29,390 |
| 16 | Dec | 2 | (h) | Southampton | D | 1-1 | Collymore | 38,007 |
| 17 | | 9 | (a) | Bolton W | W | 1-0 | Collymore | 21,042 |
| 18 | | 17 | (h) | Manchester U | W | 2-0 | Fowler 2 | 40,546 |
| 19 | | 23 | (h) | Arsenal | W | 3-1 | Fowler 3 | 39,806 |
| 20 | | 30 | (a) | Chelsea | D | 2-2 | McManaman 2 | 31,137 |
| 21 | Jan | 1 | (h) | Nottingham F | W | 4-2 | Fowler 2, Collymore, Cooper (og) | 39,206 |
| 22 | | 13 | (a) | Sheffield W | D | 1-1 | Rush | 32,747 |
| 23 | | 20 | (h) | Leeds U | W | 5-0 | Ruddock 2, Fowler 2 (1 pen), Collymore | 40,254 |
| 24 | | 31 | (a) | Aston Villa | W | 2-0 | Collymore, Fowler | 39,332 |
| 25 | Feb | 3 | (h) | Tottenham H | D | 0-0 | | 40,628 |
| 26 | | 11 | (a) | QPR | W | 2-1 | Wright, Fowler | 18,405 |
| 27 | | 24 | (a) | Blackburn R | W | 3-2 | Collymore 2, Thomas | 30,895 |
| 28 | Mar | 3 | (h) | Aston Villa | W | 3-0 | McManaman, Fowler 2 | 39,508 |
| 29 | | 13 | (h) | Wimbledon | D | 2-2 | McManaman, Collymore | 34,063 |
| 30 | | 16 | (h) | Chelsea | W | 2-0 | Wright, Fowler | 40,820 |
| 31 | | 23 | (a) | Nottingham F | L | 0-1 | | 29,058 |
| 32 | Apr | 3 | (h) | Newcastle U | W | 4-3 | Fowler 2, Collymore 2 | 40,702 |
| 33 | | 6 | (a) | Coventry C | L | 0-1 | | 23,037 |
| 34 | | 8 | (h) | West Ham U | W | 2-0 | Collymore, Barnes | 40,326 |
| 35 | | 16 | (a) | Everton | D | 1-1 | Fowler | 40,120 |
| 36 | | 27 | (h) | Middlesbrough | W | 1-0 | Collymore | 40,782 |
| 37 | May | 1 | (a) | Arsenal | D | 0-0 | | 38,323 |
| 38 | | 5 | (a) | Manchester C | D | 2-2 | Lomas (og), Rush | 31,436 |

FINAL LEAGUE POSITION: 3rd in F.A. Premiership

Appearances

Sub. Appearances

Goals

| James | Jones R | Harkness | Babb | Wright | Matteo | McManaman | Redknapp | Rush | Barnes | Collymore | Fowler | Thomas | Ruddock | McAteer | Scales | Kennedy | Clough | Bjornebye | No. |
|---|---|---|---|---|---|---|---|---|---|---|---|---|---|---|---|---|---|---|---|
| 1 | 2 | 3 | 4 | 5 | 6 | 7 | 8 | 9* | 10 | 11† | 12 | 13 | | | | | | | 1 |
| 1 | 2 | 3 | 4 | 5 | 6† | 7 | 8 | 9 | 10 | 11* | 12 | 13 | | | | | | | 2 |
| 1 | 2 | 3 | 4 | 5 | | 7* | 8 | 9 | 10 | | 11 | 12 | 6 | | | | | | 3 |
| 1 | 2 | 3 | 4 | 5 | | 7 | 8 | 9 | 10 | | 11 | | 6 | | | | | | 4 |
| 1 | 2 | 3* | 4 | 5 | | 7 | 8 | | 10 | 9 | 11 | 12 | 6 | | | | | | 5 |
| 1 | 2 | 3 | 4 | 5 | | 7 | 8* | | 10† | 9† | 11 | 12 | 6 | 13 | | | | | 6 |
| 1 | 2 | 3 | 4 | 5 | | 7 | 8 | | 10 | 9 | 11 | | 6 | | | | | | 7 |
| 1 | | 3 | | 5 | | 7 | 8 | 9 | | | 11 | 10 | 6 | 4 | 2 | | | | 8 |
| 1 | 2* | 3 | 4 | 5 | | 7 | 8 | 13 | 10 | 9† | 11 | | 6 | 12 | | | | | 9 |
| 1 | | 3 | 4 | 5 | | 7 | 8 | 9 | 10 | | 11 | | | 2 | 6 | | | | 10 |
| 1 | | 3 | 4 | 5 | | 7 | 8 | 9 | 10* | | 11 | 12 | | 2 | 6† | 13 | | | 11 |
| 1 | 2 | 3 | 6 | 5 | | 7 | 8 | 9* | 10 | 12 | 11 | | | 4 | | | | | 12 |
| 1 | 2 | 3† | 6* | 5 | | 7 | | 9 | 10 | | 11 | 12 | 13 | 8 | 4 | | | | 13 |
| 1 | 2 | 3 | 4 | 5 | | 7 | | | 10 | 9 | 11 | | 6 | 8 | | | | | 14 |
| 1 | 2* | 3 | 4 | 5 | | 7 | | | 10 | 9 | 11 | 12 | 6 | 8 | | | | | 15 |
| 1 | 2* | 3 | 6 | | | 7 | | | 10 | 9 | 8 | | | 4 | 5 | 11 | 12 | | 16 |
| 1 | 2 | 6 | | 5 | | 7 | | | 10 | 9 | 11 | | | 4 | 8 | | | 3 | 17 |
| 1 | | 3 | 6 | 5 | | 7 | | | 10 | 9 | 11 | | 8 | 2 | 4 | | | | 18 |
| 1 | 2 | 3 | | 5 | | 7 | | | 10 | 9 | 11 | | 8 | 4 | 6 | | | | 19 |
| 1 | 2 | 3 | | 5 | | 7 | | | 10 | 9 | 11 | | 8 | 4 | 6 | | | | 20 |
| 1 | 2 | 3 | 5 | | | 7 | | | 10 | 9 | 11 | | 8 | 4 | 6 | | | | 21 |
| 1 | 3* | | | 5 | | 7 | | 12 | 10 | 9 | 11 | 8 | 6 | 2 | 4 | | | | 22 |
| 1 | 3 | | | 5 | | 7 | | | 10 | 9 | 11 | 8 | 6 | 2 | 4 | | | | 23 |
| 1 | 3 | | | 5 | | 7 | | | 10 | 9 | 11 | 8 | 6 | 2 | 4 | | | | 24 |
| 1 | 3* | 6 | 5 | | | 7 | | 12 | 10 | 9 | 11 | 8 | | 2 | 4 | | | | 25 |
| 1 | 3 | 6 | 5 | | | 7 | | 12 | 10 | 9 | 11* | 8 | | 2 | 4 | | | | 26 |
| 1 | 3 | 6 | 5 | | | 7 | | | 10 | 9 | 11 | 8 | | 2 | 4 | | | | 27 |
| 1 | 3 | 6 | 5† | | | 7 | 13 | 12 | 10 | 9* | 11 | 8 | | 2 | 4 | | | | 28 |
| 1 | 3* | 6 | 5 | | | 7 | | 12 | 10 | 9 | 11 | 8 | | 2 | 4 | | | | 29 |
| 1 | 2 | 3 | 5 | | | 7 | | | 10 | 9 | 11 | 8 | | 4 | 6 | | | | 30 |
| 1 | | | 5 | | 3* | 7 | 12 | 13 | 10 | 9† | 11 | 8 | 6 | 2 | 4 | | | | 31 |
| 1 | 3† | 12 | 5* | | | 7 | 8 | 13 | 10 | 9 | 11 | | 6 | 2 | 4 | | | | 32 |
| 1 | 3† | 5* | | 6 | | 7 | 8 | 13 | 10 | 9 | 11 | 12 | | 2 | 4 | | | | 33 |
| 1 | | | 5 | | | 7 | 8 | | 10 | 9 | 11 | | 6 | 2 | 4 | | | 3 | 34 |
| 1 | 3 | | 5 | | | 7 | 8* | 12 | 10 | 9 | 11 | 13 | 6† | 2 | 4 | | | | 35 |
| 1 | 2 | 5 | | | | 7 | 8 | 12 | 10 | 9 | 11* | 3† | 6 | 4 | 13 | | | | 36 |
| 1 | 3 | 5 | | | | 7 | 8 | 12 | 10 | 9 | 11 | | 6 | 2 | 4 | | | | 37 |
| 1 | 3 | | 4 | 5 | | 7 | 8* | 9 | 10 | | 11 | | 6 | 2 | 12 | | | | 38 |
| 38 | 33 | 23 | 28 | 28 | 5 | 38 | 19 | 10 | 36 | 30 | 36 | 18 | 18 | 27 | 27 | 1 | 1 | 2 | |
| | | 1 | | | | | | 4 | 10 | | 1 | 2 | 9 | 2 | 2 | | 3 | 1 | |
| | | 1 | | 2 | | 6 | 3 | 5 | 3 | 14 | 28 | 1 | 5 | | | | | | |

# 1996-97

| # | Month | Date | | Opponent | Result | | Scorers | Attendance |
|---|---|---|---|---|---|---|---|---|
| 1 | Aug | 17 | (a) | Middlesbrough | D | 3-3 | Bjornebye, Barnes, Fowler | 30,039 |
| 2 | | 19 | (h) | Arsenal | W | 2-0 | McManaman 2 | 38,103 |
| 3 | | 24 | (h) | Sunderland | D | 0-0 | | 40,503 |
| 4 | Sep | 4 | (a) | Coventry C | W | 1-0 | Babb | 22,949 |
| 5 | | 7 | (h) | Southampton | W | 2-1 | Collymore, McManaman | 39,189 |
| 6 | | 15 | (a) | Leicester C | W | 3-0 | Berger 2, Thomas | 20,987 |
| 7 | | 21 | (h) | Chelsea | W | 5-1 | Fowler, Berger 2, Myers (og), Barnes | 40,739 |
| 8 | | 29 | (a) | West Ham U | W | 2-1 | Collymore, Thomas | 25,064 |
| 9 | Oct | 12 | (a) | Manchester U | L | 0-1 | | 55,128 |
| 10 | | 27 | (h) | Derby Co | W | 2-1 | Fowler 2 | 39,515 |
| 11 | Nov | 3 | (a) | Blackburn R | L | 0-3 | | 29,598 |
| 12 | | 16 | (a) | Leeds U | W | 2-0 | Ruddock, McManaman | 39,981 |
| 13 | | 20 | (h) | Everton | D | 1-1 | Fowler | 40,751 |
| 14 | | 23 | (h) | Wimbledon | D | 1-1 | Collymore | 39,027 |
| 15 | Dec | 2 | (a) | Tottenham H | W | 2-0 | Thomas, McManaman | 32,899 |
| 16 | | 7 | (h) | Sheffield W | L | 0-1 | | 39,507 |
| 17 | | 14 | (h) | Middlesbrough | W | 5-1 | Fowler 4, Bjornebye | 39,491 |
| 18 | | 17 | (h) | Nottingham F | W | 4-2 | Collymore 2, Fowler, Lyttle (og) | 36,126 |
| 19 | | 23 | (a) | Newcastle U | D | 1-1 | Fowler | 36,570 |
| 20 | | 26 | (h) | Leicester C | D | 1-1 | Collymore | 40,786 |
| 21 | | 29 | (a) | Southampton | W | 1-0 | Barnes | 15,222 |
| 22 | Jan | 1 | (a) | Chelsea | L | 0-1 | | 27,291 |
| 23 | | 11 | (h) | West Ham U | D | 0-0 | | 40,102 |
| 24 | | 18 | (h) | Aston Villa | W | 3-0 | Carragher, Collymore, Fowler | 40,489 |
| 25 | Feb | 1 | (a) | Derby Co | W | 1-0 | Collymore | 18,102 |
| 26 | | 19 | (h) | Leeds U | W | 4-0 | Fowler, Collymore 2, Redknapp | 38,957 |
| 27 | | 22 | (h) | Blackburn R | D | 0-0 | | 40,747 |
| 28 | Mar | 2 | (a) | Aston Villa | L | 0-1 | | 39,339 |
| 29 | | 10 | (h) | Newcastle U | W | 4-3 | McManaman, Berger, Fowler 2 | 40,751 |
| 30 | | 15 | (a) | Nottingham F | D | 1-1 | Fowler | 29,181 |
| 31 | | 24 | (a) | Arsenal | W | 2-1 | Collymore, McAteer | 38,068 |
| 32 | Apr | 6 | (h) | Coventry C | L | 1-2 | Fowler | 40,079 |
| 33 | | 13 | (a) | Sunderland | W | 2-1 | Fowler, McManaman | 21,889 |
| 34 | | 16 | (a) | Everton | D | 1-1 | Thomsen (og) | 40,177 |
| 35 | | 19 | (h) | Manchester U | L | 1-3 | Barnes | 40,892 |
| 36 | May | 3 | (h) | Tottenham H | W | 2-1 | Collymore, Berger | 40,003 |
| 37 | | 6 | (a) | Wimbledon | L | 1-2 | Owen | 20,194 |
| 38 | | 11 | (a) | Sheffield W | D | 1-1 | Redknapp | 38,943 |

FINAL LEAGUE POSITION: 4th in F.A. Premiership

Appearances

Sub. Appearances

Goals

136

| James | McAteer | Bjornebye | Matteo | Wright | Babb | McManaman | Collymore | Fowler | Barnes | Thomas | Jones L | Thompson | Berger | Redknapp | Ruddock | Scales | Kennedy | Carragher | Kvarme | Harkness | Jones R | Owen | # |
|---|---|---|---|---|---|---|---|---|---|---|---|---|---|---|---|---|---|---|---|---|---|---|---|
| 1 | 2 | 3 | 4 | 5 | 6 | 7 | 8 | 9 | 10 | 11 | | | | | | | | | | | | | 1 |
| 1 | 2 | 3 | 4 | 5 | 6 | 7 | 8* | 9† | 10 | 11 | 12 | 13 | | | | | | | | | | | 2 |
| 1 | 2 | 3 | 4 | 5 | 6* | 7 | 8 | 9 | 10 | 11 | 12 | | | | | | | | | | | | 3 |
| 1 | 2 | 3 | 4 | 5 | 6 | 7 | 8 | 9 | 10 | 11 | | | | | | | | | | | | | 4 |
| 1 | 2 | 3 | 4 | 5° | 6 | 7 | 8* | 9 | 10 | 11† | | | 12 | 13 | 14 | | | | | | | | 5 |
| 1 | 2 | 3 | 4 | 5 | 6 | 7 | 8* | 9 | 10 | 11 | | | 12 | | | | | | | | | | 6 |
| 1 | 2 | 3 | 4 | 5 | 6 | 7 | | 9 | 10 | 11 | | | 8* | 12 | | | | | | | | | 7 |
| 1 | 2 | 3 | 4 | | 6 | 7 | 8† | | 10 | 11 | 12 | | 9* | 13 | 14 | 5° | | | | | | | 8 |
| 1 | 2 | 3 | 4 | | 6 | 7 | 8 | | 10 | 11 | | | 9 | 12 | | 5* | | | | | | | 9 |
| 1 | 2 | 3 | 4 | | 6 | 7 | | 9 | 10 | 11 | | | 8 | | | 5 | | | | | | | 10 |
| 1 | 2 | 3† | 4 | 5 | 6 | 7 | 12 | 9 | 10 | 11 | | | 8* | 13 | | | | | | | | | 11 |
| 1 | 2 | 3 | 4 | 5 | | 7 | | 9 | 10 | 11 | | | 8 | 6 | | | | | | | | | 12 |
| 1 | 2 | 3 | 4 | 5 | | 7* | 12 | 9 | 10 | 11 | | | 8 | 6 | | | | | | | | | 13 |
| 1 | 2 | 3 | 4* | 5 | 12 | | 7 | 9 | 10 | 11† | | | 13 | 8 | 6 | | | | | | | | 14 |
| 1 | 2 | 3 | | 5 | 4 | 7 | | 9 | 10 | 11 | | | 8 | 6 | | | | | | | | | 15 |
| 1 | 2 | 3 | | 5 | 4* | 7 | | 9 | 10 | 11 | | | 8 | 6 | | 12 | | | | | | | 16 |
| 1 | 2 | 3 | | 5 | 4 | 7 | 8 | 9 | 10 | 11 | | | | 6 | | | | | | | | | 17 |
| 1 | 2 | 3 | 12 | 5* | 4 | 7 | 8 | 9† | 10 | 11 | | | 13 | 6 | | | | | | | | | 18 |
| 1 | 2 | 3 | | 5 | 4 | 7 | 8 | 9 | 10 | 11 | | | | 6 | | | | | | | | | 19 |
| 1 | 2 | 3† | 12 | 5 | 4* | 7 | 8 | | 10 | 11 | | | 9 | 6 | | 13 | | | | | | | 20 |
| 1 | 2 | 3 | | 5 | 4 | 7 | 8* | 9 | 10 | 11 | | | 12 | 6 | | | | | | | | | 21 |
| 1 | 2 | 3 | 12 | 5† | 4 | 7 | 8 | 9 | 10 | 11 | | | 13 | 6* | | | | | | | | | 22 |
| 1 | 2 | 3 | 4 | 5* | | 7 | 12 | 9 | 10† | 11 | | | 8 | 6° | | 13 | 14 | | | | | | 23 |
| 1 | 2 | 3 | 4 | 5 | | 7 | 8* | 9 | | | | | | 10 | | | 12 | 11 | 3 | | | | 24 |
| 1 | 2 | 3 | | 5 | 6 | 7 | 8 | 9 | 10 | 12 | | | | 11 | | | | | 4* | | | | 25 |
| 1 | 2 | 3 | 4 | 5 | | 7 | 8* | 9† | 10 | | | | 12 | 11 | | | | 13 | 6 | | | | 26 |
| 1 | 2 | 3 | 4 | 5 | | 7 | 8 | 9 | 10 | | | | | 11 | | | | | 6 | | | | 27 |
| 1 | 2 | 3 | 6 | 5 | | 7 | 8* | 9 | 10 | | | | 12 | 11 | | | | | 4 | | | | 28 |
| 1 | 2 | 3 | 6 | 5 | | 7 | | 9 | 10 | | | | 8 | 11 | | | | | 4 | | | | 29 |
| 1 | 2† | 3 | 6 | 5 | | 7 | 12 | 9 | 10 | | | | 8* | 11 | | | | | 4 | 13 | | | 30 |
| 1 | 2 | 3 | | 5 | | 7 | 8 | 9* | 10 | 12 | | | | 11 | | | | | 4 | 6 | | | 31 |
| 1 | 2 | 3* | 4 | | | 7 | 8 | 9 | 10 | | | | 12 | 11 | | | | | 5 | 6 | | | 32 |
| 1 | | 3 | | 5 | | 7 | | 9 | 10 | 11 | | | 8 | | | | | | 4 | 6 | 2 | | 33 |
| 1 | 12 | 3 | | 5 | | 7 | | 9 | 10 | 11 | | | 8 | | | | | | 4 | 6 | 2* | | 34 |
| 1 | 2* | 3 | | 5 | | 7 | 12 | 9 | 10† | 11 | | | 13 | 8 | | | | | 4 | 6 | | | 35 |
| 1 | 2 | 3 | | 5 | | 7 | 8 | | | 11 | | | 9 | 10 | 6 | | | | 4 | | | | 36 |
| 1 | 2 | 3 | | 5 | | 7 | 8 | | | 11 | | | 9* | 10 | 6 | | | | 4 | | 12 | | 37 |
| 1 | 2 | 3 | 12 | 5 | | 7 | 8† | | 13 | 11 | | | | 10 | 6° | | | | 4* | 14 | 9 | | 38 |
| 38 | 36 | 38 | 22 | 33 | 21 | 37 | 25 | 32 | 34 | 29 | | | 13 | 18 | 15 | 3 | | 1 | 15 | 5 | 2 | 1 | |
| | 1 | | 4 | | 1 | | 5 | | 1 | 2 | 2 | 2 | 10 | 5 | 2 | | 5 | 1 | | 2 | | 1 | |
| | 1 | 2 | | | 1 | 7 | 12 | 18 | 4 | 3 | | | 6 | 2 | 1 | | | 1 | | | | 1 | |

# 1997-98

| 1 | Aug | 9 | (a) | Wimbledon | D | 1-1 | Owen (pen) | 26,106 |
|---|---|---|---|---|---|---|---|---|
| 2 | | 13 | (h) | Leicester C | L | 1-2 | Ince | 35,007 |
| 3 | | 23 | (a) | Blackburn R | D | 1-1 | Owen | 30,187 |
| 4 | | 26 | (a) | Leeds U | W | 2-0 | McManaman, Riedle | 39,878 |
| 5 | Sep | 13 | (h) | Sheffield W | W | 2-1 | Ince, Thomas | 34,705 |
| 6 | | 20 | (a) | Southampton | D | 1-1 | Riedle | 15,242 |
| 7 | | 22 | (h) | Aston Villa | W | 3-0 | Fowler (pen), McManaman, Riedle | 34,843 |
| 8 | | 27 | (a) | West Ham U | L | 1-2 | Fowler | 25,908 |
| 9 | Oct | 5 | (h) | Chelsea | W | 4-2 | Berger 3, Fowler | 36,647 |
| 10 | | 18 | (a) | Everton | L | 0-2 | | 40,112 |
| 11 | | 25 | (h) | Derby Co | W | 4-0 | Fowler 2, Leonhardsen, McManaman | 38,017 |
| 12 | Nov | 1 | (a) | Bolton W | D | 1-1 | Fowler | 25,000 |
| 13 | | 8 | (h) | Tottenham H | W | 4-0 | McManaman, Leonhardsen, Redknapp, Owen | 38,006 |
| 14 | | 22 | (h) | Barnsley | L | 0-1 | | 41,011 |
| 15 | | 30 | (a) | Arsenal | W | 1-0 | McManaman | 38,094 |
| 16 | Dec | 6 | (h) | Manchester U | L | 1-3 | Fowler (pen) | 41,027 |
| 17 | | 13 | (a) | Crystal Palace | W | 3-0 | McManaman, Owen, Leonhardsen | 25,790 |
| 18 | | 20 | (h) | Coventry C | W | 1-0 | Owen | 39,707 |
| 19 | | 26 | (h) | Leeds U | W | 3-1 | Owen, Fowler 2 | 43,854 |
| 20 | | 28 | (a) | Newcastle U | W | 2-1 | McManaman 2 | 36,702 |
| 21 | Jan | 10 | (h) | Wimbledon | W | 2-0 | Redknapp 2 | 38,011 |
| 22 | | 17 | (a) | Leicester C | D | 0-0 | | 21,633 |
| 23 | | 20 | (h) | Newcastle U | W | 1-0 | Owen | 42,791 |
| 24 | | 31 | (h) | Blackburn R | D | 0-0 | | 43,890 |
| 25 | Feb | 7 | (h) | Southampton | L | 2-3 | Owen 2 | 43,550 |
| 26 | | 14 | (a) | Sheffield W | D | 3-3 | Owen 3 | 35,405 |
| 27 | | 23 | (h) | Everton | D | 1-1 | Ince | 44,501 |
| 28 | | 28 | (a) | Aston Villa | L | 1-2 | Owen (pen) | 39,372 |
| 29 | Mar | 7 | (h) | Bolton W | W | 2-1 | Ince, Owen | 44,532 |
| 30 | | 14 | (a) | Tottenham H | D | 3-3 | McManaman 2, Ince | 30,245 |
| 31 | | 28 | (a) | Barnsley | W | 3-2 | Riedle 2, McManaman | 18,687 |
| 32 | Apr | 10 | (a) | Manchester U | D | 1-1 | Owen | 55,171 |
| 33 | | 13 | (h) | Crystal Palace | W | 2-1 | Leonhardsen, Thompson | 43,007 |
| 34 | | 19 | (a) | Coventry C | D | 1-1 | Owen | 22,724 |
| 35 | | 25 | (a) | Chelsea | L | 1-4 | Riedle | 34,639 |
| 36 | May | 2 | (h) | West Ham U | W | 5-0 | Owen, McAteer 2, Leonhardsen, Ince | 44,414 |
| 37 | | 6 | (h) | Arsenal | W | 4-0 | Ince 2, Owen, Leonhardsen | 44,417 |
| 38 | | 10 | (a) | Derby Co | L | 0-1 | | 30,492 |

FINAL LEAGUE POSITION: 3rd in F.A. Premiership

Appearances

Sub. Appearances

Goals

138

| James | Jones R | Bjørnebye | Babb | Wright | Ruddock | McManaman | Ince | Owen | Riedle | Thomas | McAteer | Murphy | Harkness | Matteo | Carragher | Kvarme | Berger | Fowler | Thompson | Leonhardsen | Redknapp | Friedel | Kennedy | |
|---|---|---|---|---|---|---|---|---|---|---|---|---|---|---|---|---|---|---|---|---|---|---|---|---|
| 1 | 2* | 3† | 4 | 5 | 6° | 7 | 8 | 9 | 10 | 11 | 12 | 13 | 14 | | | | | | | | | | | 1 |
| 1 | 2 | 3† | 4* | 5 | | 7 | 8 | 9 | 10 | 11° | | 13 | 6 | 12 | 14 | | | | | | | | | 2 |
| 1 | 2 | 3 | | 5 | | 7 | 8 | 9 | 10* | 11 | | | 6 | | | 4 | 12 | | | | | | | 3 |
| 1 | 2 | 3 | | 5 | | 7 | 8 | 9 | 10* | 11 | | | 6 | | | 4 | 12 | | | | | | | 4 |
| 1 | 2† | 3 | | 5 | | 7 | 8 | 9 | 10* | 11 | 13 | | 6° | 14 | | 4 | 12 | | | | | | | 5 |
| 1 | | 3 | | 5 | | 7 | 8 | 9† | 10* | 11 | 2 | | | 6 | | 4 | 12 | 13 | | | | | | 6 |
| 1 | | 3 | 6 | | | 7 | | 10 | 12 | 11 | | 4† | | 5 | 2 | 8 | 9* | 13 | | | | | | 7 |
| 1 | | 3 | 6 | | | 7 | 8 | 10 | 12 | 11† | 14 | 13 | | 5 | 4° | 2* | 9 | | | | | | | 8 |
| 1 | 2* | 3 | 6 | | | 7 | 8 | | 10 | | 12 | | | 5 | 4 | 11 | 9 | | | | | | | 9 |
| 1 | | 3 | | | 6 | 7 | 8 | 12 | 10* | | 2 | | | 5 | 4 | 11† | | 9 | | 13 | | | | 10 |
| 1 | 2 | 3 | | | | 7 | 8 | 10 | | | | | | 5 | | 4 | | 9 | | 6 | 11 | | | 11 |
| 1 | 2 | 3 | | | | 7 | 8 | 10* | 12 | | | | | 5 | | 4 | | 9 | | 6 | 11 | | | 12 |
| 1 | 2† | 3 | | | | 7° | 8 | 12 | 10* | | 13 | | | 5 | | 4 | 14 | 9 | | 6 | 11 | | | 13 |
| 1 | | 3* | | | | 7 | | 9 | 10 | | 2 | 12 | | 5 | | 4 | 8 | | | 6 | 11 | | | 14 |
| 1 | | 3 | | | | 7 | | 9* | 10 | | 2 | 12 | | 5 | 8 | 4 | | | | 6 | 11 | | | 15 |
| 1 | | 3* | | | | 7 | | 10 | 12 | | 2 | | | 5 | 8 | 4† | 13 | 9 | | 6 | 11 | | | 16 |
| 1 | 12 | | | | | 7 | | 10 | | | 2 | 3* | | 5 | 8 | 4 | 13 | 9 | | 6† | 11 | | | 17 |
| 1 | | | | | | 7 | | 10 | | | 2 | 3 | | 5 | 8 | 4 | | 9 | | 6 | 11 | | | 18 |
| 1 | | | | | | 7 | 8° | 10 | 12 | | 2 | 3 | | 5 | 14 | 4 | 13 | 9* | | 6 | 11† | | | 19 |
| 1 | | | | | | 7 | 8 | 10 | | | 2 | 3 | | 5 | 12 | 4 | | 9* | | 6 | 11 | | | 20 |
| 1 | | | 4 | | | 7 | 8 | 10 | | | 2 | 3 | | 5 | | | 12 | 9 | | 6* | 11 | | | 21 |
| 1 | | | 4 | | | 7 | 8 | 10* | | | 2 | 3 | | 5 | | | 12 | 9 | | 6 | 11 | | | 22 |
| 1 | | | 4 | | | 7 | 8 | 10 | | | 2 | 3 | | 5 | | | | 9 | | 6 | 11 | | | 23 |
| 1 | 12 | | 4 | | | 7† | 8 | 10 | | | 2* | 3 | | 5 | 11 | | 13 | 9 | | 6 | | | | 24 |
| 1 | 2 | | 4 | | | 7 | 8 | 10 | | | 12 | 3 | | 5 | 11* | | 13 | 9 | | 6† | | | | 25 |
| 1 | 2† | | | | | 7 | 8 | 10 | | | 12 | 3 | | 5 | 11 | 4* | 13 | 9 | | 6 | | | | 26 |
| 1 | 2 | | | | | 7 | 8 | 10 | | | 12 | 3 | | 5 | | 4 | | 9* | | 6 | 11 | | | 27 |
| | 2* | 3 | | | | 7 | 8 | 9 | 10 | | 12 | | 4 | 5 | 13 | | | | | 6† | 11 | 1 | | 28 |
| | 2 | 3 | | | | 7 | 8 | 9 | 10* | | | | 4 | 5 | | | | | | 6 | 11 | 1 | 12 | 29 |
| | 2 | 3 | 12 | | | 7 | 8 | 9 | | | | | 4 | 5 | 10† | | | | 13 | 6* | 11 | 1 | | 30 |
| | 2 | | 4 | | | 7 | 8 | 9 | 10 | | 12 | 3 | | 5 | | | | | | 6 | 11 | 1 | | 31 |
| | 2 | | 4 | | | 7 | 8 | 9 | 10* | | | 3 | | 5 | 12 | | | | | 6 | 11 | 1 | | 32 |
| | 2 | | 4 | | | 7 | 8 | 9 | 10† | | | 3* | | 5 | 12 | | 13 | | | 6 | 11 | 1 | | 33 |
| | 2 | 3 | 4 | | | 7 | 8 | 9 | 12 | 10 | | | | 5 | | | | | | 6 | 11* | 1 | | 34 |
| | 2 | 3 | 4 | | | 7 | 8 | 9° | 12 | 10† | | | | 5 | 11 | 13 | 14 | | | 6* | | 1 | | 35 |
| | | 3 | 4 | | | | 8 | 9 | 10 | | 7 | | | 5 | 11 | 2 | | | | 6 | | 1 | | 36 |
| | | 3 | 4 | | | 7 | 8 | 9 | 10† | 12 | 2* | 13 | | 5 | 11 | | | | | 6 | | 1 | | 37 |
| | | 3 | 4 | | | | | 9 | 10 | 11 | 8 | | | 5 | 6 | 2 | | | | 7 | | 1 | | 38 |
| 27 | 20 | 24 | 18 | 6 | 2 | 36 | 31 | 34 | 18 | 10 | 15 | 8 | 24 | 24 | 17 | 22 | 6 | 19 | 1 | 27 | 20 | 11 | | |
| | | 1 | 1 | | | | 2 | 7 | 1 | 6 | 10 | 1 | 2 | 3 | 1 | 16 | 1 | 4 | | 1 | | | 1 | |
| | | | | | | 11 | 8 | 18 | 6 | 1 | 2 | | | | | | 3 | 9 | 1 | 6 | 3 | | | |

# 1998-99

| | | | | | | | | |
|---|---|---|---|---|---|---|---|---|
| 1 | Aug | 16 | (a) | Southampton | W | 2-1 | Riedle, Owen | 15,202 |
| 2 | | 22 | (h) | Arsenal | D | 0-0 | | 44,429 |
| 3 | | 30 | (a) | Newcastle U | W | 4-1 | Owen 3, Berger | 36,740 |
| 4 | Sep | 9 | (h) | Coventry C | W | 2-0 | Berger, Redknapp | 41,771 |
| 5 | | 12 | (a) | West Ham U | L | 1-2 | Riedle | 26,010 |
| 6 | | 19 | (h) | Charlton Ath | D | 3-3 | Fowler 2 (1 pen), Berger | 44,,526 |
| 7 | | 24 | (a) | Manchester U | L | 0-2 | | 55,181 |
| 8 | Oct | 4 | (h) | Chelsea | D | 1-1 | Redknapp | 44,404 |
| 9 | | 17 | (a) | Everton | D | 0-0 | | 40,185 |
| 10 | | 24 | (h) | Nottingham F | W | 5-1 | Owen 4 (1 pen), McManaman | 44,595 |
| 11 | | 31 | (a) | Leicester C | L | 0-1 | | 21,837 |
| 12 | Nov | 7 | (h) | Derby Co | L | 1-2 | Redknapp | 44,020 |
| 13 | | 14 | (h) | Leeds U | L | 1-3 | Fowler (pen) | 44,305 |
| 14 | | 21 | (a) | Aston Villa | W | 4-2 | Ince, Fowler 3 | 39,241 |
| 15 | | 29 | (h) | Blackburn R | W | 2-0 | Ince, Owen | 41,753 |
| 16 | Dec | 5 | (a) | Tottenham H | L | 1-2 | Berger | 36,125 |
| 17 | | 13 | (a) | Wimbledon | L | 0-1 | | 26,080 |
| 18 | | 19 | (h) | Sheffield W | W | 2-0 | Berger, Owen | 40,003 |
| 19 | | 26 | (a) | Middlesbrough | W | 3-1 | Owen, Redknapp, Heggem | 34,626 |
| 20 | | 28 | (h) | Newcastle U | W | 4-2 | Owen 2, Riedle 2 | 44,605 |
| 21 | Jan | 9 | (a) | Arsenal | D | 0-0 | | 38,107 |
| 22 | | 16 | (h) | Southampton | W | 7-1 | Fowler 3, Matteo, Carragher, Owen, Thompson | 44,011 |
| 23 | | 30 | (a) | Coventry C | L | 1-2 | McManaman | 23,057 |
| 24 | Feb | 6 | (h) | Middlesbrough | W | 3-1 | Owen, Heggem, Ince | 44,384 |
| 25 | | 13 | (a) | Charlton Ath | L | 0-1 | | 20,043 |
| 26 | | 20 | (h) | West Ham U | D | 2-2 | Fowler, Owen | 44,511 |
| 27 | | 27 | (a) | Chelsea | L | 1-2 | Owen | 34,822 |
| 28 | Mar | 13 | (a) | Derby Co | L | 2-3 | Fowler 2 (1 pen) | 32,913 |
| 29 | Apr | 3 | (h) | Everton | W | 3-2 | Fowler 2 (1 pen), Berger | 44,852 |
| 30 | | 5 | (a) | Nottingham F | D | 2-2 | Redknapp, Owen | 28,374 |
| 31 | | 12 | (a) | Leeds U | D | 0-0 | | 39,372 |
| 32 | | 17 | (h) | Aston Villa | L | 0-1 | | 44,306 |
| 33 | | 21 | (h) | Leicester C | L | 0-1 | | 36,019 |
| 34 | | 24 | (a) | Blackburn R | W | 3-1 | McManaman, Redknapp, Leonhardsen | 29,944 |
| 35 | May | 1 | (h) | Tottenham H | W | 3-2 | Redknapp (pen), Ince, McManaman | 44,007 |
| 36 | | 5 | (h) | Manchester U | D | 2-2 | Redknapp (pen), Ince | 44,702 |
| 37 | | 8 | (a) | Sheffield W | L | 0-1 | | 27,383 |
| 38 | | 16 | (h) | Wimbledon | W | 3-0 | Berger, Riedle, Ince | 41,902 |

FINAL LEAGUE POSITION: 7th in F.A. Premiership

Appearances

Sub. Appearances

Goals

| Friedel | Heggem | Staunton | McAteer | Carragher | Babb | McManaman | Ince | Riedle | Owen | Berger | Harkness | Redknapp | Thompson | Matteo | Fowler | Bjornebye | James | Leonhardsen | Kvarne | Murphy | Gerrard | Song | Ferri | Dundee | |
|---|---|---|---|---|---|---|---|---|---|---|---|---|---|---|---|---|---|---|---|---|---|---|---|---|---|
| 1 | 2 | 3 | 4 | 5 | 6 | 7 | 8 | 9 | 10 | 11* | 12 | | | | | | | | | | | | | | 1 |
| 1 | 2 | 3 | 4 | 5 | 6 | 7 | 8 | 9 | 10 | 11* | | 12 | | | | | | | | | | | | | 2 |
| 1 | 2 | 3 | 12 | 5 | 6 | 7† | 8 | 9 | 10 | 11 | 4* | 13 | | | | | | | | | | | | | 3 |
| 1 | 2 | 3 | | 5 | 6 | 7 | 8 | 9 | 10 | 11 | 4 | | | | | | | | | | | | | | 4 |
| 1 | 2† | 3° | 13 | 5 | 6 | 7 | 8 | 12 | 10 | 9 | 11* | 4 | | 14 | | | | | | | | | | | 5 |
| 1 | 2° | 3† | 12 | 5 | 6 | 7 | | 10 | 8 | 4* | 11 | 14 | 13 | 9 | | | | | | | | | | | 6 |
| 1 | 2 | | 5 | 6 | 7 | 8 | 9* | 10 | 11 | | 4 | | | | 12 | 3 | | | | | | | | | 7 |
| | 12 | 2* | | 5 | 6° | | 8 | 13 | 10 | 11 | 4 | | 14 | | 9 | 3 | 1 | 7† | | | | | | | 8 |
| | 2 | 6 | 12 | 5° | 7 | 8 | 13 | | 10 | 11† | 4* | | | | 9 | 3 | 1 | 14 | | | | | | | 9 |
| | 2 | 6 | 4 | 5 | 7* | 8 | 9 | | 10 | 11 | | | | | 12 | 3 | 1 | | | | | | | | 10 |
| | 2 | 6 | 4 | 5 | 7 | 8 | 9 | | 10 | 11* | | | | | 12 | 3 | 1 | | | | | | | | 11 |
| | 2† | 6 | 12 | 5 | 7 | 8 | | | 10 | 11* | 4 | 13 | | | 9 | 3 | 1 | | | | | | | | 12 |
| | 2 | 6 | | 5 | | | 8 | | 10* | 11 | 4 | 7 | | | 9 | 3 | 1 | 12 | | | | | | | 13 |
| | 2 | 6 | 12 | 5 | 4 | 8 | 13 | 10† | 11* | | 3° | 7 | | | 9 | 14 | 1 | | | | | | | | 14 |
| | 2† | 6* | 5 | 4 | | 8 | | 10 | 11 | | | 7 | | | 9 | 3 | 1 | | | 12 | 13 | | | | 15 |
| | 2 | 6 | 5 | 4 | | 8 | | 10 | 11 | | | 12 | | | 9 | 3† | 1 | | | 13 | 7* | | | | 16 |
| | 2 | 6 | 5 | 4 | | 8 | 12 | 10 | 11 | | | 7 | | | 9* | 3 | 1 | | | | | | | | 17 |
| | 2† | 6 | 5 | 4 | | 8 | 12 | 10* | 11 | | | 7 | | | 9 | 3 | 1 | | | 13 | | | | | 18 |
| | 2 | 6 | 5 | 4 | 12 | 8 | 13 | 10* | 11 | 14 | | 7° | | | 9† | 3 | 1 | | | | | | | | 19 |
| | 2 | 6 | 12 | 5 | 4* | 7† | | 9 | 10 | 11 | 8 | 14 | | | | 3 | 1 | | | 13° | | | | | 20 |
| | 2 | 6† | 5 | 4 | | 8 | 12 | 10* | 11 | 3 | | 7 | 13 | | 9 | | 1 | | | | | | | | 21 |
| | 2 | | | 5° | 6 | 8† | 12 | 10* | 11 | 7 | 13 | 4 | | | 9 | 3 | 1 | | | 14 | | | | | 22 |
| | 2 | 6° | | | 12 | 8 | 13 | 10 | 11† | 7 | | 4 | | | 9 | 3 | 1 | | | 14 | 5* | | | | 23 |
| | 2 | 6 | | 5 | 7 | 8 | 12 | 10† | 11 | | | 4 | | | 9* | 3 | 1 | | | 13 | | | | | 24 |
| | 2† | 6 | | 5 | 7 | 8 | 12 | 10* | 11 | | | 4 | | | 9 | 3° | 1 | | | 13 | 14 | | | | 25 |
| | 2 | 6 | 8 | 4 | 7† | 12 | | 10 | 13 | 11 | | | | | 9 | 3* | 1 | | | | | 5 | | | 26 |
| | 2* | | | 6 | 12 | 8° | 13 | 10 | 11† | 7 | 5 | | | | 9 | 3 | 1 | 4 | | 14 | | | | | 27 |
| | 2 | 6† | | 4 | 12 | 10* | 11 | | | 7 | 3 | | | | 9 | 13 | 1 | | | | 8 | 5 | | | 28 |
| | 2† | 6 | | 7 | 8 | 12 | 10 | 11 | | 4 | | 3 | | | 9* | | 1 | | | | 13 | 5 | | | 29 |
| | | 6 | | 5 | 7* | 8 | 12 | 10 | 11 | 4 | | 3 | | | 9† | | 1 | | | | 13 | 2 | | | 30 |
| | | | | 5 | 6 | 7 | 8 | 12 | 10* | 11 | 4 | 3 | | | 9 | | 1 | | | | | 2 | | | 31 |
| | | | | 5 | 4 | 7 | 8 | | 10 | 11 | 6 | 9 | | | 3* | | 1 | 12 | | | | 2† | 13 | | 32 |
| | | | | 5 | 4 | 7 | 8 | 9 | | 11 | | 10* | 3 | | 6 | | 1 | | | | | 2 | 12 | | 33 |
| 1 | 6 | | 5 | | | 7 | 8 | 9† | | | | 11 | 10 | 3 | | 4 | 12 | | | 2* | | 13 | | | 34 |
| 1 | 6 | | 5 | | | 7 | 8 | 9 | | | | 11 | 10* | 3 | | 4° | 2† | 12 | | 13 | 14 | | | | 35 |
| 1 | 6† | | 5 | 4 | | 7 | 8 | 9 | | 12 | | 11 | 13 | 3 | | | | 10 | | | 2* | | | | 36 |
| 1 | 6 | | 5 | | | 7 | 8 | 9 | | 11* | 4° | 12 | 3 | | | | | 10 | | 2† | 13 | 14 | | | 37 |
| 1 | 12 | 6† | 5 | 13 | 7° | 8 | 9 | | | 11 | 4 | 14 | 3 | | | | | 10 | | 2* | | | | | 38 |
| 12 | 27 | 31 | 6 | 34 | 24 | 25 | 34 | 16 | 30 | 30 | 4 | 33 | 4 | 16 | 23 | 20 | 26 | 7 | 2 | | 4 | 10 | | | |
| | 2 | | 7 | | 1 | 3 | | 18 | | 2 | 2 | 1 | 10 | 4 | 2 | 3 | | 2 | 5 | 1 | 8 | 3 | 2 | 3 | |
| | 2 | | | 1 | | 4 | 6 | 5 | 18 | 7 | | 8 | | 1 | 1 | 14 | | | | | 1 | | | | |

141

# 1999-2000

| | | | | | | | | |
|---|---|---|---|---|---|---|---|---|
| 1 | Aug | 7 | (a) | Sheffield W | W | 2-1 | Fowler, Camara | 34,853 |
| 2 | | 14 | (h) | Watford | L | 0-1 | | 44,174 |
| 3 | | 21 | (a) | Middlesbrough | L | 0-1 | | 34,783 |
| 4 | | 23 | (a) | Leeds U | W | 2-1 | Camara, Radebe (og) | 39,703 |
| 5 | | 28 | (h) | Arsenal | W | 2-0 | Fowler, Berger | 44,886 |
| 6 | Sep | 11 | (h) | Manchester U | L | 2-3 | Hyypia, Berger | 44,929 |
| 7 | | 18 | (a) | Leicester C | D | 2-2 | Owen 2 (1 pen) | 21,623 |
| 8 | | 27 | (h) | Everton | L | 0-1 | | 44,802 |
| 9 | Oct | 2 | (a) | Aston Villa | D | 0-0 | | 39,217 |
| 10 | . | 16 | (h) | Chelsea | W | 1-0 | Thompson | 44,826 |
| 11 | | 23 | (a) | Southampton | D | 1-1 | Camara | 15,241 |
| 12 | | 27 | (h) | West Ham U | W | 1-0 | Camara | 44,012 |
| 13 | Nov | 1 | (h) | Bradford C | W | 3-1 | Camara, Redknapp (pen), Heggem | 40,483 |
| 14 | | 6 | (h) | Derby Co | W | 2-0 | Murphy, Redknapp | 44,467 |
| 15 | | 20 | (a) | Sunderland | W | 2-0 | Owen, Berger | 41,511 |
| 16 | | 27 | (a) | West Ham U | L | 0-1 | | 26,043 |
| 17 | Dec | 5 | (h) | Sheffield W | W | 4-1 | Hyypia, Murphy, Gerrard, Thompson | 42,517 |
| 18 | | 18 | (h) | Coventry C | W | 2-0 | Owen, Camara | 44,024 |
| 19 | | 26 | (a) | Newcastle U | D | 2-2 | Owen 2 | 36,445 |
| 20 | | 28 | (h) | Wimbledon | W | 3-1 | Owen, Berger, Fowler | 44,107 |
| 21 | Jan | 3 | (a) | Tottenham H | L | 0-1 | | 36,044 |
| 22 | | 15 | (a) | Watford | W | 3-2 | Berger, Thompson, Smicer | 21,367 |
| 23 | | 22 | (h) | Middlesbrough | D | 0-0 | | 44,324 |
| 24 | Feb | 5 | (h) | Leeds U | W | 3-1 | Hamann, Berger, Murphy | 44,793 |
| 25 | | 13 | (a) | Arsenal | W | 1-0 | Camara | 38,098 |
| 26 | Mar | 4 | (a) | Manchester U | D | 1-1 | Berger | 61,592 |
| 27 | | 11 | (h) | Sunderland | D | 1-1 | Berger (pen) | 44,693 |
| 28 | | 15 | (h) | Aston Villa | D | 0-0 | | 43,615 |
| 29 | | 18 | (a) | Derby Co | W | 2-0 | Owen, Camara | 33,378 |
| 30 | | 25 | (h) | Newcastle U | W | 2-1 | Camara, Redknapp | 44,743 |
| 31 | Apr | 1 | (a) | Coventry C | W | 3-0 | Owen 2, Heskey | 23,084 |
| 32 | | 9 | (h) | Tottenham H | W | 2-0 | Berger, Owen | 44,536 |
| 33 | | 16 | (a) | Wimbledon | W | 2-1 | Heskey 2 | 26,102 |
| 34 | | 21 | (a) | Everton | D | 0-0 | | 40,052 |
| 35 | | 29 | (a) | Chelsea | L | 0-2 | | 34,957 |
| 36 | May | 3 | (h) | Leicester C | L | 0-2 | | 43,456 |
| 37 | | 7 | (h) | Southampton | D | 0-0 | | 44,015 |
| 38 | | 14 | (a) | Bradford C | L | 0-1 | | 18,276 |

FINAL LEAGUE POSITION: 4th in F.A. Premiership

Appearances

Sub. Appearances

Goals

| Westerveld | Heggem | Matteo | Hamann | Carragher | Hyypia | Redknapp | Smicer | Fowler | Camara | Berger | Thompson | Staunton | Meijer | Gerrard | Song | Riedle | Owen | Murphy | Henchoz | Friedel | Newby | Heskey | № |
|---|---|---|---|---|---|---|---|---|---|---|---|---|---|---|---|---|---|---|---|---|---|---|---|
| 1 | 2 | 3 | 4* | 5 | 6 | 7 | 8 | 9 | 10° | 11 | 12† | 13 | 14 | | | | | | | | | | 1 |
| 1 | 2° | 3 | | 5 | 6 | 4 | 8* | 9 | 10 | 11 | 13 | | | 7† | 14 | 12 | | | | | | | 2 |
| 1 | 2 | 3 | | 5 | 4 | 8 | | 9 | 10 | 11* | 12 | 6† | 13 | 7 | | | | | | | | | 3 |
| 1 | | 3 | | 5 | 6 | 4 | | 9 | 10 | 11 | 8 | | | 7 | 2 | | | | | | | | 4 |
| 1 | 12 | 3 | | 5 | 6 | 4 | | 9 | 10† | 11 | 8* | | | 7 | 2 | | 13 | | | | | | 5 |
| 1 | 12 | 3 | | 5 | 6 | 4 | 13 | 9 | 10° | 11 | 8† | | | 7* | 2 | | 14 | | | | | | 6 |
| 1 | 2 | 3 | | 5 | 6 | 4† | | 9* | | 11 | 8 | | 12 | 7 | | | 10 | 13 | | | | | 7 |
| 1 | 2 | | 4† | 5 | 6 | 7 | 8* | 9° | 12 | 11 | | 3 | 13 | 14 | | | 10 | | | | | | 8 |
| 1 | | | 4* | 12 | 6 | 7 | 8° | | 13 | 11 | | 3 | 9 | 14 | 2 | | 10† | | 5 | | | | 9 |
| | 12 | | | 5 | 6 | 11 | 8 | | | 7 | | 3 | 13 | | 2 | | 10† | 9* | 4 | 1 | | | 10 |
| | 12 | | | 5 | 6 | 11 | 8* | 10 | | 13 | | 3 | | 7° | 2 | | 14 | 9† | 4 | 1 | | | 11 |
| 1 | 12 | 3 | | 5 | 6 | 7 | 13 | 10† | | 11 | 8* | | | 9 | 2 | | | | 4 | | | | 12 |
| 1 | 12 | | 4 | 13 | 6 | 7† | 8° | 9 | | 11 | 10* | 3 | 14 | | 2 | | | | 5 | | | | 13 |
| 1 | 2 | | 7 | 5 | 6 | 11 | 8† | 9° | | | | 3 | 14 | 12 | | | 10* | 13 | 4 | | | | 14 |
| 1 | 12 | 3 | 4 | | 6 | 7 | | | | 11 | 13 | | 14 | 8† | 2 | | 10* | 9° | 5 | | | | 15 |
| 1 | 4 | 3 | 7 | | 6 | | | | | 11* | 12 | 13 | 14 | 8 | 2° | | 10† | 9 | 5 | | | | 16 |
| 1 | | 3 | 4 | 12 | 6 | | 13 | 9 | | 11 | | | 14 | 7 | 2* | | 10† | 8° | 5 | | | | 17 |
| 1 | 12 | 3 | 4 | 2 | 6 | | 13° | 9* | | 11 | 8† | | | 7 | | | 10 | 14 | 5 | | | | 18 |
| 1 | 12 | 3 | 4 | 5 | 6 | | 13 | 9* | | 11 | | | | 7 | 2 | | 10 | 8† | | | | | 19 |
| 1 | 2 | 3 | | 5 | 6 | 12 | 13 | 9° | | 11 | | | | 7 | | 14 | 10* | 8† | 4 | | | | 20 |
| 1 | 2 | 3 | 8 | 5† | 6 | 10* | | 9 | | 11° | 13 | | 12 | 7 | | | 14 | | 4 | | | | 21 |
| 1 | | 3 | 4* | 2 | 6 | | 12 | 9† | | 11 | 8 | | 13 | 7 | | | 10* | 14 | 5 | | | | 22 |
| 1 | | 3 | 4 | 2 | 6 | | | 9° | | 11 | 8† | | 12 | 7 | | | 10* | 13 | 5 | 14 | | | 23 |
| 1 | | 3 | 4 | 2 | 6 | | 8 | 9* | | 11 | | | | 7 | | | 10 | 12 | 5 | | | | 24 |
| 1 | 12 | 3 | 4 | 2 | 6 | | 8 | 9 | | 11 | | | | 7* | | | 10† | 13 | 5 | | | | 25 |
| 1 | 2* | 3 | 4 | 7 | 6° | | 8 | 9† | | 11 | | | | 12 | | | 10 | 13 | 5 | 14 | | | 26 |
| 1 | | 3 | 4 | 7 | 6 | | | | 12 | 11 | 8° | | | | 2* | | 10† | 13 | 5 | 14 | | 9 | 27 |
| 1 | | 3 | 4 | 2 | 6 | | 12 | | 13 | 11 | 8° | | 14 | 7* | | | 10† | | 5 | | | 9 | 28 |
| 1 | | 3 | 4 | 2 | 6 | | 12 | | 13 | 11 | 8 | | | 7 | | | 10† | | 5 | | | 9* | 29 |
| 1 | | 3 | 4 | 2 | 6 | | 12 | | 10 | 11° | 8† | | 13 | 7* | | | 14 | | 5 | | | 9 | 30 |
| 1 | | 3 | 4 | 2 | 6 | | 12 | | | 11 | 8 | | | 7° | 13 | | 10* | 14 | 5† | | | 9 | 31 |
| 1 | 12 | 3 | 4 | 2 | 6 | | 13 | | 14 | 11 | 8† | | | 7* | | | 10° | | 5 | | | 9 | 32 |
| 1 | | 3 | 4 | 2 | 6 | | 12 | | 13 | 11 | 8* | | | 7 | | | 10° | | 5 | 14 | | 9† | 33 |
| 1 | 12 | 3 | 4 | 2 | 6 | | | | 13 | 11 | 8* | | | 7 | | | 10 | | 5 | | | 9† | 34 |
| 1 | | 3 | 4* | 2 | 6 | | 13 | 14 | 12 | 11 | | | | 7† | | | 10 | 8° | 5 | | | 9 | 35 |
| 1 | | 3 | 4† | 2 | 6 | 7 | 13 | | 12 | 11 | 8° | | | | | | 10* | 14 | 5 | | | 9 | 36 |
| 1 | | 3 | 12 | 4 | 6 | 7 | 10† | 8° | | 11 | | | 13 | 14 | 2* | | | | 5 | | | 9 | 37 |
| 1 | | 3° | 4 | 2 | 6 | | 8 | 12 | 13 | 11† | | | 14 | 7* | | | 10 | | 5 | | | 9 | 38 |
| 36 | 10 | 32 | 27 | 33 | 38 | 18 | 13 | 8 | 22 | 34 | 19 | 7 | 7 | 26 | 14 | | 22 | 9 | 29 | 2 | | 12 | |
| | 12 | 1 | 3 | | 4 | 8 | 6 | 11 | | 8 | 5 | 14 | 3 | 4 | 1 | | 5 | 14 | | | 1 | | |
| 1 | | 1 | | 2 | 3 | 1 | 3 | 9 | 9 | 3 | | | 1 | | | | 11 | 3 | | | | 3 | |

143

# 2000-2001

| | | | | | | | | |
|---|---|---|---|---|---|---|---|---|
| 1 | Aug | 19 | (h) | Bradford C | W | 1-0 | Heskey | 44,183 |
| 2 | | 21 | (a) | Arsenal | L | 0-2 | | 38,014 |
| 3 | | 26 | (a) | Southampton | D | 3-3 | Owen 2, Hyypia | 15,202 |
| 4 | Sep | 6 | (h) | Aston Villa | W | 3-1 | Owen 3 | 43,360 |
| 5 | | 9 | (h) | Manchester C | W | 3-2 | Owen, Hamann 2 | 44,692 |
| 6 | | 17 | (a) | West Ham U | D | 1-1 | Gerrard | 25,998 |
| 7 | | 23 | (h) | Sunderland | D | 1-1 | Owen | 44,713 |
| 8 | Oct | 1 | (a) | Chelsea | L | 0-3 | | 34,966 |
| 9 | | 15 | (a) | Derby Co | W | 4-0 | Heskey 3, Berger | 30,532 |
| 10 | | 21 | (h) | Leicester C | W | 1-0 | Heskey | 44,395 |
| 11 | | 29 | (h) | Everton | W | 3-1 | Barmby, Heskey, Berger (pen) | 44,718 |
| 12 | Nov | 4 | (a) | Leeds U | L | 3-4 | Hyypia, Ziege, Smicer | 40,055 |
| 13 | | 12 | (h) | Coventry C | W | 4-1 | McAllister, Gerrard, Heskey 2 | 43,701 |
| 14 | | 19 | (a) | Tottenham H | L | 1-2 | Fowler | 36,051 |
| 15 | | 26 | (a) | Newcastle U | L | 1-2 | Heskey | 51,949 |
| 16 | Dec | 2 | (h) | Charlton Ath | W | 3-0 | Fish (og), Heskey, Babbel | 43,515 |
| 17 | | 10 | (h) | Ipswich T | L | 0-1 | | 43,509 |
| 18 | | 17 | (a) | Manchester U | W | 1-0 | Murphy | 67,533 |
| 19 | | 23 | (h) | Arsenal | W | 4-0 | Gerrard, Owen, Barmby, Fowler | 44,144 |
| 20 | | 26 | (a) | Middlesbrough | L | 0-1 | | 34,696 |
| 21 | Jan | 1 | (h) | Southampton | W | 2-1 | Gerrard, Babel | 38,474 |
| 22 | | 13 | (a) | Aston Villa | W | 3-0 | Murphy 2, Gerrard | 41,366 |
| 23 | | 20 | (h) | Middlesbrough | D | 0-0 | | 43,042 |
| 24 | | 31 | (a) | Manchester C | D | 1-1 | Heskey | 34,629 |
| 25 | Feb | 3 | (h) | West Ham U | W | 3-0 | Smicer, Fowler 2 | 44,045 |
| 26 | | 10 | (a) | Sunderland | D | 1-1 | Litmanen (pen) | 46,231 |
| 27 | Mar | 3 | (a) | Leicester C | L | 0-2 | | 21,924 |
| 28 | | 18 | (h) | Derby Co | D | 1-1 | Owen | 43,362 |
| 29 | | 31 | (h) | Manchester U | W | 2-0 | Gerrard, Fowler | 44,806 |
| 30 | Apr | 10 | (a) | Ipswich T | D | 1-1 | Heskey | 23,500 |
| 31 | | 13 | (h) | Leeds U | L | 1-2 | Gerrard | 44,116 |
| 32 | | 16 | (a) | Everton | W | 3-2 | Heskey, Babbel, McAllister | 40,260 |
| 33 | | 22 | (h) | Tottenham H | W | 3-1 | Heskey, McAllister (pen), Fowler | 43,547 |
| 34 | | 28 | (a) | Coventry C | W | 2-0 | Hyypia, McAllister | 23,063 |
| 35 | May | 1 | (a) | Bradford C | W | 2-0 | Owen, McAllister | 22,057 |
| 36 | | 5 | (h) | Newcastle U | W | 3-0 | Owen 3 | 44,363 |
| 37 | | 8 | (h) | Chelsea | D | 2-2 | Owen 2 | 43,588 |
| 38 | | 19 | (a) | Charlton Ath | W | 4-0 | Fowler 2, Murphy, Owen | 20,043 |

FINAL LEAGUE POSITION: 3rd in F.A. Premiership

Appearances

Sub. Appearances

Goals

| Westerveld | Babbel | Traore | Hamann | Henchoz | Hyypia | Gerrard | Smicer | Heskey | Owen | Barmby | McAllister | Berger | Carragher | Meijer | Murphy | Staunton | Song | Ziege | Diomede | Fowler | Heggem | Biscan | Litmanen | Wright | Vignal | # |
|---|---|---|---|---|---|---|---|---|---|---|---|---|---|---|---|---|---|---|---|---|---|---|---|---|---|---|
| 1 | 2 | 3 | 4 | 5 | 6 | 7* | 8 | 9† | 10° | 11 | 12 | 13 | 14 |  |  |  |  |  |  |  |  |  |  |  |  | 1 |
| 1 | 2 | 3 | 4 | 5 | 6 |  | 8* | 9° | 12 | 7† | 10 |  | 11 | 14 | 13 |  |  |  |  |  |  |  |  |  |  | 2 |
| 1 | 2 | 3 | 4 | 5 | 6 | 7 | 8* |  | 9 | 10† |  | 11 |  | 12 | 13 |  |  |  |  |  |  |  |  |  |  | 3 |
| 1 | 2 | 3 | 4 | 5 | 6 | 7 | 8* | 9† | 10 | 12 |  | 11 | 13 |  |  |  |  |  |  |  |  |  |  |  |  | 4 |
| 1 | 6 | 3 | 4 | 5 |  | 7† |  | 9 | 10* | 8 |  | 11 | 12 |  |  | 2 | 13 |  |  |  |  |  |  |  |  | 5 |
| 1 | 6 | 3 | 4 | 5 |  | 7† |  | 9 |  | 8 |  | 11 | 10* |  |  | 2 | 12 | 13 |  |  |  |  |  |  |  | 6 |
| 1 | 6 |  | 4* | 5 |  | 12 |  | 9† | 10 | 8 |  | 11 | 13 |  |  | 2 | 3 | 7° | 14 |  |  |  |  |  |  | 7 |
| 1 | 2 |  | 4 | 5 | 6 | 7 |  | 9 | 10 | 8* |  | 11† | 3 | 12 | 13 |  |  |  |  |  |  |  |  |  |  | 8 |
| 1 | 4 |  |  |  | 6 | 12 | 9 | 10† | 7* | 8 | 11 | 5 | 14 | 3 | 13 |  |  |  |  |  | 2° |  |  |  |  | 9 |
| 1 | 5 |  | 4 | 2 | 6 | 7 |  | 9 | 10 | 11 | 12 |  | 3 |  |  |  |  | 3 |  | 8* |  |  |  |  |  | 10 |
| 1 | 5 |  | 4 | 2† | 6 | 7 |  | 9 | 10 | 11 | 12 | 13 |  |  |  |  |  | 3 |  | 8* |  |  |  |  |  | 11 |
| 1 | 5 |  | 4 |  | 6 | 12 | 8 | 9 | 10* | 11† |  | 13 | 14 |  |  | 2 |  | 7° |  | 3 |  |  |  |  |  | 12 |
| 1 | 4 | 3 | 2* | 5 | 6 | 7 | 8° | 9 | 10† | 11 | 12 | 13 | 14 |  |  |  |  |  |  |  |  |  |  |  |  | 13 |
| 1 | 2 | 3* | 4 | 5 | 6 | 12 | 8† |  | 10 | 11 |  | 13 | 14 |  |  |  |  | 7° |  | 9 |  |  |  |  |  | 14 |
| 1 | 2 |  | 4 | 5 | 6 | 7† | 12 |  | 10 | 11 |  | 13 | 3 |  | 8* |  |  |  |  | 9 |  |  |  |  |  | 15 |
| 1 | 4 |  | 12 | 5 | 6 | 7 | 8 |  | 10* | 11 |  | 13 | 14 |  |  | 2 |  | 3° |  | 9† |  |  |  |  |  | 16 |
| 1 | 2 |  | 4 | 5 | 6 | 7 | 8* |  | 10† | 11 | 12 | 13 |  |  |  |  |  | 3° |  | 9 |  |  | 14 |  |  | 17 |
| 1 | 4 |  | 12 | 5 | 6 | 7 | 8 | 9 | 10* | 11† |  | 13 | 3 |  |  | 2 |  |  |  |  |  |  |  |  |  | 18 |
| 1 | 4 |  | 12 | 5 | 6 | 7† | 8 | 9 | 10° | 11* |  | 13 | 14 |  |  | 2 |  | 3 |  |  |  |  |  |  |  | 19 |
| 1 | 2° |  | 4* | 5 | 6 | 7 | 8 | 9 | 10† | 11 | 12 | 13 | 3 |  |  |  |  |  |  |  |  |  | 14 |  |  | 20 |
| 1 | 2 |  | 4 | 5 | 6 | 7† | 8* | 9° | 10 | 11 | 12 | 13 | 3 |  |  |  |  |  |  |  |  |  | 14 |  |  | 21 |
| 1 | 2 |  | 4 | 5 | 6 | 7* | 8 | 9† | 10° | 11 | 12 | 13 | 3 |  |  |  |  |  |  |  |  |  |  | 14 | 10° | 22 |
| 1 | 2 |  | 4 | 5 | 6 | 7 | 8 | 9* |  | 11† | 12 | 13 | 3 |  |  |  |  |  |  |  |  |  |  | 14 | 10° | 23 |
| 1 | 2 |  | 4 | 5 | 6 |  | 8 | 9 | 10† |  |  | 13 | 3 |  |  |  |  |  |  | 11° | 14 | 12 | 13 | 7* |  | 24 |
| 1 | 2° |  | 4 | 5 | 6 | 7 | 8 | 9 |  |  |  | 13 | 3 |  | 12† |  |  | 13 | 10 | 11* |  | 14 | 3 |  |  | 25 |
| 1 | 2 |  | 4 | 5 | 6 | 7* | 8 | 9† | 10 |  | 12 |  | 3 |  |  |  |  |  |  | 11° |  | 13 | 14 | 3 |  | 26 |
| 1 | 2 |  | 12 | 5† | 6 | 7 | 8° | 9 | 10 | 11 |  | 13 | 3 |  | 4* |  |  |  |  | 14 |  | 11 | 10 |  |  | 27 |
| 1 | 2 |  | 4 | 5 | 6 | 7° | 12 | 9 | 10 |  |  | 13 | 3 |  | 14 |  |  |  |  |  |  | 11* | 8† |  |  | 28 |
| 1 | 2 |  | 4 | 5 | 6 | 7* | 8 | 9 | 10† |  | 12 | 13 | 3 |  | 14 |  |  |  |  | 11° |  |  |  |  |  | 29 |
| 1 | 5 |  | 12 |  | 6 | 7 | 8 | 9 | 10 |  |  | 13 | 3 |  |  | 2 |  |  |  | 11* |  |  | 4† |  |  | 30 |
| 1 | 2 |  | 4† | 5 | 6 | 7 | 12 |  | 10 |  |  | 13 | 3 |  | 14 |  |  | 11* | 8° | 9 |  |  |  |  |  | 31 |
| 1 | 2 |  | 4 | 5 | 6 |  | 8 | 9 |  | 11 |  |  | 3 |  |  |  |  |  |  | 10* |  | 7 |  |  | 12 | 32 |
| 1 | 2 |  | 12 | 5 | 6 | 4* | 8 | 9† | 10 | 11 |  |  | 3° |  |  |  |  | 7 |  | 13 |  |  | 13 | 14 |  | 33 |
| 1 | 2 |  | 4 | 5 | 6 | 7 | 8 | 9° |  | 11† | 12 |  | 3 |  | 13 |  |  |  |  | 10* |  | 14 |  |  |  | 34 |
| 1 | 2 |  | 4 | 5 | 6 | 7 | 12 | 9 | 10 | 11† |  | 13 | 3 |  |  |  |  |  |  | 8* |  |  |  |  |  | 35 |
| 1 | 2 |  | 4 | 5 | 6 | 7† | 8* | 9° | 10 | 11 | 12 |  | 3 |  |  |  |  |  |  |  |  | 13 | 14 |  |  | 36 |
| 1 | 2 |  | 4† | 5 | 6 | 7 | 12 | 9° | 10 | 11* |  |  | 3 |  |  |  |  |  |  |  |  | 13 | 14 |  |  | 37 |
| 1 | 5 |  | 4† |  | 6 | 7 | 12 | 8 | 10 | 11 |  | 13 | 3 |  | 13 |  |  |  |  | 9 |  |  |  |  | 2 | 38 |
| 38 | 38 | 8 | 26 | 32 | 35 | 29 | 16 | 33 | 20 | 21 | 21 | 11 | 30 |  | 13 |  | 3 | 11 | 1 | 15 | 1 | 8 | 4 |  | 4 |  |
|  |  |  | 4 |  |  | 4 | 11 | 3 | 8 | 5 | 9 | 3 | 4 | 3 | 14 | 1 |  | 5 | 1 | 12 | 2 | 5 | 1 | 2 | 2 |  |
|  | 3 |  | 2 |  |  | 3 | 7 | 2 | 14 | 16 | 2 | 5 | 2 |  | 4 |  |  | 1 |  | 8 |  |  | 1 |  |  |  |

# 2001-2002

| | | | | | | | | |
|---|---|---|---|---|---|---|---|---|
| 1 | Aug | 18 | (h) | West Ham U | W | 2-1 | Owen 2 | 43,935 |
| 2 | | 27 | (a) | Bolton W | L | 1-2 | Heskey | 27,205 |
| 3 | Sep | 8 | (h) | Aston Villa | L | 1-3 | Gerrard | 44,102 |
| 4 | | 15 | (a) | Everton | W | 3-1 | Gerrard, Owen (pen), Riise | 39,554 |
| 5 | | 22 | (h) | Tottenham H | W | 1-0 | Litmanen | 44,116 |
| 6 | | 30 | (a) | Newcastle U | W | 2-0 | Riise, Murphy | 52,095 |
| 7 | Oct | 13 | (h) | Leeds U | D | 1-1 | Murphy | 44,352 |
| 8 | | 20 | (a) | Leicester C | W | 4-1 | Fowler 3, Hyypia | 21,886 |
| 9 | | 27 | (a) | Charlton Ath | W | 2-0 | Redknapp, Owen | 22,658 |
| 10 | Nov | 4 | (h) | Manchester U | W | 3-1 | Owen 2, Riise | 44,361 |
| 11 | | 17 | (a) | Blackburn R | D | 1-1 | Owen | 28,859 |
| 12 | | 25 | (h) | Sunderland | W | 1-0 | Heskey | 43,537 |
| 13 | Dec | 1 | (a) | Derby Co | W | 1-0 | Owen | 33,289 |
| 14 | | 8 | (h) | Middlesbrough | W | 2-0 | Owen, Berger | 43,674 |
| 15 | | 12 | (h) | Fulham | D | 0-0 | | 37,163 |
| 16 | | 16 | (a) | Chelsea | L | 0-4 | | 41,175 |
| 17 | | 23 | (h) | Arsenal | L | 1-2 | Litmanen | 44,297 |
| 18 | | 26 | (a) | Aston Villa | W | 2-1 | Litmanen, Smicer | 42,602 |
| 19 | | 29 | (a) | West Ham U | D | 1-1 | Owen | 35,103 |
| 20 | Jan | 1 | (h) | Bolton W | D | 1-1 | Gerrard | 43,710 |
| 21 | | 9 | (a) | Southampton | L | 0-2 | | 31,527 |
| 22 | | 13 | (a) | Arsenal | D | 1-1 | Riise | 38,132 |
| 23 | | 19 | (h) | Southampton | D | 1-1 | Owen | 43,710 |
| 24 | | 22 | (a) | Manchester U | W | 1-0 | Murphy | 67,599 |
| 25 | | 30 | (h) | Leicester C | W | 1-0 | Heskey | 42,305 |
| 26 | Feb | 3 | (a) | Leeds U | W | 4-0 | Ferdinand (og), Heskey 2, Owen | 40,216 |
| 27 | | 9 | (a) | Ipswich T | W | 6-0 | Xavier, Heskey 2, Hyypia, Owen 2 | 25,607 |
| 28 | | 23 | (h) | Everton | D | 1-1 | Anelka | 44,371 |
| 29 | Mar | 2 | (a) | Fulham | W | 2-0 | Anelka, Litmanen | 21,103 |
| 30 | | 6 | (h) | Newcastle U | W | 3-0 | Murphy 2, Hamann | 44,204 |
| 31 | | 16 | (a) | Middlesbrough | W | 2-1 | Heskey, Riise | 31,253 |
| 32 | | 24 | (h) | Chelsea | W | 1-0 | Smicer | 44,203 |
| 33 | | 30 | (h) | Charlton Ath | W | 2-0 | Smicer, Owen | 44,094 |
| 34 | Apr | 13 | (a) | Sunderland | W | 1-0 | Owen | 46,062 |
| 35 | | 20 | (h) | Derby Co | W | 2-0 | Owen 2 | 43,510 |
| 36 | | 27 | (a) | Tottenham H | L | 0-1 | | 36,017 |
| 37 | May | 8 | (h) | Blackburn R | W | 4-3 | Murphy, Anelka, Hyypia, Heskey | 40,663 |
| 38 | | 11 | (h) | Ipswich T | W | 5-0 | Riise 2, Owen, Smicer, Anelka | 44,088 |

FINAL LEAGUE POSITION: 2nd in F.A. Premiership

Appearances

Sub. Appearances

Goals

| Arphexad | Babbel | Carragher | Hamann | Henchoz | Hyypia | Murphy | Litmanen | Owen | McAllister | Biscan | Riise | Redknapp | Barmby | Westerveld | Gerrard | Fowler | Heskey | Dudek | Vignal | Smicer | Wright | Berger | Anelka | Xavier | Kirkland | # |
|---|---|---|---|---|---|---|---|---|---|---|---|---|---|---|---|---|---|---|---|---|---|---|---|---|---|---|
| 1 | 2* | 3 | 4 | 5 | 6 | 7† | 8 | 9 | 10 | 11° | 12 | 13 | 14 |  |  |  |  |  |  |  |  |  |  |  |  | 1 |
|  | 2* | 3 | 4 | 5 | 6 | 11 |  | 10 | 8 |  | 12 |  |  | 1 | 7 | 9† | 13 |  |  |  |  |  |  |  |  | 2 |
|  |  | 2 | 4 | 5† | 6 | 13 |  | 12 | 8 |  | 3° |  | 11* |  | 7 | 10 | 9 | 1 |  | 14 |  |  |  |  |  | 3 |
|  |  | 2 | 4 | 5 | 6 | 11* |  | 10 | 12 |  | 3 |  |  |  | 7† | 9 |  | 1 |  | 8 | 13 |  |  |  |  | 4 |
|  |  | 2 |  | 5 | 6 | 10* | 12† | 13 | 11 |  | 3 |  |  |  | 8 | 9° | 14 | 1 | 7 |  |  |  |  |  |  | 5 |
|  |  | 2 |  | 5 | 6 | 7 | 8 | 11 |  |  | 3 |  |  |  | 10 | 9 |  | 1 | 4 |  |  |  |  |  |  | 6 |
|  |  | 2 |  | 5 | 6 | 7* | 13 | 11° |  |  | 3 | 14 | 12 |  | 4 | 10 | 9† | 1 |  | 8 |  |  |  |  |  | 7 |
|  |  | 5 |  |  | 6 | 11 | 12 | 8 |  |  | 3 | 4† |  |  | 7° | 10 | 9* | 1 |  | 13 | 2 | 14 |  |  |  | 8 |
|  |  | 6 | 4 | 5 |  | 11 | 9* | 10† |  |  | 3 | 8° |  |  | 7 | 13 | 12 | 1 |  | 2 | 14 |  |  |  |  | 9 |
|  |  | 2 | 4 | 5 | 6 | 11 |  | 10* |  |  | 3 |  |  |  | 7 | 12 | 9 | 1 |  | 8† | 13 |  |  |  |  | 10 |
|  |  | 2 | 4 | 5 | 6 | 12 | 8 | 10† |  |  | 3 |  |  |  | 7 | 9 | 13 | 1 |  |  | 11* |  |  |  |  | 11 |
|  |  | 2 | 4 | 5 | 6 | 11° |  | 12 |  |  | 3 |  |  |  | 7 | 10* | 9 | 1 |  | 8† | 13 | 14 |  |  |  | 12 |
|  |  | 2 | 4 | 5 | 6 | 8 | 12 | 10* | 13 |  | 3 |  |  |  | 7 |  | 9 | 1 |  |  | 11† |  |  |  |  | 13 |
|  |  | 2 | 4 | 5 | 6 | 7 | 9 | 10* | 8 |  | 3 |  |  |  |  | 12 |  | 1 |  |  | 11 |  |  |  |  | 14 |
|  |  | 2 |  | 5 | 6 | 8† | 12 | 10 | 4 | 13 | 3 |  |  |  | 7 |  | 9 | 1 |  |  | 11* |  |  |  |  | 15 |
|  |  | 2 |  | 5 | 6 | 11 |  | 10 | 8 | 4* | 3 |  |  |  | 7 |  | 9 | 1 |  | 12 |  |  |  |  |  | 16 |
|  |  | 2 |  | 5 | 6 | 7 | 12 | 10 | 8* |  | 3 |  |  |  | 4 | 9† |  | 1 |  | 13 | 11 |  |  |  |  | 17 |
|  |  | 2 | 4 | 5 | 6 | 12 | 9° | 10 | 13 |  | 3 |  |  |  | 7* |  |  | 1 |  | 8† | 11 | 14 |  |  |  | 18 |
|  |  | 2 |  | 5 | 6 | 7† | 12 | 13 | 4° |  | 3 |  |  |  | 14 | 9 |  | 1 |  | 8* | 11 | 10 |  |  |  | 19 |
|  |  |  | 4 | 5 | 6 | 12 |  | 10 |  |  | 3 |  |  |  | 7 | 9 |  | 1 |  | 8† | 2 | 11* | 13 |  |  | 20 |
|  |  | 3 | 4 | 5 | 6 | 11° | 9 |  |  |  | 12 |  |  |  | 7 | 13 |  | 1 |  | 8† | 2* | 14 | 10 |  |  | 21 |
|  |  | 2 | 4 | 5 | 6 | 8† |  | 10 | 12 |  | 3 |  |  |  | 7 | 13 |  | 1 |  |  | 11 | 9* |  |  |  | 22 |
|  |  | 2 | 4 | 5 | 6 | 8* |  | 10 | 12 |  | 3 |  |  |  | 7† | 9 |  | 1 |  | 13° | 11 | 14 |  |  |  | 23 |
|  |  | 3 | 4 | 5 | 6 | 8* |  | 10† | 11 |  | 7 |  |  |  |  | 9 |  | 1 |  | 2 | 12 | 13 |  |  |  | 24 |
|  |  | 3 | 4 | 5 | 6 | 12 |  | 8* | 13 |  |  |  |  |  |  | 9 |  | 1 | 7 | 2 | 11† | 10 |  |  |  | 25 |
|  |  | 3 | 4 | 5 | 6 | 8 |  | 10 | 12 | 11 | 7* |  |  |  |  | 9 |  | 1 |  | 2 |  |  |  |  |  | 26 |
| 14 |  |  | 4 | 5 | 6 | 8 |  | 10 | 12 | 11† | 7* |  |  |  | 9 | 1° |  |  |  | 2 | 13 | 3 |  |  |  | 27 |
|  |  |  | 4 | 5 | 6 | 7 |  | 10 | 8† | 11 | 12 |  |  |  |  | 13 | 3* | 9 |  | 2 | 1 |  |  |  |  | 28 |
|  |  |  | 4 | 5 | 6 | 7 | 12 |  |  | 11 | 13 |  |  |  | 9 | 1 | 8† | 3 | 10* | 2 |  |  |  |  |  | 29 |
|  |  |  | 4 | 5 | 6 | 7 | 12 | 10* |  | 3 | 13 |  |  |  | 11 | 1 | 8† | 9 | 2 |  |  |  |  |  |  | 30 |
|  |  | 3 | 4 | 5 | 6 | 7 |  |  |  | 11 | 12 |  |  |  | 9 | 1 | 8* | 10 | 2 |  |  |  |  |  |  | 31 |
|  |  | 3 | 4 | 5 | 6 | 8 | 12 | 13 |  | 11 | 7° |  |  |  | 9 | 1 | 14 | 10* | 2† |  |  |  |  |  |  | 32 |
|  |  | 2 | 4 | 5 | 6 | 7 | 12 | 10* | 13 | 3 | 9° |  |  |  | 1 | 14 | 11† | 8 |  |  |  |  |  |  |  | 33 |
|  |  | 3 | 4 | 5 | 6 | 12 | 9* | 10† | 11 | 7 |  |  |  | 1 | 13 | 8 | 2 |  |  |  |  |  |  |  |  | 34 |
|  |  | 2 | 4 | 5 | 6 | 11* | 12 | 10 |  | 3 | 7 | 13 | 1 | 8° | 14 | 9† |  |  |  |  |  |  |  |  |  | 35 |
|  |  | 3 | 4 | 5 | 6 | 7* | 12 | 10 |  | 11 | 9° | 1 | 8 | 13 | 14 | 2† |  |  |  |  |  |  |  |  |  | 36 |
|  |  | 2 | 4† | 5 | 6 | 11 |  | 10* |  | 3 | 7 | 9 | 1 | 12 | 8 | 13 |  |  |  |  |  |  |  |  |  | 37 |
|  |  | 3 | 4 | 5 | 6 | 8* |  | 10 | 12 | 11 | 7† | 9 | 1 | 13 | 14 | 2° |  |  |  |  |  |  |  |  |  | 38 |
| 1 | 2 | 33 | 31 | 37 | 37 | 31 | 8 | 25 | 14 | 4 | 34 | 2 | 2 | 1 | 26 | 8 | 26 | 35 | 3 | 13 | 10 | 12 | 13 | 9 | 1 |  |
| 1 |  |  |  |  | 5 | 13 | 4 | 11 | 1 | 4 | 2 | 4 |  | 2 | 2 | 9 |  | 1 | 9 | 2 | 9 | 7 | 1 |  |  |  |
|  |  | 1 |  | 3 | 6 | 4 | 19 |  | 7 | 1 |  | 3 | 3 | 9 |  | 4 |  | 1 | 4 | 1 |  |  |  |  |  |  |

## Season 1977/78

### DIVISION ONE

| | | | | | | | |
|---|---|---|---|---|---|---|---|
| Nottingham Forest | 42 | 25 | 14 | 3 | 69 | 24 | 64 |
| **Liverpool** | **42** | **24** | **9** | **9** | **65** | **34** | **57** |
| Everton | 42 | 22 | 11 | 9 | 76 | 45 | 55 |
| Manchester City | 42 | 20 | 12 | 10 | 74 | 51 | 52 |
| Arsenal | 42 | 21 | 10 | 11 | 60 | 37 | 52 |
| West Bromwich Albion | 42 | 18 | 14 | 10 | 62 | 53 | 50 |
| Coventry City | 42 | 18 | 12 | 12 | 75 | 62 | 48 |
| Aston Villa | 42 | 18 | 10 | 14 | 57 | 42 | 46 |
| Leeds United | 42 | 18 | 10 | 14 | 63 | 53 | 46 |
| Manchester United | 42 | 16 | 10 | 16 | 67 | 63 | 42 |
| Birmingham City | 42 | 16 | 9 | 17 | 55 | 60 | 41 |
| Derby County | 42 | 14 | 13 | 15 | 54 | 59 | 41 |
| Norwich City | 42 | 11 | 18 | 13 | 52 | 66 | 40 |
| Middlesbrough | 42 | 12 | 15 | 15 | 42 | 54 | 39 |
| Wolverhampton Wands. | 42 | 12 | 12 | 18 | 51 | 64 | 36 |
| Chelsea | 42 | 11 | 14 | 17 | 46 | 69 | 36 |
| Bristol City | 42 | 11 | 13 | 18 | 49 | 53 | 35 |
| Ipswich Town | 42 | 11 | 13 | 18 | 47 | 61 | 35 |
| Queen's Park Rangers | 42 | 9 | 15 | 18 | 47 | 64 | 33 |
| West Ham United | 42 | 12 | 8 | 22 | 52 | 69 | 32 |
| Newcastle United | 42 | 6 | 10 | 26 | 42 | 78 | 22 |
| Leicester City | 42 | 5 | 12 | 25 | 26 | 70 | 22 |

## Season 1979/80

### DIVISION ONE

| | | | | | | | |
|---|---|---|---|---|---|---|---|
| **Liverpool** | **42** | **25** | **10** | **7** | **81** | **30** | **60** |
| Manchester United | 42 | 24 | 10 | 8 | 65 | 35 | 58 |
| Ispwich | 42 | 22 | 9 | 11 | 68 | 39 | 53 |
| Arsenal | 42 | 18 | 16 | 8 | 52 | 36 | 52 |
| Nottingham Forest | 42 | 20 | 8 | 14 | 63 | 43 | 48 |
| Wolverhampton Wands. | 42 | 19 | 9 | 14 | 58 | 47 | 47 |
| Aston Villa | 42 | 16 | 14 | 12 | 51 | 50 | 46 |
| Southampton | 42 | 18 | 9 | 15 | 65 | 53 | 45 |
| Middlesbrough | 42 | 16 | 12 | 14 | 50 | 44 | 44 |
| West Bromwich Albion | 42 | 11 | 19 | 12 | 54 | 50 | 41 |
| Leeds United | 42 | 13 | 14 | 15 | 46 | 50 | 40 |
| Norwich City | 42 | 13 | 14 | 15 | 58 | 66 | 40 |
| Crystal Palace | 42 | 12 | 16 | 14 | 41 | 50 | 40 |
| Tottenham Hotspur | 42 | 15 | 10 | 17 | 52 | 62 | 40 |
| Coventry City | 42 | 16 | 7 | 19 | 56 | 66 | 39 |
| Brighton & Hove Albion | 42 | 11 | 15 | 16 | 47 | 57 | 37 |
| Manchester City | 42 | 12 | 13 | 17 | 43 | 66 | 37 |
| Stoke City | 42 | 13 | 10 | 19 | 44 | 58 | 36 |
| Everton | 42 | 9 | 17 | 16 | 43 | 51 | 35 |
| Bristol City | 42 | 9 | 13 | 20 | 37 | 66 | 31 |
| Derby County | 42 | 11 | 8 | 23 | 47 | 67 | 30 |
| Bolton Wanderers | 42 | 5 | 15 | 22 | 38 | 73 | 25 |

## Season 1978/79

### DIVISION ONE

| | | | | | | | |
|---|---|---|---|---|---|---|---|
| **Liverpool** | **42** | **30** | **8** | **4** | **85** | **16** | **68** |
| Nottingham Forest | 42 | 21 | 18 | 3 | 61 | 26 | 60 |
| West Bromwich Albion | 42 | 24 | 11 | 7 | 72 | 35 | 59 |
| Everton | 42 | 17 | 17 | 8 | 52 | 40 | 51 |
| Leeds United | 42 | 18 | 14 | 10 | 70 | 52 | 50 |
| Ipswich Town | 42 | 20 | 9 | 13 | 63 | 49 | 49 |
| Arsenal | 42 | 17 | 14 | 11 | 61 | 48 | 48 |
| Aston Villa | 42 | 15 | 16 | 11 | 59 | 49 | 46 |
| Manchester United | 42 | 15 | 15 | 12 | 60 | 63 | 45 |
| Coventry City | 42 | 14 | 16 | 12 | 58 | 68 | 44 |
| Tottenham Hotspur | 42 | 13 | 15 | 14 | 48 | 61 | 41 |
| Middlesbrough | 42 | 15 | 10 | 17 | 57 | 50 | 40 |
| Bristol City | 42 | 15 | 10 | 17 | 47 | 51 | 40 |
| Southampton | 42 | 12 | 16 | 14 | 47 | 53 | 40 |
| Manchester City | 42 | 13 | 13 | 16 | 58 | 56 | 39 |
| Norwich City | 42 | 7 | 23 | 12 | 51 | 57 | 37 |
| Bolton Wanderers | 42 | 12 | 11 | 19 | 54 | 75 | 35 |
| Wolverhampton Wands. | 42 | 13 | 8 | 21 | 44 | 68 | 34 |
| Derby County | 42 | 10 | 11 | 21 | 44 | 71 | 31 |
| Queen's Park Rangers | 42 | 6 | 13 | 23 | 45 | 73 | 25 |
| Birmingham City | 42 | 6 | 10 | 26 | 37 | 64 | 22 |
| Chelsea | 42 | 5 | 10 | 27 | 44 | 92 | 20 |

## Season 1980/81

### DIVISION ONE

| | | | | | | | |
|---|---|---|---|---|---|---|---|
| Aston Villa | 42 | 26 | 8 | 8 | 72 | 40 | 60 |
| Ipswich Town | 42 | 23 | 10 | 9 | 77 | 43 | 56 |
| Arsenal | 42 | 19 | 15 | 8 | 61 | 45 | 53 |
| West Bromwich Albion | 42 | 20 | 12 | 10 | 60 | 42 | 52 |
| **Liverpool** | **42** | **17** | **17** | **8** | **62** | **42** | **51** |
| Southampton | 42 | 20 | 10 | 12 | 76 | 56 | 50 |
| Nottingham Forest | 42 | 19 | 12 | 11 | 62 | 44 | 50 |
| Manchester United | 42 | 15 | 18 | 9 | 51 | 36 | 48 |
| Leeds United | 42 | 17 | 10 | 15 | 39 | 47 | 44 |
| Tottenham Hotspur | 42 | 14 | 15 | 13 | 70 | 68 | 43 |
| Stoke City | 42 | 12 | 18 | 12 | 51 | 60 | 42 |
| Manchester City | 42 | 14 | 11 | 17 | 56 | 59 | 39 |
| Birmingham City | 42 | 13 | 12 | 17 | 50 | 61 | 38 |
| Middlesbrough | 42 | 16 | 5 | 21 | 53 | 61 | 37 |
| Everton | 42 | 13 | 10 | 19 | 55 | 58 | 36 |
| Coventry City | 42 | 13 | 10 | 19 | 48 | 68 | 36 |
| Sunderland | 42 | 14 | 7 | 21 | 52 | 53 | 35 |
| Wolverhampton Wands. | 42 | 13 | 9 | 20 | 43 | 55 | 35 |
| Brighton & Hove Albion | 42 | 14 | 7 | 21 | 54 | 67 | 35 |
| Norwich City | 42 | 13 | 7 | 22 | 49 | 73 | 33 |
| Leicester City | 42 | 13 | 6 | 23 | 40 | 67 | 32 |
| Crystal Palace | 42 | 6 | 7 | 29 | 47 | 83 | 19 |

## Season 1981/82

### DIVISION ONE

| | P | W | D | L | F | A | Pts |
|---|---|---|---|---|---|---|---|
| Liverpool | 42 | 26 | 9 | 7 | 80 | 32 | 87 |
| Ipswich Town | 42 | 26 | 5 | 11 | 75 | 53 | 83 |
| Manchester United | 42 | 22 | 12 | 8 | 59 | 29 | 78 |
| Tottenham Hotspur | 42 | 20 | 11 | 11 | 67 | 48 | 71 |
| Arsenal | 42 | 20 | 11 | 11 | 48 | 37 | 71 |
| Swansea City | 42 | 21 | 6 | 15 | 58 | 51 | 69 |
| Southampton | 42 | 19 | 9 | 14 | 72 | 67 | 66 |
| Everton | 42 | 17 | 13 | 12 | 56 | 50 | 64 |
| West Ham United | 42 | 14 | 16 | 12 | 66 | 57 | 58 |
| Manchester City | 42 | 15 | 13 | 14 | 49 | 50 | 58 |
| Aston Villa | 42 | 15 | 12 | 15 | 55 | 53 | 57 |
| Nottingham Forest | 42 | 15 | 12 | 15 | 42 | 48 | 57 |
| Brighton & Hove Albion | 42 | 13 | 13 | 16 | 43 | 52 | 52 |
| Coventry City | 42 | 13 | 11 | 18 | 56 | 62 | 50 |
| Notts County | 42 | 13 | 8 | 21 | 61 | 69 | 47 |
| Birmingham City | 42 | 10 | 14 | 18 | 53 | 61 | 44 |
| West Bromwich Albion | 42 | 11 | 11 | 20 | 46 | 57 | 44 |
| Stoke City | 42 | 12 | 8 | 22 | 44 | 63 | 44 |
| Sunderland | 42 | 11 | 11 | 20 | 38 | 58 | 44 |
| Leeds United | 42 | 10 | 12 | 20 | 39 | 61 | 42 |
| Wolverhampton Wands. | 42 | 10 | 10 | 22 | 32 | 63 | 40 |
| Middlesbrough | 42 | 8 | 15 | 19 | 34 | 52 | 39 |

## Season 1982/83

### DIVISION ONE

| | P | W | D | L | F | A | Pts |
|---|---|---|---|---|---|---|---|
| Liverpool | 42 | 24 | 10 | 8 | 87 | 37 | 82 |
| Watford | 42 | 22 | 5 | 15 | 74 | 57 | 71 |
| Manchester United | 42 | 19 | 13 | 10 | 56 | 38 | 70 |
| Tottenham Hotspur | 42 | 20 | 9 | 13 | 65 | 50 | 69 |
| Nottingham Forest | 42 | 20 | 9 | 13 | 62 | 50 | 69 |
| Aston Villa | 42 | 21 | 5 | 16 | 62 | 50 | 68 |
| Everton | 42 | 18 | 10 | 14 | 66 | 48 | 64 |
| West Ham United | 42 | 20 | 4 | 18 | 68 | 62 | 64 |
| Ipswich Town | 42 | 15 | 13 | 14 | 64 | 50 | 58 |
| Arsenal | 42 | 16 | 10 | 16 | 58 | 56 | 58 |
| West Bromwich Albion | 42 | 15 | 12 | 15 | 51 | 49 | 57 |
| Southampton | 42 | 15 | 12 | 15 | 54 | 58 | 57 |
| Stoke City | 42 | 16 | 9 | 17 | 53 | 64 | 57 |
| Norwich City | 42 | 14 | 12 | 16 | 52 | 58 | 54 |
| Notts County | 42 | 15 | 7 | 20 | 55 | 71 | 52 |
| Sunderland | 42 | 12 | 14 | 16 | 48 | 61 | 50 |
| Birmingham City | 42 | 12 | 14 | 16 | 40 | 55 | 50 |
| Luton Town | 42 | 12 | 13 | 17 | 65 | 84 | 49 |
| Coventry City | 42 | 13 | 9 | 20 | 48 | 59 | 48 |
| Manchester City | 42 | 13 | 8 | 21 | 47 | 70 | 47 |
| Swansea City | 42 | 10 | 11 | 21 | 51 | 69 | 41 |
| Brighton & Hove Albion | 42 | 9 | 13 | 20 | 38 | 68 | 40 |

## Season 1983/84

### DIVISION ONE

| | P | W | D | L | F | A | Pts |
|---|---|---|---|---|---|---|---|
| Liverpool | 42 | 22 | 14 | 6 | 73 | 32 | 80 |
| Southampton | 42 | 22 | 11 | 9 | 66 | 38 | 77 |
| Nottingham Forest | 42 | 22 | 8 | 12 | 76 | 45 | 74 |
| Manchester United | 42 | 20 | 14 | 8 | 71 | 41 | 74 |
| Queen's Park Rangers | 42 | 22 | 7 | 13 | 67 | 37 | 73 |
| Arsenal | 42 | 18 | 9 | 15 | 74 | 60 | 63 |
| Everton | 42 | 16 | 14 | 12 | 44 | 42 | 62 |
| Tottenham Hotspur | 42 | 17 | 10 | 15 | 64 | 65 | 61 |
| West Ham United | 42 | 17 | 9 | 16 | 60 | 55 | 60 |
| Aston Villa | 42 | 17 | 9 | 16 | 59 | 61 | 60 |
| Watford | 42 | 16 | 9 | 17 | 68 | 77 | 57 |
| Ipswich Town | 42 | 15 | 8 | 19 | 55 | 57 | 53 |
| Sunderland | 42 | 13 | 13 | 16 | 42 | 53 | 52 |
| Norwich City | 42 | 12 | 15 | 15 | 48 | 49 | 51 |
| Leicester City | 42 | 13 | 12 | 17 | 65 | 68 | 51 |
| Luton Town | 42 | 14 | 9 | 19 | 53 | 66 | 51 |
| West Bromwich Albion | 42 | 14 | 9 | 19 | 48 | 62 | 51 |
| Stoke City | 42 | 13 | 11 | 18 | 44 | 63 | 50 |
| Coventry City | 42 | 13 | 11 | 18 | 57 | 77 | 50 |
| Birmingham City | 42 | 12 | 12 | 18 | 39 | 50 | 48 |
| Notts County | 42 | 10 | 11 | 21 | 50 | 72 | 41 |
| Wolverhampton Wands. | 42 | 6 | 11 | 25 | 27 | 80 | 29 |

## Season 1984/85

### DIVISION ONE

| | P | W | D | L | F | A | Pts |
|---|---|---|---|---|---|---|---|
| Everton | 42 | 28 | 6 | 8 | 88 | 43 | 90 |
| Liverpool | 42 | 22 | 11 | 9 | 68 | 35 | 77 |
| Tottenham Hotspur | 42 | 23 | 8 | 11 | 78 | 51 | 77 |
| Manchester United | 42 | 22 | 10 | 10 | 77 | 47 | 76 |
| Southampton | 42 | 19 | 11 | 12 | 56 | 47 | 68 |
| Chelsea | 42 | 18 | 12 | 12 | 63 | 48 | 66 |
| Arsenal | 42 | 19 | 9 | 14 | 61 | 49 | 66 |
| Sheffield Wednesday | 42 | 17 | 14 | 11 | 58 | 45 | 65 |
| Nottingham Forest | 42 | 19 | 7 | 16 | 56 | 48 | 64 |
| Aston Villa | 42 | 15 | 11 | 16 | 60 | 60 | 56 |
| Watford | 42 | 14 | 13 | 15 | 81 | 71 | 55 |
| West Bromwich Albion | 42 | 16 | 7 | 19 | 58 | 62 | 55 |
| Luton Town | 42 | 15 | 9 | 18 | 57 | 61 | 54 |
| Newcastle United | 42 | 13 | 13 | 16 | 55 | 70 | 52 |
| Leicester City | 42 | 15 | 6 | 21 | 65 | 73 | 51 |
| West Ham United | 42 | 13 | 12 | 17 | 51 | 68 | 51 |
| Ipswich Town | 42 | 13 | 11 | 18 | 46 | 57 | 50 |
| Coventry City | 42 | 15 | 5 | 22 | 47 | 64 | 50 |
| Queen's Park Rangers | 42 | 13 | 11 | 18 | 53 | 72 | 50 |
| Norwich City | 42 | 13 | 10 | 19 | 46 | 64 | 49 |
| Sunderland | 42 | 10 | 10 | 22 | 40 | 62 | 40 |
| Stoke City | 42 | 3 | 8 | 31 | 24 | 91 | 17 |

## Season 1985/86

### DIVISION ONE

| | | | | | | | |
|---|---|---|---|---|---|---|---|
| Liverpool | 42 | 26 | 10 | 6 | 89 | 37 | 88 |
| Everton | 42 | 26 | 8 | 8 | 87 | 41 | 86 |
| West Ham United | 42 | 26 | 6 | 10 | 74 | 40 | 84 |
| Manchester United | 42 | 22 | 10 | 10 | 70 | 36 | 76 |
| Sheffield Wednesday | 42 | 21 | 10 | 11 | 63 | 54 | 73 |
| Chelsea | 42 | 20 | 11 | 11 | 57 | 56 | 71 |
| Arsenal | 42 | 20 | 9 | 13 | 49 | 47 | 69 |
| Nottingham Forest | 42 | 19 | 11 | 12 | 69 | 53 | 68 |
| Luton Town | 42 | 18 | 12 | 12 | 61 | 44 | 66 |
| Tottenham Hotspur | 42 | 19 | 8 | 15 | 74 | 52 | 65 |
| Newcastle United | 42 | 17 | 12 | 13 | 67 | 72 | 63 |
| Watford | 42 | 16 | 11 | 15 | 69 | 62 | 59 |
| Queen's Park Rangers | 42 | 15 | 7 | 20 | 53 | 64 | 52 |
| Southampton | 42 | 12 | 10 | 20 | 51 | 62 | 46 |
| Manchester City | 42 | 11 | 12 | 19 | 43 | 57 | 45 |
| Aston Villa | 42 | 10 | 14 | 18 | 51 | 67 | 44 |
| Coventry City | 42 | 11 | 10 | 21 | 48 | 71 | 43 |
| Oxford United | 42 | 10 | 12 | 20 | 62 | 80 | 42 |
| Leicester City | 42 | 10 | 12 | 20 | 54 | 76 | 42 |
| Ipswich Town | 42 | 11 | 8 | 23 | 32 | 55 | 41 |
| Birmingham City | 42 | 8 | 5 | 29 | 30 | 73 | 29 |
| West Bromwich Albion | 42 | 4 | 12 | 26 | 35 | 89 | 24 |

## Season 1986/87

### DIVISION ONE

| | | | | | | | |
|---|---|---|---|---|---|---|---|
| Everton | 42 | 26 | 8 | 8 | 76 | 31 | 86 |
| Liverpool | 42 | 23 | 8 | 11 | 72 | 42 | 77 |
| Tottenham Hotspur | 42 | 21 | 8 | 13 | 68 | 43 | 71 |
| Arsenal | 42 | 20 | 10 | 12 | 58 | 35 | 70 |
| Norwich City | 42 | 17 | 17 | 8 | 53 | 51 | 68 |
| Wimbledon | 42 | 19 | 9 | 14 | 57 | 50 | 66 |
| Luton Town | 42 | 18 | 12 | 12 | 47 | 45 | 66 |
| Nottingham Forest | 42 | 18 | 11 | 13 | 64 | 51 | 65 |
| Watford | 42 | 18 | 9 | 15 | 67 | 54 | 63 |
| Coventry City | 42 | 17 | 12 | 13 | 50 | 45 | 63 |
| Manchester United | 42 | 14 | 14 | 14 | 52 | 45 | 56 |
| Southampton | 42 | 14 | 10 | 18 | 69 | 68 | 52 |
| Sheffield Wednesday | 42 | 13 | 13 | 16 | 58 | 59 | 52 |
| Chelsea | 42 | 13 | 13 | 16 | 53 | 64 | 52 |
| West Ham United | 42 | 14 | 10 | 18 | 52 | 67 | 52 |
| Queen's Park Rangers | 42 | 13 | 11 | 18 | 48 | 64 | 50 |
| Newcastle United | 42 | 12 | 11 | 19 | 47 | 65 | 47 |
| Oxford United | 42 | 11 | 13 | 18 | 44 | 69 | 46 |
| Charlton Athletic | 42 | 11 | 11 | 20 | 45 | 55 | 44 |
| Leicester City | 42 | 11 | 9 | 22 | 54 | 76 | 42 |
| Manchester City | 42 | 8 | 15 | 19 | 36 | 57 | 39 |
| Aston Villa | 42 | 8 | 12 | 22 | 45 | 79 | 36 |

## Season 1987/88

### DIVISION ONE

| | | | | | | | |
|---|---|---|---|---|---|---|---|
| Liverpool | 40 | 26 | 12 | 2 | 87 | 24 | 90 |
| Manchester United | 40 | 23 | 12 | 5 | 71 | 38 | 81 |
| Nottingham Forest | 40 | 20 | 13 | 7 | 67 | 39 | 73 |
| Everton | 40 | 19 | 13 | 8 | 53 | 27 | 70 |
| Queen's Park Rangers | 40 | 19 | 10 | 11 | 48 | 38 | 67 |
| Arsenal | 40 | 18 | 12 | 10 | 58 | 39 | 66 |
| Wimbledon | 40 | 14 | 15 | 11 | 58 | 47 | 57 |
| Newcastle United | 40 | 14 | 14 | 12 | 55 | 53 | 56 |
| Luton Town | 40 | 14 | 11 | 15 | 57 | 58 | 53 |
| Coventry City | 40 | 13 | 14 | 13 | 46 | 53 | 53 |
| Sheffield Wednesday | 40 | 15 | 8 | 17 | 52 | 66 | 53 |
| Southampton | 40 | 12 | 14 | 14 | 49 | 53 | 50 |
| Tottenham Hotspur | 40 | 12 | 11 | 17 | 38 | 48 | 47 |
| Norwich City | 40 | 12 | 9 | 19 | 40 | 52 | 45 |
| Derby County | 40 | 10 | 13 | 17 | 35 | 45 | 43 |
| West Ham United | 40 | 9 | 15 | 16 | 40 | 52 | 42 |
| Charlton Athletic | 40 | 9 | 15 | 16 | 38 | 52 | 42 |
| Chelsea | 40 | 9 | 15 | 16 | 50 | 68 | 42 |
| Portsmouth | 40 | 7 | 14 | 19 | 36 | 66 | 35 |
| Watford | 40 | 7 | 11 | 22 | 27 | 51 | 32 |
| Oxford United | 40 | 6 | 13 | 21 | 44 | 80 | 31 |

## Season 1988/89

### DIVISION ONE

| | | | | | | | |
|---|---|---|---|---|---|---|---|
| Arsenal | 38 | 22 | 10 | 6 | 73 | 36 | 76 |
| Liverpool | 38 | 22 | 10 | 6 | 65 | 28 | 76 |
| Nottingham Forest | 38 | 17 | 13 | 8 | 64 | 43 | 64 |
| Norwich City | 38 | 17 | 11 | 10 | 48 | 45 | 62 |
| Derby County | 38 | 17 | 7 | 14 | 40 | 38 | 58 |
| Tottenham Hotspur | 38 | 15 | 12 | 11 | 60 | 46 | 57 |
| Coventry City | 38 | 14 | 13 | 11 | 47 | 42 | 55 |
| Everton | 38 | 14 | 12 | 12 | 50 | 45 | 54 |
| Queen's Park Rangers | 38 | 14 | 11 | 13 | 43 | 37 | 53 |
| Millwall | 38 | 14 | 11 | 13 | 47 | 52 | 53 |
| Manchester United | 38 | 13 | 12 | 13 | 45 | 35 | 51 |
| Wimbledon | 38 | 14 | 9 | 15 | 50 | 46 | 51 |
| Southampton | 38 | 10 | 15 | 13 | 52 | 66 | 45 |
| Charlton Athletic | 38 | 10 | 12 | 16 | 44 | 58 | 42 |
| Sheffield Wednesday | 38 | 10 | 12 | 16 | 34 | 51 | 42 |
| Luton Town | 38 | 10 | 11 | 17 | 42 | 52 | 41 |
| Aston Villa | 38 | 9 | 13 | 16 | 45 | 56 | 40 |
| Middlesbrough | 38 | 9 | 12 | 17 | 44 | 61 | 39 |
| West Ham United | 38 | 10 | 8 | 20 | 37 | 62 | 38 |
| Newcastle United | 38 | 7 | 10 | 21 | 32 | 63 | 31 |

## Season 1989/90

### DIVISION ONE

| | | | | | | | |
|---|---|---|---|---|---|---|---|
| **Liverpool** | 38 | 23 | 10 | 5 | 78 | 37 | 79 |
| Aston Villa | 38 | 21 | 7 | 10 | 57 | 38 | 70 |
| Tottenham Hotspur | 38 | 19 | 6 | 13 | 59 | 47 | 63 |
| Arsenal | 38 | 18 | 8 | 12 | 54 | 38 | 62 |
| Chelsea | 38 | 16 | 12 | 10 | 58 | 50 | 60 |
| Everton | 38 | 17 | 8 | 13 | 57 | 46 | 59 |
| Southampton | 38 | 15 | 10 | 13 | 71 | 63 | 55 |
| Wimbledon | 38 | 13 | 16 | 9 | 47 | 40 | 55 |
| Nottingham Forest | 38 | 15 | 9 | 14 | 55 | 47 | 54 |
| Norwich City | 38 | 13 | 14 | 11 | 44 | 42 | 53 |
| Queen's Park Rangers | 38 | 13 | 11 | 14 | 45 | 44 | 50 |
| Coventry City | 38 | 14 | 7 | 17 | 39 | 59 | 49 |
| Manchester United | 38 | 13 | 9 | 16 | 46 | 47 | 48 |
| Manchester City | 38 | 12 | 12 | 14 | 43 | 52 | 48 |
| Crystal Palace | 38 | 13 | 9 | 16 | 42 | 66 | 48 |
| Derby County | 38 | 13 | 7 | 18 | 43 | 40 | 46 |
| Luton Town | 38 | 10 | 13 | 15 | 43 | 57 | 43 |
| Sheffield Wednesday | 38 | 11 | 10 | 17 | 35 | 51 | 43 |
| Charlton Athletic | 38 | 7 | 9 | 22 | 31 | 57 | 30 |
| Millwall | 38 | 5 | 11 | 22 | 39 | 65 | 26 |

## Season 1990/91

### DIVISION ONE

| | | | | | | | |
|---|---|---|---|---|---|---|---|
| Arsenal | 38 | 24 | 13 | 1 | 74 | 18 | 83 |
| **Liverpool** | 38 | 23 | 7 | 8 | 77 | 40 | 76 |
| Crystal Palace | 38 | 20 | 9 | 9 | 50 | 41 | 69 |
| Leeds United | 38 | 19 | 7 | 12 | 65 | 47 | 64 |
| Manchester City | 38 | 17 | 11 | 10 | 64 | 53 | 62 |
| Manchester United | 38 | 16 | 12 | 10 | 58 | 45 | 60 |
| Wimbledon | 38 | 14 | 14 | 10 | 53 | 46 | 56 |
| Nottingham Forest | 38 | 14 | 12 | 12 | 65 | 50 | 54 |
| Everton | 38 | 13 | 12 | 13 | 50 | 46 | 51 |
| Tottenham Hotspur | 38 | 11 | 16 | 11 | 51 | 50 | 49 |
| Chelsea | 38 | 13 | 10 | 15 | 58 | 69 | 49 |
| Queen's Park Rangers | 38 | 12 | 10 | 16 | 44 | 53 | 46 |
| Sheffield United | 38 | 13 | 7 | 18 | 36 | 55 | 46 |
| Southampton | 38 | 12 | 9 | 17 | 58 | 69 | 45 |
| Norwich City | 38 | 13 | 6 | 19 | 41 | 64 | 45 |
| Coventry City | 38 | 11 | 11 | 16 | 42 | 49 | 44 |
| Aston Villa | 38 | 9 | 14 | 15 | 46 | 58 | 41 |
| Luton Town | 38 | 10 | 7 | 21 | 42 | 61 | 37 |
| Sunderland | 38 | 8 | 10 | 20 | 38 | 60 | 34 |
| Derby County | 38 | 5 | 9 | 24 | 37 | 75 | 24 |

Arsenal had 2 points deducted
Manchester United had 1 point deducted

## Season 1991/92

### DIVISION ONE

| | | | | | | | |
|---|---|---|---|---|---|---|---|
| Leeds United | 42 | 22 | 16 | 4 | 74 | 37 | 82 |
| Manchester United | 42 | 21 | 15 | 6 | 63 | 33 | 78 |
| Sheffield Wednesday | 42 | 21 | 12 | 9 | 62 | 49 | 75 |
| Arsenal | 42 | 19 | 15 | 8 | 81 | 46 | 72 |
| Manchester City | 42 | 20 | 10 | 12 | 61 | 48 | 70 |
| **Liverpool** | 42 | 16 | 16 | 10 | 47 | 40 | 64 |
| Aston Villa | 42 | 17 | 9 | 16 | 48 | 44 | 60 |
| Nottingham Forest | 42 | 16 | 11 | 15 | 60 | 58 | 59 |
| Sheffield United | 42 | 16 | 9 | 17 | 65 | 63 | 57 |
| Crystal Palace | 42 | 14 | 15 | 13 | 53 | 61 | 57 |
| Queen's Park Rangers | 42 | 12 | 18 | 12 | 48 | 47 | 54 |
| Everton | 42 | 13 | 14 | 15 | 52 | 51 | 53 |
| Wimbledon | 42 | 13 | 14 | 15 | 53 | 53 | 53 |
| Chelsea | 42 | 13 | 14 | 15 | 50 | 60 | 53 |
| Tottenham Hotspur | 42 | 15 | 7 | 20 | 58 | 63 | 52 |
| Southampton | 42 | 14 | 10 | 18 | 39 | 55 | 52 |
| Oldham Athletic | 42 | 14 | 9 | 19 | 63 | 67 | 51 |
| Norwich City | 42 | 11 | 12 | 19 | 47 | 63 | 45 |
| Coventry City | 42 | 11 | 11 | 20 | 35 | 44 | 44 |
| Luton Town | 42 | 10 | 12 | 20 | 38 | 71 | 42 |
| Notts County | 42 | 10 | 10 | 22 | 40 | 62 | 40 |
| West Ham United | 42 | 9 | 11 | 22 | 37 | 59 | 38 |

## Season 1992/93

### F.A. PREMIER LEAGUE

| | | | | | | | |
|---|---|---|---|---|---|---|---|
| Manchester United | 42 | 24 | 12 | 6 | 67 | 31 | 84 |
| Aston Villa | 42 | 21 | 11 | 10 | 57 | 40 | 74 |
| Norwich City | 42 | 21 | 9 | 12 | 61 | 65 | 72 |
| Blackburn Rovers | 42 | 20 | 11 | 11 | 68 | 46 | 71 |
| Queen's Park Rangers | 42 | 17 | 12 | 13 | 63 | 55 | 63 |
| **Liverpool** | 42 | 16 | 11 | 15 | 62 | 55 | 59 |
| Sheffield Wednesday | 42 | 15 | 14 | 13 | 55 | 51 | 59 |
| Tottenham Hotspur | 42 | 16 | 11 | 15 | 60 | 66 | 59 |
| Manchester City | 42 | 15 | 12 | 15 | 56 | 51 | 57 |
| Arsenal | 42 | 15 | 11 | 16 | 40 | 38 | 56 |
| Chelsea | 42 | 14 | 14 | 14 | 51 | 54 | 56 |
| Wimbledon | 42 | 14 | 12 | 16 | 56 | 55 | 54 |
| Everton | 42 | 15 | 8 | 19 | 53 | 55 | 53 |
| Sheffield United | 42 | 14 | 10 | 18 | 54 | 53 | 52 |
| Coventry City | 42 | 13 | 13 | 16 | 52 | 57 | 52 |
| Ipswich Town | 42 | 12 | 16 | 14 | 50 | 55 | 52 |
| Leeds United | 42 | 12 | 15 | 15 | 57 | 62 | 51 |
| Southampton | 42 | 13 | 11 | 18 | 54 | 61 | 50 |
| Oldham Athletic | 42 | 13 | 10 | 19 | 63 | 74 | 49 |
| Crystal Palace | 42 | 11 | 16 | 15 | 48 | 61 | 49 |
| Middlesbrough | 42 | 11 | 11 | 20 | 54 | 75 | 44 |
| Nottingham Forest | 42 | 10 | 10 | 22 | 41 | 62 | 40 |

## Season 1993/94
### F.A.PREMIERSHIP

| | | | | | | | |
|---|---|---|---|---|---|---|---|
| Manchester United | 42 | 27 | 11 | 4 | 80 | 38 | 92 |
| Blackburn Rovers | 42 | 25 | 9 | 8 | 63 | 36 | 84 |
| Newcastle United | 42 | 23 | 8 | 11 | 82 | 41 | 77 |
| Arsenal | 42 | 18 | 17 | 7 | 53 | 28 | 71 |
| Leeds United | 42 | 18 | 16 | 8 | 65 | 39 | 70 |
| Wimbledon | 42 | 18 | 11 | 13 | 56 | 53 | 65 |
| Sheffield Wednesday | 42 | 16 | 16 | 10 | 76 | 54 | 64 |
| Liverpool | 42 | 17 | 9 | 16 | 59 | 55 | 60 |
| Queen's Park Rangers | 42 | 16 | 12 | 14 | 62 | 61 | 60 |
| Aston Villa | 42 | 15 | 12 | 15 | 46 | 50 | 57 |
| Coventry City | 42 | 14 | 14 | 14 | 43 | 45 | 56 |
| Norwich City | 42 | 12 | 17 | 13 | 65 | 61 | 53 |
| West Ham United | 42 | 13 | 13 | 16 | 47 | 58 | 52 |
| Chelsea | 42 | 13 | 12 | 17 | 49 | 53 | 51 |
| Tottenham Hotspur | 42 | 11 | 12 | 19 | 54 | 59 | 45 |
| Manchester City | 42 | 9 | 18 | 15 | 38 | 49 | 45 |
| Everton | 42 | 12 | 8 | 22 | 42 | 63 | 44 |
| Southampton | 42 | 12 | 7 | 23 | 49 | 66 | 43 |
| Ipswich Town | 42 | 9 | 16 | 17 | 35 | 58 | 43 |
| Sheffield United | 42 | 8 | 18 | 16 | 42 | 60 | 42 |
| Oldham Athletic | 42 | 9 | 13 | 20 | 42 | 68 | 40 |
| Swindon Town | 42 | 5 | 15 | 22 | 47 | 100 | 30 |

## Season 1995/96
### F.A. PREMIERSHIP

| | | | | | | | |
|---|---|---|---|---|---|---|---|
| Manchester United | 38 | 25 | 7 | 6 | 73 | 35 | 82 |
| Newcastle United | 38 | 24 | 6 | 8 | 66 | 37 | 78 |
| Liverpool | 38 | 20 | 11 | 7 | 70 | 34 | 71 |
| Aston Villa | 38 | 18 | 9 | 11 | 52 | 35 | 63 |
| Arsenal | 38 | 17 | 12 | 9 | 49 | 32 | 63 |
| Everton | 38 | 17 | 10 | 11 | 64 | 44 | 61 |
| Blackburn Rovers | 38 | 18 | 7 | 13 | 61 | 47 | 61 |
| Tottenham Hotspur | 38 | 16 | 13 | 9 | 50 | 38 | 61 |
| Nottingham Forest | 38 | 15 | 13 | 10 | 50 | 54 | 58 |
| West Ham United | 38 | 14 | 9 | 15 | 43 | 52 | 51 |
| Chelsea | 38 | 12 | 14 | 12 | 46 | 44 | 50 |
| Middlesbrough | 38 | 11 | 10 | 17 | 35 | 50 | 43 |
| Leeds United | 38 | 12 | 7 | 19 | 40 | 57 | 43 |
| Wimbledon | 38 | 10 | 11 | 17 | 55 | 70 | 41 |
| Sheffield Wednesday | 38 | 10 | 10 | 18 | 48 | 61 | 40 |
| Coventry City | 38 | 8 | 14 | 16 | 42 | 60 | 38 |
| Southampton | 38 | 9 | 11 | 18 | 34 | 52 | 38 |
| Manchester City | 38 | 9 | 11 | 18 | 33 | 58 | 38 |
| Queen's Park Rangers | 38 | 9 | 6 | 23 | 38 | 57 | 33 |
| Bolton Wanderers | 38 | 8 | 5 | 25 | 39 | 71 | 29 |

## Season 1994/95
### F.A. PREMIERSHIP

| | | | | | | | |
|---|---|---|---|---|---|---|---|
| Blackburn Rovers | 42 | 27 | 8 | 7 | 80 | 39 | 89 |
| Manchester United | 42 | 26 | 10 | 6 | 77 | 28 | 88 |
| Nottingham Forest | 42 | 22 | 11 | 9 | 72 | 43 | 77 |
| Liverpool | 42 | 21 | 11 | 10 | 65 | 37 | 74 |
| Leeds United | 42 | 20 | 13 | 9 | 59 | 38 | 73 |
| Newcastle United | 42 | 20 | 12 | 10 | 67 | 47 | 72 |
| Tottenham Hotspur | 42 | 16 | 14 | 12 | 66 | 58 | 62 |
| Queen's Park Rangers | 42 | 17 | 9 | 16 | 61 | 59 | 60 |
| Wimbledon | 42 | 15 | 11 | 16 | 48 | 65 | 56 |
| Southampton | 42 | 12 | 18 | 12 | 61 | 63 | 54 |
| Chelsea | 42 | 13 | 15 | 14 | 50 | 55 | 54 |
| Arsenal | 42 | 13 | 12 | 17 | 52 | 49 | 51 |
| Sheffield Wednesday | 42 | 13 | 12 | 17 | 49 | 57 | 51 |
| West Ham United | 42 | 13 | 11 | 18 | 44 | 48 | 50 |
| Everton | 42 | 11 | 17 | 14 | 44 | 51 | 50 |
| Coventry City | 42 | 12 | 14 | 16 | 44 | 62 | 50 |
| Manchester City | 42 | 12 | 13 | 17 | 53 | 64 | 49 |
| Aston Villa | 42 | 11 | 15 | 16 | 51 | 56 | 48 |
| Crystal Palace | 42 | 11 | 12 | 19 | 34 | 49 | 45 |
| Norwich City | 42 | 10 | 13 | 19 | 37 | 54 | 43 |
| Leicester City | 42 | 6 | 11 | 25 | 45 | 80 | 29 |
| Ipswich Town | 42 | 7 | 6 | 29 | 36 | 93 | 27 |

## Season 1996/97
### F.A. PREMIERSHIP

| | | | | | | | |
|---|---|---|---|---|---|---|---|
| Manchester United | 38 | 21 | 12 | 5 | 76 | 44 | 75 |
| Newcastle United | 38 | 19 | 11 | 8 | 73 | 40 | 68 |
| Arsenal | 38 | 19 | 11 | 8 | 62 | 32 | 68 |
| Liverpool | 38 | 19 | 11 | 8 | 62 | 37 | 68 |
| Aston Villa | 38 | 17 | 10 | 11 | 47 | 34 | 61 |
| Chelsea | 38 | 16 | 11 | 11 | 58 | 55 | 59 |
| Sheffield Wednesday | 38 | 14 | 15 | 9 | 50 | 51 | 57 |
| Wimbledon | 38 | 15 | 11 | 12 | 49 | 46 | 56 |
| Leicester City | 38 | 12 | 11 | 15 | 46 | 54 | 47 |
| Tottenham Hotspur | 38 | 13 | 7 | 18 | 44 | 51 | 46 |
| Leeds United | 38 | 11 | 13 | 14 | 28 | 38 | 46 |
| Derby County | 38 | 11 | 13 | 14 | 45 | 58 | 46 |
| Blackburn Rovers | 38 | 9 | 15 | 14 | 42 | 43 | 42 |
| West Ham United | 38 | 10 | 12 | 16 | 39 | 48 | 42 |
| Everton | 38 | 10 | 12 | 16 | 44 | 57 | 42 |
| Southampton | 38 | 10 | 11 | 17 | 50 | 56 | 41 |
| Coventry City | 38 | 9 | 14 | 15 | 38 | 54 | 41 |
| Sunderland | 38 | 10 | 10 | 18 | 35 | 53 | 40 |
| Middlesbrough | 38 | 10 | 12 | 16 | 51 | 60 | 39 |
| Nottingham Forest | 38 | 6 | 16 | 16 | 31 | 59 | 34 |

Middlesbrough had 3 points deducted

## Season 1997/98
### F.A. PREMIERSHIP

| | | | | | | | |
|---|---|---|---|---|---|---|---|
| Arsenal | 38 | 23 | 9 | 6 | 68 | 33 | 78 |
| Manchester United | 38 | 23 | 8 | 7 | 73 | 26 | 77 |
| **Liverpool** | **38** | **18** | **11** | **9** | **68** | **42** | **65** |
| Chelsea | 38 | 20 | 3 | 15 | 71 | 43 | 63 |
| Leeds United | 38 | 17 | 8 | 13 | 57 | 46 | 59 |
| Blackburn Rovers | 38 | 16 | 10 | 12 | 57 | 52 | 58 |
| Aston Villa | 38 | 17 | 6 | 15 | 49 | 48 | 57 |
| West Ham United | 38 | 16 | 8 | 14 | 56 | 57 | 56 |
| Derby County | 38 | 16 | 7 | 15 | 52 | 49 | 55 |
| Leicester City | 38 | 13 | 14 | 11 | 51 | 41 | 53 |
| Coventry City | 38 | 12 | 16 | 10 | 46 | 44 | 52 |
| Southampton | 38 | 14 | 6 | 18 | 50 | 55 | 48 |
| Newcastle United | 38 | 11 | 11 | 16 | 35 | 44 | 44 |
| Tottenham Hotspur | 38 | 11 | 11 | 16 | 44 | 56 | 44 |
| Wimbledon | 38 | 10 | 14 | 14 | 34 | 46 | 44 |
| Sheffield Wednesday | 38 | 12 | 8 | 18 | 52 | 67 | 44 |
| Everton | 38 | 9 | 13 | 16 | 41 | 56 | 40 |
| Bolton Wanderers | 38 | 9 | 13 | 16 | 41 | 61 | 40 |
| Barnsley | 38 | 10 | 5 | 23 | 37 | 82 | 35 |
| Crystal Palace | 38 | 8 | 9 | 21 | 37 | 71 | 33 |

## Season 1998/99
### F.A. PREMIERSHIP

| | | | | | | | |
|---|---|---|---|---|---|---|---|
| Manchester United | 38 | 22 | 13 | 3 | 80 | 37 | 79 |
| Arsenal | 38 | 22 | 12 | 4 | 59 | 17 | 78 |
| Chelsea | 38 | 20 | 15 | 3 | 57 | 30 | 75 |
| Leeds United | 38 | 18 | 13 | 7 | 62 | 34 | 67 |
| West Ham United | 38 | 16 | 9 | 13 | 46 | 53 | 57 |
| Aston Villa | 38 | 15 | 10 | 13 | 51 | 46 | 55 |
| **Liverpool** | **38** | **15** | **9** | **14** | **68** | **49** | **54** |
| Derby County | 38 | 13 | 13 | 12 | 40 | 45 | 52 |
| Middlesbrough | 38 | 12 | 15 | 11 | 48 | 54 | 51 |
| Leicester City | 38 | 12 | 13 | 13 | 40 | 46 | 49 |
| Tottenham Hotspur | 38 | 11 | 14 | 13 | 47 | 50 | 47 |
| Sheffield Wednesday | 38 | 13 | 7 | 18 | 41 | 42 | 46 |
| Newcastle United | 38 | 11 | 13 | 14 | 48 | 54 | 46 |
| Everton | 38 | 11 | 10 | 17 | 42 | 47 | 43 |
| Coventry City | 38 | 11 | 9 | 18 | 39 | 51 | 42 |
| Wimbledon | 38 | 10 | 12 | 16 | 40 | 63 | 42 |
| Southampton | 38 | 11 | 8 | 19 | 37 | 64 | 41 |
| Charlton Athletic | 38 | 8 | 12 | 18 | 41 | 56 | 36 |
| Blackburn Rovers | 38 | 7 | 14 | 17 | 38 | 52 | 35 |
| Nottingham Forest | 38 | 7 | 9 | 22 | 35 | 69 | 30 |

## Season 1999/2000
### F.A. PREMIERSHIP

| | | | | | | | |
|---|---|---|---|---|---|---|---|
| Manchester United | 38 | 28 | 7 | 3 | 97 | 45 | 91 |
| Arsenal | 38 | 22 | 7 | 9 | 73 | 43 | 73 |
| Leeds United | 38 | 21 | 6 | 11 | 58 | 43 | 69 |
| **Liverpool** | **38** | **19** | **10** | **9** | **51** | **30** | **67** |
| Chelsea | 38 | 18 | 11 | 9 | 53 | 34 | 65 |
| Aston Villa | 38 | 15 | 13 | 10 | 46 | 35 | 58 |
| Sunderland | 38 | 16 | 10 | 12 | 57 | 56 | 58 |
| Leicester City | 38 | 16 | 7 | 15 | 55 | 55 | 55 |
| West Ham United | 38 | 15 | 10 | 13 | 52 | 53 | 55 |
| Tottenham Hotspur | 38 | 15 | 8 | 15 | 57 | 49 | 53 |
| Newcastle United | 38 | 14 | 10 | 14 | 63 | 54 | 52 |
| Middlesbrough | 38 | 14 | 10 | 14 | 46 | 52 | 52 |
| Everton | 38 | 12 | 14 | 12 | 59 | 49 | 50 |
| Coventry City | 38 | 12 | 8 | 18 | 47 | 54 | 44 |
| Southampton | 38 | 12 | 8 | 18 | 45 | 62 | 44 |
| Derby County | 38 | 9 | 11 | 18 | 44 | 57 | 38 |
| Bradford City | 38 | 9 | 9 | 20 | 38 | 68 | 36 |
| Wimbledon | 38 | 7 | 12 | 19 | 46 | 74 | 33 |
| Sheffield Wednesday | 38 | 8 | 7 | 23 | 38 | 70 | 31 |
| Watford | 38 | 6 | 6 | 26 | 35 | 77 | 24 |

## Season 2000/2001
### F.A. PREMIERSHIP

| | | | | | | | |
|---|---|---|---|---|---|---|---|
| Manchester United | 38 | 24 | 8 | 6 | 79 | 31 | 80 |
| Arsenal | 38 | 20 | 10 | 8 | 63 | 38 | 70 |
| **Liverpool** | **38** | **20** | **9** | **9** | **71** | **39** | **69** |
| Leeds United | 38 | 20 | 8 | 10 | 64 | 43 | 68 |
| Ipswich Town | 38 | 20 | 6 | 12 | 57 | 42 | 66 |
| Chelsea | 38 | 17 | 10 | 11 | 68 | 45 | 61 |
| Sunderland | 38 | 15 | 12 | 11 | 46 | 41 | 57 |
| Aston Villa | 38 | 13 | 15 | 10 | 46 | 43 | 54 |
| Charlton Athletic | 38 | 14 | 10 | 14 | 50 | 57 | 52 |
| Southampton | 38 | 14 | 10 | 14 | 40 | 48 | 52 |
| Newcastle United | 38 | 14 | 9 | 15 | 44 | 50 | 51 |
| Tottenham Hotspur | 38 | 13 | 10 | 15 | 47 | 54 | 49 |
| Leicester City | 38 | 14 | 6 | 18 | 39 | 51 | 48 |
| Middlesbrough | 38 | 9 | 15 | 14 | 44 | 44 | 42 |
| West Ham United | 38 | 10 | 12 | 16 | 45 | 50 | 42 |
| Everton | 38 | 11 | 9 | 18 | 45 | 59 | 42 |
| Derby County | 38 | 10 | 12 | 16 | 37 | 59 | 42 |
| Manchester City | 38 | 8 | 10 | 20 | 41 | 65 | 34 |
| Coventry City | 38 | 8 | 10 | 20 | 36 | 63 | 34 |
| Bradford City | 38 | 5 | 11 | 22 | 30 | 70 | 26 |

153

# Season 2001/2002

## F.A. PREMIERSHIP

| | | | | | | | |
|---|---|---|---|---|---|---|---|
| Arsenal | 38 | 26 | 9 | 3 | 79 | 36 | 87 |
| **Liverpool** | **38** | **24** | **8** | **6** | **67** | **30** | **80** |
| Manchester United | 38 | 24 | 5 | 9 | 87 | 45 | 77 |
| Newcastle United | 38 | 21 | 8 | 9 | 74 | 52 | 71 |
| Leeds United | 38 | 18 | 12 | 8 | 53 | 37 | 66 |
| Chelsea | 38 | 17 | 13 | 8 | 66 | 38 | 64 |
| West Ham United | 38 | 15 | 8 | 15 | 48 | 57 | 53 |
| Aston Villa | 38 | 12 | 14 | 12 | 46 | 47 | 50 |
| Tottenham Hotspur | 38 | 14 | 8 | 16 | 49 | 53 | 50 |
| Blackburn Rovers | 38 | 12 | 10 | 16 | 55 | 51 | 46 |
| Southampton | 38 | 12 | 9 | 17 | 46 | 54 | 45 |
| Middlesbrough | 38 | 12 | 9 | 17 | 35 | 47 | 45 |
| Fulham | 38 | 10 | 14 | 14 | 36 | 44 | 44 |
| Charlton Athletic | 38 | 10 | 14 | 14 | 38 | 49 | 44 |
| Everton | 38 | 11 | 10 | 17 | 45 | 57 | 43 |
| Bolton Wanderers | 38 | 9 | 13 | 16 | 44 | 62 | 40 |
| Sunderland | 38 | 10 | 10 | 18 | 29 | 51 | 40 |
| Ipswich Town | 38 | 9 | 9 | 20 | 41 | 64 | 36 |
| Derby County | 38 | 8 | 6 | 24 | 33 | 63 | 30 |
| Leicester City | 38 | 5 | 13 | 20 | 30 | 64 | 28 |

---

# LIVERPOOL CUP RESULTS – 1977-78 to 2001-2002

## F.A. CUP COMPETITION

### 1977/78 SEASON
**3rd Round**
Jan 7 vs Chelsea (a) 2-4
*Att: 45,449    Johnson, Dalglish*

### 1978/79 SEASON
**3rd Round**
Jan 10 vs Southend United (a) 0-0
*Att: 31,033*
**Replay**
Jan 17 vs Southend United (h) 3-0
*Att: 37,797    Case, Dalglish, R. Kennedy*
**4th Round**
Jan 30 vs Blackburn Rovers (h) 1-0
*Att: 43,432    Dalglish*
**5th Round**
Feb 28 vs Burnley (h) 3-0
*Att: 47,161    Johnson 2, Souness*
**6th Round**
Mar 10 vs Ipswich Town (a) 1-0
*Att: 31,322    Dalglish*
**Semi-Final (at Maine Road)**
Mar 31 vs Manchester United 2-2
*Att: 52,584    Dalglish, Hansen*
**Semi-Final (at Goodison Park)**
Apr 4 vs Manchester United 0-1
*Att: 53,069*

### 1979/80 SEASON
**3rd Round**
Jan 5 vs Grimsby Town (h) 5-0
*Att: 49,706    Souness, Johnson 3, Case*
**4th Round**
Jan 26 vs Nottingham Forest (a) 2-0
*Att: 33,277    Dalglish, McDermott (pen)*
**5th Round**
Feb 16 vs Bury (h) 2-0
*Att: 43,769    Fairclough 2*

**6th Round**
Mar 8 vs Tottenham Hotspur (a) 1-0
*Att: 48,033    McDermott*
**Semi-Final (at Hillsborough)**
Apr 12 vs Arsenal 0-0
*Att: 50,174*
**Replay (at Villa Park)**
Apr 16 vs Arsenal 1-1 (aet.)
*Att: 40,679    Fairclough*
**2nd Replay (at Villa Park)**
Apr 28 vs Arsenal 1-1 (aet.)
*Att: 42,975    Dalglish*
**3rd Replay (at Coventry)**
May 1 vs Arsenal 0-1
*Att: 35,335*

### 1980/81 SEASON
**3rd Round**
Jan 3 vs Altrincham (h) 4-1
*Att: 37,170    McDermott, Dalglish 2,
R. Kennedy*
**4th Round**
Jan 24 vs Everton (a) 1-2
*Att: 53,084    Case*

### 1981/82 SEASON
**3rd Round**
Jan 2 vs Swansea City (a) 4-0
*Att: 24,179    Hansen, Rush 2, Lawrenson*
**4th Round**
Jan 23 vs Sunderland (a) 3-0
*Att: 28,582    Dalglish 2, Rush*
**5th Round**
Feb 13 vs Chelsea (a) 0-2
*Att: 41,422*

### 1982/83 SEASON
**3rd Round**
Jan 8 vs Blackburn Rovers (a) 2-1
*Att: 21,966    Hodgson, Rush*
**4th Round**
Jan 29 vs Stoke City (h) 2-0
*Att: 36,666    Dalglish, Rush*

**5th Round**
Feb 20 vs Brighton & Hove Albion (h) 1-2
*Att: 44,868    Johnston*

### 1983/84 SEASON
**3rd Round**
Jan 6 vs Newcastle United (h) 4-0
*Att: 33,566    Robinson, Rush 2, Johnston*
**4th Round**
Jan 29 vs Brighton & Hove Albion (a) 0-2
*Att: 19,057*

### 1984/85 SEASON
**3rd Round**
Jan 5 vs Aston Villa (h) 3-0
*Att: 36,877    Rush 2, Wark*
**4th Round**
Jan 27 vs Tottenham Hotspur (h) 1-0
*Att: 27,905    Rush*
**5th Round**
Feb 15 vs York City (a) 1-1
*Att: 13,485    Rush*
**Replay**
Feb 20 vs York City (h) 7-0
*Att: 43,010    Whelan 2, Wark 3, Neal, Walsh*
**6th Round**
Mar 10 vs Barnsley (a) 4-0
*Att: 19,838    Whelan, Rush 3*
**Semi-Final (at Goodison Park)**
Apr 13 vs Manchester United 2-2 (aet.)
(score after 90 minutes 1-1)
*Att: 51,690    Whelan, Walsh*
**Replay (at Maine Road)**
Apr 17 vs Manchester United 1-2
*Att: 45,775    McGrath (og)*

### 1985/86 SEASON
**3rd Round**
Jan 4 vs Norwich City (h) 5-0
*Att: 29,082    MacDonald, Walsh, McMahon,
Whelan, Wark*
**4th Round**
Jan 26 vs Chelsea (a) 2-1
*Att: 33,625    Rush, Lawrenson*

**5th Round**
Feb 15 vs York City (a) 1-1
*Att: 12,443   Molby (pen)*
**Replay**
Feb 18 vs York City (h) 3-1
*Att: 19,326   Wark, Molby, Dalglish*
**6th Round**
Mar 11 vs Watford (h) 0-0
*Att: 36,775*
**Replay**
Mar 17 vs Watford (a) 2-1
*Att: 28,097   Molby (pen), Rush*
**Semi-Final (at White Hart Lane)**
Apr 5 vs Southampton 2-0 (aet.)
*Att: 44,605   Rush 2*
**FINAL (at Wembley)**
May 10 vs Everton 3-1
*Att: 98,000   Rush 2, Johnston*

## 1986/87 SEASON
**3rd Round**
Jan 11 vs Luton Town (a) 0-0
*Att: 11,085*
**Replay**
Jan 26 vs Luton Town (h) 0-0 (aet.)
*Att: 34,822*
**2nd Replay**
Jan 28 vs Luton Town (a) 0-3
*Att: 14,687*

## 1987/88 SEASON
**3rd Round**
Jan 9 vs Stoke City (a) 0-0
*Att: 31,979*
**Replay**
Jan 12 vs Stoke City (h) 1-0
*Att: 39,147   Beardsley*
**4th Round**
Jan 31 vs Aston Villa (a) 2-0
*Att: 46,324   Barnes, Beardsley*
**5th Round**
Feb 21 vs Everton (a) 1-0
*Att: 48,270   Houghton*
**6th Round**
Mar 13 vs Manchester City (a) 4-0
*Att: 44,047   Houghton, Beardsley (pen),
Johnston, Barnes*
**Semi-Final (at Hillsborough)**
Apr 9 vs Nottingham Forest 2-1
*Att: 51,627   Aldridge 2 (1 pen)*
**FINAL (at Wembley)**
May 14 vs Wimbledon 0-1
*Att: 98,203*

## 1988/89 SEASON
**3rd Round**
Jan 7 vs Carlisle United (a) 3-0
*Att: 18,556   Barnes, McMahon 2*
**4th Round**
Jan 29 vs Millwall (a) 2-0
*Att: 23,615   Aldridge, Rush*
**5th Round**
Feb 18 vs Hull City (a) 3-2
*Att: 20,058   Barnes, Aldridge 2*
**6th Round**
Mar 18 vs Brentford (h) 4-0
*Att: 42,376   McMahon, Barnes, Beardsley 2*
**Semi-Final (at Hillsborough)**
Apr 15 vs Nottingham Forest
(Abandoned after 6 minutes)
*Att: 53,000*
**Replay (at Old Trafford)**
May 7 vs Nottingham Forest 3-1
*Att: 38,000   Aldridge 2, Laws (og)*
**FINAL (at Wembley)**
May 20 vs Everton 3-2 (aet.)
(score after 90 minutes 1-1)
*Att: 82,800   Aldridge, Rush 2*

## 1989/90 SEASON
**3rd Round**
Jan 6 vs Swansea City (a) 0-0
*Att: 16,098*
**Replay**
Jan 9 vs Swansea City (h) 8-0
*Att: 29,149   Barnes 2, Whelan, Beardsley,
Nicol, Rush 3*
**4th Round**
Jan 28 vs Norwich City (a) 0-0
*Att: 23,162*
**Replay**
Jan 31 vs Norwich City (h) 3-1
*Att: 29,339   Nicol, Barnes,
Beardsley (pen)*
**5th Round**
Feb 17 vs Southampton (h) 3-0
*Att: 35,961   Rush, Beardsley, Nicol*
**6th Round**
Mar 11 vs Queen's Park Rangers (a) 2-2
*Att: 21,057   Barnes, Rush*
**Replay**
Mar 14 vs Queen's Park Rangers (h) 1-0
*Att: 38,090   Beardsley*
**Semi-Final (at Villa Park)**
Apr 8 vs Crystal Palace 3-4 (aet.)
(score after 90 minutes 3-3)
*Att: 38,389   Rush, McMahon, Barnes (pen)*

## 1990/91 SEASON
**3rd Round**
Jan 5 vs Blackburn Rovers (a) 1-1
*Att: 18,845   Atkins (og)*
**Replay**
Jan 8 vs Blackburn Rovers (h) 3-0
*Att: 34,175   Houghton, Rush, Staunton*
**4th Round**
Jan 26 vs Brighton & Hove Albion (h) 2-2
*Att: 32,670   Rush 2*
**Replay**
Jan 30 vs Brighton & Hove Alb. (a) 3-2 (aet.)
*Att: 14,392   McMahon 2, Rush*
**5th Round**
Feb 17 vs Everton (h) 0-0
*Att: 38,323*
**Replay**
Feb 20 vs Everton (a) 4-4 (aet.)
(score after 90 minutes 3-3)
*Att: 37,766   Beardsley 2, Rush, Barnes*
**2nd Replay**
Feb 27 vs Everton (a) 0-1
*Att: 40,201*

## 1991/92 SEASON
**3rd Round**
Jan 6 vs Crewe Alexandra (a) 4-0
*Att: 7,457   McManaman, Barnes 3 (1 pen)*
**4th Round**
Feb 5 vs Bristol Rovers (a) 1-1
*Att: 9,464   Saunders*
**Replay**
Feb 11 vs Bristol Rovers (h) 2-1
*Att: 30,142   McManaman, Saunders*
**5th Round**
Feb 16 vs Ipswich Town (h) 0-0
*Att: 26,140*
**Replay**
Feb 26 vs Ipswich Town (h) 3-2 (aet.)
*Att: 27,355   Houghton, Molby, McManaman*
**6th Round**
Mar 8 vs Aston Villa (h) 1-0
*Att: 29,109   Thomas*
**Semi-Final (at Highbury)**
Apr 5 vs Portsmouth 1-1 (aet.)
(score after 90 minutes 0-0)
*Att: 41,869   Whelan*
**Replay (at Villa Park)**
Apr 13 vs Portsmouth 0-0 (aet.)
*Att: 40,077   Liverpool won 3-1 on penalties*

**FINAL (at Wembley)**
May 9 vs Sunderland 2-0
*Att: 79,544   Thomas, Rush*

## 1992/93 SEASON
**3rd Round**
Jan 3 vs Bolton Wanderers (a) 2-2
*Att: 21,502   Winstanley (og), Rush*
**Replay**
Jan 13 vs Bolton Wanderers (h) 0-2
*Att: 34,790*

## 1993/94 SEASON
**3rd Round**
Jan 19 vs Bristol City (a) 1-1
*Att: 21,718   Rush*
**Replay**
Jan 25 vs Bristol City (h) 0-1
*Att: 36,720*

## 1994/95 SEASON
**3rd Round**
Jan 7 vs Birmingham City (a) 0-0
*Att: 25,326*
**Replay**
Jan 18 vs Birmingham City (h) 1-1 (aet.)
*Att: 36,275   Redknapp*
*Liverpool won 2-0 on penalties*
**4th Round**
Jan 28 vs Burnley (a) 0-0
*Att: 20,551*
**Replay**
Feb 7 vs Burnley (h) 1-0
*Att: 32,109   Barnes*
**5th Round**
Feb 19 vs Wimbledon (h) 1-1
*Att: 25,124   Fowler*
**Replay**
Feb 28 vs Wimbledon (a) 2-0
*Att: 12,553   Barnes, Rush*
**6th Round**
Mar 11 vs Tottenham Hotspur (h) 1-2
*Att: 39,592   Fowler*

## 1995/96 SEASON
**3rd Round**
Jan 6 vs Rochdale (h) 7-0
*Att: 28,126   Fowler, Collymore 3, Valentine
(og), Rush, McAteer*
**4th Round**
Feb 18 vs Shrewsbury Town (a) 4-0
*Att: 7,752   Collymore, Watson (og), Fowler,
McAteer*
**5th Round**
Feb 28 vs Charlton Athletic (h) 2-1
*Att: 36,818   Fowler, Collymore*
**6th Round**
Mar 10 vs Leeds United (a) 0-0
*Att: 24,632*
**Replay**
Mar 20 vs Leeds United (h) 3-0
*Att: 30,812   McManaman 2, Fowler*
**Semi-Final (at Old Trafford)**
Mar 31 vs Aston Villa 3-0
*Att: 39,021   Fowler 2, McAteer*
**FINAL (at Wembley)**
May 11 vs Manchester United 0-1
*Att: 79,007*

## 1996/97 SEASON
**3rd Round**
Jan 4 vs Burnley (h) 1-0
*Att: 33,352   Collymore*
**4th Round**
Jan 26 vs Chelsea (a) 2-4
*Att: 27,950   Fowler, Collymore*

## 1997/98 SEASON
**3rd Round**
Jan 3 vs Coventry City (h) 1-3
*Att: 33,888   Redknapp*

155

## 1998/99 SEASON

**3rd Round**
Jan 3 vs Port Vale (a)  3-0
*Att: 16,557   Owen (pen), Ince, Fowler*

**4th Round**
Jan 24 vs Manchester United (a)  1-2
*Att: 54,591   Owen*

## 1999/2000 SEASON

**3rd Round**
Dec 12 vs Huddersfield Town (a)  2-0
*Att: 23,678   Camara, Matteo*

**4th Round**
Jan 10 vs Blackburn Rovers (h)  0-1
*Att: 32,839*

## 2000/2001 SEASON

**3rd Round**
Jan 6 vs Rotherham United (h)  3-0
*Att: 30,689   Heskey 2, Hamann*

**4th Round**
Jan 27 vs Leeds United (a)  2-0
*Att: 37,108   Barmby, Heskey*

**5th Round**
Feb 18 vs Manchester City (h)  4-2
*Att: 36,231   Litmanen (pen), Heskey, Smicer (pen), Babbel*

**6th Round**
Mar 11 vs Tranmere Rovers (a)  4-2
*Att: 16,342   Murphy, Owen, Gerrard, Fowler (pen)*

**Semi-Final (at Villa Park)**
Apr 8 vs Wycombe Wanderers 2-1
*Att: 40,037   Heskey, Fowler*

**FINAL (at the Millennium Stadium)**
May 12 vs Arsenal  2-1
*Att: 74,200   Owen 2*

## 2001/2002 SEASON

**3rd Round**
Jan 5 vs Birmingham City (h)  3-0
*Att: 40,875   Owen 2, Anelka*

**4th Round**
Jan 27 vs Arsenal (a)  0-1
*Att: 38,092*

# LEAGUE CUP COMPETITION

## 1977/78 SEASON

**2nd Round**
Aug 30 vs Chelsea (h)  2-0
*Att: 33,170   Dalglish, Case*

**3rd Round**
Oct 26 vs Derby County (h)  2-0
*Att: 30,400   Fairclough 2*

**4th Round**
Nov 29 vs Coventry City (h)  2-2
*Att: 33,817   Fairclough, Neal (pen)*

**Replay**
Dec 20 vs Coventry City (a)  2-0
*Att: 36,105   Case, Dalglish*

**5th Round**
Jan 17 vs Wrexham (h)  3-1
*Att: 25,641   Dalglish 3*

**Semi-Final (1st leg)**
Feb 7 vs Arsenal (h)  2-1
*Att: 44,764   Dalglish, Kennedy*

**Semi-Final (2nd leg)**
Feb 14 vs Arsenal (a)  0-0  (aggregate 2-1)
*Att: 49,561*

**FINAL (at Wembley)**
Mar 18 vs Nottingham Forest  0-0  (aet.)
*Att: 100,000*

**Replay (at Old Trafford)**
Mar 22 vs Nottingham Forest  0-1
*Att: 54,375*

## 1978/79 SEASON

**2nd Round**
Aug 28 vs Sheffield United (a)  0-1
*Att: 35,753*

## 1979/80 SEASON

**2nd Round (1st leg)**
Aug 29 vs Tranmere Rovers (a)  0-0
*Att: 16,759*

**2nd Round (2nd leg)**
Sep 4 vs Tranmere Rovers (h)  4-0  (agg. 4-0)
*Att: 24,785   Thompson, Dalglish 2, Fairclough*

**3rd Round**
Sep 25 vs Chesterfield (h)  3-1
*Att: 20,960   Fairclough, Dalglish, McDermott*

**4th Round**
Oct 30 vs Exeter City (h)  2-0
*Att: 21,019   Fairclough 2*

**5th Round**
Dec 5 vs Norwich City (a)  3-1
*Att: 23,000   Johnson 2, Dalglish*

**Semi-Final (1st leg)**
Jan 22 vs Nottingham Forest (a)  0-1
*Att: 32,234*

**Semi-Final (2nd leg)**
Feb 12 vs Nottingham Forest (h)  1-1
(aggregate 1-2)
*Att: 50,880   Fairclough*

## 1980/81 SEASON

**2nd Round (1st leg)**
Aug 27 vs Bradford City (a)  0-1
*Att: 16,232*

**2nd Round (2nd leg)**
Sep 2 vs Bradford City (h)  4-0  (agg. 4-1)
*Att: 21,107   Dalglish 2, R. Kennedy, Johnson*

**3rd Round**
Sep 23 vs Swindon Town (h)  5-0
*Att: 16,566   Lee 2, Dalglish, Fairclough 2*

**4th Round**
Oct 28 vs Portsmouth (h)  4-1
*Att: 32,021   Dalglish, Johnson 2, Souness*

**5th Round**
Dec 5 vs Birmingham City (h)  3-1
*Att: 30,236   Dalglish, McDermott, Johnson*

**Semi-Final (1st leg)**
Jan 14 vs Manchester City (a)  1-0
*Att: 48,045   R. Kennedy*

**Semi-Final (2nd leg)**
Feb 10 vs Manchester City (h)  1-1  (agg. 2-1)
*Att: 46,711   Dalglish*

**FINAL (at Wembley)**
Mar 14 vs West Ham United  1-1  (aet.)
*Att: 100,000   A. Kennedy*

**Replay (at Villa Park)**
Apr 1 vs West Ham United  2-1
*Att: 36,693   Dalglish, Hansen*

## 1981/82 SEASON

**2nd Round (1st leg)**
Oct 7 vs Exeter City (h)  5-0
*Att: 11,478   Rush 2, McDermott, Dalglish, Whelan*

**2nd Round (2nd leg)**
Oct 28 vs Exeter City (a)  6-0  (agg. 11-0)
*Att: 11,740   Rush 2, Dalglish, Neal, Sheedy, Marker (og)*

**3rd Round**
Nov 10 vs Middlesbrough (h)  4-1
*Att: 16,145   Sheedy, Rush, Johnson 2*

**4th Round**
Dec 1 vs Arsenal (a)  0-0
*Att: 37,917*

**Replay**
Dec 8 vs Arsenal (h)  3-0  (aet.)
*Att: 21,375   Johnston, McDermott (pen), Dalglish*

**5th Round**
Jan 12 vs Barnsley (h)  0-0
*Att: 33,707*

**Replay**
Jan 19 vs Barnsley (a)  3-1
*Att: 29,639   Souness, Johnson, Dalglish*

**Semi-Final (1st leg)**
Feb 2 vs Ipswich Town (a)  2-0
*Att: 26,690   McDermott, Rush*

**Semi-Final (2nd leg)**
Feb 9 vs Ipswich Town (h)  2-2
(aggregate 4-2)
*Att: 34,933   Rush, Dalglish*

**FINAL (at Wembley)**
Mar 13 vs Tottenham Hotspur 3-1 (aet.)
*Att: 100,000   Whelan 2, Rush*

## 1982/83 SEASON

**2nd Round (1st leg)**
Oct 5 vs Ipswich Town (a)  2-1
*Att: 19,329   Rush 2*

**2nd Round (2nd leg)**
Oct 26 vs Ipswich Town (h)  2-0  (agg. 4-1)
*Att: 17,698   Whelan, Lawrenson*

**3rd Round**
Nov 11 vs Rotherham United (h)  1-0
*Att: 20,412   Johnston*

**4th Round**
Nov 30 vs Norwich City (h)  2-0
*Att: 13,235   Lawrenson, Fairclough*

**5th Round**
Jan 18 vs West Ham United (h)  2-1
*Att: 23,953   Hodgson, Souness*

**Semi-Final (1st leg)**
Feb 8 vs Burnley (h)  3-0
*Att: 33,520   Souness, Neal (pen), Hodgson*

**Semi-Final (2nd leg)**
Feb 15 vs Burnley (a)  0-1  (agg. 3-1)
*Att: 22,350*

**FINAL (at Wembley)**
Mar 26 vs Manchester United  2-1  (aet)
(score after 90 minutes 1-1)
*Att: 100,000   Kennedy, Whelan*

## 1983/84 SEASON

**2nd Round (1st leg)**
Oct 5 vs Brentford (a)  4-1
*Att: 17,859   Rush 2, Robinson, Souness*

**2nd Round (2nd leg)**
Oct 25 vs Brentford (h)  4-0  (agg. 8-1)
*Att: 9,092   Souness (pen), Hodgson, Dalglish, Robinson*

**3rd Round**
Nov 8 vs Fulham (a)  1-1
*Att: 20,142   Rush*

**Replay**
Nov 22 vs Fulham (h)  1-1  (aet.)
(score after 90 minutes 1-1)
*Att: 15,783   Dalglish*

**2nd Replay**
Nov 29 vs Fulham (a)  1-0  (aet.)
(score after 90 minutes 0-0)
*Att: 20,905   Souness*

**4th Round**
Dec 20 vs Birmingham City (a)  1-1
*Att: 17,405   Souness*

**Replay**
Dec 22 vs Birmingham City (h)  3-0
*Att: 11,638   Nicholl, Rush 2 (1 pen)*

**5th Round**
Jan 17 vs Sheffield Wednesday (a)  2-2
*Att: 49,357   Nicol, Neal (pen)*

**Replay**
Jan 25 vs Sheffield Wednesday (h)  3-0
*Att: 40,485   Rush 2, Robinson*

**Semi-Final (1st leg)**
Feb 7 vs Walsall (h)  2-2
*Att: 31,073   Whelan 2*

**Semi-Final (2nd leg)**
Feb 14 vs Walsall (a)  2-0  (agg. 4-2)
*Att: 40,006   Sheedy, Richardson*

**FINAL (at Wembley)**
Mar 25 vs Everton 0-0 (aet.)
*Att: 100,000*
**Replay (at Maine Road)**
Mar 28 vs Everton 1-0
*Att: 52,089 Souness*

## 1984/85 SEASON
**2nd Round (1st leg)**
Sep 24 vs Stockport County (a) 0-0
*Att: 11,169*
**2nd Round (2nd leg)**
Oct 9 vs Stockport County (h) 2-0 (agg. 2-0)
*Att: 13,422 Robinson, Walsh*
**3rd Round**
Oct 31 vs Tottenham Hotspur (a) 0-1
*Att: 38,690*

## 1985/86 SEASON
**2nd Round (1st leg)**
Sep 23 vs Oldham Athletic (h) 3-0
*Att: 16,150 McMahon 2, Rush*
**2nd Round (2nd leg)**
Oct 7 vs Oldham Athletic (a) 5-2
(aggregate 8-2)
*Att: 7,719 Whelan 2, Wark, Rush, MacDonald*
**3rd Round**
Oct 29 vs Brighton & Hove Albion (h) 4-0
*Att: 15,291 Walsh 3, Dalglish*
**4th Round**
Nov 26 vs Manchester United (h) 2-1
*Att: 41,291 Molby 2 (1 pen)*
**Quarter-Final**
Jan 21 vs Ipswich Town (h) 3-0
*Att: 19,762 Walsh, Whelan, Rush*
**Semi-Final (1st leg)**
Feb 12 vs Queen's Park Rangers (a) 0-1
*Att: 15,051*
**Semi-Final (2nd leg)**
Mar 5 vs Queen's Park Rangers (h) 2-2
(aggregate 2-3)
*Att: 23,863 McMahon, Johnston*

## 1986/87 SEASON
**2nd Round (1st leg)**
Sep 23 vs Fulham (h) 10-0
*Att: 13,498 Rush 2, Wark 2, Whelan, McMahon 4, Nicol*
**2nd Round (2nd leg)**
Oct 7 vs Fulham (a) 3-2 (agg. 13-2)
*Att: 7,864 McMahon, Parker (og), Molby (pen)*
**3rd Round**
Oct 29 vs Leicester City (h) 4-1
*Att: 20,248 McMahon 3, Dalglish*
**4th Round**
Nov 19 vs Coventry City (a) 0-0
*Att: 26,385*
**Replay**
Nov 26 vs Coventry City (h) 3-1
*Att: 19,179 Molby 3 (3 pens)*
**Quarter-Final**
Jan 21 vs Everton (a) 1-0
*Att: 53,323 Rush*
**Semi-Final (1st leg)**
Feb 11 vs Southampton (a) 0-0
*Att: 22,818*
**Semi-Final (2nd leg)**
Feb 25 vs Southampton (h) 3-0
*Att: 38,481 Whelan, Dalglish, Molby*
**FINAL (at Wembley)**
Apr 5 vs Arsenal 1-2
*Att: 96,000 Rush*

## 1987/88 SEASON
**2nd Round (1st leg)**
Sep 23 vs Blackburn Rovers (a) 1-1
*Att: 13,924 Nicol*
**2nd Round (2nd leg)**
Oct 6 vs Blackburn Rovers (h) 1-0 (agg. 2-1)
*Att: 28,994 Aldridge*

**3rd Round**
Oct 27 vs Everton (h) 0-1
*Att: 44,071*

## 1988/89 SEASON
**2nd Round (1st leg)**
Sep 28 vs Walsall (h) 1-0
*Att: 18,084 Gillespie*
**2nd Round (2nd leg)**
Oct 12 vs Walsall (a) 3-1 (agg. 4-1)
*Att: 12,015 Barnes, Rush, Molby (pen)*
**3rd Round**
Nov 2 vs Arsenal (h) 1-1
*Att: 31,961 Barnes*
**Replay**
Nov 9 vs Arsenal (a) 0-0 (aet.)
*Att: 54,029*
**2nd Replay (at Villa Park)**
Nov 23 vs Arsenal 2-1
*Att: 21,708 McMahon, Aldridge*
**4th Round**
Nov 30 vs West Ham United (a) 1-4
*Att: 26,971 Aldridge (pen)*

## 1989/90 SEASON
**2nd Round (1st leg)**
Sep 19 vs Wigan Athletic (h) 5-2
*Att: 19,231 Hysen, Rush 2, Beardsley, Barnes*
**2nd Round (2nd leg) (at Anfield)**
Oct 4 vs Wigan Athletic (a) 3-0 (agg. 8-2)
*Att: 17,954 Staunton 3*
**3rd Round**
Oct 25 vs Arsenal (a) 0-1
*Att: 40,814*

## 1990/91 SEASON
**2nd Round (1st leg)**
Sep 25 vs Crewe Alexandra (h) 5-1
*Att: 17,228 McMahon, Gillespie, Houghton, Rush 2*
**2nd Round (2nd leg)**
Oct 9 vs Crewe Alexandra (a) 4-1 (agg. 9-2)
*Att: 7,200 Rush 3, Staunton*
**3rd Round**
Oct 31 vs Manchester United (a) 1-3
*Att: 42,033 Houghton*

## 1991/92 SEASON
**2nd Round (1st leg)**
Sep 25 vs Stoke City (h) 2-2
*Att: 18,389 Rush 2*
**2nd Round (2nd leg)**
Oct 9 vs Stoke City (a) 3-2 (agg. 5-4)
*Att: 22,335 McManaman, Saunders, Walters*
**3rd Round**
Oct 29 vs Port Vale (h) 2-2
*Att: 21,553 McManaman, Rush*
**Replay**
Nov 20 vs Port Vale (a) 4-1
*Att: 18,725 McManaman, Walters, Houghton, Saunders*
**4th Round**
Dec 3 vs Peterborough United (a) 0-1
*Att: 14,114*

## 1992/93 SEASON
**2nd Round (1st leg)**
Sep 22 vs Chesterfield (h) 4-4
*Att: 12,533 Rosenthal, Hutchison, Walters, Wright*
**2nd Round (2nd leg)**
Oct 6 vs Chesterfield (a) 4-1 (agg. 8-5)
*Att: 10,632 Hutchison, Redknapp, Walters, Rush*
**3rd Round**
Oct 28 vs Sheffield United (a) 0-0
*Att: 17,856*
**Replay**
Nov 11 vs Sheffield United (h) 3-0
*Att: 17,654 McManaman 2, Marsh (pen)*

**4th Round**
Dec 1 vs Crystal Palace (h) 1-1
*Att: 18,525 Marsh (pen)*
**Replay**
Dec 16 vs Crystal Palace (a) 1-2 (aet.)
*Att: 16,622 Marsh (pen)*

## 1993/94 SEASON
**2nd Round (1st leg)**
Sep 22 vs Fulham (a) 3-1
*Att: 13,599 Clough, Rush, Fowler*
**2nd Round (2nd leg)**
Oct 5 vs Fulham (h) 5-0 (agg. 8-1)
*Att: 12,541 Fowler 5*
**3rd Round**
Oct 27 vs Ipswich Town (h) 3-2
*Att: 19,058 Rush 3*
**4th Round**
Dec 1 vs Wimbledon (h) 1-1
*Att: 19,290 Molby (pen)*
**Replay**
Dec 14 vs Wimbledon (a) 2-2 (aet.)
*Att: 11,343 Ruddock, Segers (og)*
*Wimbledon won 4-3 on penalties*

## 1994/95 SEASON
**2nd Round (1st leg)**
Sep 21 vs Burnley (h) 2-0
*Att: 23,359 Scales, Fowler*
**2nd Round (2nd leg)**
Oct 5 vs Burnley (a) 4-1 (agg. 6-1)
*Att: 19,032 Redknapp 2, Fowler, Clough*
**3rd Round**
Oct 25 vs Stoke City (h) 2-1
*Att: 32,060 Rush 2*
**4th Round**
Nov 30 vs Blackburn Rovers (a) 3-1
*Att: 30,115 Rush 3*
**5th Round**
Jan 11 vs Arsenal (h) 1-0
*Att: 35,026 Rush*
**Semi-Final (1st leg)**
Feb 15 vs Crystal Palace (h) 1-0
*Att: 25,480 Fowler*
**Semi-Final (2nd leg)**
Mar 8 vs Crystal Palace (a) 1-0
(aggregate 2-0)
*Att: 18,224 Fowler*
**FINAL (at Wembley)**
Apr 2 vs Bolton Wanderers 2-1
*Att: 75,595 McManaman 2*

## 1995/96 SEASON
**2nd Round (1st leg)**
Sep 20 vs Sunderland (h) 2-0
*Att: 25,579 McManaman, Thomas*
**2nd Round (2nd leg)**
Oct 4 vs Sunderland (a) 1-0 (agg. 3-0)
*Att: 20,560 Fowler*
**3rd Round**
Oct 25 vs Manchester City (h) 4-0
*Att: 29,394 Scales, Fowler, Rush, Harkness*
**4th Round**
Nov 29 vs Newcastle United (h) 0-1
*Att: 40,077*

## 1996/97 SEASON
**3rd Round**
Oct 23 vs Charlton Athletic (a) 1-1
*Att: 15,000 Fowler*
**Replay**
Nov 13 vs Charlton Athletic (h) 4-1
*Att: 20,714 Wright, Redknapp, Fowler 2*
**4th Round**
Nov 27 vs Arsenal (h) 4-2
*Att: 32,814 McManaman, Fowler 2 (1 pen), Berger*
**5th Round**
Jan 8 vs Middlesbrough (a) 1-2
*Att: 28,670 McManaman*

## 1997/98 SEASON

**3rd Round**
Oct 15 vs West Bromwich A. (a) 2-0
*Att: 21,986    Berger, Fowler*

**4th Round**
Nov 18 vs Grimsby Town (h) 3-0
*Att: 28,515    Owen 3 (1 pen)*

**5th Round**
Jan 7 vs Newcastle United (h) 2-0 (aet.)
*Att: 33,207    Owen, Fowler*

**Semi-Final (1st leg)**
Jan 27 vs Middlesbrough (h) 2-1
*Att: 33,438    Redknapp, Fowler*

**Semi-Final (2nd leg)**
Feb 18 vs Middlesbrough (a) 0-2 (agg. 2-3)
*Att: 29,828*

## 1998/99 SEASON

**3rd Round**
Oct 27 vs Fulham (h) 3-1
*Att: 22,296    Morgan (og), Fowler (pen), Ince*

**4th Round**
Nov 10 vs Tottenham Hotspur (h) 1-3
*Att: 20,772    Owen*

## 1999/2000 SEASON

**2nd Round (1st leg)**
Sep 14 vs Hull City (a) 5-1
*Att: 10,034    Murphy 2, Meijer 2, Staunton*

**2nd Round (2nd leg)**
Sep 21 vs Hull City (h) 4-2 (agg. 9-3)
*Att: 24,318    Murphy, Maxwell, Riedle 2*

**3rd Round**
Oct 13 vs Southampton (a) 1-2
*Att; 13,822    Owen*

## 2000/2001 SEASON

**3rd Round**
Nov 1 vs Chelsea (h) 2-1 (aet.)
(score after 90 minutes 1-1)
*Att: 29,370    Murphy, Fowler*

**4th Round**
Nov 29 vs Stoke City (a) 8-0
*Att: 27,109    Ziege, Smicer, Babbel, Fowler 3
(1 pen), Hyypia, Murphy*

**5th Round**
Dec 13 vs Fulham (h) 3-0 (aet.)
*Att: 20,144    Owen, Smicer, Barmby*

**Semi-Final (1st leg)**
Jan 10 vs Crystal Palace (a) 1-2
*Att: 25,933    Smicer*

**Semi-Final (2nd leg)**
Jan 24 vs Crystal Palace (h) 5-0
(aggregate 6-2)
*Att: 41,854    Smicer, Murphy 2, Biscan, Fowler*

**FINAL (at The Millennium Stadium)**
Feb 25 vs Birmingham City 1-1 (aet.)
*Att: 73,500    Fowler*
*Liverpool won 5-4 on penalties*

## 2001/2002 SEASON

**3rd Round**
Oct 9 vs Grimsby Town (h) 1-2 (aet.)
(score after 90 minutes 0-0)
*Att: 32,672    McAllister (pen)*

# EUROPEAN CHAMPIONS CUP

## 1977/78 SEASON

**2nd Round (1st leg)**
Oct 19 vs Dynamo Dresden (h) 5-1
*Att: 39,835    Hansen, Case 2, Neal (pen),
Kennedy*

**2nd Round (2nd leg)**
Nov 2 vs Dynamo Dresden (a) 1-2
(aggregate 6-3)
*Att: 33,000    Heighway*

**Quarter-Final (1st leg)**
Mar 1 vs Benfica (a) 2-1
*Att: 70,000    Case, Hughes*

**Quarter-Final (2nd leg)**
Mar 15 vs Benfica (h) 4-1 (agg. 6-2)
*Att: 48,364    Callaghan, Dalglish, McDermott,
Neal*

**Semi-Final (1st leg)**
Mar 29 vs Bor. Moenchengladbach (a) 1-2
*Att: 67,000    Johnson*

**Semi-Final (2nd leg)**
Apr 12 vs Bor. Moenchengladbach (h) 3-0
(aggregate 4-2)
*Att: 51,500    Kennedy, Dalglish, Case*

**FINAL (at Wembley)**
May 10 vs FC Brugge 1-0
*Att: 92,000    Dalglish*

## 1978/79 SEASON

**1st Round (1st leg)**
Sep 13 vs Nottingham Forest (a) 0-2
*Att: 38,316*

**1st Round (2nd leg)**
Sep 27 vs Nottingham Forest (h) 0-0
(aggregate 0-2)
*Att: 51,679*

## 1979/80 SEASON

**1st Round (1st leg)**
Sep 27 vs Dynamo Tbilisi (h) 2-1
*Att: 35,270    Johnson, Case*

**1st Round (2nd leg)**
Oct 3 vs Dynamo Tbilisi (a) 0-3 (agg. 2-4)
*Att: 80,000*

## 1980/81 SEASON

**1st Round (1st leg)**
Sep 17 vs OPS Oulu (a) 1-1
*Att: 8,400    Dalglish*

**1st Round (2nd leg)**
Oct 1 vs OPS Oulu (h) 10-1 (agg. 11-2)
*Att: 21,013    Souness 3, McDermott 2,
Dalglish, Lee, R. Kennedy, Fairclough 2*

**2nd Round (1st leg)**
Oct 22 vs Aberdeen (a) 1-0
*Att: 24,000    McDermott*

**2nd Round (2nd leg)**
Nov 5 vs Aberdeen (h) 4-0 (agg. 5-0)
*Att: 36,182    Miller (og), Neal, Dalglish,
Hansen*

**Quarter-Final (1st leg)**
Mar 4 vs CSKA Sofia (h) 5-1
*Att: 37,259    Souness 3, Lee, McDermott*

**Quarter-Final (2nd leg)**
Mar 18 vs CSKA Sofia (a) 1-0 (agg. 6-1)
*Att: 60,000    Johnson*

**Semi-Final (1st leg)**
Apr 8 vs Bayern Munich (h) 0-0
*Att: 44,543*

**Semi-Final (2nd leg)**
Apr 22 vs Bayern Munich (a) 1-1 (agg. 1-1)
*Att: 75,000    R. Kennedy*
*Liverpool won on Away Goals*

**FINAL (at Paris)**
May 27 vs Real Madrid 1-0
*Att: 48,360    A. Kennedy*

## 1981/82 SEASON

**1st Round (1st leg)**
Sep 16 vs OPS Oulu (a) 1-0
*Att: 8,400    Dalglish*

**1st Round (2nd leg)**
Sep 30 vs OPS Oulu (h) 7-0 (agg. 8-0)
*Att: 20,789    Dalglish, McDermott 2,
R. Kennedy, Johnson, Rush, Lawrenson*

**2nd Round (1st leg)**
Oct 21 vs AZ67 Alkmaar (a) 2-2
*Att: 15,000    Johnson, Lee*

**2nd Round (2nd leg)**
Nov 4 vs AZ67 Alkmaar (h) 3-2 (agg. 5-4)
*Att: 29,703    McDermott (pen), Rush, Hansen*

**Quarter-Final (1st leg)**
Mar 3 vs CSKA Sofia (h) 1-0
*Att: 27,388    Whelan*

**Quarter-Final (2nd leg)**
Mar 17 vs CSKA Sofia (a) 0-2 (aet.)
(aggregate 1-2)
*Att: 60,000*

## 1982/83 SEASON

**1st Round (1st leg)**
Sep 15 vs Dundalk (a) 4-1
*Att: 16,500    Whelan 2, Rush, Hodgson*

**1st Round (2nd leg)**
Sep 29 vs Dundalk (h) 1-0 (agg. 5-1)
*Att: 12,021    Whelan*

**2nd Round (1st leg)**
Oct 20 vs HJK Helsinki (a) 0-1
*Att: 5,722*

**2nd Round (2nd leg)**
Nov 3 vs HJK Helsinki (h) 5-0 (agg. 5-1)
*Att: 16,434    Dalglish, Johnston, Neal,
A. Kennedy 2*

**Quarter-Final (1st leg)**
Mar 2 vs Widzew Lodz (a) 0-2
*Att: 40,000*

**Quarter-Final (2nd leg)**
Mar 16 vs Widzew Lodz (h) 3-2 (agg. 3-4)
*Att: 44,949    Neal (pen), Rush, Hodgson*

## 1983/84 SEASON

**1st Round (1st leg)**
Sep 14 vs Odense BK (a) 1-0
*Att: 30,000    Dalglish*

**1st Round (2nd leg)**
Sep 28 vs Odense BK (h) 5-0 (agg. 6-0)
*Att: 14,985    Robinson 2, Dalglish 2, Clausen
(og)*

**2nd Round (1st leg)**
Oct 19 vs Athletic Bilbao (h) 0-0
*Att: 33,063*

**2nd Round (2nd leg)**
Nov 2 vs Athletic Bilbao (a) 1-0 (agg. 1-0)
*Att: 47,500    Rush*

**Quarter-Final (1st leg)**
Mar 7 vs Benfica (h) 1-0
*Att: 39,096    Rush*

**Quarter-Final (2nd leg)**
Mar 21 vs Benfica (a) 4-1 (agg. 5-1)
*Att: 70,000    Whelan 2, Johnston, Rush*

**Semi-Final (1st leg)**
Apr 11 vs Dynamo Bucharest (h) 1-0
*Att: 36,941    Lee*

**Semi-Final (2nd leg)**
Apr 25 vs Dynamo Bucharest (a) 2-1
(aggregate 3-1)
*Att: 60,000    Rush 2*

**FINAL (at Rome)**
May 30 vs AS Roma 1-1 (aet.)
(score after 90 minutes 1-1)
*Att: 69,693    Neal*
*Liverpool won 4-2 on penalties*

## 1984/85 SEASON

**2nd Round (1st leg)**
Oct 24 vs Benfica (h) 3-1
*Att: 27,733    Rush 3*

**2nd Round (2nd leg)**
Nov 7 vs Benfica (a) 0-1 (agg. 3-2)
*Att: 35,000*

**Quarter-Final (1st leg)**
Mar 6 vs FK Austria (a) 1-1
*Att: 20,000    Nicol*

**Quarter-Final (2nd leg)**
Mar 20 vs FK Austria (h) 4-1 (agg. 5-2)
*Att: 32,761    Walsh 2, Nicol, Obermayer (og)*

**Semi-Final (1st leg)**
Apr 10 vs Panathinaikos (h) 4-0
*Att: 39,488    Wark, Rush 2, Beglin*

**Semi-Final (2nd leg)**
Apr 24 vs Panathinaikos (a)  1-0  (agg. 5-0)
*Att: 60,000   Lawrenson*

**FINAL (in Brussels)**
May 29 vs Juventus  0-1
*Att: 58,000   Platini (pen)*

## 2001/2001 SEASON
**3rd Qualifying Round (1st leg)**
Aug 8 vs Haka (a)  5-0
*Att: 33,217   Heskey, Owen 3, Hyypia*

**3rd Qualifying Round (2nd leg)**
Aug 21 vs Haka (h)  4-1  (agg. 9-1)
*Att: 31,602   Fowler, Redknapp, Heskey,
Wilson (og)*

**Group B, Game 1**
Sep 11 vs Boavista (h)  1-1
*Att: 30,015   Owen*

**Group B, Game 2**
Sep 19 vs Borussia Dortmund (a)  0-0
*Att: 46,000*

**Group B, Game 3**
Sep 26 vs Dynamo Kiev (h)  1-0
*Att: 33,513   Litmanen*

**Group B, Game 4**
Oct 16 vs Dynamo Kiev (a)  2-1
*Att: 50,000   Murphy, Gerrard*

**Group B, Game 5**
Oct 24 vs Boavista (a)  1-1
*Att: 6,000   Murphy*

**Group B, Game 6**
Oct 30 vs Borussia Dortmund (h)  2-0
*Att: 41,507   Smicer, Wright*

**2nd Stage Group B, Game 1**
Nov 20 vs Barcelona (h)  1-3
*Att: 41,521   Owen*

**2nd Stage Group B, Game 2**
Dec 5 vs Roma (a)  0-0
*Att: 57,819*

**2nd Stage Group B, Game 3**
Feb 20 vs Galatasaray (h)  0-0
*Att: 41,605*

**2nd Stage Group B, Game 4**
Feb 26 vs Galatasaray (a)  1-1
*Att: 39,362   Heskey*

**2nd Stage Group B, Game 5**
Mar 13 vs Barcelona (a)  0-0
*Att: 75,362*

**2nd Stage Group B, Game 6**
Mar 19 vs Roma (h)  2-0
*Att: 41,794   Litmanen (pen), Heskey*

**Quarter-Final (1st leg)**
Apr 3 vs Bayer Leverkusen (h)  1-0
*Att: 42,454   Hyypia*

**Quarter-Final (2nd leg)**
Apr 9 vs Bayer Leverkusen (a)  2-4  (agg. 3-4)
*Att: 22,500   Xavier, Litmanen*

## EUROPEAN CUP-WINNERS CUP

### 1992/93 SEASON
**1st Round (1st leg)**
Sep 16 vs Apollon Limassol (h)  6-1
*Att: 12,769   Stewart 2, Rush 4*

**1st Round (2nd leg)**
Sep 29 vs Apollon Limassol (a)  2-1
(aggregate 8-2)
*Att: 12,000   Rush, Hutchison*

**2nd Round (1st leg)**
Oct 22 vs Spartak Moscow (a)  2-4
*Att: 55,000   Wright, McManaman*

**2nd Round (2nd leg)**
Nov 4 vs Spartak Moscow (h)  0-2  (agg. 2-6)
*Att: 37,993*

## 1996/97 SEASON
**1st Round (1st leg)**
Sep 12 vs MyPa (a)  0-1
*Att: 5,500   Bjornebye*

**1st Round (2nd leg)**
Sep 26 vs MyPa (h)  3-1  (agg. 4-1)
*Att: 39,013   Berger, Collymore, Barnes*

**2nd Round (1st leg)**
Oct 17 vs Sion (a)  2-1
*Att: 16,500   Fowler, Barnes*

**2nd Round (2nd leg)**
Oct 31 vs Sion (h)  6-3  (aggregate 8-4)
*Att: 38,514   McManaman, Bjornebye, Barnes,
Fowler 2, Berger*

**Quarter-Final (1st leg)**
Mar 6 vs Brann (a)  1-1
*Att: 12,700   Fowler*

**Quarter-Final (2nd leg)**
Mar 20 vs Brann (h)  3-0  (agg. 4-1)
*Att: 40,326   Fowler 2 (1 pen), Collymore*

**Semi-Final (1st leg)**
Apr 10 vs Paris St. Germain (a)  0-3
*Att: 35,142*

**Semi-Final (2nd leg)**
Apr 24 vs Paris St. Germain (h)  2-0
(aggregate 2-3)
*Att: 38,984   Fowler, Wright*

## UEFA CUP COMPETITION

### 1991/92 SEASON
**1st Round (1st leg)**
Sep 18 vs Kuusysi Lahti (h)  6-1
*Att: 17,131   Saunders 4, Houghton 2*

**1st Round (2nd leg)**
Oct 2 vs Kuusysi Lahti (a)  0-1  (agg. 6-2)
*Att: 8,000*

**2nd Round (1st leg)**
Oct 23 vs Auxerre (a)  0-2
*Att: 20,000*

**2nd Round (2nd leg)**
Nov 6 vs Auxerre (h)  3-0  (agg. 3-2)
*Att: 23,094   Molby (pen), Marsh, Walters*

**3rd Round (1st leg)**
Nov 27 vs Tirol (a)  2-0
*Att: 13,500   Saunders 2*

**3rd Round (2nd leg)**
Dec 11 vs Tirol (h)  4-0  (agg. 6-0)
*Att: 16,007   Saunders 3, Venison*

**Quarter-Final (1st leg)**
Mar 4 vs Genoa (a)  0-2
*Att: 40,000*

**Quarter-Final (2nd leg)**
Mar 18 vs Genoa (h)  1-2  (agg. 1-4)
*Att: 38,840   Rush*

### 1995/96 SEASON
**1st Round (1st leg)**
Sep 12 vs Spartak Vladikavkaz (a)  2-1
*Att: 43,000   McManaman, Redknapp*

**1st Round (2nd leg)**
Sep 26 vs Spartak Vladikavkaz (h)  0-0
(aggregate 2-1)
*Att: 35,042*

**2nd Round (1st leg)**
Oct 17 vs Brondby (a)  0-0
*Att: 37,648*

**2nd Round (2nd leg)**
Oct 31 vs Brondby (h)  0-1  (agg. 0-1)
*Att: 35,878*

### 1997-98 SEASON
**1st Round (1st leg)**
Sep 16 vs Celtic (a)  2-2
*Att: 48,526   Owen, McManaman*

**1st Round (2nd leg)**
Sep 30 vs Celtic (h)  0-0  (agg. 2-2)
*Att: 38,205*

*Liverpool won on Away Goals*

**2nd Round (1st leg)**
Oct 21 vs Strasbourg (a)  0-3
*Att: 18,813*

**2nd Round (2nd leg)**
Nov 4 vs Strasbourg (h)  2-0  (agg. 2-3)
*Att: 32,426   Fowler (pen), Riedle*

### 1998/99 SEASON
**1st Round (1st leg)**
Sep 15 vs Kosice (a)  3-0
*Att: 4,500   Berger, Riedle, Owen*

**1st Round (2nd leg)**
Sep 29 vs Kosice (h)  5-0  (agg. 8-0)
*Att: 23,792   Redknapp 2, Ince, Fowler 2*

**2nd Round (1st leg)**
Oct 20 vs Valencia (h)  0-0
*Att: 26,004*

**2nd Round (2nd leg)**
Nov 3 vs Valencia (a)  2-2  (agg. 2-2)
*Att: 53,000   McManaman, Berger*
*Liverpool won on Away Goals*

**3rd Round (1st leg)**
Nov 24 vs Celta Vigo (a)  1-3
*Att: 24,600   Owen*

**3rd Round (2nd leg)**
Dec 8 vs Celta Vigo (h)  0-1  (agg. 1-4)
*Att: 30,289*

### 2000/2001
**1st Round (1st leg)**
Sep 14 vs Rapid Bucharest (a)  1-0
*Att: 9,782   Barmby*

**1st Round (2nd leg)**
Sep 28 vs Rapid Bucharest (h)  0-0  (agg. 1-0)
*Att: 37,954*

**2nd Round (1st leg)**
Oct 26 vs Slovan Liberec (h)  1-0
*Att: 29,662   Heskey*

**2nd Round (2nd leg)**
Nov 9 vs Slovan Liberec (a)  3-2  (agg. 4-2)
*Att: 6,808   Barmby, Heskey, Owen*

**3rd Round (1st leg)**
Nov 23 vs Olympiakos (a)  2-2
*Att: 43,855   Barmby, Gerrard*

**3rd Round (2nd leg)**
Dec 7 vs Olympiakos (h)  2-0  (agg. 4-2)
*Att: 35,484   Heskey, Barmby*

**Quarter-Final (1st leg)**
Mar 8 vs Porto (a)  0-0
*Att: 22,000*

**Quarter-Final (2nd leg)**
Mar 15 vs Porto (h)  2-0  (agg. 2-0)
*Att: 40,502   Murphy, Owen*

**Semi-Final (1st leg)**
Apr 5 vs Barcelona (h)  0-0
*Att: 90,000*

**Semi-Final (2nd leg)**
Apr 19 vs Barcelona (h)  1-0  (agg. 1-0)
*Att: 44,203   McAllister (pen)*

**FINAL (in Dortmund)**
May 16 vs Alaves  5-4  (aet.)
(90 minutes 4-4)
*Att: 65,000   Babbel, Gerrard, McAllister
(pen), Fowler, Geli (og)*
*Liverpool won by the Golden Goal rule*

# SOCCER BOOKS LIMITED
## 72 ST. PETERS AVENUE (Dept. SBL)
## CLEETHORPES
## N.E. LINCOLNSHIRE
## DN35 8HU
## ENGLAND
### Tel. 01472 696226   Fax 01472 698546
Web site http://www.soccer-books.co.uk
e-mail info@soccer-books.co.uk

Established in 1982, Soccer Books Limited has the biggest range of English-Language soccer books and videos available. We are now expanding our stocks even further to include many more titles including German, French, Spanish and Italian-language books.

With over 100,000 satisfied customers already, we supply books to virtually every country in the world but have maintained the friendliness and accessibility associated with a small family-run business. The range of titles we sell includes:

**YEARBOOKS** – All major yearbooks including Rothmans (many editions), Calcios (many editions), Supporters' Guides, Playfair Annuals, North & Latin American Guides (all editions), African Guides, Non-League Directories.

**CLUB HISTORIES** – Complete Records, Official Histories, 25 Year Records, Definitive Histories plus many more.

**WORLD FOOTBALL** – World Cup books, International Line-up & Statistics Series, European Championships History, International Statistical Histories (many titles) and much more.

**BIOGRAPHIES & WHO'S WHOS** – on Managers and Players plus Who's Whos etc.

**ENCYCLOPEDIAS & GENERAL TITLES** – Books on Stadia, Hooligan studies, Histories and dozens of others.

**VIDEOS** – Season's highlights, histories, big games, World Cup, European Championships, player profiles, F.A. Cup Finals – including many back items.

For a current listing of our titles, please contact us using the information at the top of the page.